Lonely Planet Publications
Melbourne | Oakland | London

Sandra Bao &
Sally O'Brien

Sydney

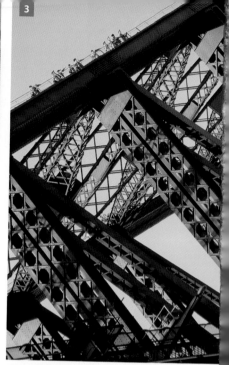

The Top Five

1 Sydney Opera House
Savour the views at the Sydney Opera House (pp70-1)

2 Taronga Zoo
Stroll in good company at Taronga Zoo (pp86-7)

3 Sydney Harbour Bridge
Clamber up the iconic Sydney Harbour Bridge (pp68-9)

4 Bondi Beach
Bathe or bask at Bondi Beach (p82)

5 The Rocks
Ponder the past in The Rocks historic precinct (pp50-9)

Contents

Published by Lonely Planet Publications Pty Ltd
ABN 36 005 607 983

Australia Head Office, Locked Bag 1, Footscray,
Victoria 3011, ☎ 03 8379 8000, fax 03 8379 8111,
talk2us@lonelyplanet.com.au

USA 150 Linden St, Oakland, CA 94607,
☎ 510 893 8555, toll free 800 275 8555,
fax 510 893 8572, info@lonelyplanet.com

UK 72–82 Rosebery Ave, Clerkenwell, London,
EC1R 4RW, ☎ 020 7841 9000, fax 020 7841 9001,
go@lonelyplanet.co.uk

The Authors

Sandra Bao

An inveterate traveller, Sandra has seen many beautiful cities in her life, but Sydney remains among her favourites. Perhaps it's her southern hemisphere connection – she was, after all, born in another beautiful down-under city, Buenos Aires – and with it, the joy of experiencing winter in July and summer in December (sweaty Christmas shoppers? Why of course, I remember that!).

Sydney gets under the skin. Despite spending the equivalent of three months here within a year, Sandra hasn't tired of visiting this charmed city. Locals may tell her where to go, but it's likely she's already been there ('yeah, I've already *researched* the Lord Dudley Hotel – twice.'), and she often finds herself giving them advice on their own city ('Why, I've never even *heard* of Edna's Table!' or 'It's been *years* since I've been to the North Shore', they might exclaim). It all comes with the territory of being a Lonely Planet researcher.

Sandra's other Australian guidebook credits include *Australia, Australia & New Zealand on a Shoestring* and *East Coast Australia*.

Sally O'Brien

Sally has flitted back and forth between Sydney and other cities from a young age. One memorable stint in the harbour city lasted 25 years and saw her living in the eastern suburbs, southeastern suburbs and inner west (never the North Shore). Despite attending schools near Coogee, Bronte and Bondi, she didn't cut class, only learned to surf when she moved to Victoria, and never appreciated beer gardens until she realised Melbourne's weather conspired against them.

CONTRIBUTING AUTHORS
EOGHAN LEWIS

Eoghan Lewis is a trained architect and Utzon obsessive who practises, teaches, and conducts tours on architecture. He is in love with cities, with the trashy and raw as much as the beautiful and the refined and reckons a city's architecture is there to be clambered over and walked (and talked) about.

PHOTOGRAPHER
Greg Elms

Greg Elms' interest in photography began during a stint of winery work in South Australia's Barossa Valley, where regular consumption of the local wines forced him to lie on his back and gaze skyward at the spectacular cloudscapes above the valley. Knowing his memory would be somewhat wine-soaked, he grabbed a camera. Greg has contributed to numerous Lonely Planet guidebooks over the past 13 years.

Introducing Sydney

If the world were a catwalk, Sydney would be its celebrity supermodel. Sparkling in the sunshine, this is a city full of gleaming skyline, lush parklands, refined inhabitants and zany neighbourhoods – all centred on a gorgeous and curvaceous harbour. It exudes optimism, hedonism and a carefree style that's way too full of itself, but needs – and offers – no excuses. Style over substance? Maybe. Unrefined edges? So what. After Sydney casts her spell, you won't even care.

The emerald city is bewitching, and has an infinite variety of faces that translates into a different experience for every visitor. History buff? You can go back 200 years to when the First Fleet landed right here, or 50,000 years to Australia's first inhabitation. Nature fan? A plethora of extensive gardens and native parklands are only a short walk or ferry ride away. Compulsive shopper? Fancy department stores and boutiques abound, both in the centre and charming surrounding 'hoods. Sophisticated arts? You'd better believe it; after all, Sydney's key symbol is a famous opera house. Great weather? Over 300 days of sunshine every year means the outdoors are a part of the indoors, and practically every café and restaurant has a breezy terrace. Beaches? Oh please, just *try* to find another city with as many heavenly sweeps of sands so very close to its heart. Sydney is that rare example of great things coming together in ringing harmony.

But it's also the smaller details that make this city great. That nostalgic smell of jasmine on a balmy summer night. All the different cultures and the vitality of its colourful neighbourhoods. The romantic air on a ferry as it slices through sparkling harbour waters. The friendly laughs of the drinkers at the next table in the pub. That tingling sensation when you first clap eyes on a world icon you've only ever seen in pictures. Are we starting to get the picture?

It's not as if there's no poverty, cynicism or urban sprawl to mar this pretty picture, but this is a city that bounces back quickly. Whether for good or bad, Sydney eagerly looks to its progressive future rather than its convict past. The influx of immigrants has made this megalopolis into a flexible, mostly tolerant society full of hope and enthusiasm and willing to take on all comers. Sydney has finally come of age, and – never quite satisfied with what it has – keeps wanting more.

Sydney's cheeks are *still* flushed from its incredibly successful 2000 Olympic Games, which saw the city swell with pride, confidence and smiles. This new millennium brought with it a stable local government, an economy that's stronger than it should

be and a gaggle of open-minded entrepreneurial types itching to show the whole place off. Sydney may have its critics, but these will be the types easily intimidated by the city's 'brash, flash, trash' façade. After all, it's not as if only the beautiful people are let in the gates, though it may seem that way after the umpteenth überpunk glides by on rollerblades or in a convertible.

Sydney is as sexy and sassy as the letter 'S' – sinewy streets wind around hills and hug sandstone cliffs; sparkling seascapes and spectacular views fill the sky; scrumptious cuisine stimulates the senses and a sun-drenched atmosphere satisfies the soul. (Meanwhile, everyone sports sunglasses, sensuous swimwear and soy lattes!) Fight for a window seat on your flight in, because you're landing somewhere special.

SANDRA'S TOP SYDNEY DAY

It's a beautifully sunny Saturday (big surprise! The sun's out so often these warm autumn days) and I'm in good spirits. I bus over to Bondi to meet my old friend Dilip for brunch at Brown Sugar (damn those long lines), then we walk off the pancakes by strolling the glorious Bondi to Coogee coastal walk, taking a cool dip at Giles Baths along the way. In Coogee we part ways and I head to the Paddington Markets on Oxford Street, browsing for the next hot fashion accessory. The crowds are heavy, so I take my leave and target Circular Quay, where I toss some coins at busker's hats and, along with hundreds of tourists, rest up and enjoy the shimmer on the harbour. It's getting towards dinnertime, so I hop the train to Newtown and meet my buddies Richie and Juliette for some scrumptious Thai food. They're going to the movies at Dendy, but I have a goal in mind so say goodbye and take off back into the city centre. I arrive in the Domain just as dusk falls, and plant myself in a strategic spot to watch as thousands of flying foxes start their nightly commute out of the Royal Botanic Gardens, flapping their way to the south.

ESSENTIAL SYDNEY

- Royal Botanic Gardens (p68)
- Sydney Aquarium (p74)
- Chinatown (p72)
- Surry Hills restaurants (p76)
- Art Gallery of New South Wales (p60)

City Life

City Life

SYDNEY TODAY

To say that Sydney has come a long way since its convict beginnings is something of an understatement. While there are rough edges here and there, today's Sydney is mostly an invigorating blend of shiny newness and vibrant energy that hangs eagerly in the air – just daring the outsider to challenge it. The perennial sunshine means that shrinking violets tend to stay indoors, the buildings are downright bombastic in their use of colour, form and materials, straights and gays alike don't mind sprinkling a few sequins on an outfit to attract attention (after all, the harbour sparkles in the morning) and the landscape just *knows* you're looking at it. After all, confidence is a quintessential Sydney trait, and locals either have it in spades or can fake it like pros.

Speaking of locals, Sydney's got quite a few – nearly 4½ million at last count – and they represent the world's rainbow of cultures. The majority of Australia's immigrants make a beeline to this pot of gold, and the city's mixture of pragmatic egalitarianism and natural indifference has lit a beacon of pluralism. Despite some definite bumps in the road of tolerance, over the last 200 years this former British colony has been transformed into one of the world's most diverse societies. A potpourri of ethnic groups contributes to the city's cultural life; Chinese newspapers, Lebanese restaurants and Greek Orthodox churches are as much a part of the city as its English and Irish traditions. Evidence of the region's original inhabitation survives in the Aboriginal stencils to be found in coastal caves, and in the indigenous names of many streets and suburbs.

Sydneysiders tend to be casual, forthright, irreverent, curious and friendly. They're also passionate about the price of real estate (especially waterfront – who's got a view?) but despite this obsession they have always been comforted by the knowledge that the best things about life here – the beaches, the mountains, the surf and the much-loved

HOT CONVERSATION TOPICS

- **That damn moisture-free weather** Drought, dam levels and desalination plants for drinking water.
- **Train delays** When trains skip stations to keep on schedule, and arrive 10 minutes late (still considered 'on time'), something's amiss.
- **Tasmania's Crown Princess Mary and Denmark's Crown Prince Frederik** Now starting a family!
- **Real estate, real estate, real estate** Who's got what, and does it come with a water view?
- **Celebrity gossip** Or just chat about any colourful and prominent personality – legal eagles, racing heads, media owners or stockbrokers.

Statue of Captain Arthur Phillip (p41) in the Royal Botanic Gardens (p68)

TOP FIVE SYDNEY GRUNGE NOVELS

- *Candy*, Luke Davies (1998) A harrowing and tragic debut novel which follows two heroin addicts caught in the grey space of a black and white world. Told by an unknown narrator, which gives a sense of detachment, this is a story of love, despair and dark humour.
- *Chemical Palace*, Fiona McGregor (2002) Follows the creative endeavours of a group of queer friends, while capturing the magic, myth and moodiness of Sydney's dance-party scene. Brings out the friends' bacchanalian struggle against the backdrop of Sydney's harshness, excesses, sweat and hedonism.
- *The Empty Beach*, Peter Corris (1983) Australia's favourite private eye, Cliff Hardy, takes on a case in Bondi and falls into its murky underworld, all the while trying to stay alive and battling his inner demons. Adapted for film in the 1980s, with Bryan Brown in the lead role.
- *The Monkey's Mask*, Dorothy Porter (1994) Written entirely in poetry, this thriller mixes lesbian erotica and crime to stunning effect. The staccato verse, salty language and Aussie slang are hard to resist, as is the idea of a lesbian detective as protagonist.
- *Pig's Blood*, Peter Robb (1999) A raucous, hard-hitting set of three pulp crime novellas that follows incompetent hit men, bad chefs, tarty young women and the more idiotic aspects of modern life. Violent and humorous and not for the squeamish.

harbour – are free. These natural assets are what make Sydney one of the greatest cities in the world, and so supremely outdoors-focused. Whether it's yacht racing on the harbour, bushwalking in Sydney Harbour National Park or the Blue Mountains, or body-surfing at an iconic Sydney beach like Bondi, there's no shortage of ways for visitors or locals to get out into that fresh, life-giving air.

But despite the gleaming façade and billowing hot air prevalent in Sydneysiders' words and in the media, you can spot patches of grey in the cloud's lining. Every election gives a thorough workout to the 'law and order' clichés and 'tough on crime' rhetoric. And while Bob Carr resigned in 2005 after 10 years as premier – making some Sydneysiders' day a happy one – his replacement, Morris Iemma, offers only a relatively unknown personality with lacklustre background. Iemma has promised to deal with Sydney's crumbling railway and public health systems, but this may be more than the former health minister can handle. Breakdowns in the political and social machines, along with the occasional allegation of police corruption, add to the feeling that Sydney's convict shackles can never be completely shaken off. This is one of Sydney's least attractive sides – despite a 'she'll be right' attitude to many things, Sydney doesn't cope well with what is perceived to be failure. To be upwardly mobile is everything, and those who fall between the cracks are shown little sympathy (though at least there are charities to pick up the pieces).

In the end, however, Sydney's relentlessly cheery 'bread and circuses' attitude tends to bowl over any obstacle. A glorious display of fireworks over the harbour and a general back-thumping over how great the city is does wonders for everyone's spirits, and inadvertently slaps a quick band-aid over any ill that dares to show its ugly head.

CITY CALENDAR

Sydney loves a party, and any excuse will do. Events can range from the pissed-up appropriation of another country's national day (St Patrick's Day) to the resolutely high-brow (see the Biennale of Sydney, p12). For a full list of public holidays, refer to p207.

JANUARY & FEBRUARY

AUSTRALIA DAY

www.nadc.com.au

Australia's 'birthday' is 26 January (the day the First Fleet landed in Sydney in 1788), and Sydneysiders celebrate with barbecues, picnics and fireworks on the harbour. This day is also notable for the Survival Day Concert (or just 'Survival'), which takes place at Woomera Reserve in La Perouse. This is a vitally important celebration of Aboriginal and Torres Strait Islander survival of the European invasion, with music performances and art exhibits on display. It's alcohol-free and goes from about 10am until sunset.

A TALE OF TWO CITIES

Athens and Sparta, Paris and Milan, Springfield and Shelbyville – their struggles pale beside the epic 150-year rivalry between Sydney and Melbourne. Australia's biggest city, Sydney is also its oldest, having begun in 1788 as a convict colony. Melbourne, currently in the number-two slot, was founded in 1835. Sixteen years later prospectors struck gold in Victoria, and the ensuing rush rocketed Melbourne ahead of Sydney in both wealth and population. The SMR (Sydney-Melbourne Rivalry) had begun.

Competition flared when Melbourne became Australia's temporary capital following nationhood in 1901. Purpose-built Canberra didn't replace Melbourne until 1927, by which time a driven Sydney had begun catching up financially, having already retaken the lead in human numbers.

These days, the SMR plays out for the most part as friendly chaffing, though discussions can get heated. Melburnians will point to Sydney's convict origins, its high housing prices and what they see as a lack of culture, while talking up their own city's multi-ethnicity, great pubs and lively arts scene. Sydneysiders will often either feign ignorance of any rivalry, or maintain that it's one-sided, an invention of envious Melburnians deluded enough to compare their boring burgh with the obviously superior Sydney.

If you should get caught in the middle between such types, don't try to pour oil on the waters by saying the two cities are nearing parity in their cultural diversity and culinary sophistication, or claiming that Sydney's scenery and glorious weather is balanced by Melbourne's being Lonely Planet HQ and the birthplace of footy.

Just put on your most innocent face and ask, 'Hey, does Canberra really suck as much as they say?'

BIG DAY OUT
Sydney Showground; www.bigdayout.com
This touring concert series, which has gone from strength to strength since its inception in the early 1990s, features popular alternative music acts from Australia and abroad. Tickets sell fast, so book in advance. It plays in Sydney on the Australia Day long weekend.

CHINESE NEW YEAR
www.sydneychinesenewyear.com.au
Kung hei fat choy! Depending on the phase of the moon, this fantastic celebration is held in either January or February. The Lunar New Year arrives (literally with a bang!) in Chinatown, and you can also catch dragon-boat races and eat some fabulous food.

FLICKERFEST
☎ 9365 6877; www.flickerfest.com.au
This international short film festival has been going for about 15 years, with almost a thousand entries competing for a slot. It runs for 10 days and takes place at Bondi Pavilion.

STREETS FERRYTHON
www.sydneyfestival.org.au
Held on Australia Day (26 January) as part of the Sydney Festival, four First Fleet catamarans are decorated with balloons and streamers for the race from Circular Quay around Shark Island and back to the Sydney Harbour Bridge. Sydneysiders are still getting over the excitement of the 1983 Great Ferry Race Sinking!

SYDNEY FESTIVAL
☎ 8248 6500; www.sydneyfestival.org.au
Held throughout January for the last 25 or so years, this is probably Australia's largest cultural happening. A wide range of events are scheduled, from art exhibits and street theatre to huge, free concerts in The Domain. Any performance at the Opera House forecourt is also worth looking into.

TROPFEST
www.tropfest.com
The world's largest short-film festival is held on the last Sunday in February each year in Sydney's Domain and selected cafés on Victoria St, Darlinghurst. A compulsory prop appears in each entry (which encourages creativity and discourages cheating) and some famous people from the film world are involved in the judging (think Russell Crowe and Nicole Kidman).

MARCH & APRIL
GAY & LESBIAN MARDI GRAS
www.mardigras.org.au
This world-famous festival, held from late February to early March, attracts more visitors and brings in more tourist dollars

Drag queen performs at Stonewall (p123)

than any other event in Australia. It runs for a month and includes a sports carnival, the Blessing of the Mardi Gras, theatre performances, a film festival and lots of parties culminating in an amazingly sequinned parade along Oxford Street (first Saturday in March) and the bacchanalian Mardi Gras Party. Tickets for this final party normally sell out by mid-January and are usually only available to Mardi Gras members, though interstate and overseas visitors can get temporary membership.

GOLDEN SLIPPER FESTIVAL
☎ 9930 4000; www.theraces.com.au
This major Sydney horse race, held at Rosehill Gardens and involves a 1200m track and two-year-old thoroughbreds. Prize money on the day hits about $3 million – putting it firmly in the big time. General admission is $25 (concession $5). It takes place in late March or early April.

ROYAL EASTER SHOW
www.eastershow.com.au
This wonderful Sydney tradition takes place at the Sydney Showground at Homebush Bay. It's a 12-day event beginning with a massive parade of farm animals and has a distinctly agricultural flavour throughout – although there are plenty of events to entertain even the most urban city slickers. Bring the kids and pat the baby animals.

ST PATRICK'S DAY
Not a public holiday, but it may as well be one. On 17 March, a large part of Sydney's population adds an 'O' to its surname (if they don't already have one) and gets blotto on Guinness in The Rocks. Festivities start early in the morning and continue until well into the night. Rowdy.

SYDNEY CUP
www.ajc.org.au
Australia's second most popular horse race (after the Melbourne Cup) is held at Royal Randwick in April. Expect big hats, big horses and big money to jostle for attention.

MAY
MERCEDES AUSTRALIAN FASHION WEEK
www.mafw.com.au
The gaunt, pert and pubescent tread the catwalk wearing local designer duds. Who's wearing this stuff in real life? Expect plenty of skin, impracticality and mundane bitchy gossip, plus the usual round of 'Australian fashion has come of age' PR speak. It's held in early May in Circular Quay.

SYDNEY WRITERS' FESTIVAL
☎ 9252 7729; www.swf.org.au
This excellent, week-long event is generally held in mid-May or late May and brings to-

---

TOP FIVE UNUSUAL HOLIDAYS & EVENTS
- **Streets Ferrython** Endearingly geeky and swash-buckling all at the same time. Bring a picnic and cheer on your boat. Unmissable.
- **Mardi Gras** Bare chests, bare breasts and bare you-don't-wanna-know, with a political vibe true to the 1970s. Film, cabaret, theatre, music and the Sleaze Ball – yeah.
- **Tropfest** A great short-film festival. Compulsory props (say, an umbrella) must feature prominently, so everyone has the same amount of time to make the movie. Brilliant.
- **Yulefest** Christmas in winter, just like it should be. Except that it's in July. What doesn't make sense about that?
- **Queer Screen Festival** Held during Mardi Gras, the biggest gay and lesbian festival in the world, so expect the unexpected – and more.

gether local and international writing talent to discuss a broad range of literary topics. It gets bigger every year. Talks and forums take place, with guest authors as highlights; there are children's books authors for the kids, also.

JUNE
STATE OF ORIGIN SERIES
http://aus.rleague.com/origin/
Rugby league fanatics unite for this gripping series of three games between Queensland (the Maroons, or Cane Toads) and New South Wales (the Blues, or Cockroaches). It's considered the height of rugby league, and worth catching for dazzling displays of speed, tactics and bloody-nosed aggression. It happens anytime from late May to July, and either one or two games are played in Sydney, depending on who won the series the previous year.

SYDNEY BIENNALE
☎ 9368 1411; www.biennaleofsydney.com.au
In even-numbered years this international arts festival, held at the Art Gallery of NSW and other city venues, showcases the bold, the brilliant and the downright mind-boggling. The curator for the 2006 exhibition is Charles Merewether, an art historian and ex-curator at Los Angeles' Getty Center.

SYDNEY FILM FESTIVAL
☎ 9660 3844; www.sydneyfilmfestival.org
Held at the magnificent State Theatre or at Dendy Opera Quays, this excellent, highly regarded film festival screens new-release gems from Australia and around the world. Subscribe to the whole season or buy tickets to special screenings (tickets can be hard to come by, so be sure to book). It starts in early June and runs for two weeks.

JULY
YULEFEST
www.katoomba-nsw.com/yulefest.html
Christmas comes in July and is as close to white as Australia gets in this popular Blue Mountains celebration. Think traditional holiday beverages, roaring fires, a carol or two and Christmas dinner with all the trimmings.

Reserve accommodation in Katoomba and surrounding towns way ahead of time.

AUGUST
CITY TO SURF RUN
www.city2surf.sunherald.com.au
On the second Sunday in August some 50,000 runners pound the 14km from Park St in the city to Bondi Beach; some are deadly serious, some are in costume and in it for fun, and everyone gets their name and finishing position published in the paper. Entry forms appear in the *Sun Herald* months before the race, but you can enter on the day. All-time record to beat: 40.04 minutes by Steve Moneghetti in 1991.

SEPTEMBER & OCTOBER
CARNIVALE
☎ 9251 7974; www.carnivale.com.au
You want multicultural colour? You got it! From September to October, food, folk dancing and a bewildering array of cultures (over 150 countries' worth!) will remind you that for all the bad press Australians get about being racist, there are plenty who think Australia's a hell of a lot better off thanks to immigration. Various venues hold events.

FESTIVAL OF THE WINDS
☎ 8362 3400; www.aks.org.au
Held on the second Sunday in September, this kite-flying festival – sporting a multicultural theme – includes competitions for the best home-made kites and music and dance performances. Its Bondi Beach location adds to the fun.

SPILLING A DROP OR TWO
Australians may be famous for their beer-drinking prowess, but they're no wimps when it comes to squeezing little grapes into big wines. While the Barossa Valley in South Australia is the heftiest grape-growing region, the Hunter Valley (just outside Sydney, see p196) produces some of the best Sémillon, Chardonnay and Shiraz in the world. Eating out in Sydney will provide plenty of opportunity to try these wines, either by BYO (bringing your own bottle) or by utilising the services of a sommelier.

MANLY INTERNATIONAL JAZZ FESTIVAL

☎ 9977 1088; www.manly.nsw.gov.au/manlyjazz
This enjoyable local event takes place on the Labour Day long weekend (early October), and, as you can imagine, offers plenty of jazz (mostly free). Styles range from traditional and big band to fusion, bop and contemporary.

QUEER SCREEN FILM FESTIVAL

☎ 9332 4938; www.queerscreen.com.au
Generally held in early September, this film fest also features the only queer documentary festival in the world; catch shows at the Valhalla Cinema in Glebe. Queer Screen also runs a film fest during the Mardi Gras celebrations (late February–early March); various venues across the city participate. Contact them for their monthly screenings also.

RUGBY LEAGUE GRAND FINAL

www.nrl.com.au
Once a year, two of the national rugby league tribes meet face to face to battle out the title of 'team of the year', in what's probably the toughest rugby league comp in the world. Tickets sell fast, so be sure to book. Games are generally played in September or October at Aussie Stadium or Sydney Stadium.

SLEAZE BALL

www.mardigras.org.au
Early October provides the perfect excuse for gay, lesbian, transgender, bisexual and queer Sydney to dust off the nipple clamps, chaps and handlebar moustaches and party like it's still 1999. Recent debates about the event have included 'should it have a theme?' Der. As if the word 'sleaze' isn't theme enough… The venue varies.

NOVEMBER
HOMEBAKE

www.homebake.com.au
This concert has showcased Aussie bands like Grinspoon, Powderfinger, You Am I, Something for Kate and John Butler Trio for over a decade. It takes place in The Domain around late November or early December.

Enjoying one of the cafés in upmarket Paddington (p77)

SCULPTURE BY THE SEA

☎ 9357 1457; www.sculpturebythesea.com
This outdoor sculpture exhibition utilises one of Sydney's greatest natural settings, part of the Bondi to Coogee coastal walk, to display stunning and creative artworks from local and international artists. Free, open 24 hours and great for starting debates!

DECEMBER
CHRISTMAS PARTY

While others are sequestered with their families on 25 December, the international family of travellers stages a party at Bondi Beach. Christmas Day 2004 saw gloomy skies, a ban on alcohol and hardly any revellers on the cold sands, but the sun and the party got going the next day – better late than never, one supposes.

SYDNEY TO HOBART YACHT RACE

www.rolexsydneyhobart.com
On 26 December Sydney Harbour is crowded with boats farewelling the international yachts competing in the race, a gruelling 628-nautical-mile course. It's an event that melds the city's psyche, despite

the disastrous events (thanks to grim weather conditions) of recent years.

NEW YEAR'S EVE

With hundreds of thousands of revellers pouring into vantage points like Circular Quay and Darling Harbour, the City of Sydney gives them something to ooh and aah about on 31 December. Expect a magnificent fireworks display from the stroke of midnight. And yes, they really are worth the headache of nabbing a spot hours beforehand.

CULTURE

IDENTITY

Sydney's residents (known as 'Sydneysiders') comprise nearly 4½ million, out of Australia's total population of 20 million people. It's become a very multicultural city, and today, one in four Sydneysiders was born overseas. More than 200 nationalities are represented, with over 20 languages in widespread use. Sydney is about as colourful a place as you can get.

Before WWII, however, most Sydneysiders had British or Irish ancestry. This changed dramatically after the war, with many Italian and Greek immigrants entering the country, along with significant populations of Yugoslavian, Lebanese and Turkish people. Asian migration into Australia goes back even further; the 1850s saw a surge in Chinese migrants as the gold rush bloomed, and there were also large influxes of Vietnamese people shortly after the Vietnam War. More recently, the majority of Sydney's immigrants have come from China and New Zealand, with others arriving from Thailand, Cambodia and the Philippines.

As for religion, most Australians are at least nominally Christian (though this majority is shrinking). Most Protestant churches merged to form the Uniting Church, with the Anglican Church of Australia remaining independent. The Catholic Church is popular due to a large population with Irish or Mediterranean heritage.

Non-Christian minorities abound in Sydney. Islam, Hinduism and Buddhism are the fastest-growing religions, while the spiritual beliefs of paganism and Scientology have claimed quite a few followers in the recent past. About 15% of Australians have no stated religion.

Australia's relationship with its indigenous cultures is multifaceted. Although many non-Aborigines have come to recognise the complexities of indigenous culture, many people are

PLACES OF WORSHIP

Auburn Gallipoli Mosque (☎ 9646 5972; www.gallipolimosque.org.au; 15-19 North Pde, Auburn; train Auburn) This glorious mosque is open to non-Muslim visitors. Call ahead for weekday tours, $3 per person.

Bahá'í House of Worship (☎ 9998 9222; www.bahai.org.au; 173 Mona Vale Rd, Ingleside; ⌚ 9am-5pm; train Chatswood, then Forst Coach Line bus 285) This stunning nondenominational place is open to everyone for prayer or meditation. Services take place at 11am on Sunday.

Great Synagogue (Map pp228–9; ☎ 9267 2477; 187A Elizabeth St, City; ⌚ services 6.45pm Fri, 8.45am Sat; train Museum) An impressive 1878 synagogue which houses Sydney's longest-running congregation. Tours Tuesday and Thursday (adult/child $5/3; enter at 166 Castlereagh St).

Mahamakut Buddhist Temple (☎ 9557 2039; 88 Stanmore Rd, Stanmore; train Stanmore) Call for details of opening times and access.

St Andrew's Cathedral (Map pp228–9; ☎ 9265 1661; www.sydney.anglican.asn.au/andrews; cnr George & Bathurst Sts, City; ⌚ 7.30am-5.30pm; train Town Hall) This twin-spired Anglican cathedral is the oldest cathedral in Australia, founded in 1819 and consecrated in 1868.

St Mary's Cathedral (Map pp228–9; ☎ 9220 0400; www.sydney.catholic.org.au; cnr College St & St Marys Rd, City; ⌚ 6.30am-6pm; train Museum) Across College St from the park's northeastern corner, the neogothic St Mary's Cathedral (1882) is Sydney's Catholic cathedral.

still intolerant of the culture of urban Aborigines and their strong traditional links. Frequent misunderstandings occur, with urban Aborigines often labelled troublemakers because they don't conform to the 'norms' of modern Australia.

Sydney's inner-city suburb of Redfern has a large Koori (indigenous Australian) population, though as real estate prices skyrocket even this area is seeing its share of property developers and yuppie home renovators.

LIFESTYLE

Australians are typically seen by the world as beer-swilling, crocodile-wrestling, Akubra hat–wearing yahoos with a penchant for the rough outdoors and even rougher sports. Well, this stereotype is about as common as bald albino wombats, especially in cosmopolitan Sydney. In fact, if you were to construct an image of the 'typical' (ie clichéd) Sydney-sider then you'd get something like this: works as a real-estate agent, mobile phone glued to the ear, plenty of product in the hair, maybe a piercing, perhaps a discreet tattoo, lots of designer labels in the wardrobe. Lives in a smartly decorated apartment on the inner city's fringes. Drives a Corolla; dreams of driving a BMW convertible and having a place to park it. Has put off having a child for now because it's too expensive and private-school fees are crippling. When a child does make an appearance, though, you can bet there's a novelty name involved – something like Mink or Otis. Nonwork play-time is spent at the beach, shopping for clothes and homewares, at the gym, jogging around Centennial Park or boning up on which places are the hippest right now. At night, it's dinner in Surry Hills or somewhere that's just poached yet another Melbourne chef, and then drinks around Darlinghurst or Potts Point (don't call it Kings Cross – it sounds too 'buck's night'). Oh, and by the way, this person can be straight or gay, male or female.

TOP FIVE SYDNEY COOKBOOKS

- *Open Kitchen*, Bill Granger (2004) Bill Granger is one of Australia's most famous chefs (see boxed text, p16) and this is his third book. Inside are simple, easy-to-prepare recipes fusing Asian and Mediterranean flavours into fresh, quality dishes. Rich and innovative.
- *Recipes & Stories*, Kylie Kwong (2003) A celebration of Chinese culture and cuisine, with Kylie Kwong recollecting stories ranging from her grandmother's mah jong meetings to Chinatown shopping rituals. Memorable photos and diverse recipes complement this great read.
- *Spice*, Christine Manfield (1999) Still mourning the close of Christine Manfield's restaurant Paramount? At least with this cookbook you can replicate her flavour-packed creations with recipes like pickled beetroot, peppered kangaroo fillet and prawn risotto with saffron.
- *Longrain*, Martin Boetz (2004) One hundred of Martin Boetz' favourite Modern Thai dishes. If you can't get into his award-winning restaurant in Surry Hills, whip up these spicy treats for yourself. Also a how-to on Longrain's famous cocktail concoctions.
- *Tetsuya*, Tetsuya Wakuda (2000) The first cookbook by Tetsuya Wakuda, widely considered Australia's finest and most innovative chef. Recipes are a fusion of Japanese and European flavours, highly artistic in their aesthetic and incredibly complex in their unconventional flavours. A must for the serious chef.

FOOD

The days of bland, insipid, Anglo-derived 'meat and potatoes' dinners followed by cheap vanilla ice cream are long over. Sydney has spent the last three decades splashing onto the international scene with Australia's freshest, most innovative cuisine. Some of the world's best chefs have been lured to Sydney's rich culinary pastures, mixing European traditions with exotic flavours to create what is casually termed 'Mod Oz' (Modern Australian) cuisine – an amalgamation of Mediterranean, Asian, Middle Eastern and Californian cooking practices that emphasise lightness, experimentation and healthy eating. It's a hybrid style, shaped by migrant influences, climatic conditions and local ingredients.

SKILLS TO COOK AT BILLS

The New York Times dubbed him the 'egg master of Sydney'. Abandoning British reserve, the London *Times* anointed him 'the god of Australian cooking'. A lot of Sydneysiders just call him bill, and they can't get enough of the food at any of his restaurants (see p107 and p110). When they're not sampling his food, they may be listening to him on the radio, watching him on TV, or reading one of his cookbooks.

This culinary phenomenon is Bill Granger, a cheerful transplanted Melburnian with massive gastronomical talent and an aversion to capital letters and apostrophes. Bill moved to Sydney to study fine art, but happily was sidetracked by his love of cooking, and opened his first restaurant (bills) in 1993, at the tender age of 22.

The bedrock of bills is breakfast, and folks queue up to chow down on the famously creamy scrambled eggs and such delights as sweet corn fritters and ricotta hotcakes with fresh banana and honeycomb butter. Bill stretches his New Australian legs at lunch, serving up dishes that combine the likes of blood orange, Gorgonzola, goat's curd, aïoli, wagyu beef, free-range chicken and seafood galore. Since 2004, he's been pulling out all the stops and serving dinner as well.

Bill does Australian radio, and featured in a six-part BBC Two TV series, bills food. He's even been known to pop up on PBS in the States. The media blitz was rounded off with three cookbooks at last count, and Bill shows no signs of slowing down.

In Sydney this style has filtered down from sophisticated restaurants to modest corner bistros and pub grub.

Think of this style as 'magpie' cuisine. Eyeing the surroundings carefully, determining what to steal from this neighbour and that neighbour and weaving it all into something better than the sum of its parts – something just right for its location and climate. This is essentially a culinary adventure built around local, seasonal produce which plays freely with imported ingredients, along with their accompanying cooking techniques and traditions. Yes, it's 'fusion' and 'eclectic', but not so much 'Australian' (which implies the expectation of 'bush tucker'). Not that there's anything *wrong* with this term – you may well come across indigenous Australian meats on some menus, such as kangaroo, crocodile or even emu. (Kangaroo is quite tasty and has a gamey quality, reminiscent of venison, and if it's not cooked properly can be awfully tough. But try it!)

So what it comes down to is this: when in Sydney, you can expect cuisine as stunning as any you've had in Paris, Rome, San Francisco or Tokyo. Add a dazzling harbour, bounteous raw produce and the vast reservoir of food knowledge that comes from its celebrated multicultural population and there's something special in the air. Sydney's chefs are continuously eager to make their mark on the international stage by experimenting with all things new, and a still-sizzling economy means there will be equally eager diners to support them (people seem to want to eat out for about half the week despite crippling mortgage repayments and the sort of credit-card debts our parents would be mortified by). After all, 'food is the new porn' – or sex, depending on who's writing the reviews – and fashionable Sydneysiders would demand nothing less than one of the world's most creative and vibrant food scenes.

What does this boil down to for you, the inquiring visitor to Sydney? It means a dazzling choice of cuisine in everything from fight-for-a-sticky-table food courts to the ritziest, most beautifully designed temples of eating you've seen – and at a price to

Delicious food at Boathouse Blackwattle Bay (p115)

suit any budget, from a $10 steaming-hot bowl of *pho* or freshly put-together *gyro* to 'what Gewürztraminer would you recommend with the lobster?'

Breakfast is generally an important meal for Sydneysiders, and has become an increasingly social event. Many people might now choose to conduct business over a *macchiato* and a bowl of porridge just as they would over an upmarket power lunch or a fine steak dinner, and friends often choose to start the day with scrambled eggs, gossip and giggling. The prime area for this is Darlinghurst and Potts Point, and with good reason: great coffee abounds and some wonderful early-morning dishes are served up. Breakfast time can start around 6am, and extend until late in the morning (say 11am), although many cafés serve all-day breakfasts, especially on weekends.

For most working Sydneysiders, lunch means a quick sandwich or salad gobbled at the desk, though many good restaurants in the city centre are there to offer something special (with a view). Chinatown sees huge crowds jamming its good-value eateries between noon and 2pm – it's a great place to go for a casual and delicious meal. Dinner is more important on the social scale, with people sampling a variety of cuisines on any one of Sydney's 'eat streets', such as King St, Newtown, or Crown St, Surry Hills. A good website to visit is www.eatstreetsatnight.com.au, which has plenty of information about the city's various dining precincts and some good tips for getting a decent bite late into the night.

FASHION

Sydney's fashion scene is definitely cutting edge – body-conscious Sydneysiders make sure they step out of their doorways as sleek and svelte as their wallets and thrice-weekly (well, maybe *twice*-weekly) workouts can possibly make them. Invariably it's Sydney's special climate which proves the major determining factor in many wardrobe decisions. While there are plenty of over-the-shoulder glances towards Europe and the States for fashion ideas, no one's going to go crazy and start wearing floor-length fur coats to Puccini at the Opera House.

The city's fashion scene began to stretch its wings back in the 1970s, when stalwart designers such as Prue Acton, George Gross, Trent Nathan and Carla Zampatti won nods of approval from well-dressed locals who'd previously relied on foreign labels to grace their wardrobes. Australian designers, after all, were better placed to judge the needs of Australians when it came to getting dressed in a city where humidity and strong sunlight combine to create a 'tropical' vibe for much of the year.

This laid-back ethos extends to the office, where pantyhose are not compulsory business attire for many women. While some ultra-conservative law firms or financial institutions may frown on women wearing trousers, this is not the norm. Some offices adopt the practice of 'casual Friday', but then, some seem to have a policy of 'casual Monday to Friday'.

WALKING ON (EXPENSIVE) SUNSHINE

'At the end of the day, it's all about the shoe,' says Terry Biviano, once the professional girlfriend of high-profile actor Alex Dimitriades and now one of the hippest shoe designers in town. She's been described as Australia's answer to Manolo Blahnik, but no one seems to notice that she hasn't had a job before – other than looking good. Now she's starting on everyone else, from the ground up. After all, 'if you have a really great shoe, you can be wearing anything and look fabulous,' claims Biviano.

For Biviano, a fabulous shoe must have at least a 10cm heel. She believes the curvy lines show off a woman's sexy foot best – comfort and orthopaedics be damned. She has, however, recently relented somewhat by producing a 7.5cm heel. 'Wait till you see it. You will die. It's so low,' she once told a fashion writer.

Biviano's career took off after launching her label at Australia's Fashion Week in 2002. Her signature creations are graced by the aforementioned sky-high stilettos, fragile straps, exotic skins, sparkling crystals and wispy feathers. They are sleek, Italian-made, artfully balanced and a wonderfully luxurious footwear experience for those who can dish out the bucks.

Expect to pay about $600 for a pair of her creations – more if they're in must-have barramundi skin (about $900). Special fish skin boots go for $1400. Find them at Myer (p161) and other specialty shoe stores in town.

If you're conducting business here, you may want to dress up, but be prepared to remove your jacket or tie early on in the day.

While many local designers may sometimes seem too imitative to truly warrant their job description of 'designer', the one area where they are head and shoulders above the rest is swimwear. Australian designers' use of colour, cut and fabric make a trip to the beach that much more exciting, and labels to look for include Zimmermann Swim, Tiger Lily and Expozay, which you'll find in department stores, surf shops and boutiques throughout the city. Other hot designers (and fashion show darlings) include Sass & Bide and Jayson Brunsdon.

One fashion personality who could sum up the Sydney experience is South African–born, New Zealand–raised Collette Dinnigan. A broken limb saw her housebound, with plenty of free time to start creating fastidiously detailed and sexy lingerie. Word spread, and after being besieged with requests Dinnigan decided to establish her namesake label in 1990. Enraptured women (and more than a few men) have flocked to her stores for her creations, which have come to include beautifully beaded and embroidered dresses and separates – and not just for stick figures either. The rich and famous have also discovered this treasure; join the ranks of Jade Jagger, Angelina Jolie and Halle Berry by donning one of Dinnigan's famous frocks. See p164 for details on her Sydney store.

SPORT

Sydneysiders – like most Aussies – are mad for sport, whether it's watching it, playing it or betting on it. In fact you'll often get the feeling that they would prefer physical activity to mental activity any day of the week. It's even been suggested that Australians would rather succeed in sports than in business. At least this national obsession makes for exciting times at the local pub (with sport on TV and pokies out the back) – and certainly contributed to Sydney's overwhelmingly successful 2000 Olympic Games.

No matter when you're visiting, there's probably some exciting football (p150) going on. Rugby league (www.nrl.com.au) is especially popular in New South Wales (NSW) and considered one of the most violent sports in the world (no doubt the reason for its popularity). Rugby union (www.rugby.com.au) is represented in Sydney by the Waratahs. Australian Football League (or Aussie rules football; www.afl.com.au) is the most-watched sport in the country; Sydney's beloved Swans won the 2005 premiership. Soccer in Australia (www.socceraustralia.com.au) has seen some of its best players drawn away to Europe. All these sports are referred to as 'footy' more often than not.

But there's more to Sydney (and Australia) than these macho-saturated 'run 'em down' games. Other spectator sports like swimming, basketball, cricket, tennis, hockey and surfing all have their avid fans. There are even surf life-saving competitions that many relish – not unexpected considering the relationship between Australia and its massive coastline.

GO RABBITOHS!

For a rugby league team that needed friends in high places, South Sydney (also known as Souths or the Rabbitohs) certainly managed to pull a few bunnies out of the hat. Try these names on for size: Ray Martin (host of *A Current Affair*), Andrew Denton (host of *Enough Rope*), Russell Crowe *(Gladiator)* and Tom Cruise (Australia's favourite ex-son-in-law).

Despite holding the record for more first-grade rugby league premierships than any other club (although the last one was in 1971), South Sydney was relegated to the scrap heap in the late 1990s. This was thanks to Super League and the business interests of the very rich, who had the local competition reduced from 17 teams to 14 in 1998. However, the Souths' passionate supporters did not appreciate this 'redundancy' and weren't going to go quietly. In June 2001, 80,000 green-and-red-clad supporters paraded from Redfern Oval through the streets of Sydney to the Town Hall at a 'Save the Game' rally. On 6 July 2001 the Federal Court of Australia gave the bunnies back their footy-playing rights and the number of teams in the comp was raised to 15. 'Power to the people' has never quite meant so much in sport.

While the Rabbitohs aren't usually at the top of the National Rugby League (NRL) ladder – you're more likely to find them at the bottom – it's good to know they're here to stay, and that a slice of local history is continuing. For current bunny stats see www.souths.com.au.

SYDNEY LOVES A SHOCK JOCK... *Sally O'Brien*

God only knows why, but Sydneysiders love having a dose of just-right-of-Genghis-Khan opinion rammed down their throats. Radio-dial stars to look out for (or avoid, depending on your political leanings) include the 'Golden Tonsils' (and ego) of John Laws on 2UE AM 954 between 9am and noon Monday to Friday (or just visit www.johnlaws.com.au). You'll recognise him by his chocolate-tinged baritone (if only that heavenly voice had been used for good instead of evil!) and plugs that give you the feeling he'd sell his gran for a quid.

Outrageously opinionated (even for Sydney) Stan Zemanek can be found keeping Sydney's cabbies company between 9pm and midnight on 2UE. Stan's well-known zingers cover topics as diverse as asylum seekers, hairy feminists and dole bludgers (people drawing unemployment benefits without making any attempt to work).

King of the jocks though is Alan Jones, whose defection from 2UE to archrival 2GB sent shockwaves through radio's corridors of power. With an opinion on everything and a tendency towards grandstanding, he rules the roost from 5.30am to 9am on the AM dial at 873. He can also be found delivering rapid-fire editorials on Channel 9's *Today* show.

As for participation in sport, well, there's lots of that too. Netball (similar to basketball), swimming, tennis and golf are all well liked, and it's not unusual for workmates to band together and form their own league or 'comp' against workers from rival organisations. And of course gambling is another event that requires personal 'involvement', with plenty of horse and greyhound racing venues (along with pokies at the pub) to feed the monster.

See p150 for more details.

MEDIA

Kerry Packer is Australia's richest man and Sydney's major player in the media, and via his enormous media empire Publishing & Broadcasting Ltd (PBL) he owns Channel 9 (TV) and Australian Consolidated Press. All in all Packer owns 60% of all magazines sold in Australia, including the Sydney-based *Bulletin* (news and current affairs), *Woman's Day* (celebrity gossip and local battler tales), *Australian Gourmet Traveller* (lovingly detailed food and wine escapes), *Cleo* (fashion and orgasms for young women) and the *Picture* (light-blue porn with a distinctly ocker flavour). The other player is none other than Rupert Murdoch, whose News Corporation publishes the *Australian* and the *Daily Telegraph* newspapers.

Another media heavyweight is John Fairfax Holdings, the publishers of the *Sydney Morning Herald* (a centre-left broadsheet), the *Australian Financial Review* (financial news), *Business Review Weekly* (business) and the *Sun-Herald* (Sunday tabloid).

The Australian media relies heavily on foreign newspapers, especially British and American ones, for its international coverage. Bylines attributing news stories to the *Guardian*, the *New York Times*, the *Washington Post*, the *Daily Telegraph* and *The Times* (of London) are fairly common. Having said that, foreign correspondents such as the *Sydney Morning Herald*'s Paul McGeough provide excellent independent coverage of, for example, the happenings in Iraq.

For more information on TV, see p29 and p210.

LANGUAGE

English is the official language in Australia. Although Australia's English-speaking immigrants have mainly come from the UK, the ever-increasing contact with the USA through military activity, tourism and popular culture has led to a noticeable Americanisation of Australian English.

About 15% of people in NSW speak a language other than English at home, and the proportion is much higher in Sydney, where you may well stumble across an Iranian cabbie, Chinese massage therapist, Korean

TOP FIVE MEDIA WEBSITES

- www.smh.com.au *Sydney Morning Herald* (newspaper)
- www.dailytelegraph.com.au *Daily Telegraph* (newspaper)
- www.chaser.com.au *The Chaser* (newspaper)
- www.abc.com.au ABC (TV & radio)
- www.sbs.com.au SBS (TV & radio)

grocer, Turkish doctor, Lebanese restaurateur, Vietnamese communications consultant, Serbian real-estate agent, Greek photographer or Brazilian beer-puller.

Another thing you may notice about Australian English is the differences between the language of the older generation and that of the younger generation. Much of the colloquial language that's regarded as distinctly Australian might not be so popular with young Sydneysiders, who tend to take their fashionable colloquialisms from the US or UK.

The Australian accent (and it is an *Australian* accent – trying to identify a Sydney, Perth or Melbourne accent is near impossible) has often been regarded as a national embarrassment, but has proved remarkably resistant to various attempts to correct those 'twisted vowels' that are such a hallmark of speaking 'Strine' (Australian).

ECONOMY & COSTS

Sydney is Australia's chief commercial, financial and industrial centre and is responsible for about a quarter of Australia's economic activity. The city's economic growth rate is routinely above the national average, at over 5% most years. Sydney is also an important transport centre, with two harbours – Sydney Harbour (also known as Port Jackson) and, about 15km south, Botany Bay – plus Australia's busiest airport and a network of roads and rail. Most of Australia's foreign trade is conducted in Sydney and NSW.

Sydney is not a cheap city to visit. If you bed down in hostel dorms, eat inexpensive takeaway and use public transport you can get away with spending $40 to $50 per day. Staying at a budget hotel with a friend and sitting down for a nice meal once a day kicks this up to about $80 to $100 per person. Those needing a few more luxuries (say a double room at a three-star hotel) and fancier grub can expect to pay at least $150 per person.

As accommodation will be your biggest expense, you should ask around for deals if

HOW MUCH?
Litre of unleaded petrol $1
Litre of bottled water $2.50
Copy of the Sydney Morning Herald $1.20
Schooner of beer $4
Souvenir T-shirt $8
Short taxi ride $10
Movie ticket $14
Hostel dorm bed about $24
Opera house tour ticket $23
BridgeClimb tour $160

staying for a week or more; hostels and hotels often give significant discounts for longer-term stays. If travelling with your family, be aware that some attractions and transport options offer family rates. And while many sights cost money to see, quite a few others are free of charge (see the boxed text on p48).

GOVERNMENT & POLITICS

Sydney is the capital of NSW and the seat of the state government, which conducts its business at Parliament House (p62) on Macquarie St. The system of government is a combination of the British Westminster system and the US system.

There are two main political groupings in NSW: the Australian Labor Party (ALP), and a coalition of the Liberal and National Parties (usually just called 'the coalition'). Minor parties with parliamentary representation include the Greens (who are going from strength to strength in the new millennium), the Christian Democratic Party and the Shooters Party.

State elections are held every four years; the most recent NSW election was held in March 2003, when Bob Carr won re-election. He then became NSW's longest continually-serving premier, but in July 2005 Carr suddenly resigned after 10 years in office. He was replaced by former NSW health minister Morris Iemma, of the Labor party.

At local government level, the various districts of Sydney are controlled by city councils, often operating out of Victorian-era town halls, such as Sydney Town Hall on the

Kirribilli House (p85), residence of the prime minister

corner of George and Druitt Sts. Sydney's mayor is Clover Moore, an independent pollie and almost punk-styled figure who stands for strong inner-city services, gay rights and the environment. Her stance on limiting development has put her on big business' shit list, however.

Those expecting salacious media coverage of politicians' sex lives and personal peccadilloes will be disappointed – Australians don't seem to want to read about the behind-the-scenes intimate activities of their elected representatives, and a certain respectful distance is generally maintained between the press gallery and the pollies. If it's saturation coverage of a Clinton/Lewinsky-style scandal or a 'Tory sex romp' fiasco you're after, you'll be hard-pressed to find it applied to local politicians – possibly because Aussies can hardly bear the idea of their local leaders involved in sex.

ENVIRONMENT

THE LAND

Sydney lies on Australia's populous east coast, about 870km north of Melbourne by road, and almost 1000km south of Brisbane.

The city is centred on the harbour of Port Jackson, but Greater Sydney sprawls over 1800 sq km and has grown to encompass Botany Bay in the south, the foothills of the Blue Mountains in the west and the fringes of the national parks to the north.

Sydney is hilly, and its layout is complicated by the harbour's numerous bays and headlands. It's built on a vast sandstone shelf, the rocky outcrops of which provide a dramatic backdrop to the harbour.

GREEN SYDNEY

Sydney's residents are generally a pretty environmentally sensitive bunch (when you start with such a glorious setting, you have a lot of incentive to keep things nice). Many households and businesses recycle paper, glass and plastic. Parks and bushland in and around Sydney act as animal and plant habitats, recreation reserves and the city's 'lungs'.

Sydney's glorious beaches are fairly clean but can become polluted after heavy rainfalls, when city runoff streams into the city's harbour and coastal waters. Millions have been spent installing litter and pollution traps, but it's still best not to swim at harbour beaches for about two days after rain. You can drink tap water without fear, however.

There is controversy around plans to build a desalination plant to overcome Sydney's falling dam levels during the ongoing drought. A desalination plant is an extremely energy-intensive way to provide drinking water, and the energy required is most likely to be provided by burning fossil fuels – adding to the already high greenhouse emissions.

Sydney's love affair with the car and the city's high humidity mean that air pollution can be sometimes be bad, but it's nothing compared to Los Angeles, Bangkok or Buenos Aires. Those seriously affected by allergies and asthma, however, should check the daily air pollution levels in newspaper weather sections. The world's biggest ozone hole – a gaping 26 million sq km – is above Australia, making sun block a necessity.

URBAN PLANNING & DEVELOPMENT

Despite Sydney's overall beauty, this modern city was originally built with very little urban planning. You wouldn't think it, but Circular Quay is a prime example of muddy vision; it's been the victim of more architectural abortions and near-sighted planning initiatives than is decent for what should be the city's showcase.

CUTE CRAWLY CRITTERS

Australia is famous for harbouring a lion's share of the world's most poisonous creatures. You might hear that eight out of 10 of the world's most poisonous snakes live in Australia, or that an innocent-looking cone snail could kill you with one prick, or that there are crocodiles that hunt out in the ocean – and of course all of these would be true. But don't panic yet; the chances of you running into any of these critters, especially in downtown Sydney, are pretty darn near zero.

Although there are many venomous snakes in the outback, few are aggressive, and unless you have the bad fortune to tread on one you're unlikely to be bitten. Taipans and tiger snakes, however, will attack if alarmed (it's a good idea to wear boots and long pants in the undergrowth, *not* to poke hands into holes, and to be careful when collecting firewood). Snake bites don't cause instantaneous death and antivenins are usually available. Keep the victim calm and still, wrap the bitten limb tightly, as you would for a sprained ankle, then attach a splint to immobilise it. Then seek medical help, with the dead snake for identification, if possible.

There are a few nasty spiders around also, including the funnel-web and the redback. The funnel-web bite is treated in the same way as a snake bite. For redback bites, apply ice and seek medical attention. Again, these are not creatures you're likely to find snuggling up to you in bed; these spiders like to hang around gardens and wood piles, not in hotel rooms or under restaurant chairs.

Shark attacks are relatively rare in Australia (about a dozen annually), with an average of one fatality per year. But this is out of the hundreds of thousands people who swim, scuba or snorkel every year in Australian waters. Just remember that, world-wide, more people get killed by lightning, elephants and bees than they do by sharks. And that for every human killed by a shark, two million sharks get killed by humans. The odds are very much against you encountering that large toothy smile, but you're worried, find a beach with a shark net.

Other waterside critters to watch for include the stone fish (with poisonous spines) and the deadly blue-ringed octopus (they're small and hang around in rock pools – signs will be posted if there's a danger). Another threat is the small bluebottle jellyfish, which you can often find washed up on the shores of Sydney's beaches (don't touch it!). In the water they look like bright blue sacs with trailing tentacles up to two metres long. Stings aren't fatal but do cause severe pain and leave red welts. Carefully rub the area with wet sand (to remove stingers) and apply ice and an anaesthetic cream. And of course, go see the doc!

Sydney just keeps getting bigger too, stretching its boundaries and seeing just how many people can cram into the one space. From the original colony at The Rocks, things developed out in ever-expanding circles, and now the city is reaching its limits to the north and south (abutting national parks) and to the west (edging the Blue Mountains). This only leaves the agricultural southwest and northwest corridors open for expansion, and development plans into these areas will no doubt become politically controversial. And with regards to the city proper, as recently as 2003 its boundaries have been expanded to include Glebe, Forest Lodge, Woolloomooloo, Potts Point, Elizabeth Bay, Darlinghurst, Rushcutters Bay, Chippendale and smidgins of Camperdown and Darlington.

Good planning developments are currently in the works, however, such as the commitment to improve the major road network in Sydney's western suburbs. And by the time you hold this book, the Cross City Tunnel, a 2km-long underground stretch of toll road that will connect Kings Cross and Darling Harbour (thus linking the eastern suburbs to the inner West) may already be transporting happy commuters. Current improvement projects at Dawes Point and East Darling Harbour are also in the pipeline.

Arts

Arts

While it's not about to match New York City or London for sheer volume in terms of theatres, galleries, or performance venues, Sydney nevertheless lays claim to a very healthy and robust arts scene – what else could you expect from a major city with an opera house as its most popular symbol? And as opposed to taking the sniffy, superior attitude so prevalent in many artsy societies, Sydney instead has a laid-back, open-minded view of its artistic pursuits – perhaps a fortunate consequence of relaxing sand, surf and sea elements being so close by. Also influencing the city's arts scene is a constant pursuit of identity, with its many multicultural facets constantly chiming in. Does this cultural mix work out for the best? You bet it does.

Sydney's blessed environment offers another pleasant bonus for art lovers. Outdoor events are a common theme, especially when the weather turns warm and sultry. Don't be surprised to see sculpture by the sea, hear an author read at an alfresco luncheon, watch cinema in the park under the stars, or witness modern dance outside the Opera House on Circular Quay's promenade.

You won't find yourself waiting for cultural events to fall into your lap, either – Sydney's sociable 'get out and be seen' nature keeps gallery openings, theatrical first nights, film screenings and book readings firmly entrenched in many local diaries (see p9 for festivals and events). So whether you're staying just a few days or a few months, be sure to take full advantage of what Sydney's arts scene has to offer – it won't let you down.

MUSIC

Sydney offers the traveller everything from world-class opera and intimate jazz to urban indigenous hip-hop and live electronic beats. This vibrant music culture attracts musicians from all over the world, and many international acts often kick off Australian tours in Sydney.

Songs are an incredibly important part of traditional Aboriginal culture. Aboriginal mythology tells of the Dreamtime or Dreaming, the time when totemic spirits created the world with song. These spirits left emblems behind, and connecting them are songlines or invisible pathways that tell the story of this creation. For Aborigines these integral songs also function as totems, maps and a guiding system of land tenure.

Most recently traditional Aboriginal music has been hybridised with modern sounds to create a new and popular musical 'fusion' that blends didgeridoo notes with reggae, rock, blues, country and pop. Aboriginal group Yothu Yindi and Torres Strait Islander singer Christine Anu are performers known Australia-wide in this relatively new genre.

Hip-hop has proven enormously popular as a means of expression for many indigenous and Islander youth, and vital acts such as MC Wire and MC Trey (the latter a Sydney-based woman) have had rave reviews for both their lyrical skills and stimulating performances.

The first European settlers' ballads and songs about the bush comprise a uniquely Australian folklore, and mark the first attempt to adapt European cultural forms to the Australian environment. These creative efforts evolved from convict ditties, campfire yarns and English, Scottish and Irish folk songs. Part poetry and part music-hall romp, they paint an evocative picture of life

Lyric Theatre (p128)

SYDNEY-CENTRIC CDS

- *Here's To The Start Of Something Beautiful* (Todd Sparrow) Sparkling, angular pop album with incredible production work; a great example of the amazing things achieved by local acts with no major record company backing. A tribute to the small but hard-working independent music scene.
- *Hourly, Daily* (You Am I) This mid-1990s album, recorded in Sydney and oozing a certain inner-city sensibility, was a soundtrack of sorts to the lives of innumerable young Sydneysiders.
- *Love This City* (The Whitlams) Named after Australia's grooviest ever prime minister (and Sydney stalwart) Gough Whitlam and exhorting its listeners to love this city, this band portrays Sydney's best ('God Drinks at the Sando') and worst ('Blow Up the Pokies').
- *Skeleton Jar* (Youth Group) Introspective, intelligent pop songs laden with references to Sydney's hip inner west and the isolation often felt in the heart of big cities.
- *Stomp on Tripwires* (The Cops) A perfect example of the meeting of cultures found in Sydney—US R&B grooves plus UK Punk plus Euro synth-pop equals one big, bold album of irresistible tunes and street-smart style.

in the bush in the 19th century. You can sometimes hear these old songs at several venues in The Rocks area.

Popular new acts to watch out for in the rock, pop and alternative music spheres include Sarah Blasko, Missy Higgins, The Waifs, Xavier Rudd, Ash Grunwald, The Scare, Midnight Juggernaughts, Dallas Crane and The City Lights.

Cabaret performers (for want of a better term) of note include energetically wild Christa Hughes (who also sings with Machine Gun Fellatio) and the amazingly talented Paul Capsis, whose husky, soulful vocals need to be heard to be believed.

Sydney has some excellent local DJs, and frequent appearances by international guests liven things up. There are clubs and dance parties catering to every subgenre, from hip-hop to drum 'n' bass, funk, techno, electroclash, handbag and house.

Sydney also has a healthy jazz and blues scene, centred on city venues (jazz) and the inner west (blues) and attracting local and international luminaries. Local performers to look out for include the internationally-recognised Mike Nock (and his trio), and the unique cult band The Necks.

Classical music can be heard at the Sydney Opera House, at nearby universities and at various city venues like the exceptional City Recital Hall. Opera Australia is Australia's national opera company and one of the busiest in the world, giving around 250 performances per year. It's based at the Sydney Opera House for seven months of the year (and in Melbourne the rest of the time). Some notable Australian opera singers you may be able to catch performing include Amelia Farrugia, Cheryl Barker, David Hobson and Joan Carden.

See p128 for more detailed listings of various companies and venues.

LITERATURE

Australia's literary history could be said to have started with the convict colony in Sydney in the late 18th century. New adventures and landscapes inspired the colonists to tell stories and eventually to record them with the written word. By mid-19th century the Australian storytelling tradition was becoming established, and though many early works have been lost, some – like Marcus Clarke's *For the Term of his Natural Life* (1870) – managed to survive.

In the late 19th century a more formal Australian literary movement began to develop with *The Bulletin,* an influential publication that promoted an egalitarian and unionist school of thought (and survives to this day). Well-known contributing authors of the time included Henry Lawson (1867–1922), who wrote short stories about the Australian bush, and AB 'Banjo' Paterson (1864–1941), famous for his poems – especially *Waltzing Matilda* and *The Man from Snowy River.*

Miles Franklin (1879–1954) wrote *My Brilliant Career* (1901), considered the first authentic Australian novel. After coming out it caused a sensation, especially when it was revealed that

READING SYDNEY

- *A Private Man*, Malcolm Knox (2004) A profound tale of a family's dark side, involving a strange death, skeletons in the closet, Internet pornography and the cult of Sydney's cricket test match. It takes place in Sydney and depicts both the city's shiny and seedy sides.
- *Camille's Bread*, Amanda Lohrey (1995) A love story set in Glebe, Leichhardt and Chinatown, this tender novel tells the story of Marita and Stephen's love affair and Marita's relationship with her 8-year-old daughter Camille. The themes of food, dreams and responsibilities are explored in wry vignettes and observations.
- *The Cross*, Mandy Sayer (1995) Based on the life and disappearance of Juanita Nelson – an unsolved mystery still – this gritty novel has Kings Cross as a central character and is an illuminating treatment of a nasty period in Sydney's history (the 1970s), when organised crime and property development led to murder.
- *The Glass Canoe*, David Ireland (1976) Ireland explores Sydney's larrikin, and at times aimless, pub culture in this dark yet humorous work. Both a graphic depiction of isolation and an insight into suburban life. Won the Miles Franklin award in 1976.
- *Hell has Harbour Views*, Richard Beasley (2001) Sydney-based barrister Richard Beasley writes about a young lawyer caught in a powerful legal world, symbolised by Sydney's thin exterior and complex core, which challenges his morals and ambitions. Made into a telemovie in 2004.
- *The Service of Clouds*, Delia Falconer (1997) A powerful debut novel set in the Blue Mountains in 1907, this is a deft and thrilling exercise in magic realism. It captures the allure of the area and of love itself in a coming-of-age yarn. Romance with a capital 'R'.
- *Seven Poor Men of Sydney*, Christina Stead (1934) Expatriate Christina Stead's debut novel is a poetic and impressionistic tale of seven revolutionary men held together by the bonds of friendship and their associations with Sydney. Depicts the isolation of Australia and the cultural growth of its population.
- *Snugglepot and Cuddlepie*, May Gibbs (1918) May Gibbs' much-loved bush-baby creations Snugglepot and Cuddlepie are a staple of Australian childhood, with endearing illustrations (the originals are the best). You can visit Gibbs' North Shore home, Nutcote (p86), while in Sydney.
- *30 Days in Sydney*, Peter Carey (2001) A rich and nostalgic account of Peter Carey's return to Sydney after ten years of living in New York City. His emotions and experiences read like a diary, with full descriptions and a theme covering the four elements of earth, air, fire and water. A skilled observer and historian.
- *Voss*, Patrick White (1957) Nobel Prize–winner White contrasts the harsh and unforgiving outback with colonial life in Sydney in this modern masterpiece. It tells the story of German obsessive explorer Voss, who plans to cross Australia from coast to coast. In the 1980s *Voss* was transformed into an opera, with a libretto by David Malouf.

Miles was a woman. Another gender bender was Ethel Florence Lindesay Richardson, who worked under the pseudonym of Henry Handel Richardson and is now regarded as one of Australia's most important early-20th-century writers.

Multi-award-winning Australian writers of international stature include Patrick White (the only Australian ever to have won the Nobel Prize in Literature, in 1973), Thomas Keneally, Peter Carey, David Malouf and Tim Winton. Also good to read are Thea Astley, Frank Moorhouse, Robert Drewe, David Foster, Helen Garner, Elizabeth Jolley, Lily Brett and Rodney Hall. For poetry look out for the works of Les Murray, Robert Gray, John Tranter, Kate Lilley and Jill Jones, among others.

One worthy literary journal that regularly showcases excellent Australian writing talent is *Heat*, which is edited by Sydney-raised Ivor Indyk and features poetry, fiction and nonfiction. It's available at many bookshops around Sydney and is published regularly by Giramondo.

See p11 for details on the annual Sydney Writers' Festival.

VISUAL ARTS

Sydney's first artists were the members of the indigenous Eora tribe. Figures of animals and humans were engraved into the area's rock outcroppings, offering a tiny insight into the Dreamtime, social systems and occupational patterns. Although Sydney claims more engraving sites than any other city in Australia, many have been covered by modern construction. One place you can still see some engravings is in **Bondi** (see p82). For more on Aboriginal art see the boxed text on p28.

Traditional European arts didn't quite mesh with the strange and beguiling Australian landscape. The first European landscape painters used colours and features that didn't authentically represent this new land, and today they wouldn't be regarded as typically 'Australian'. This was mainly due to the fact that European aesthetic standards were being applied to a non-European landscape. Some early painters, however, made an effort to approach the Australian landscape on its own terms.

In the early 19th century John Glover (a convict) was an early adopter of the Australian landscape painting style, using warm earth tones and accurate depictions of gum trees and distant mountains in his work. Colonial artists such as Conrad Martens (a friend of Charles Darwin) painted Turneresque landscapes of Sydney Harbour in the 1850s, startling current Sydneysiders used to seeing a foreshore dominated by exclusive housing rather than miles of bush.

The first significant art movement in Australia, the Heidelberg School, emerged around the 1890s. Using impressionistic techniques and favouring outdoor painting, the school represented a major break with prevailing British and Germanic tastes. Painters such as Tom Roberts and Arthur Streeton were the first to render Australian light and colour in this naturalistic fashion. Originally from Melbourne, they came to Sydney and established an artists' camp at Little Sirius Cove in Mosman in 1891, which became a focal point for Sydney artists. Roberts and Streeton depicted what are now considered typically Australian scenes of sheepshearers, pioneers and bushrangers. Their paintings were powerful stimulants to the development of an enduring national mythology.

Frederick McCubbin was also associated with the Heidelberg School, and became the first significant white artist born in Australia. His impressionistic work was influenced by his association with Roberts, and his most famous work *Lost* was inspired by a young girl lost in the bush for three weeks.

At the beginning of the 20th century Australian painters began to flirt with modernism, which originally started in Sydney. French-influenced Nora Simpson kick-started the innovative movement, which experimented with cubism and expressionism. Grace Cossington Smith and Margaret Preston were other highly-regarded early modernists, both based in Sydney.

In the 1940s there began a flowering of symbolic surrealism in the work of such painters as Sidney Nolan, Arthur Boyd, Albert Tucker and Russell Drysdale. This movement used a spontaneous and transcendent approach to the visual arts, and added another dimension to the Australian creative process through the level of mythology.

Museum of Contemporary Art (p66)

In the 1960s Australian art drew on a wide range of cultures and abstract trends. This eclecticism is best represented by the work of Sydney artist Brett Whiteley, who died in 1992 and was an internationally celebrated *enfant terrible* (though it doesn't take much to get called that in these parts). He painted bold, colourful canvases, often with distorted figures, as well as landscapes of Sydney Harbour and Lavender Bay. His studio, containing many of his works, has been preserved as a gallery in Surry Hills (see p76).

Drawing on popular cultural images for much of his work, Martin Sharp first rose to prominence in the 1960s as cofounder of the satirical magazine *Oz*. In the 1970s he helped restore the 'face' at Luna Park, but is especially famous for his theatrical posters and record covers.

Other modern artists of note include Sandy Bruch, Ian Fairweather, Keith Looby, Ian Grant, Judy Cassab, Lindy Lee and John Olsen. On the design front, Australia's most successful export has been the work of Marc Newson. His aerodynamic Lockheed Lounge (1985-86) has been snapped up by savvy furniture collectors and design buffs the world over. A graduate of the Sydney College of the Arts, he has long resided overseas.

Sydney is no slouch when it comes to exhibiting sculpture in its public spaces. Exceptional pieces to keep an eye out for include *Edge of Trees* (Janet Laurence and Fiona Foley) in front of the Museum of Sydney; *Touchstones* (Kan Yasuda) in the Aurora Place plaza at Phillip and Bent Sts; *Three Wheeler* (Tim Prentice) in reception at Aurora Place; and *Canoe* (Richard Goodwin) at 30 Hickson Rd. Clusters of interesting pieces can also be seen in the Royal Botanic Gardens, The Domain and Martin Place. For a self-guided sculpture walk in these areas, see the boxed text on p60. Sydney Architecture Walks (p49) offers a guided tour of public art and its place within Sydney's landscape.

Some of Sydney's buildings have incorporated sculptural pieces, such as the Art Gallery of NSW (p60), whose façade features four bronze relief panels by four different sculptors. The 2000 Olympics saw three athletic sculptures by Dominique Sutton temporarily perched on the Sydney Tower, and the Opera House shows obvious sculptural influences in its design.

The world's largest outdoor sculpture exhibition is Sculpture by the Sea (p13), which takes place in November on the stunningly gorgeous seaside walk between Bondi and Tamarama beaches. Don't miss it if you're in the area during this time.

Performance art can be found at galleries such as Artspace (p75) in Woolloomooloo – and some of it's certainly not for the faint-hearted. In 2003 Mike Parr performed a piece at Artspace titled *Democratic Torture*, in which people could deliver electric shocks to him via the Internet; he's also nailed himself to a wall here in *Malevich: A Political Arm*.

ABORIGINAL ART

Aboriginal art is one of the oldest forms of creativity in the world, dating back more than 50,000 years. It has always been an integral part of Aboriginal life, forming a connection between the past and the present, the supernatural and the earthly, the people and the land. This art is a reflection of Aboriginal people's ancestral Dreaming, or the 'Creation', when the earth's physical features were formed by the struggles between powerful supernatural ancestors. Ceremonies, rituals and sacred paintings are all based on the Dreaming.

Aboriginal art is widely varied and includes dot paintings from the central deserts, bark paintings and weavings from Arnhem Land, woodcarving and silk-screen printing from the Tiwi Islands, and batik printing and woodcarving from central Australia. Warmun artists are known for their ochres, while the Wangkatjunkga community is famous for abstract paintings. Many great young artists are based out of Lockhart River in north Queensland.

Dot and canvas paintings especially have become very popular in the last 25 years, which has given Aboriginal artists both a means with which to preserve their ancient Dreaming values and a way to share this rich cultural heritage with the wider community in Australia. Modern materials like glass, fibre and aluminium have also been incorporated by recent Aboriginal artists, encompassing traditional themes with contemporary expression.

The best way to support Aboriginal artists is to buy their art at a reputable store that guarantees authenticity (and has the papers to prove it) and from Aboriginal-owned galleries and outlets. Some top Aboriginal artists include Mabel Juli, Eubena Nampitjin, Rosella Namok, Gloria Petyarre, Kathleen Petyarre, Minnie Pwerle, Jimmy Pike, Paddy Japaljarri Stewart, Rover Thomas, Mick Namarari Tjapaltjarri and Judy Napangardi Watson. See the Shopping chapter (p158) for some store recommendations.

Photographic exhibitions are always on at the **Australian Centre for Photography** (p78) in Woollahra. The Australian Photographic Portrait Prize is a popular $15,000 competition – catch it at the Art Gallery of NSW in March or April (p60). Finally, some of Sydney's quirkiest and most idiosyncratic art can be found in the fashion choices of locals – artist Reg Mombasa's work regularly pops up in the designs of surfwear label Mambo (for store locations see p166).

DANCE

Always aware of its physicality, sexy Sydney is an exceptional place to see cutting-edge dance performances. And while contemporary dance companies are hailed for their creative choreography and intrepid performers, traditional practitioners continue to be revered for their relentless hard work in pursuit of formal excellence.

The Australian Ballet, based in Melbourne, is the national ballet company and one of the finest and most prolific in the world. It often performs at the Sydney Opera House, as well as in other major Australian and international cities, and offers a mixed program of classical and modern ballets. Since being established by artistic director Peggy van Praagh in 1962, the Australian Ballet flourished under the direction of Maina Gielgud, whose creativity and insight saw the company's repertoire solidify and its reputation expand. Following a difficult period in the mid- to late 1990s, the company is stable once again, and since 2001 has been under the watchful eye of principal-artist-turned-artistic-director David McAllister.

The Sydney Dance Company (SDC) has become Australia's leading contemporary dance company since being founded in 1976. Artistic director and choreographer Graeme Murphy, along with former dancer and now associate director Janet Vernon, have guided the company to stunning recent successes. The year 2004 saw Murphy's clever and daunting *Shades of Grey* (inspired by Oscar Wilde's *The Picture of Dorian Gray*) and, in 2005, *Grand* explored the relationship between dance and the piano (and included costumes by renowned fashion designer Akira Isogawa). Beg, borrow or steal a ticket to any sultry SDC performance.

The prestigious Bangarra Dance Theatre has proclaimed itself to be 'one of the youngest and oldest of Australia's dance companies' by combining 50,000 years of Aboriginal and Torres Strait Islands performance tradition with fresh, bold choreography. It has been led by former SDC dancer and choreographer Stephen Paige since 1991, and has galvanised audiences both domestically and internationally with stunning and spiritual performances that honour Australia's indigenous past. From their original production *Rites* (done in collaboration with the Australian Ballet) to 2004's mesmerizing *Spirits* and 2005's captivating *Boomerang*, this company puts out stuff definitely worth attending.

See the p130 for more detailed listings of these various companies and other venues.

CINEMA & TV

Australia experienced some of the world's earliest attempts at cinematography. In 1896, just one year after the Lumiere brothers opened the world's first cinema in Paris, Maurice Sestier (one of the Lumieres'

TOP FIVE MUSEUMS & GALLERIES

- **Art Gallery of NSW** (p60) Everything from classic to modern and local to international, plus an exceptional collection of Aboriginal and Torres Strait Islander works.
- **Powerhouse Museum** (p73) Wonderful hands-on displays and thought-provoking exhibitions. You'll need hours to go through it all.
- **Object Gallery** (p77) Gorgeous crafts and contemporary household designs on display at this new Surry Hills centre. Their store is located in The Rocks.
- **Museum of Contemporary Art** (p66) Marvellous temporary exhibitions complement the permanent works at this large modern art museum. Great café also.
- **Australian Museum** (p61) A fun wander through the natural history of Australia, with plenty of cultural artefacts, taxidermy and interactive displays.

photographers) came to Sydney and made the country's first films. Sestier also opened Australia's first cinema in Sydney – Salon Lumiere on Pitt St – during this time, and on 17 October premiered the landmark *Passengers Alighting from Ferry 'Brighton' at Manly*.

One of the most successful of the early Australian feature films was *The Sentimental Bloke* (1919), which premiered in Melbourne but included scenes shot in Manly, the Sydney Royal Botanic Gardens and Woolloomooloo.

The Calvary epic *Forty Thousand Horsemen* (1940), directed by the great filmmaker Charles Chauvel, was a highlight of locally produced and financed films of the 1930s to 1950s (which were often based on Australian history or literature). Chauvel also made the country's first colour movie, the Aboriginal-themed *Jedda* (1955), which was also the first Australian flick to make an appearance at the Cannes film festival. The final scenes were reshot in the Blue Mountains after original footage was lost in a plane crash.

Government intervention in the form of both state and federal subsidies (as well as tax breaks) reshaped the future of the country's film industry from 1969 through the 1970s, with the Australian Film Commission (AFC) being created in 1975. An ongoing 'renaissance' of Australian cinema was thus established, and today Sydney is a major centre for feature-film making.

One director who gained fame during this period and continues to be successful in Hollywood is Sydney-born Peter Weir, who oversaw films like *Gallipoli* (1981), *Dead Poets Society* (1989) and, more recently, *Master and Commander* (2003).

The 1990s saw films that cemented Australia's reputation as a producer of quirky comedies about local misfits: *Strictly Ballroom* (with locations in Pyrmont and Marrickville), *Muriel's Wedding* (Parramatta, Oxford St, Darling Point and Ryde) and *Priscilla – Queen of the Desert* (Erskineville). Actors who got their cinematic start around this time include Russell Crowe, Cate Blanchett, Heath Ledger, Toni Collette and Rachel Griffiths.

Sydney's flashest film studio, **Fox Studios** (p131), was once the site of Sydney's much-loved Royal Easter Show. It's now the multimillion-dollar centre of a revitalised and flourishing local industry, and many movies financed with overseas money have recently been shot and produced here. These include big-budget extravaganzas like the trilogy *The Matrix* (featuring numerous Sydney skyscrapers), *Mission Impossible 2* (Elizabeth Bay and Sydney Harbour) and the *Star Wars* prequels. Sydneysider Baz Luhrmann's *Moulin Rouge* was also made here, and starred Sydney's favourite celebrity Nicole Kidman.

Films with Aboriginal themes had mixed success in the past, but have recently gained ground. Sydneysider Phillip Noyce's *Rabbit Proof Fence* (2002) broke open Australian

TOP TEN SYDNEY FILMS

- *Finding Nemo* (2003) Excellent animated feature that follows the adventures of a wild clownfish who suddenly finds himself captive in an aquarium. Directed by Andrew Stanton.
- *Lantana* (2001) Touted as a 'mystery for grownups', this is an extraordinary ensemble piece and deeply moving meditation on life, love, truth and grief. Directed by Ray Lawrence.
- *Looking for Alibrandi* (2000) A charming story of what it's like to grow up Italian in modern Sydney. Directed by Kate Woods.
- *The Matrix* (1999–2003) A trio of futuristic mind-bending flicks with plenty of martial-arts action, slick costumes and dark themes. Filmed in Sydney's streets and soundstages. Directed by Andy and Larry Wachowski.
- *Mission Impossible 2* (2000) An ex-secret agent plans to unleash a killer virus on the streets of Sydney, with only agent Ethan Hunt to stop him. Directed by John Woo.
- *Moulin Rouge* (2001) Sydney's golden girl Nicole Kidman stars in this frilly musical, with plenty of singing and dancing all around. Partly made in Sydney; directed by Baz Luhrmann.
- *Newsfront* (1978) The story of rival newsreel companies in the mid-20th century, this film was a vital part of the renaissance of Australian cinema in the 1970s. Directed by Phillip Noyce.
- *Puberty Blues* (1981) Southern Sydney's 1970s surf culture at its most 'perf'. Directed by Bruce Beresford.
- *Two Hands* (1999) A humorous look at Sydney's surprisingly daggy criminal underworld. Directed by Gregor Jordan.
- *Star Wars* prequels (2002-2005) The last two prequels of this massively popular film saga were produced at Fox Studios in Sydney. Directed by George Lucas.

cinematic racial barriers to become the year's most successful film. David Gulpilil, the most well-known Aboriginal actor, has charmed audiences in *Walkabout* (1971), *The Last Wave* (1977), *Crocodile Dundee* (1986), *Rabbit Proof Fence* and *The Tracker* (2002). Parramatta's annual Indigenous Arts Festival (early July; www.parracity. nsw.gov.au) showcases Aboriginal filmmakers and their work. For more information on other local film festivals and cinemas, see p131.

Giant video screen on a building at Fox Studios (p131)

Sydney's three commercial TV stations (channels 7, 9 and 10) serve up a steady diet of reality TV dross, soap operas, American comedy imports, sensationalistic news, plenty of sports and enough 'home/garden makeover' shows to make you wonder if Australians ever leave their domiciles to savour all that beautiful weather. One local production that has added to this sunny perception of Oz is *Home and Away,* which is often filmed at Palm Beach on Sydney's Northern Beaches.

ABC (channel 2) is the national broadcaster and specialises in BBC-related programs (along with more local news and current affairs) that appeal to a wide sector of Australian society. SBS, the multicultural broadcaster, is the thinking person's TV station and a national gem: their 6.30pm news bulletin is easily the best in the country. For more on TV, see p210.

THEATRE

Sydney has something for all mainstream tastes, from imported blockbuster musicals at major venues like the State Theatre to solid, crowd-friendly productions in well-built theatres in the city. While there are a few small theatre companies staging more experimental, exciting works in inner-city suburbs, Sydney's theatrical tastes tend towards, well, the unadventurous end of the spectrum, and sometimes appear to be riding the wave from its 1970s glory days.

While the bulk of Australian actors live and work in Sydney, Australia's geographic isolation and a lingering sense of the 'cultural cringe' mean that truly local theatre gigs are few and far between, and not particularly well paid. Thus, many actors prefer to get as much film and TV work as they can, or better yet, go overseas. The National Institute of Dramatic Art (NIDA) in Kensington is a breeding ground for new talent, and stages performances of students' work. For more details on theatre venues see p129.

The city's biggest name in theatre is the popular Sydney Theatre Company (STC), at Miller's Point. Established in 1978, it provides a balanced program of modern, classical, local and foreign drama and attracts solid talent across the board. The company is still radiant from the opening of its state-of-the-art Sydney Theatre in 2004. There are also many smaller theatre companies presenting genuinely innovative work: Sydney's much-loved Company B at the Belvoir St Theatre; Griffin at the Stables; Tamarama Rock Surfers at the Old Fitzroy and various local independent companies at the Darlinghurst Theatre. The independent scene also supports 'boutique' companies like Pact Youth Theatre and the Sidetrack Performance group, which emphasise multicultural issues.

Sydney-based writers and directors of note include the acclaimed John Bell, who often takes the reins (when he's not appearing on stage) of his Bell Shakespeare Company; Neil Armfield, the prolific artistic director of Company B; Kate Gaul, who is known for interpreting new works; Adam Cook, who took on the challenging task of adapting and directing Patrick White's *The Aunt's Story* for the stage in 2001; and the political Stephen Sewell, who wrote the multi-award-winning play *Myth, Propaganda and Disaster in Nazi Germany and Contemporary America.*

Stage performers to keep an eye out for in local productions include Angie Millikin, Jackie Weaver, Marcus Graham, Gillian Jones, John Gaden, Wendy Hughes, Angela Punch-MacGregor and Barry Otto.

Sydney is still recovering from the deaths of two of its brightest theatre stars in recent times, former STC founder Richard Wherrett (1940-2001), who might have been Australia's most successful and controversial theatrical director, and the much-loved playwright and teacher Nick Enright (1950-2003), whose legacy includes the musical *The Boy from Oz* and the Oscar-nominated screenplay *Lorenzo's Oil.* Both men contributed to the flourishing of the Sydney theatrical scene from the 1970s onwards.

Architecture

Architecture

LANDSCAPE & HISTORY

As a land colonised from the sea, the pattern of settlement and development in Sydney has been determined by water in all its forms. The freshwater Tank Stream, which cuts Circular Quay in half (now in brick culverts beneath city streets) is the reason the city is here at all, and it inspired the first planning initiatives. Governor Phillip used the stream to divide the convicts on the rocky west from the officers on the gentler eastern slopes. Following this pattern, government institutions concentrated on the east of the stream, while industry was attracted to the western side of the city. So social differences were articulated in the layout of the settlement and set a pattern that continued as the city grew, a class distinction that has had a lasting effect and can be seen in Sydney almost 220 years later.

Sydney Opera House (p70)

Sydney conforms to an Aboriginal pattern of human occupation. Scientist and author Dr Tim Flannery observes that like many Aboriginal campsites, the city lies near fresh water on a north-facing shore where it catches winter sun, while being sheltered from the chilling southerly and the bullying westerly winds. The northeasterly breeze, meanwhile, comes straight through the mouth of the harbour, delivering warm winter and cool summer breezes.

The gentler topography and northern aspect resulted in dense development to the south of the harbour. This area enjoys a romantic view of the bushland vista of the north.

THE SYDNEY OPERA HOUSE

Frank Lloyd Wright called it a 'circus tent' and Mies van der Rohe thought it the work of the devil, yet Danish architect Jørn Utzon bequeathed Sydney one of the 20th century's defining architectural moments.

Utzon was 38 when he entered the Opera House competition, and remarkably, had only realised a few small houses. Working from navigational maps of the site and memories of his travels to the great pre-Columbian platforms in Mexico, Utzon achieved the unimaginable. His great architectural gesture – billowing white clouds hovering above a heavy stone platform – tapped into the essence of Sydney, almost as if building and site had grown out of the same founding principles.

Eight years on, having realised his designs for the platform, concrete shells and ceramic skin, Utzon found himself with a new client, NSW Premier and Liberal Party scoundrel Robert Askin. By April 1966, owed hundreds of thousands of dollars in unpaid fees, Utzon was unceremoniously forced to leave his building half finished. He says now that the six years he spent developing his House's interiors and glass walls, of which there is nothing to show, were the most productive of his working life.

Now a spritely octogenarian, Utzon is again working on his Opera House, this time with his architect son Jan Utzon and Sydney architect Richard Johnson. The majority of the new work concerns the interiors, most notably the design of a completely new acoustic interior for the Opera Shell. We are led to believe that although there is money to pay Utzon to design the work there is no money to do the work itself. Bring back the state lottery we say!

The **Sydney Opera House** (☎ 9250 7250) conducts regular tours of the building including tours of the new 'Utzon Room'. The architect-led **Sydney Architecture Walks** (☎ 8239 2211; www.sydneyarchitecture.org) run comprehensive tours that discuss Utzon's work and ideas.

TOP FIVE PUBLIC BUILDINGS (APART FROM THE OPERA HOUSE)

- **Aurora Place office and apartment buildings** (Map pp228–9; cnr Phillip and Bent Sts, City; 2000; Renzo Piano Building Workshop) This is Piano's homage to 'the grand old lady down the road', a radical, very fine and very feminine take on corporate space. You can even have coffee in the foyer!
- **Arthur and Yvonne Boyd Education Centre** (☎ 4423 0433; sonya@bundanon.com.au; Riversdale; 2000; Glenn Murcutt) Pritzker-prizewinning Australian architect Glenn Murcutt's best building, and it's public! A few hours out of town but well worth the trip.
- **Australia Square** (Map pp228–9; cnr George and Pitt Sts, City; 1967; Harry Seidler) A 183m-high Seidler–PL Nervi modernist classic. The Calder stabile located near the George St entrance and the foyer mural by New York artist Sol LeWitt are also well worth a look.
- **Wylie's Sea Baths** (Map p238; South Coogee; 1907; HA Wylie) A delicate timber structure clinging to the cliffs of South Coogee. Do the two-hour cliff walk from Bondi for full effect.
- **QVB** (Map pp228–9; George St, Sydney; 1898; George McRae) And to think it was almost pulled down to make way for a car park.

The ridges were tracks for the indigenous people, a quick and energy-efficient way to cross the hilly terrain. Roads followed the pathways of the original inhabitants, quickly leading to a seemingly haphazard street pattern, the fortunate legacy of an unplanned city.

In one of history's greatest coincidences, Frenchman Jean Compte de la Perouse arrived at Botany Bay days after the First Fleet, so from the outset there was a perceived threat of invasion. As a consequence, the navy appropriated much of the harbour foreshore, which was truly fortunate because they resisted the temptation to build on the land. Recently six key harbour sites, including the North Head and Cockatoo Island, were returned to the people of Sydney under the control of the Harbour Trust. See www.harbourtrust.gov.au.

AN ANTIPODEAN BRITAIN

During the 18th and 19th centuries, Sydney sought to make itself an antipodean Britain, denying its social, environmental and geographic context. As a result, the city has an architecture that is largely derived from European and North American sources and that is often anachronistic and developed for quite a different climate. Two such examples are the **Museum of Contemporary Art** (Map pp228–9) at East Circular Quay, built in the early 1950s to a 1930s Art Deco style, and the pompous **Chifley Tower** (Map pp228–9), at the time the country's most expensive building, built in the late 1980s to a 1920s Art Deco Manhattan style. In many ways it is the erosion of these styles and their adaptation in response to local materials and climatic conditions, such as the use of the veranda or the predominant use of Sydney sandstone, that make Sydney's architecture most fascinating.

UTILITARIAN

Historically Sydney has relied on and been nourished by its harbour, and cargo in all its forms (including human) have been unloaded on its shores. Some of the most interesting city buildings are the utilitarian wharves and warehouse structures that still line parts of the city's western shore. The arrival of the bubonic plague at the wharves in 1900 (which killed 103 Sydneysiders in eight months) was used as the excuse for the government to resume the old, privately-owned wharves and clean up The Rocks slums, and the new industrial buildings reflected a turn to utilitarian simplicity, in contrast to the previous obsession with neoclassical forms. The 'containerisation' of shipping in the 1960s and 1970s made many of these sites redundant overnight and the current obsession for harbourside living is the latest development wave sweeping the city and putting many of these historic sites at risk. One of the qualities that makes the harbour so extraordinary is the juxtaposition of buildings of all scales and myriad uses. The city's challenge will be to retain the richness a working harbour brings while infusing these industrial sites with new uses and ideas. The **Woolloomooloo** (Map pp228–9) and **Walsh Bay finger wharves** (Map pp228–9) are the most dramatic examples of the new uses of these structures.

MODERN

Between the two world wars, Australia looked to the US for architectural inspiration and a building boom took place. **Martin Place** (Map pp228–9), with its granite-bedecked Art Deco temples to commerce and big business, is a well-preserved example of such prosperity. Similarly lavish buildings began to dot the eastern suburban skyline, giving a stylish look to many suburbs, despite some hideous modern incursions.

Some good news in the 1950s and 1960s came via the 'Sydney School', which pioneered a distinctively Australian architecture, characterised by the appreciation of native landscapes and natural materials and the avoidance of conventional and historic language. Further steps were taken as 'new Australians' like Harry Seidler, Hugh Buhrich and Jørn Utzon brought to the local architectural scene a sensitivity to place, infused with Bauhaus and modernist-inspired concepts.

Since the early 1960s, central Sydney has become a mini-Manhattan of tall buildings vying for harbour views, thanks to the lifting in the late 1950s of the 150ft height limit. Best early modernist examples are Harry Seidler's **Australia Square** (Map pp228–9) and **MLC** buildings. Plans for an almost total redevelopment of the city's historic districts were afoot in the 1960s as the irascible Askin Liberal Government (who kicked Utzon out of

FIND IT

The key historic precinct is the area around Circular Quay and The Rocks. Wander down Bridge and Macquarie Streets (Map 000) and look for the gorgeous old Georgian government buildings like the **Department of Land & Water Conservation** (Map pp228–9). Grand Victorian structures include the **Town Hall** (Map pp228–9), **Queen Victoria Building (QVB)** (Map pp228–9) and the **General Post Office** (Map pp228–9) on Martin Place. Wander through the Rocks, up Observatory Hill and on to Millers Point to find Sydney's gritty industrial/maritime heritage. The Appian Way in Burwood is a great place to find turn-of-the-century Federation-style homes. Macleay St, Potts Point, is a wonderful place to source Art Deco apartment blocks, as are parts of Elizabeth Bay, Kings Cross and Edgecliff. The **Historic Houses Trust** (☎ 8239 2288; www.hht.net.au) is a great resource.

Art Deco architecture in Kings Cross (above)

TOP FIVE EYESORES

- **McMansions** In the last 30 years the average suburban block has halved in size, whilst the average home has doubled! It seems Sydneysiders' addiction to bigness is matched only by their hunger for real estate and their reluctance to waver from the brick 'n' tile formula of the project home. You don't have to go far to see the bloated expression of the neoclassical and Federation Australian Dream. **Homeworld** (www.homeworld.com.au) at Kellyville in Sydney's western suburbs is a good place to start.
- **Darling Harbour** (Map pp228–9) A tacky, dislocated theme park of postmodern buildings traversed by freeways, desperately referencing a long-since-erased maritime/industrial past. We only hope that nearby Millers Point, Sydney's next great piece of contested real estate, won't be subsumed by the culture of ordinariness that is so rampant here.
- **The 'temporary' tents on the Sydney Opera House northern boardwalk** These have been there for as long as we can remember and are a disgrace. Perhaps they will look all right when the pot plants grow!
- **The Toaster** (Map pp228–9; East Circular Quay) Once, there were some nasty buildings along this stretch, then in the 1990s they were pulled down, opening up the views to and from the Royal Botanic Gardens and creating a warm, fuzzy glow as locals looked at the jewel in the crown anew. Then some even uglier buildings were erected, despite sustained and vociferous protests. Sydneysiders are still waiting for a proper answer as to how this was allowed to happen.
- **The Monorail** From god knows where and back again. Sydneysiders sure don't use it and tourists spend as much time looking for the stations as they do riding on it.

Sydney) deemed many Victorian and early-20th-century buildings undesirable in the race to construct an 'all new' metropolis. Thankfully, the 'green bans' campaign and plenty of vocal protests managed to save large chunks of The Rocks and areas such as Kings Cross, Paddington and Woolloomooloo.

Many buildings from the 1970s and 1980s are forgettable, but there are striking exceptions such as the **Capita Centre** on Castlereagh St and **Governors Phillip and Macquarie Towers** (Map pp228–9) on Phillip Street.

CONTEMPORARY

There is a freshness and a sense of optimistic pluralism to contemporary Sydney architecture that at its best embraces new ideas while still deferring to its own architectural traditions, particularly the sensitive, site-specific concerns of the 'Sydney School'. The

TOP FIVE AREAS TO EXPLORE

- **Castlecrag** (Map pp226–7) Having won the competition for the design of Canberra, then having been unceremoniously dumped before their vision was complete (a great tradition in Australia), the Burley Griffins chose to stay in Australia and carved this remarkable suburb out of 'goat country'. Refer to a useful map in the back of *A Guide to Sydney Architecture* by Graham Jahn.
- **Millers Point** (Map pp228–9) The genuine egalitarian-ness of the *Western* Rocks with its intact industrial maritime heritage, social housing, corner pubs and dramatic sandstone cut-and-fill edge are Sydney's best-kept secret. Have a beer at the Palisade Hotel or a kangaroo or crocodile pizza at the Australia Hotel.
- **Sydney Olympic Park** (Map pp224–5) Sure, it's not Barcelona or Munich, but full of impressive post-Olympic follies nonetheless. Catch a ferry from Circular Quay or arrive by train at the notable Olympic Park railway (designed by Hassell). Other architectural highlights include the Newington sustainable suburb (Bruce Eeles), the Archery Pavilion (Peter Stutchbury) and the Amenities Blocks (Durbach and Block).
- **Potts Point and Elizabeth Bay** (Map pp228–9) Wander the backstreets of the densest suburbs in Australia. Superb Art Deco apartments, modern housing, coffee shops, boutique eateries and surprising harbour glimpses abound.
- **Walsh Bay Finger Wharves** (Map pp228–9) A family of stunning wharf buildings, among the largest timber structures in the world, neglected since the 1960s and recently converted into a cultural and residential precinct.

most innovative work happens far from the public gaze in the realm of the single-family house, where enlightened clients can bankroll the creative ambition of their architects. Leading figures include Richard Leplastrier, Glenn Murcutt, Peter Stutchbury, Neil Durbach and Richard Francis-Jones.

An encouraging trend helping retain some of Sydney's historic character is towards adapting and appropriating old buildings for a new use. Historic buildings like **The Mint** (Map pp228–9) and the **Sydney Conservatorium of Music** (Map pp228–9) on Macquarie Street, the **Customs House** (Map pp228–9) at Circular Quay and the **Walsh Bay Finger Wharves** (Map pp228–9) are great examples of how thoughtful and sympathetic contemporary additions can bring new life and energy to their historic context.

Environmental concerns are slowly influencing the domain of public architecture and a number of recent buildings stand out from the pack. Renzo Piano's stunning **Aurora Place** (Map pp228–9) and apartment buildings are exemplary. **The Mint** (Map pp228–9), by FJMT, on Macquarie Street, and Sydney's first 'five-star' green-energy-rated building **30 The Bond** on Hickson Rd push boundaries and press all the right buttons at urban, environmental and social levels, suggesting ways towards a more sustainable future.

TOP FIVE BOOKS ON SYDNEY ARCHITECTURE

- *A Guide to Sydney Architecture*, Graham Jahn (1997) – Ten years out of date but still the best architecture guide. Some good driving tours and maps in the back.
- *Celebrating Sydney 2000: 100 Legacies*, Chris Johnson (2000) – A surprisingly good little guide with some very useful maps to facilitate archiwanderings.
- *Jørn Utzon: The Sydney Opera House*, Francoise Fromonot (1998) – The best-value book on the Opera House, it touches on social and political topics as well as Utzon's work before and after the Opera House.
- *Glenn Murcutt*, Haig Beck and Jackie Cooper (2002) – Glenn Murcutt is the most influential Australian architect of his generation and won the 2002 Pritzker Prize.
- *New Directions in Australian Architecture*, Philip Goad (2001) – A beautiful book covering the best of the new generation of Australian architects.

History ▮

History

THE RECENT PAST

Today's Sydney is a glittering example of commercial achievement and the decadent pleasures of life in a fun-loving city. The wildly successful 2000 Olympic Games gave Sydney an economic and psychological boost, placing it right in the world's face. Its population is growing, its real estate has taken off, the building boom continues and arts are flourishing. Sydney has finally reached its full potential as an international destination and power-player city.

Sydneysiders have been somewhat cynical about their state politics, however. Bob Carr, NSW's longest continually-serving premier, resigned suddenly in July 2005 after 10 years in office. Many people were glad to see him go, blaming Carr for Sydney's ongoing transport and public health services problems. Labor's Morris Iemma, previously NSW's health minister, replaced Carr as premier and has promised to tackle these issues head-on – and we all wish him luck.

Another recent political figure is the colourful and punky Clover Moore, elected in 2004 as Sydney's first female lord mayor. Moore is a strong advocate of gay rights, the environment and inner city services, but her anti-'over'development stance has riled the big business people. It's also ruffled feathers in the Labor and Liberal party camps, since Moore is an independent pollie – and despite her new employment, remains a member of parliament.

FROM THE BEGINNING

ABORIGINAL SETTLEMENT

Australia was the last great landmass to be claimed by Europeans, but the first inhabitants of this country were here for tens of thousands of years before the First Fleet stomped a foot down under. Australian Aboriginal society has the longest continuous cultural history in the world, its origins dating to at least the last ice age. Although mystery shrouds many aspects of Australian prehistory, it is thought that the first humans probably came here across the sea from Southeast Asia, more than 50,000 years ago.

Archaeological evidence suggests that descendants of these first settlers colonised the continent within a few thousand years. They were the first people in the world to make polished, edge-ground, stone tools; to cremate their dead; and to engrave and paint representations of themselves and the animals they hunted.

Aborigines were traditionally tribal people, living in extended family groups. Knowledge and skills obtained over millennia enabled them to use their environment extensively and in a sustainable manner. Their intimate knowledge of animal behaviour and plant harvesting ensured that food shortages were rare.

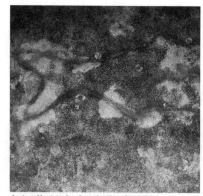

Ancient Aboriginal rock art (p97) at Grotto Point

TIMELINE **40,000 BC**

Dharug people live in Sydney, hunting and painting rock art

AD 1770

Captain James Cook lands at Botany Bay and claims Australia for the British Crown

FROM THE BEGINNING

TOP FIVE BOOKS ON SYDNEY'S HISTORY

- *The Birth of Sydney*, Tim Flannery (2000)
- *The Fatal Shore*, Robert Hughes (1987)
- *Leviathan*, John Birmingham (1999)
- *Sydney*, Jan Morris (1992)
- *Sydney's Aboriginal Past*, Val Attenbrow (2002)

The simplicity of the Aborigines' technology contrasted with their sophisticated cultural life. Religion, history, law and art were integrated in complex ceremonies, which not only depicted ancestral beings who created the land and its people, but also prescribed codes of behaviour. Aborigines continue to perform traditional ceremonies in many parts of Australia.

When the British arrived at Sydney Cove in 1788 there were somewhere between 500,000 and one million Aborigines in Australia, and between 200 and 250 distinct regional languages. Around what is now Sydney, there were approximately 3000 Aborigines using three main languages to communicate, encompassing several dialects and subgroups. Although there was considerable overlap, Ku-ring-gai was generally spoken on the northern shore, Dharawal along the coast south of Botany Bay and Dharug and its dialects on the plains at the foot of the Blue Mountains.

Because Aboriginal society was based on family groups with an egalitarian political structure, a coordinated response to the European colonisers wasn't possible. Without any 'legal right' to the lands they once lived on, Aborigines became dispossessed. Some were driven away by force, some were killed, many were shifted onto government reserves and missions, and thousands succumbed to foreign diseases introduced by the Europeans. Others voluntarily left tribal lands and travelled to the fringes of settled areas to obtain new commodities such as steel and cloth, and, once there, were vulnerable to drugs such as alcohol, tea, tobacco and opium.

THE EUROPEANS COME KNOCKING

When the American War of Independence disrupted the transportation of convicts to North America, Britain lost its main rubbish tip for undesirables and needed somewhere else to chuck them. Joseph Banks, who had been Captain James Cook's scientific leader during the expedition in 1770, piped up with the suggestion that Botany Bay would be a fine new site for criminals.

The First Fleet landed at Botany Bay in January 1788. This motley, dubious group comprised 11 ships carrying 730 male and female convicts, 400 sailors, four companies of marines and enough livestock and booze to last two years. Captain Arthur Phillip, eager to be the colony's first governor, didn't take to Botany Bay's meagre natural supplies, however, so weighed anchor after only a few days and sailed 25km north to the harbour Cook had named Port Jackson and renamed it Sydney Harbour.

The settlers liked Sydney Cove much better, and from this settlement the town of Sydney grew. Word spread, and the Second Fleet came around in 1790 with more convicts and supplies. A year later, following the landing of the Third Fleet, Sydney's population had swollen to around 4000. The early days of the colony weren't for softies and the threat of starvation hung over the settlement for at least 16 years.

Convicts were put to work on farms, roads and government building projects, but Governor Phillip was convinced that the colony wouldn't progress if it relied solely on convict blood and sweat. He believed prosperity depended on attracting free settlers, to whom convicts would be assigned as labourers, and on the granting of land to officers, soldiers and worthy emancipists (convicts who had served their time). In 1792 James Ruse was the first former convict to be granted land by Governor Phillip. He was given 12 hectares as reward for his successful work in agriculture (see p92).

When Governor Phillip had had enough, Francis Grose took over. Grose granted land to officers of the New South Wales Corps, nicknamed the Rum Corps. With so much money,

1851	1918
Australia's first gold rush takes place in the Blue Mountains near Bathurst	WWI ends; Aboriginal children are removed from their families if the father is non-Aboriginal – this continues until at least the late 1960s

PEMULWUY: THE PATH OF MOST RESISTANCE

Aboriginal resistance to European colonisation was a subject long glossed over in Australian history books, although it began pretty much at first contact. Dutch sailors in the early 17th century had violent run-ins on the west coast, and after Captain Cook came ashore in 1770 and had a rock chucked at him, he wrote of the locals 'all they seem'd to want was us to be gone'. (Apparently not one to take a hint, Cook was stoned, clubbed and stabbed to death nine years later in Hawai'i.)

Pemulwuy, a member of the Bidjigal group of Dharug-speakers from near Botany Bay, very much wanted the British to be gone. He was around 10 years old when Cook visited, and pushing 30 by the time Arthur Phillip and the new arrivals from the First and Second Fleets had begun killing and kidnapping his countrymen and generally acting like they owned the place.

Pemulwuy branded himself as a troublemaker in 1790 by killing Governor Phillip's game shooter with a spear. The shooter, John McIntyre, was a convict who reportedly brutalised Aboriginal people, but this didn't keep Phillip from getting royally pissed off. He sent out the first-ever punitive force against the locals, at first with orders to kill ten Bidjigals and bring their heads back to Sydney in sacks. Phillips soon relented and issued milder orders to capture six for possible hanging.

The mission was an utter flop in any case, and Pemulwuy's 12 years as leader of the struggle against the British began in earnest. At first he limited his guerrilla campaign to small, sporadic raids on farms, stealing livestock and crops, but eventually worked up to leading attacks by groups of more than a hundred men – a huge number, by Aboriginal standards of the time.

During his career as a badass Pemulwuy survived being shot, as well as having his skull fractured in a rumble with the enormous 'Black Caesar', a bushranger of African descent. He thoroughly cemented his reputation in 1797 in a bloody battle against soldiers and settlers at Parramatta. During the fracas, Pemulwuy took seven pellets of buckshot to the head and body and went down. Bleeding severely and near death, he was captured and placed in hospital. Within weeks he managed to escape, while still wearing the leg irons he'd been shackled with.

Pemulwuy's luck ran out in 1802, when he was ambushed and shot dead. It's not entirely clear by whom, but there *was* a price on Pemulwuy's head – which was cut off, pickled in alcohol and sent to England. (A similar fate befell Yagan, an Aboriginal resistance leader in southwestern Australia, some 30 years later. The thrifty Perthians smoke-cured his head, however, rather than use up the alcohol.) Pemulwuy's son Tedbury carried on the fight until 1805.

For further reading, check out *Pemulwuy: The Rainbow Warrior*, by Eric Willmot.

land and cheap labour in their hot little hands, this military leadership made huge profits at the expense of small farmers. They began paying for labour and local products in rum. Meeting little resistance, they managed to upset, defy, outmanoeuvre and outlast three governors, including William Bligh, the unlucky leader of the infamous *Bounty*.

The Rum Rebellion was the final straw for the British government, and in 1809 it decided to punish its unruly child. Lieutenant Colonel Lachlan Macquarie was dispatched with his own regiment and ordered the New South Wales Corps to return to London for a spanking. Having broken the stranglehold of the Rum Corps, Governor Macquarie began laying the groundwork for social reforms.

WILD COLONIAL BOYS...

In 1800 there were still only two small settlements in the Australian colony – Sydney Cove, and Norfolk Island in the Pacific Ocean. Inroads were only made into the vast interior of the continent in the ensuing 40 years.

In 1851 the discovery of large gold deposits near Bathurst, 200km west of Sydney, caused an exodus of hopeful miners from the city and forced the government to abandon the law of ownership of gold discoveries. Instead, it introduced a compulsory digger's-licence fee of 30 shillings a month. The fee was payable whether the miner found gold or not, to ensure the country earned revenue from the incredible wealth being unearthed.

1932	1942
Sydney Harbour Bridge opens	Sydney Harbour is entered by Japanese midget submarines

Due to another massive gold rush in Victoria, Sydney (the capital of NSW) remained of secondary size and importance to Melbourne (the capital of the southern colony of Victoria) from the 1850s until the economic depression of the 1890s. And thus the Sydney-Melbourne rivalry began (see p10).

MOVING ON TO THE 20TH CENTURY...

The Commonwealth of Australia came into being on 1 January 1901, and NSW became a state of the new Australian nation. However, Australia's legal ties with, loyalty to and dependency on Britain remained strong. When WWI broke out in Europe, Australian troops were sent to fight in the trenches of France, at Gallipoli in Turkey and in the Middle East. Although almost 60,000 of the 330,000 troops perished in the war, for Australia this was a first test of physical stamina and strength – and they held their own. A renewed patriotism cemented the country's confidence in itself.

Australia continued to grow in the 1920s until the Great Depression hit the country hard. By 1932, however, Australia's economy was starting to recover as a result of rises in wool prices and a revival of manufacturing. With the opening of the Harbour Bridge in the same year, Sydney's building industry revived, and its northern suburbs began to develop.

Things weren't going quite so well within Aboriginal communities, though, as discontent continued to escalate. On 26 January 1938 a Day of Mourning was established, attended by Aborigines from NSW, Victoria and Queensland. However, it wasn't until 1967 that Aboriginal people were given the right to vote. More than 90% of white Australians voted for the change in a national referendum on the issue, altering the constitution to count Aboriginals as full citizens.

In the years before WWII, Australia became increasingly fearful of the threat to national security posed by expansionist Japan. When war broke out, Australian troops again fought beside the British in Europe. Only after the Japanese bombed Pearl Harbour did Australia's own national security begin to take priority. A boom with a net barrage was stretched across the entrance channels of Sydney Harbour and gun emplacements were set up on the rocky headlands.

Sydney escaped WWII comparatively unscathed, although on 31 May 1942 several Japanese midget submarines were destroyed after becoming trapped in the harbour boom. A week later, another Japanese submarine entered the harbour, sank a small supply vessel and lobbed a few shells into the suburbs of Bondi and Rose Bay.

THE CHINESE IN SYDNEY & AUSTRALIA

Colourful Sydney and many other large cities have come to realise the benefits of having a multicultural society, but Australia hasn't always been so racially tolerant (and still has a way to go, in fact).

Chinese immigrants came to Australia around 1840, when convict shipments stopped and labouring jobs became more freely available. Initially Chinese immigrants were considered a solution to the labour shortages, but as gold rush greed came on racial intolerance grew. The tireless Chinese were seen as competitive threats, and state entry restrictions were in place from the early 19th century into much of the 20th century. In 1861 the NSW Government put in place the now shameful 'White Australia Policy', aimed at reducing the influx of Chinese immigrants. This included a refusal of naturalisation, restricted work permits and acts such as the 1861 *Chinese Immigration Regulation and Restriction Act* (a tax on Chinese immigrants). As a result of this policy (and the fact many Chinese returned to China after the gold rush) the Chinese population remained low.

Sydney's Chinese community gravitated to Dixon St around 1870, and soon this area became a bustling commercial centre known for its opium dens and gambling. While the opium dens are long gone (sorry), you'll still find plenty of action in the area (now called Chinatown), along with plenty of Australians of Chinese descent. For the traveller, this translates into some really tasty and great-value food, so don't miss out!

1978	1988
The first gay protest march takes place – a precursor to the infamous annual Mardi Gras parade	Bicentenary of Australia's European settlement; the Sydney monorail begins operation

43

ABORIGINAL LAND ISSUES & THE STOLEN GENERATIONS

In 1992 the Mabo case (named after indigenous activist Eddie Mabo) was one of the most sensational issues in recent Australian history. It involved an attack on the principle of *terra nullius* – the idea that Australia was uninhabited at the time of British colonisation. The High Court ruled that Aborigines once 'owned' Australia, and that where there was continuous association with the land they had the right to claim it back.

Then, in 1996, the High Court handed down the Wik decision, which established that pastoral leases don't necessarily extinguish native title. This resulted in an uproar on both sides, which threatened to undermine the reconciliation process between Aboriginal and non-Aboriginal Australians.

Another issue that remains unresolved is that of the stolen generations. In the early 1900s legislation was created that allowed the forcible removal of indigenous children from their families. These stolen children, whose fathers were non-Aboriginal, were then fostered, adopted or placed in an institution. The idea was to assimilate them into Australian mainstream society (slowly wiping out their Aboriginal blood), but this idea never really worked. The trauma of separation from family and culture brought about wide-ranging effects on Aboriginal society, causing suicide, substance abuse, social pathologies and a vicious cycle of poor parenting skills, which in turn caused even more 'removals'. Up to a quarter of the kidnapped children had been physically or sexually abused.

Surprisingly, this abhorrent practice continued until the late 1960s, and even today the Howard government refuses to apologise or even acknowledge the full extent of what was essentially an attempt at cultural genocide. The mainstream movie *Rabbit Proof Fence* tells an emotional story about this issue; for more information see Lonely Planet's *Aboriginal Australia & the Torres Strait Islands*.

Ultimately, US victory in the Battle of the Coral Sea helped protect Australia from a Japanese invasion and marked the beginning of Australia's shift of allegiance from mother Britain to the USA.

The aftermath of WWII, along with postwar immigration programs, made Australia more appealing to migrants from Britain, Germany, Italy, Poland, Greece and Ireland, among other places. Australia experienced new growth and prosperity, and Sydney gained a jump in its population as its borders spread west rapidly.

Despite the influx of these new immigrants and a strong trade-union movement, Australia came to accept the US view that communism threatened the increasingly Americanised Australian way of life. In 1965 the conservative government sent troops to serve in the Vietnam War, even when Britain did not.

During these Vietnam War years the face of Sydney changed as American GIs flooded the city for R&R (rest and recreation). Kings Cross became an entertaining playground for US troops on leave, giving rise to its sleazy reputation as a den of drinking and bordellos.

Civil unrest over the issue of conscription eventually brought about the election of the Australian Labor Party (ALP) in 1972, the first time in 23 years that it had been in power. The government, under the leadership of Gough Whitlam, withdrew Australian troops from Vietnam and abolished national service. Unfortunately Whitlam's reign only lasted until he was ousted in 1975 by Governor General John Kerr, which in itself created an uproar since Kerr was the British monarch's representative and thus not an Australian-elected official.

The booming economy of the 1980s saw Sydney skyscrapers shoot up, while the Bicentennial celebrations in 1988 boosted the city's confidence. A subsequent bust in 1989 left a number of holes in the city centre, but with the announcement of the 2000 Olympics Sydney renewed itself and put on a great show for the world. Sydney was left with a glowing image and vigorous tourist trade, and hasn't stopped shining since.

2000	2005
Sydney stages a dazzling Olympic Games	Bob Carr, NSW's premier, resigns; Morris Iemma is sworn in to replace him

Sights

Sights

Sydney is smack-bang on Australia's populous east coast, and its centre is located within the protected harbour of Port Jackson – about seven kilometres inland (as the kookaburra flies). Greater Sydney, however, sprawls over 1800 sq km and has grown to encompass Botany Bay in the south, the foothills of the Blue Mountains in the west and the fringes of the national parks to the north.

Sydney was not a planned city (the first streets were essentially Aboriginal paths and bullock trails), and its layout is further complicated by hills and the numerous inlets of the harbour. The city is divided into northern and southern halves, which are connected by the prominent Sydney Harbour Bridge and the not-so-prominent Harbour Tunnel. Most places of interest to the tourist are located south of the bridge.

Hundreds of neighbourhoods and suburbs, some with more spice and charm than others, unite to form the multifaceted personality that is Sydney. We've broken down the most interesting into 10 manageable regions.

The **City Centre, The Rocks and Circular Quay** encompass the heart of Sydney, and all are within reasonable walking distance of each other. Most of the city's traditional tourist attractions and services are also here, such as museums, parks and historic buildings. Further south are bustling **Darling Harbour and Chinatown**, both within a 20-minute walk of Circular Quay. East of here are the lively areas of **Darlinghurst to Potts Point**, which include serene Woolloomooloo and raunchy Kings Cross. Nearby are multicultural **Surry Hills and East Sydney**, and to the east are upmarket and yuppie **Paddington and Woollahra**. As you keep going east the houses get even more exclusive as you hit the aloof **eastern suburbs**. At the end of the eastern line are the breezy, balmy **Eastern Beaches**, which extend from Bondi to Coogee.

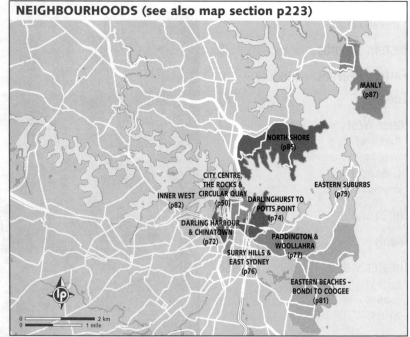

NEIGHBOURHOODS (see also map section p223)

MANLY (p87)

NORTH SHORE (p85)

CITY CENTRE, THE ROCKS & CIRCULAR QUAY (p50)

INNER WEST (p82)

DARLINGHURST TO POTTS POINT (p74)

EASTERN SUBURBS (p79)

DARLING HARBOUR & CHINATOWN (p72)

PADDINGTON & WOOLLAHRA (p77)

SURRY HILLS & EAST SYDNEY (p76)

EASTERN BEACHES – BONDI TO COOGEE (p81)

0 [=========] 2 km
0 [=========] 1 mile

SYDNEY FOR CHILDREN

If you've landed in Sydney with the little ones, take heart because this city is full of ways to keep them busy, happy and worn out by day's end. Look for the excellent and free **Sydney's Child magazine** (www.sydneyschild.com.au), found at tot-oriented businesses, libraries and schools, or the **kidfriendly minimagazine** (www.kidfriendly.com.au), available at tourist offices. For a general guide get Lonely Planet's *Travel with Children*. Need babysitting services? Look in the Directory at the back of this book (p205).

Many of Sydney's attractions have good children's exhibits; check out the **Powerhouse Museum** (p73) and the **Australian Museum** (p61). The **Art Gallery of NSW** (p60) offers special kids' tours and workshops, while the **Sydney Opera House** (p70) often puts on events for children. Star gazers will appreciate the **Sydney Observatory** (p67) and its educational events; thrill-seekers will love **Luna Park** (p86) and its roller coasters. Finally, no child should leave the city without a visit to **Taronga Zoo** (p86), with its grand views and well-tended animals.

Darling Harbour (p72) is a wonderful destination for families. There are kids' rides, playgrounds and activities, along with plenty of fast food outlets. Big draws include the **Sydney Aquarium** (p74), an **IMAX theatre** (p132), the **Chinese Garden of Friendship** (p73) and the **Australian National Maritime Museum** (p72). A trackless train called the People Mover connects most attractions within Darling Harbour.

Further outside the city are some other good destinations. Manly's **Quarantine Station** (p87) offers kids' ghost tours, along with its own dinky aquarium, **Oceanworld** (p88).

Some of Sydney's best kids' fun is free, however. There are always the popular beaches like **Bondi** (p82), **Bronte** (p81) or **Manly** (p87) – just be sure to keep a wary eye on warning flags, and don't let your children wander too far into the water by themselves. Its glorious, grassy parks include the **Royal Botanic Gardens** (p68), with its riveting flying fox population; **Centennial Park** (p79), which offers activities along with picnic areas; and **Moore Park** (p78), which includes the Fox Studios complex.

Whichever way you look at it, your kids will have a ball in Sydney – just make sure you've got the energy to keep up with them!

At the other side of town are the distinct and pleasant **inner west** suburbs of Balmain, Glebe, Leichhardt and Newtown. Across the harbour are the upmarket neighbourhoods of the **North Shore** and then the laid-back beach resort of **Manly**. We finish with **greater Sydney**, which covers the western and southern suburbs and the northern beaches. See each section and the Directory (p200) for transport details.

ITINERARIES

One Day

Sydney Harbour is the heart and soul of the city, and you can spend hours wandering around **Circular Quay** (p68) watching buskers, visiting museums, taking in the views or enjoying a drink or meal. Tour the **Sydney Opera House** (p129), stroll the nearby historic **Rocks** (p65) and walk through the lush **Royal Botanic Gardens** (p68). Scoot off to **Bondi beach** (p82) for a late afternoon dip and dinner, then head to **Kings Cross** (p75) for some bright lights and raucous nightlife.

Three Days

This is a good amount of time to really start getting the feel of the city. After following the One Day itinerary, start your second day with a ferry ride to **Manly** (p87). Find yourself a café close to the beach for an open-air breakfast then go for a swim or long walk along the **Manly Scenic Walkway** (p96). That night, head out to **Surry Hills** (p76) for dinner and drinks.

On the third day, get a different view of Sydney; either climb the stairs to **Pylon Lookout** (p69) or cough up the dough for a 'BridgeClimb' tour (p49). You'll need some serious sustenance after that, so lunch (preferably *yum cha*) in **Chinatown** (p105) is looking good. Follow this with a **shopping spree** along Oxford St, Paddington (p77) or King St, Newtown (p83). That night, take in a show at the **Sydney Opera House** (p71) or other entertainment venues throughout the city (p128).

One Week

On your fourth day, get out of town by taking the train to the majestic Blue Mountains and gaze upon the monumental **Three Sisters** (p189). Have lunch in **Katoomba** (p190) before heading back to Sydney, or stay the night in one of the mountain villages. On the fifth day rent a car and explore the **northern beaches** (p90) at your own pace. The next day, explore one of **Sydney Harbour National Park**'s attractions (p70), before a ferry ride to Watsons Bay transports you to beer-garden heaven at the **Doyles Palace Hotel** (p178).

Head back to Bondi on your last day and stroll the stunning **Bondi to Coogee coastal walk** (p95). Do some final shopping for cheap souvenirs at **Paddy's Markets** (p159) right before your special dinner at Circular Quay – try **Aria** (p103) or **Guillaume at Bennelong** (p104) for exceptional food and stellar views, a great way to end your trip to Sydney.

ORGANISED TOURS

Harbour Cruises

There's a range of cruises on the harbour, from tour cruisers to paddle steamers to sailing yachts. If you're pinching pennies, take the $6 ferry to Manly and call it a night.

HARBOURSIGHTS CRUISES

☎ 131 500; www.sydneyferries.info; adult/child/family from $18/9/45

Run by the State Transit Authority (STA), these excellent short cruises allow you to take in the sights, sounds and, sometimes, smells of the harbour. Take your pick from the Morning Cruise (one hour), Afternoon Cruise (2½ hours) or Evening Harbour Lights Cruise (1½ hours). Tickets can be bought at ferry ticket offices in Circular Quay.

MAGISTIC CRUISES

☎ 8296 7222; www.magisticcruises.com.au; King St, Wharf 5, Darling Harbour or Wharf 6, Circular Quay; adult/child/family $22/16.50/60

With regular daily departures and all the Sydney Harbour icons on the itinerary, the fancy boats of Magistic are a good way to see the sights (with a free beer) in one hour.

MATILDA ROCKET EXPRESS

☎ 9264 7377; www.matilda.com.au; Aquarium Wharf, Darling Harbour; adult/child/family $22/14/50

Another good option for those wanting to savour the harbour quickly. You can start from Circular Quay or Darling Harbour. Commentary and refreshments provided.

CAPTAIN COOK CRUISES

☎ 9206 1111; www.captaincook.com.au; Aquarium Wharf, Darling Harbour or Wharf 6, Circular Quay; adult/child/family from $22/19/59

Competing with the rest of the pack is this outfit (and the hawkers are indeed outfitted), which offers café and buffet lunch cruises, a Harbour Highlights cruise and Sydney Harbour Explorer cruise (this last one lets you disembark at any destination and reboard on the next boat).

City Bus Tours

The best bus tours are operated by the STA.

BONDI EXPLORER

☎ 131 500; www.sydneypass.info; adult/child/family $36/18/90; ☽ 8.45am-4.15pm

The Bondi Explorer runs along a large circuit from Circular Quay to Kings Cross, Double Bay, Rose Bay, Vaucluse, Watsons Bay, the Gap, Bondi Beach and Coogee, returning to the city along Oxford St. Just riding around the circuit takes two hours, so if you want to get off at many of the 19 places of interest along the way, start early. Buses depart every 30 minutes or so, and tickets can be purchased on board or at STA offices.

THE BEST OF SYDNEY – FOR FREE!

- A swim in an enclosed saltwater pool at one of Sydney's great **beaches** (p69)
- A walk across the **Sydney Harbour Bridge** (p69) and around the **Opera House** (opposite)
- A stroll around the beautiful **Royal Botanic Gardens** (p68)
- **Government House** (p61)
- **Art Gallery of NSW** (p60)
- **Museum of Contemporary Art** (p66)
- **Australian National Maritime Museum** (p72)
- **Sydney Observatory** (p67)

SYDNEY EXPLORER

☎ 131 500; www.sydneypass.info; adult/child/family $36/18/90; ⏱ 8.40am-5.20pm

Red STA tourist buses navigate the inner city on a route designed to pass most central attractions. A bus departs from Circular Quay every 20 minutes, but you can board at any of the 26 clearly marked red bus stops on the route. Tickets are sold on board and at STA offices and entitle you to get on and off the bus as often as you like. Commentary is provided, and sights include the Opera House, the Art Gallery of NSW, Kings Cross and the Powerhouse Museum.

Tours on Foot

There are plenty of tours for those who prefer to pound the pavement while sightseeing. Here are just a few:

BRIDGECLIMB Map pp228-9

☎ 8274 7777; www.bridgeclimb.com; 5 Cumberland St, The Rocks; adult $160-225, child $100-175

A once-in-a-lifetime experience and worth the bucks for the unforgettable views. Even if you're afraid of heights, the scariest part is crossing over the grates while *under* the bridge; on the curved span itself the track is wide enough that you never look straight down. Plus, you're securely attached to a safety cable at all times. The 3½-hour tour includes safety checks, your own climbing suit and an enthusiastic guide. You'll also get a complimentary group photo, but you can't take a camera so any other photos you'll have to purchase (at premium prices).

MAUREEN FRY

☎ 9660 7157; www.ozemail.com.au/~mpfry

Maureen caters mainly for groups, but she can take individuals or perhaps fit you in with a group. A two-hour guided walk costs $18 per person (minimum 10 people or $180 per tour). Options include Sydney and its suburbs, or lesser-known destinations within a few hours' reach of Sydney.

THE ROCKS WALKING TOURS

Map pp228-9

☎ 9247 6678; 23 Playfair St, The Rocks; adult/child $19/10.50

With regular 90-minute tours, this outfit will lead you through the historical Rocks area, point out details you'd never see on

your own and tell you tales of the colourful characters that once lived here. Tours run weekdays at 10.30am, 12.30pm and 2.30pm (January just 10.30am and 2.30pm) and weekends at 11.30am and 2pm.

SYDNEY ABORIGINAL DISCOVERIES

☎ 9599 1693; www.sydneyaustour.com.au/Abordiscover.html; adult $65-180

This outfit offers a variety of interesting tours focused on indigenous culture and history. Options include a harbour cruise, an enjoyable walkabout tour, a feast of native Australian foods, and a Dreamtime cruise. We've had good feedback about these tours.

SYDNEY ARCHITECTURE WALKS

☎ 8239 2211; www.sydneyarchitecture.org; adult/concession $20/15

These enthusiastic building buffs will open your eyes to Sydney's architecture, both old and new. Those who are into the Sydney Opera House will love the Utzon walk. Strolls last two hours, leave rain or shine and depart from the Museum of Sydney (p66).

Other Tours

BIKESCAPE

☎ 1300 736 869; www.bikescape.com.au; unit 17, 566 Gardeners Rd, Alexandria; tours from $100, rentals $270-350/day; train Mascot

Bikescape is a trustworthy source of motorcycles for hire, and offers a wide range of tours (from a whirl round town to the wine country to the 'tropical north') and rentals (Hondas, BMWs, PGOs – even Harleys).

OZ TRAILS

☎ 9387 8390; www.oztrails.com.au

This reader-recommended tour operator specialises in small-group trips within Sydney, the Blue Mountains, the Hunter Valley and other choice spots. Charter group prices range from $660 to $880 for one to 10 people.

SYDNEY NIGHT CAT TOURS

☎ 1300 551 608; www.nightcattours.com; adult/child/concession $65/50/55

Like the name says, offers tours (via bus) at night. Check out some of Sydney's famous quirky nightspots, along with the inner city suburbs. Offers plenty of opportunities to stop for snacks and drinks. Chartered day trips to the Blue Mountains and Hunter Valley are also available.

SYDNEY BY SEAPLANE

☎ 1300 656 787; www.sydneybyseaplane.com; Rose Bay Seaplane Base, Lyne Park, Rose Bay; adult $145-620, child $70-310; bus 324, ferry Rose Bay

If you think Sydney looks beautiful from the ground, a scenic flight will knock your socks off. This organisation has a variety of scenic flights (from 15 to 90 minutes) which offer views of Sydney Harbour, the northern beaches and coastline, plus areas further afield like the Hawkesbury River and Ku-ring-gai National Park.

DESTINY TOURS

☎ 9943 0167; www.destinytours.com.au; adult $49-72, child $25-36

Quirky as all hell, this company offers night-time ghost and history tours in a black Cadillac hearse named Elvira. Discover the unwritten side of Sydney while rattling some skeletons in the city's murky closets.

The Rocks (right)

CITY CENTRE, THE ROCKS & CIRCULAR QUAY

Eating p103; Drinking p121; Shopping p159; Sleeping p170

Australia (as white people know it) was born at The Rocks. This was where Britain's first colony was established: on a rocky spur of land at the base of the Sydney Harbour Bridge sporting the prominent cliffs of sandstone that inspired its name. Today the site is unrecognisable as the squalid and overcrowded place it was when the sewers were open and the residents were raucous.

Soon after settlement The Rocks became the centre of the colony's maritime and commercial enterprises. Warehouses and bond stores were built and the area thronged with convicts, officers, ticket-of-leavers (convicts with permits to leave prison), whalers, sailors and street gangs. Not surprisingly, brothels and inns soon followed.

In the 1820s and 1830s the nouveaux riches built three-storey houses on what is now Lower Fort St (overlooking the slums), but the area remained notorious right into the 20th century. In the 1870s and 1880s the infamous Rocks 'pushes' (gangs) haunted the area, snatching purses, holding up pedestrians, feuding with each other and generally creating havoc. The area fell into decline when modern shipping and storage facilities moved away from Circular Quay, and slumped further following the 1900 outbreak of the bubonic plague that led to whole streets being razed. The construction of the Harbour Bridge two decades later resulted in further demolition.

CITY CENTRE, THE ROCKS & CIRCULAR QUAY TOP FIVE

- Walking through the historical **Rocks** (p49)
- Enjoying the affordable view from **Pylon Lookout** (p69)
- Gliding over Sydney Harbour on a **Manly ferry** (p69)
- Picnicking at or walking through the **Royal Botanic Gardens** (p68)
- Touring the **Sydney Opera House** (p34)

(Continued on page 59)

1 *Performance artist miming at Circular Quay (p59)* **2** *Passengers on a harbour ferry (p201)* **3** *Drinkers at Green Park Hotel (p123), Darlinghurst* **4** *Joggers and walkers at Bondi Beach promenade (p82)*

1 *Sydney Philharmonic Motet Choir (p147) at the City Recital Hall* **2** *Cadigal Place at the Museum of Sydney (pp66-7)* **3** *Sydney Opera House (pp70-1) performance of* Testimony: The Legend of Charlie Parker **4** *Puppet show at The Rocks (p50)*

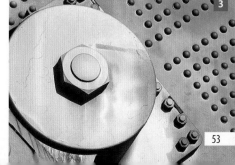

1 *Governors Phillip and Macquarie Towers (p37)* **2** *St Mary's Cathedral (p63)* **3** *Some of the Sydney Harbour Bridge's six million rivets (pp68-9)* **4** *The Sydney Opera House (pp70-1) in front of Sydney's skyline*

1 North Shore (p85) at sunset
2 Camp Cove Beach (p81) 3 Manly
(pp87-8) 4 Surf boat race (p18)

OZ CUT
Concrete Cutting Services

MANLY WHARF

1 *View of Darling Harbour (p72) complex from IMAX Theatre*
2 *Sydney Harbour (p201) life ring*
3 *Approaching Sydney's central business district (CBD) on Anzac Bridge (pp83-4)* **4** *Darling Harbour (p72) ferry*

1 *Historic terrace houses in Paddington (p77)* **2** *Centennial Park (p79)* **3** *Art Deco apartments in Bondi (pp81-2)* **4** *Cadmans Cottage (p65), built in 1816, houses the Sydney Harbour National Park Information Centre*

1 *Bamboo at the Chinese Garden of Friendship (p73)* 2 *Lightshades on Commonwealth Bank Building, Martin Place (p36)* 3 *Colonial remnants sculpture park, Royal Botanic Gardens (p68)* 4 *'Il Porcellino' wild boar sculpture outside Sydney Hospital (p64)*

1 *The monorail (pp203-5) at Darling Harbour* 2 *Martin Place (p36)* 3 *Darlinghurst Rd (p75), Kings Cross* 4 *One of Sydney's main thoroughfares (p59)*

TRANSPORT

Bus Dozens of buses go to Circular Quay from other parts of the city.

Ferry Circular Quay has six wharves with ferries that go to/from the eastern suburbs, the North Shore, the inner west, Manly and Parramatta.

Monorail The monorail loop encompasses Central City stations like World Square, Galeries Victoria, and City Centre.

Train Busy train stations like Martin Place (Illawarra line), Town Hall, Wynyard (Western Line, Northern Line, South Line, Inner West Line), Circular Quay, St James and Museum (both Cumberland Line and South Line) to/from a variety of suburbs.

Parking The Cook + Phillip underground car park has space for 360 cars. Try parking in The Domain, where there's metered car parking that hardly ever seems to get checked. Other car parks in the *Yellow Pages*.

Redevelopment in the 1970s turned The Rocks into a sanitised, historical tourist precinct full of narrow cobbled streets, fine colonial buildings, converted warehouses and souvenir shops. Ignore or embrace the kitsch, but either way it's a delightful place to stroll around, especially in the narrow backstreets and in the less touristy, tightly knit community of Millers Point (just east of The Rocks). Here you'll find charming old terrace houses and the lofty and peaceful Sydney Observatory.

Circular Quay is built around Sydney Cove and attracts tourists with its broad pedestrian promenades, which serve as backdrop for buskers, a plethora of services and some of Sydney's sunniest cafés. It also boasts spine-tingling views of the Opera House and the bridge, and connects The Rocks with the city centre and the Royal Botanic Gardens.

The quay was created by a huge landfill built using convict labour between 1837 and 1844, and was originally (and more accurately) called Semi Circular Quay. In the 1850s it was extended further, covering the Tank Stream (Sydney's first water supply), and was given its present name. Circular Quay was for many years the shipping centre of Sydney; early photographs and paintings show a forest of masts crowding the skyline.

Circular Quay is the departure point for all harbour ferries, the starting point of many city bus routes, and a train station on the City Circle. The elevated Cahill Expressway, running above Alfred St behind the ferry wharves, is one of Sydney's most notorious eyesores.

The City Centre, or Central Business District (CBD), lies just inland from Circular Quay. It contains most of Sydney's business offices, historic buildings, notable museums and department stores. As far as downtowns go it's a pleasant place to wander around on foot, and the sizable Hyde Park offers plenty of greenery in which to relax those tired feet.

Orientation

The city centre is long and narrow, and George and Pitt Sts (the main thoroughfares) run 3km from Circular Quay to Central Station. The Rocks and Circular Quay, where you'll find the Sydney Opera House and the Harbour Bridge, mark the northern boundary of the city centre. Darling Harbour forms the western boundary while the Royal Botanic Gardens and Hyde Park border the area's east side.

The main street leading into The Rocks is crooked George St, which is essentially Australia's first 'street'. Cumberland St is parallel to the northern top end of George St, and almost all of the area's attractions are jammed into the narrow paths and alleyways between the two. The Argyle Cut on Argyle St is the short cut between the eastern and western sides of the peninsula.

Circular Quay is basically the U-shaped edges of Sydney Cove; there's East Circular Quay (which contains the Opera House) and West Circular Quay (which borders The Rocks).

CITY CENTRE

ANZAC WAR MEMORIAL Map pp228-9

☎ 9267 7668; Hyde Park; admission free; ☻ 9am-5pm daily

A dramatic and moving monument holds centre stage on the ground floor of this tastefully designed building. An eternal flame burns nearby, and you can visit the museum, which holds well-displayed photos, video and lots of memorabilia and paraphernalia from the many wars Australia

SYDNEY SCULPTURE WALK

One thing that makes Sydney such a pleasant city to stroll around is the Sydney Sculpture Walk, an excellent collection of 10 intriguing artworks created by local and overseas artists. They're dotted around central Sydney, mostly in its parks and gardens.

In the Royal Botanic Gardens you'll stumble upon Bronwyn Oliver's sculptures, *Magnolia* and *Palm,* which depict over-sized seedlike matter. Nearby in Farm Cove, Brenda Croft pays tribute to the area's indigenous clans with *Wuganmagulya.* Look down for this – it's a mix of coloured concrete and tile work in the footpath. More traditional is Fiona Hall's *Folly for Mrs Macquarie,* a beautifully symbolic birdcagelike gazebo. It's on Lawn 62 of the Botanic Gardens.

In the Domain is Debra Phillips' *Viva Voce* at Speaker's Corner, a fitting tribute to the soapboxers. Nearby is the large-scale *Veil of Trees* by Janet Laurence and Jisuk Han, which features clear glass, opaque steel and 100 eucalyptus trees native to the area. Also in The Domain is a sandstone spiral entitled *Memory is Creation Without End,* by Kimio Tsuchiya, which uses its surrounding space beautifully.

The Archaeology of Bathing, by Robyn Backen, evokes the elements of the former Woolloomooloo baths of the 1830s. The site was used for bathing by the indigenous Cattigal people. Close by is Nigel Helyer's *Dual Nature,* which features water- and land-based works, some of which feature the effective use of soundscapes.

Lynne Robert-Goodwin's *Tank Stream – Into the Head of the Cove* does stream-spotters a great favour by placing five illuminated markers at street level to highlight the route of the Tank Stream, which runs under central Sydney. Last but not least, *Passage* by Anne Graham marks out the borders and some of the features of a Georgian-era house that once stood in what we now call Martin Place.

has fought in. Every day at 11am an Act of Remembrance is conducted.

ART GALLERY OF NSW Map pp228-9
☎ 9225 1744; www.artgallery.nsw.gov.au; Art Gallery Rd; admission free; ⏰ 10am-5pm, till 9pm Wed
The AGNSW, in The Domain, east of Macquarie St, has an excellent permanent display of 19th- and 20th-century Australian art, Aboriginal and Torres Strait Islander art, 15th- to 19th-century European and Asian art, and some inspired temporary exhibits. The frequently controversial, much-debated Archibald Prize exhibition is held here annually, with portraits of the famous and not-so-famous bringing out the art critic in almost every Sydneysider. Temporary exhibitions usually incur a charge. Free guided tours are held at 1pm (call for days), and wheelchair access is good.

ARTHOUSE HOTEL Map pp228-9
☎ 9284 1200; www.thearthousehotel.com.au; 275 Pitt St; ⏰ 11am-midnight Mon-Tue, till 1am Wed & Thu, till 3am Fri, 5pm-6am Sat
Once the School of Arts (1836), this beautifully restored, heritage-listed building houses an artful combination of the artistic and the alcoholic. There are regular exhibitions by emerging Australian artists in the Gallery bar, and the Verge bar once housed

a chapel. Upstairs is a restaurant and lounge; for more information see p121.

AURORA PLACE Map pp228-9
☎ 8243 4400; 88 Phillip St
Renzo Piano designed this complex of offices (purported to be Australia's most expensive), apartments and shops, and its bold lines and graceful mass still look pretty impressive from a distance. Up closer it looks like they're having trouble keeping some of the windows and the Perspex awnings clean. Comparing Aurora Place with the simple timelessness of Australia Square makes for an interesting architectural study.

AUSTRALIA SQUARE Map pp228-9
Cnr George & Bond Sts
Generally acknowledged as Sydney's first major office block, Australia Square was designed by local phenomenon Harry Seidler in the early 1960s. His timeless 47-storey design, with its distinctive circular form and airy open plaza at the base, has aged beautifully. The Alexander Calder sculpture on the plaza outside (one of his stabiles) looks somewhat dated in contrast, while the colourful Sol LeWitt mural in the lobby makes you pray that the 1960s die with the last baby-boomer. A rare Le Corbusier tapestry that hung in the lobby for decades

was recently auctioned off by the building's owner, GPT/Deutsche Bank.

AUSTRALIAN MUSEUM Map pp228-9
☎ 9320 6000; www.amonline.net.au; 6 College St; adult/child/family $10/5/17.50-25, over 55 free; ⏲ 9.30am-5pm
This natural-history museum, established only 40 years after the First Fleet dropped anchor, has an excellent Australian wildlife collection (including some cool skeletons) and a gallery tracing Aboriginal history and the Dreamtime. It's on the eastern flank of Hyde Park, on the corner of College and William Sts. There's an indigenous performance at noon and 2pm every Sunday, and a range of exciting kids' activities in the holidays. It's also wheelchair accessible.

THE DOMAIN Map pp228-9
The Domain is a large, grassy and tree-dotted area east of Macquarie St. It contained Australia's first farm and was set aside by Governor Phillip in 1788 for public recreation. Today, The Domain is used by workers for lunchtime sport and as a place to escape the bustle of the city. It's also the Sunday afternoon gathering place for impassioned soapbox speakers who do their best to entertain or enrage their listeners. **Tropfest film festival** (p10) is held here, as are free events during the **Sydney Festival** (p10). The **Art Gallery of NSW** (opposite) is located here as well.

The Domain is separated from the Royal Botanic Gardens by the Cahill Expressway, but you can cross via the Art Gallery Rd bridge. At dusk the large flying fox colony that lives in the RBG flies over the Domain; it's quite an eerie and spectacular sight.

GOVERNMENT HOUSE Map pp228-9
☎ 9931 5222; www.hht.net.au; Macquarie St; admission free; ⏲ grounds 10am-4pm, house 10am-3pm Fri-Sun
Government House, completed in 1845, is the third of five structures that have served as the official residence of the governor of New South Wales (another is in Parramatta). It dominates the western headland of Farm Cove and plays host to visiting dignitaries, including heads of state and royalty (the governor uses it for weekly meetings as well). It's a marvellous example of the Gothic Revival style. Tours of the house depart every half-hour from 10.30am. They're

the only way to see the opulent interior, and can be extremely entertaining and informative. Disabled access is OK, but it's always best to call in advance and let staff help with arrangements.

GREAT SYNAGOGUE Map pp228-9
☎ 9267 2477; 187A Elizabeth St; adult/concession $5/3; ⏲ tours noon Tue & Thu (enter at 166 Castlereagh St), services 5.30pm Fri, 8.45am Sat
The Great Synagogue was built in 1878 and houses Sydney's longest-running congregation. The impressive ceiling features gold-leaf stars on a night-blue background. The general public can only visit via the tours.

HISTORY HOUSE Map pp228-9
☎ 9247 8001; 133 Macquarie St
This beautiful Victorian townhouse, completed in 1872 by architect George Allen Mansfield for his uncle, the politician George Oakes, has housed the Royal Australian Historical Society since 1970. The library is open to researchers, for a fee; otherwise there's no public access. Just down the block at 145 Macquarie St is a similar building quartering the Royal Australian College of Physicians. Australia Place looms behind it, affording an interesting contrast.

HYDE PARK Map pp228-9
Hyde Park is a refreshing green space within the city centre. Much more domesticated than The Domain, it still offers something of a break from the surrounding traffic and crowds, and a home to many small creatures. The tree-formed tunnel running down the middle is particularly lovely to walk through at night, when it's illuminated by fairy lights. Make the amble from south to north, in order to best appreciate the richly symbolic Art Deco **Archibald Memorial Fountain** at the northern end.

HYDE PARK BARRACKS MUSEUM
Map pp228-9
☎ 8239 2311; www.hht.net.au; Queens Sq, Macquarie St; adult/child & concession/family $7.50/3/17; ⏲ 9.30am-5pm
Francis Greenway designed this squarish, decorously Georgian structure (1819) as convict quarters. It later served in turn as an immigration depot, an asylum for women, and even law courts. Now it's a fascinating if not entirely cheerful museum, focusing

on the various phases of the barracks' history and the archaeological efforts made to learn that history in depth. Be sure to read about some of the offences that got people transported to Australia to begin with, or added to their time and punishment once they arrived; many of them were of an astoundingly petty nature. Cheapskates can wander the exterior courtyard and look at the display in the museum's foyer for free.

MACQUARIE STREET Map pp228-9
Sydney's early public buildings graces Macquarie St, which runs along the eastern edge of the city from Hyde Park to the Opera House. The street is named after Governor Lachlan Macquarie, the first governor to have a vision of the city extending beyond a convict colony. Macquarie commissioned convicted forger Francis Greenway to design this street in the early 19th century.

MARBLE BAR Map pp228-9
Hilton Hotel Sydney, 259 Pitt St
Long delays in the Hilton Hotel Sydney's renovation have kept this extravagant piece of Victoriana under wraps since 2002, but with luck it should be back on display by the time you read this. The bar, now situated under the Hilton, was built by George Adams, founder of Tattersalls lotteries. When the old Adams Hotel was torn down to build the Hilton, the bar was carefully dismantled and then reassembled.

MARTIN PLACE Map pp228-9
This grand mall extends from Macquarie St to George St and is lined with monuments to imperialism past and present, including several financial institutions and the enormous, beautifully colonnaded Victorian building at No. One Martin Pl. Formerly the General Post Office (GPO), it underwent an enormously expensive renovation and now houses a hotel, shops and restaurants as well as a postal facility. The Commonwealth Bank, corner of Martin Pl and Elizabeth St, and the Westpac Bank on George St, opposite the western end of Martin Pl, have impressive old bank chambers.

The vehicle-free mall is a low-stress route across five busy downtown blocks. It has a has a couple of fountains, plenty of public seating and an amphitheatre – a popular lunchtime entertainment spot, especially during the Sydney Festival (p10) in January, when there's free entertainment daily. Near the George St end of Martin Place is the Cenotaph, commemorating Australia's war dead. This is where Sydney's Christmas tree is placed in December.

MINT BUILDING Map pp228-9
☎ 8239 2288; 10 Macquarie St; admission free; ☾ 9am-5pm Mon-Fri
The handsome main building (1811–16) in the Mint complex was the southern wing of the infamous Rum Hospital, built by two Sydney merchants in return for a monopoly on the rum trade (Sydney's *real* form of currency in those days!). It became a branch of the Royal Mint in 1854, the first to be established outside London. It's now head office for the Historic Houses Trust (HHT), with cheerful, very knowledgable staff, a small historical collection on the premises and a lovely café. You're welcome to peruse those areas not posted off-limits, including the serene rear courtyard and parts of the large stone building behind it. In the upstairs library there you can see the old prefab cast iron framework of the structure.

PARLIAMENT HOUSE Map pp228-9
☎ 9230 2047; www.parliament.nsw.gov.au; Macquarie St; admission free; ☾ 9.30am-4pm Mon-Fri; train Martin Place
Twin of the Mint (above), Parliament House (1816), used by the Legislative Council of the colony from 1829, is still used by the Parliament of New South Wales, making it the world's oldest continually operating parliament building. The front section is an elegant two-storey, sandstone, verandaed building, originally the northern wing of the Rum Hospital. It blends seamlessly into a modern addition on the east side. You'll need to go through a very sensitive metal detector and get a pass to gain access to the public gallery, open on days when Parliament is sitting, but once you're in you can nearly reach out and touch the pollies. Wheelchair access is excellent.

QUEEN VICTORIA BUILDING (QVB)
Map pp228-9
☎ 9265 6869; 455 George St; ☾ bldg 24hr, shops 9am-6pm Mon-Wed, Fri & Sat, 9am-9pm Thu, 11am-5pm Sun
They don't build 'em like this anymore! The lavish QVB, next to Town Hall, takes up the

entire long block bordered by George, Market, York and Druitt Sts, and houses some 200 shops (p162), cafés and restaurants. It was originally built in 1898 for the city's fruit and vegetable market.

The becolumned façade and multiple verdigrised copper domes are meant to evoke a Byzantine palace. **Guided tours** (☎ 9264 9209; ⏱ 11.30am & 2.30pm Mon-Sat, noon & 2.30pm Sun) depart from the Information Desk just south of the building's middle, on the ground level. Among the interior features to keep an eye out for are the two large suspended clocks, one in fake sandstone, one in the shape of a castle. Outside the QVB is an imposing statue of Queen Victoria herself, and nearby is a wishing well featuring a small bronze statue of her beloved pooch, Islay (which, quite disconcertingly, speaks aloud in the deep baritone voice of radio shock jock John Laws).

ST ANDREW'S CATHEDRAL Map pp228-9
☎ 9265 1661; www.cathedral.sydney.anglican
.asn.au; cnr George & Bathurst Sts; admission free;
⏱ 10am-4pm Mon & Tue, Fri & Sat, 8am-8pm Wed,
10am-6.30pm Thu, 7.30am-8pm Sun
Sporting beautiful stained glass and twin spires inspired by England's York Minster, St Andrew's is the oldest cathedral in Australia, founded in 1819 and consecrated in 1868. It's been tastefully renovated and disabled access is good. Organ recitals (donations appreciated) take place here at 1.10pm Friday, and during term time, free 'Young Music' concerts are held Thursday at 1.10pm.

ST JAMES' CHURCH Map pp228-9
☎ 9232 3022; www.stjameschurchsydney.org.au;
Queens Sq; admission free; ⏱ 8am-6pm Mon-Fri,
8am-4.30 Sat, 7am-4pm Sun
Another Greenway gem, St James' Church (1819–24) was originally designed to be a courthouse, but was consecrated by the Reverend Marsden in 1824. Restored in the 1950s, it contains traditional stained glass, but also the more modern, striking 'creation window' in the Chapel of the Holy Spirit, as well as a choir loft of dark wood and a lovely pipe organ. Free half-hour organ recitals are given at 1.15pm Wednesday from March to December and free tours at 2.30pm Monday to Friday.

ST MARY'S CATHEDRAL Map pp228-9
☎ 9220 0400; www.sydney.catholic.org.au; cnr
College St & Prince Albert Rd; admission free;
⏱ 6.30am-6.30pm Sun-Fri, 7am-7pm Sat
Begun in 1868 and consecrated in 1905, St Mary's is the seat of the Archbishop of Sydney who, traditionally, is eventually elevated to the cardinalate of Australia. Which means that, technically, he could be elected Pope. (Hey, stranger things have happened!) As you might expect given its importance, the Gothic Revival cathedral is imposingly large, and has oodles of stained glass (crafted in Birmingham, England); its 75m-high spires were only completed in 2000. A free tour of the cathedral and impressive crypt (whose terrazzo mosaic floor depicts *The Creation* and was inspired by the *Book of Kells*) is held at noon Sunday, departing from the College St entrance.

ST PHILIP'S CHURCH Map pp228-9
☎ 9247 1071; www.stphilips-sydney.org.au; cnr
York, Jamison & Clarence Sts; ⏱ 9am-5pm Mon-Fri
Completed in 1856 by architect Edmund Blacket in the High Victorian style, St Philip's is the current successor in a line descending from Sydney's original Anglican parish church (1793). In 1841 it was the first church building in the city to be lit by gas. Today it's a pleasing and unobtrusive church dwarfed by the area's surrounding skyscrapers.

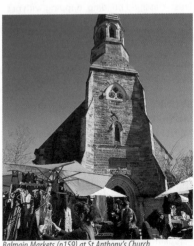
Balmain Markets (p159) at St Anthony's Church

STATE LIBRARY OF NSW Map pp228-9
☎ 9273 1414; Macquarie St; 🕑 9am-5pm Mon-Fri, 11am-5pm Sat & Sun

Situated between Shakespeare Pl and Parliament House, the library holds over five million tomes, and has one of the best collections of early works on Australia, including Captain Cook's and Joseph Banks' journals and Captain Bligh's log from the *Bounty*. It hosts innovative temporary exhibitions in its **galleries** (🕑 9am-5pm Mon-Fri, 10am-5pm Sat & Sun). The library's modern wing, adjoining Parliament, also has a great bookshop, filled with Australian titles, and disabled access is excellent.

The venerable old Mitchell Wing, to the north, has a statue of Matthew Flinders on its Macquarie St side. Behind Flinders, beneath a window of the wing, is a statue of his intrepid cat, Trim, who, as the plaque nearby explains, 'circumnavigated Australia with his master 1801–1803 and thereafter shared his exile on the isle of Mauritius where he met his untimely death.' To clarify: it was little Trim who met his maker, not Flinders.

STATE THEATRE Map pp228-9
☎ 9373 6652; www.statetheatre.com.au; 49 Market St; tours $15; box office 🕑 9am-5pm Mon-Fri & from 9pm on performance nights

The splendidly elaborate State (1929) is the city's most ostentatious theatre. It was originally built as a movie palace during Hollywood's heyday and is now a National Trust–classified building, dripping with gilt and velveteen. These days it stages live shows nearly exclusively, except during the Sydney Film Festival in June (p12).Recommended; **Guided tours** (☎ 9373 6861) require groups of ten or more; smaller parties may be able to arrange self-guided tours.

SYDNEY CONSERVATORIUM OF MUSIC Map pp228-9
☎ 9351 1222; www.usyd.edu.au/su/conmusic/; Macquarie St

'The Con' was built by convict designer Francis Greenway as the stables and servants' quarters of Macquarie's planned new government house. Partly because of the project's extravagance, Macquarie was replaced as governor before the house could be completed. Greenway's life ended in poverty because he couldn't recoup the money he had invested in the building. Past renovations (at a cost of $145 million) have the venue back in the business of showcasing student talents (see p129).

SYDNEY HOSPITAL & SYDNEY EYE HOSPITAL Map pp228-9
☎ 9382 7111; 8 Macquarie St

Just south of Parliament, the country's oldest hospital has a grand Victorian sandstone façade and an interesting history. Dating from the early 1880s, it was the site of the first Nightingale school, and the home of nursing in Australia. In front of the hospital is the large bronze **Il Porcellino**, a copy of a statue of a boar in Florence, with water dripping from its mouth. Rubbing its polished snout – coupled with a donation that goes to the hospital – is said to grant you a wish. Call the hospital for details of guided tours, but don't go wandering in off the street.

SYDNEY TOWER Map pp228-9
☎ 9223 0933; www.sydneyskytour.com.au; Podium Level, Sydney Tower, 100 Market St; adult/child/concession/family $22/13.20/16.50/57; 🕑 9am-10.30pm Sun-Fri, 9am-11.30pm Sat

The unobstructed view of Sydney that you get up here, 250m above the Central Business District (CBD), is rivalled only by that from atop the Harbour Bridge, and here you're indoors. (Whether this is in fact an advantage is a matter of individual taste, but being indoors is certainly quieter.) The needle-shaped tower stands 300m high and on clear days the views take in the Blue Mountains, Botany Bay and the length of Sydney Harbour to the headlands. The admission price entitles you to a goofy but fun virtual-reality ride through Australia's history and landscape. At ground level is the Centrepoint shopping complex, which comprises four storeys of fashion, food and other shops.

TOWN HALL Map pp228-9
☎ 9265 9189; 483 George St; 🕑 8am-6pm Mon-Fri

The High Victorian sandstone wedding-cake exterior of the Town Hall (1874), on the corner of George and Druitt Sts, is matched by the elaborate chamber room and wood-lined concert hall inside. The stupendous **concert hall** (☎ 9265 9007) houses an impressive 8000-pipe organ and is a venue for free, monthly lunchtime concerts. Private functions sometimes see Town Hall closed to the casual visitor.

THE ROCKS

ARGYLE CUT Map pp228-9
Convict labourers excavated this canal-like roadway connecting Sydney Cove and Millers Point on the other side of the peninsula. The work began in 1843 with hand tools, and was completed (with the aid of dynamite) in 1867. The cut sandstone frames scenery and greenery in a dramatic fashion, especially when the light and clouds are right, and makes for a very atmospheric stroll.

ARGYLE PLACE Map pp228-9
Argyle Pl, Millers Point
A quiet, English-style village green in a district of early colonial homes, Argyle Place offers the sacred appeal of the **Garrison Church** and the more secular delights of the **Lord Nelson Brewery** hotel. Both the Lord Nelson and the **Hero of Waterloo** (p121) hotel a block north lay claim to being Sydney's oldest pub.

ARGYLE STORES Map pp228-9
☎ 9240 8800; 18-24 Argyle St; admission free; ◷ 10am-6pm
This was originally a bond store between 1826 and 1881, holding imported goods in storage until duty was paid. Today the complex houses shops, studios, a beer garden and eateries, many of which specialise in local produce.

CADMANS COTTAGE Map pp228-9
☎ 9247 5033; 110 George St; ◷ 9.30am-4.30pm Mon-Fri, 10am-4.30pm Sat & Sun
John Cadman, the last government coxswain, once lived here in what is now Sydney's oldest house (1816). When the cottage was built, it was actually on the waterfront, and the arches on its south side housed longboats. The cottage is now the home of the Sydney Harbour National Park Information Centre, which helps organise tours of the harbour islands (see p70). There's also a 'dig' visible on the lower levels, giving you a good look at a mass of old drain work, as well as a small museum with a few exhibits.

CAMPBELL'S STOREHOUSES
Map pp228-9
7 Circular Quay West
In 1839, Scottish merchant Robert Campbell commenced construction of these storehouses and a private wharf in order to hold supplies of tea, alcohol, sugar and fabric. Construction eventually finished in 1861, and a brick storey was added in 1890. Such storehouses were a common feature of the area into the early 20th century. The surviving 11 storehouses here are now given over to restaurants.

DAWES POINT Map pp228-9
This waterfront was Sydney's busiest before container shipping and the construction of new port facilities at Botany Bay. Today many wharves and warehouses around Dawes Point are in a state of decay, though others have had the 'luxury waterfront apartments' treatment that is so Sydney. **Wharf Theatre** (also known as Pier 4; p129) is home to the renowned **Sydney Theatre Company** (p130), **Sydney Dance Company** (p131) and **Bangarra Dance Theatre** (p131).

GARRISON CHURCH Map pp228-9
☎ 9247 1268; 62 Lower Fort St, Millers Point; admission free; ◷ 9am-5pm
Also known as Holy Trinity (1848), this church at the west end of the Argyle Cut was the first in Australia. Soldiers of the 50th Queen's Own Regiment once said their prayers here, and the first prime minister of Australia, Edmund Barton, received his primary education in the now-demolished parish hall. It's a charming place of worship, and it is also wheelchair accessible.

GOVERNORS PHILLIP & MACQUARIE TOWERS Map pp228-9
Phillip, Bridge, Young & Bent Sts
Governor Phillip Tower, at 64 storeys, is Sydney's tallest office block, while Governor Macquarie Tower boasts 39 storeys. They loom large just behind the Museum of Sydney, and are clad in steel, granite and glass that may well stand the test of time aesthetically, unlike many of Sydney's other high-rise buildings. The towers were constructed in the early 1990s after there had been much fuss over the need to rehabilitate the semiderelict **First Government**

House Plaza, site of the first and infamously fetid government house (1788). The best view of the towers is probably from the edge of the Botanic Gardens, near Government House.

JUSTICE & POLICE MUSEUM
Map pp228-9

☎ 9252 1144; cnr Alfred & Phillip Sts; adult/child & concession/family $7/3/17; ☼ 10am-5pm Sat & Sun
This museum is in the old Water Police Station, in use until 1979 and now set up as a late-19th-century police station and court. Like the Hyde Park Barracks Museum (p61), it can be at once fascinating and depressing.

The various exhibits focus on past and present criminal activity, policing, and the Australian legal and penal system. Is it comforting to learn that the last hanging for carnal knowledge in Sydney occurred in 1901, or horrifying? Displays include forensic evidence from famous crimes of the past, some nasty-looking weapons, lots of mug shots and at least two stuffed dogs. The museum has wheelchair access to the ground floor only, but Braille and audio guides are available.

KEN DONE GALLERY Map pp228-9

☎ 9247 2740; www.done.com.au; 1 Hickson Rd, The Rocks; admission free; ☼ 10am-5.30pm
The cheerful, almost childlike work of Sydney artist Ken Done is displayed in a gallery in the wonderfully restored Australian Steam Navigation Building. Expect plenty of vividly coloured, uniquely Australian landscapes and seascapes, plus plenty of works that depict the daily minutiae of Done's rather charmed existence.

MACQUARIE PLACE Map pp228-9
cnr Loftus & Bridge Sts
Under the shady Moreton Bay figs is this historic little area. Look for the cannon and anchor from the First Fleet flagship (HMS Sirius), an ornate drinking fountain (1857), a National Trust–classified gentlemen's convenience (not open), and an obelisk erected in 1818 and inscribed with the words 'to record that all the public roads leading to the interior of the colony are measured from it'.

The square is overlooked by the back of the imposing 19th-century Lands Department Building (home of the Department of Land

and Water Conservation map shop, p208). Nip round to the south façade, which bears statues of Blaxland, Wentworth, Lawson and other notables from the history of Australia's exploration.

MUSEUM OF CONTEMPORARY ART
Map pp228-9

☎ 9245 2456; www.mca.com.au; 140 George St; admission free, exhibition prices vary; ☼ 10am-5pm
Fronting West Circular Quay and set in a stately Art Deco building, the MCA can make your spirit soar, or bring out your inner Philistine. Case in point: the 2005 video installation of an artist's colonoscopy. Art really is whatever you can get away with!

A broad collection of modern art from Australia and around the world (sculpture, painting, installation and the moving image) is augmented by temporary exhibitions on a variety of themes. The MCA store (☼ 10am-5.30pm) has a good range of postcards and gifts, and the on-site café (☼ 10am-5pm) serves classy food. Disabled access throughout the building is excellent.

MUSEUM OF SYDNEY Map pp228-9
☎ 9251 5988; www.hht.net.au; cnr Phillip & Bridge Sts; adult/child & concession/family $7/3/17; ☼ 9.30am-5pm
The MOS is a top-notch museum that uses installation and multiple-perspective art to

Museum of Contemporary Art (above)

explore Sydney's early history – including the early natural environment, the culture of the indigenous Eora people and convict life. Sydney's early history comes to life in whisper, argument, gossip and artefacts, displayed in clever and engaging ways. Be sure to open some of the many stainless steel and glass drawers (they close themselves).

OVERSEAS PASSENGER TERMINAL

Map pp228-9

Passengers from luxury cruise ships like the *QEII* disembark here, so what better place to site ultrafancy drinking and dining establishments? **Doyles** (p103), Quay and Wildfire are among the occupants of the architecturally dynamic new terminal that typifies dockside development in so many parts of Sydney.

SH ERVIN GALLERY Map pp228-9

☎ 9258 0173; www.nsw.nationaltrust.org.au /ervin.html; Watson Rd, Observatory Hill; adult/ child & concession $6/4; ⏰ 11am-5pm Tue-Fri, noon-5pm Sat & Sun

This small gallery is located in the old military hospital building, close to the Sydney Observatory. Its temporary exhibitions of Australian art invariably prove popular, and every year it hosts the Salon des Refusés show, for rejected Archibald and Wynne Prize contenders. Disabled access is good.

SUEZ CANAL Map pp228-9

One of few remaining such lanes, the Suez Canal tapers as it goes downhill until at the eastern end it's less than a metre wide (thus the name). Constructed in the 1840s, it was notorious as a lurking point for members of The Rocks push gang throughout the 19th century. Where the Canal intersects Nurses Walk, another old cobbled thoroughfare, there's an interesting building with exposed timbers and an old-style hoist consisting of a wooden beam and eye bolt, used for moving goods into and out of the upper floor.

SUSANNAH PLACE MUSEUM

Map pp228-9

☎ 9241 1893; 58-64 Gloucester St; general/concession/family $7/3/17; ⏰ 10am-5pm Sat & Sun, by reservation Mon-Fri Feb-Dec, 10am-5pm Dec

Visits to this row of tiny 1844 terrace houses take the form of semi-self-guided tours. You start by watching a video in the dilapidated parlour of the first house, which illustrates the state of disrepair all had fallen into. The next two houses are in progressively better shape, and you get an idea of what life was like for the working-class folk who lived here during different periods, cooking in basement or outdoor kitchens, laundering clothes using a wood-fired copper out the back (near the dunny).

The curators wear 19th-century dress and run the corner shop that sells wares from the period. They'll get you started on your tour and help you move from house to house.

SYDNEY OBSERVATORY Map pp228-9

☎ 9217 0485; www.sydneyobservatory.com.au; Watson Rd, Observatory Hill; admission free; day tours adult/child & concession/family $6/4/16; night tours adult/child/concession/family $15/10/12/40; ⏰ 10am-5pm

The historically and architecturally interesting Sydney Observatory, built in the 1850s, occupies a commanding position atop Observatory Hill, overlooking Millers Point and the harbour. This was the second observatory to be built on the hill – the first was constructed in 1821. Before that, Sydneysiders took advantage of the hill's exposed position: it was an ideal site for a windmill to grind wheat. The colony's first windmill was built here in 1796, but its canvas sails were stolen and the structure eventually collapsed.

This observatory-cum-astronomy-museum features an interesting exhibition about astronomy in Australia, covering Aboriginal sky stories and the technology and science of astronomy, with interactive displays and videos, and a great variety of vintage apparatus, ranging from chronometers to telescopes large and small. **Night tours** (bookings essential) include the exhibition, a viewing through the telescopes and a screening in the 3-D Space Theatre. **Day tours** also include a Space Theatre screening and they are the only way to visit the copper dome and its big telescope.

Observatory Hill is surrounded by enormous-trunked Moreton Bay fig trees, and it has some wonderfully peaceful spots great for just sitting and taking in the views.

CIRCULAR QUAY

CUSTOMS HOUSE Map pp228-9

☎ 9247 2285; 31 Alfred St; admission free;
🕙 10am-5pm

In June of 2005, 120 years after its construction, Customs House reopened following a major renovation that turned the first three floors into a municipal library (☎ 9242 8555). The grand old building offers attractions for visitors and locals alike. The City Exhibition Space (☎ 9242 8555; level 4) has displays and exhibitions on Sydney's architecture and you can organise an excellent Sydney Architecture Walk (p49) here, though the walks now leave from the Museum of Sydney. Café Sydney, on the top floor, has sweeping views of the quay and good jazz on Fridays (see p137).

ROYAL BOTANIC GARDENS Map pp228-9

☎ 9231 8111; Mrs Macquaries Rd; admission free;
🕙 gardens 7am-sunset, visitors centre 9.30am-5pm

The expansive green area of the gardens makes them the city's favourite picnic spot, jogging route and strolling venue. Bordering Farm Cove, east of the Sydney Opera House, the enchanting gardens were established in 1816 and feature plant life from the South Pacific and around the world. They include the site of the colony's first paltry vegetable patch, which has been preserved as the First Farm exhibit.

Overlooking spectacular views of the bay is Mrs Macquarie's Chair, which the governor ordered to be carved out of the sandstone ledge for his wife.

The fabulous Sydney Tropical Centre (adult/child & concession $2.20/1.10; 🕙 10am-4pm daily) is housed in the interconnecting Arc and Pyramid glasshouses. It's a great place to visit on a cool, grey day, with the added advantage of always being warm. The multistorey Arc has a collection of rampant climbers and trailers from the world's rainforests, while the Pyramid houses the Australian collection, including monsoonal, woodland and tropical rainforest plants. Other attractions in the gardens include the Fernery, the Succulent Garden and the Rose Garden.

Free guided walks (10.30am Monday to Sunday and 1pm Monday to Friday) depart from the information booth at the Gardens Shop, and last about an hour and a half. As far as wildlife goes, you can't fail to notice the gardens' resident colony of grey-headed flying foxes (Pteropus ploiocephalus; see boxed text, below), or the large flocks of sulphur-crested cockatoos, whose raucous squawks can be heard for blocks.

The park's paths are for the most part wheelchair accessible, although there are some flights of stairs scattered about. Attractions are well signposted throughout, although the estimated walking times are best described as pessimistic. If a sign says something is five minutes away, bank on only about two minutes.

SYDNEY HARBOUR

Sydney's stunning harbour has melded and shaped the local psyche since the first days of settlement, and today it's both a major working port and the city's sparkling playground. Its waters, beaches, islands and shorefront parks offer all the swimming, sailing, picnicking, walking and real estate fantasies you could wish for.

Officially called Port Jackson, Sydney's extravagantly colourful harbour stretches some 20km inland to join the mouth of the

FLYING FOXINESS

If you're not expecting it, a walk around the Royal Botanic Gardens (RBG) can bring on a small fright (or glee, depending on your stance). The trees around the visitors centre and café are the leafy homes of the grey-headed flying fox (or Pteropus ploiocephalus) – giant bats with metre-long wingspans. You'll have to see them to believe them.

By day the bats hang around (literally) in their thousands, chittering madly and wrestling for the best roost. Towards dusk they'll take to the air in impressive numbers, commuting to Sydney's suburbs in their search for ripe fruit and nectar. It's an amazing and incongruous sight to watch as they stream over the CBD and its shiny high-rises.

Unlike other bats, flying foxes don't live in caves; they also don't use echolocation and can't see in complete darkness. Also, they don't fly in a jerky manner like their smaller cousins, but rather flap around gracefully, much like birds do. These bats are an important part of the region's ecology, spreading seeds and pollinating flowers as they feed.

For more information on these amazing creatures, stop by the RBG visitors centre or check out www.sydneybats.org.au.

SYDNEY HARBOUR BEACHES

Balmoral (Map pp226–7) A large, sweeping beach on the North Shore near Mosman with several fancy restaurants and cafés, grassy parkland for picnics and a small island peninsula to explore. Popular on weekends.

Camp Cove (Map pp226–7) Near Lady Bay, this is a quiet family-friendly beach with kiosk and historic past. Close to some pleasant walks.

Chinaman's Beach (Map pp226–7) Gorgeous, peaceful and serene, despite its proximity to busy Balmoral. Good for picturesque swimming.

Clontarf (Map pp224–5) Another popular and sheltered beach for families, with large grassy areas for picnics. Not very isolated, however.

Lady Bay Beach (Map pp226–7) Nudist beach (mostly males), with boulders on which to sun and great views of the harbour. On a popular path, but mostly private.

Manly Cove (Map p240) A decent suburban beach in Manly, protected with netting. Close to services; for more party action simply cross the peninsula (p87).

Parsley Bay (Map pp226–7) A real gem, with large calm lagoon to swim in, grassy areas for picnics and a cute suspension bridge to cross.

Reef Beach (Map pp224–5) On the stunning Manly Scenic Walkway, this beach is not nudist, despite what you may have heard.

Shark Beach (Map pp226–7) Despite its name, this easily-accessible beach is netted and safe. It's in Nielsen Park and popular for family picnics; there are services and lush walks nearby.

Parramatta River. The headlands at the entrance are stunning North Head and South Head (the latter holding the unsavoury reputation as a suicide spot). The city centre is about 8km inland and the most scenic area is on the ocean side, although some coves further inland offer pleasant little getaways. The harbour has multiple sandstone headlands, beautiful bays and beaches, numerous inlets and several islands. Glorious **Middle Harbour** is a large inlet that heads northwest 2km inside the Heads.

The best way to view the harbour is by private yacht (yeah, right). Lacking this, just take a harbour cruise or catch any one of the many ferries that ply its waters (see p201). You can also fly above it via a scenic flight (p50). The Manly ferry offers vistas of the harbour east of the bridge, while the Parramatta RiverCats cover the west. You can also visit some of the small islands, which are part of the stupendous **Sydney Harbour National Park** (p70).

SYDNEY HARBOUR BRIDGE & PYLON LOOKOUT Map pp228-9
Sydney's second most famous icon is this massive steel bridge that's visible from a surprising number of spots around the city. Nicknamed 'the coat hanger,' this much-

loved icon crosses the harbour at one of its narrowest points, linking the southern and northern shores and joining central Sydney with north Sydney. It's the largest and heaviest (but not longest) steel arch in the world. Sydneysiders hold it dear to their hearts – partly because of its sheer size, simplicity and symmetry, partly because of its function in uniting the city, and partly because it kept many people employed during the Depression.

The two halves of the mighty arch were built out from each shore, supported by cranes. After nine years of work, when the ends of the arches were only centimetres apart and ready to be bolted together, gale force winds of over 100km/h (62mph) set them swaying. But the bridge survived and the arch was soon completed. The bridge cost $20 million, a bargain in today's money, but took until 1988 to pay off. Giving it a new coat of paint takes four years and 80,000L, making a change of colour a difficult prospect indeed.

You can climb almost 200 stairs to the top of the southeastern **Pylon Lookout** (☎ 9240 1100; www.pylonlookout.com .au; adult/child $8.50/3; ☽ 10am-5pm); it has awesome views and a good museum with exhibits explaining how the bridge was built. The pylons may look as though

69

they're shouldering the weight of the Harbour Bridge, but they're largely decorative – right down to their granite facing. Get to the lookout via the Argyle St stairs to Cumberland St, then follow the Bridge Stairs signs.

Cars, trains, cyclists, joggers and pedestrians all use the bridge. The cycleway is on the western side, the pedestrian footpath on the eastern. The best way to experience the bridge is on foot; views of the bridge suck when crossing by car or train. Driving south there's a $3 toll.

The adventurous and vertigo-free can climb to the apex of the bridge itself on a fabulous BridgeClimb tour (p49).

SYDNEY HARBOUR NATIONAL PARK

Map pp226-7

☎ 9247 5033; Park Office, Cadmans Cottage, 110 George St, The Rocks; ☻ park office 9.30am-4.30pm Mon-Fri, 10am-4.30pm Sat & Sun; parking at Bradleys Head, North Sydney & North Head, Manly $3

One of the qualities that makes Sydney such a wonderful city is its close proximity (and easy access) to beautiful bushland, historic attractions and stunning seascapes. The Sydney Harbour National Park protects the scattered pockets of bushland around the harbour and includes several small islands. It offers some great walking tracks, scenic lookouts, Aboriginal carvings, beaches and a handful of historic sites. On the south shore, the park incorporates South Head and delightful Nielsen Park; on the North Shore it includes North Head,

Dobroyd Head, Middle Head and Ashton Park. George's Head, Obelisk Bay and Middle Head, northeast of Taylors Bay, are also part of the park, as are the islands (see the boxed text, below).

SYDNEY OPERA HOUSE Map pp228-9

☎ 9250 7111; www.sydneyoperahouse.com; Bennelong Point

Gazing upon the Sydney Opera House with virgin eyes is a sure way to get a tingle up your spine; it's akin to seeing the Taj Mahal or Machu Picchu for the very first time. Gloriously white and brilliantly sharp, Australia's most recognisable icon sits dramatically at the tip of Bennelong Point, almost like a sentinel standing watch over Circular Quay. On a sunny day (and there are many in Sydney) the Opera House is postcard-perfect, its soaring shell-like roofs a pinnacle of architectural genius.

The history of the Opera House's construction, however, is a tangled tale. The $7-million design was the winner of an international competition, with Danish Jørn Utzon as top dog. Construction of Utzon's unique design began in 1959, but the project soon became a nightmare of cost overruns and building difficulties. After political interference and disagreement over construction methods, Utzon quit in disgust in 1966. The interior ended up being designed by three other architects and the building was finally finished in 1973, at a cost of $102 million.

The Opera House has four main auditoriums, and hosts dance, theatre, concerts

SYDNEY HARBOUR'S ISLANDS

Previously known as Pinchgut, **Fort Denison** (Map pp228–9) is a small, fortified island off Mrs Macquaries Point. It was originally used as a punishment 'cell' to isolate troublesome convicts, until it was fortified in the mid-19th century during the Crimean War, amid fears of a Russian invasion (seriously!). It now has a café, which may be one of the best places to have coffee in all of Sydney, in terms of views and location. Take your pick of tours, including the **heritage tour** (adult/child/family $22/18/72) or the **brunch tour** (adult/child $47/43).

The largest island in the bay, **Goat Island** (Map pp228–9), west of Sydney Harbour Bridge, has been a shipyard, quarantine station and gunpowder depot in its previous lives. There are tours of Goat Island – a **Heritage tour** (adult/child/family $20/16/62), **Gruesome Tales tour** ($25) or **Picnic Day tour** (adult/child/family $22/18/72). All tours are booked at and depart from the park's office at **Cadmans Cottage** (p65).

Clark Island off Darling Point, Rodd Island at Iron Cove near Birkenhead Point and Shark Island off Rose Bay make great picnic getaways, but you'll need to hire a water taxi or have access to a boat to reach them (see p201). To visit these islands you need a permit from Cadmans Cottage. Landing fees are $3 per person. These three islands are open from 9am to sunset daily; for more information contact **Cadmans Cottage** (p65).

SEEING A SHOW AT THE SYDNEY OPERA HOUSE

Seeing a show at the Sydney Opera House is a real treat, and you can book tickets through the **box office** (☎ 9250 7777; www.sydneyoperahouse.com /boxoffice; ⏱ 9am-8.30pm Mon-Sat & 2½ hrs before Sun performance). Children under five aren't admitted to most performances, so check before you book. And don't get there late, or you'll be shut out until the first intermission!

Popular operas sell out quickly, but there are often 'partial view' tickets available for a discount. A rough guide of opera ticket prices are adult $90 to $195 and concession $80 to $170. For a performance by, say, the Sydney Symphony Orchestra, you're probably looking at adult $45 to $75 and concession $35 to $65.

Performance of Testimony: The Legend of Charlie Parker *at the Sydney Opera House (left)*

and films, as well as opera. Over 2000 events are staged every year. It's truly memorable to see a performance here, so if you have a chance, take it (see above). Otherwise there's a very informative, hour-long **tour** (☎ 9250 7250; adult/concession $23/16; ⏱ 9am-5pm) available; not all tours can visit all theatres because of rehearsals, but you're more likely to see everything if you go early. Tours run every half hour and include a free drink; phone beforehand if you need wheelchair access.

On Sunday there's a market near the front entrance selling Australian-made arts and crafts. Every two months *Opera House Diary* details forthcoming performances and is available free inside. *Kids at the House* is the Opera House's pint-size entertainment program, with music, dance and drama on offer, including the delightful Babies' Proms series.

Disabled access is good for the most part, although some areas of the building still require staff assistance. Subtitles are a feature of opera performances and guide dogs are welcome throughout the building and at performances.

TANK STREAM FOUNTAIN
Map pp228-9
Alfred St
This elaborate, four-part bronze fountain in Herald Square near Circular Quay incorporates dozens of sculptures of native Australian animals. It was designed by Stephen Walker and installed in 1981. See if you can find the echidna.

WRITERS WALK Map pp228-9
Circular Quay
A series of round metal plaques set into the promenade alongside the wharves hold ruminations from a handful of prominent Australian writers (and the odd literary visitor). The likes of Robert Hughes, Germaine Greer, Thea Astley, Peter Carey, Dorothy Hewitt and James Michener wax lyrical on subjects ranging from indigenous rights and identity to the paradoxical nature of glass. Genres vary from eloquent poems addressing the human condition to an irreverent ditty about a meat pie by Barry Humphries.

A wistful entry from the expatriate (and apparently homesick) author and entertainer Clive James reads:

> In Sydney Harbour the yachts will be racing on the crushed diamond water under a sky the texture of powdered sapphires. It would be churlish not to concede that the same abundance of natural blessings which gave us the energy to leave has every right to call us back.

On one of James' visits to Sydney, he saw a group of tourists bowing over his plaque, believing it was the site of his grave!

This heady bunch was recently joined by even more illustrious company – namely, famous Australian *supermodels* (who's spinning in their grave?), several of whose plaques are embedded in the pavement near the Overseas Terminal.

DARLING HARBOUR & CHINATOWN

Eating p105; Drinking p122; Shopping p162; Sleeping p174

West of central Sydney is long, protected Darling Harbour. This large and touristy (but pleasant) area was once a thriving dockland with factories, warehouses and shipyards lining Cockle Bay. Having been a state of decline for many years, it was reinvented and opened in 1988 as a Bicentennial gift to Sydney. Today Darling Harbour holds good restaurants, great museums, family-oriented attractions, a large shopping centre, a gigantic casino complex and some humungous entertainment venues. It's mostly accessible to pedestrians (even Pyrmont bridge) and plays host to many outdoor festivals and other events.

Bustling Chinatown, with its exuberant capitalism, buzzes with activity at any time of day or night. Lively crowds look for a late-night bit and the hippest techno-kid accessories, or just hang around entertainment hot spots and get into the groove. It's a great spot for quick and cheap (but excellent) Chinese food – especially in shopping centre food courts – and *yum cha* (or dim sum) is worthy as well. The much smaller and less obvious Spanish Quarter (or Latin Quarter) is only a block long, along Liverpool St between George and Sussex Sts; this contains most of Sydney's Spanish restaurants.

Central Station (1906; Map pp232–3), south of Chinatown, teems with daily commuters;

TRANSPORT

Bus Any bus running to/from Circular Quay along George St; to/from Railway Square take bus 888.

Ferry Darling Harbour, Pyrmont Bay.

Monorail Darling Park, Harbourside, Convention, Powerhouse Museum, Garden Plaza, World Square.

MLR Metro Light Rail stations Haymarket, Exhibition, Convention, Pyrmont Bay.

Train Central or Town Hall; from Town Hall walk down Druitt or Market Sts; from Central Station walk to George St, turn right and head to Hay St, then turn left.

Parking Harbourside car park, under Novotel; entry via Murray St.

Railway Sq is actually one of Sydney's bus terminals and located west of Central Station. At the turn of the 20th century, this area was Sydney's business district. Running beneath Central Station from Railway Square is a long pedestrian subway, emerging at Devonshire St in Surry Hills. It's usually crowded with commuters (and buskers), but late at night it can be a tad spooky.

Orientation

Darling Harbour is, of course, a harbour, but the name also refers to the large claw-shaped pedestrian area surrounding Cockle Bay. Chinatown is contained within the odd shape made by Liverpool, George, Quay and Harbour Sts. A monorail circles Darling Harbour and the northwest edges of Chinatown, providing easy passage between key attractions.

Although this section covers a large area, it's easy to see on foot (or monorail!). The two main pedestrian approaches to Darling Harbour are footbridges from Market and Liverpool Sts (though current renovations may provide more access). The one from Market St leads onto the lovely Pyrmont Bridge, a pedestrian- and monorail-only span that crosses Cockle Bay. It was famous in its day as the first electrically operated swing span bridge in the world, and these days is often accented by festively colourful flags.

AUSTRALIAN NATIONAL MARITIME MUSEUM Map pp228-9

☎ 9298 3777; www.anmm.gov.au; 2 Murray St, Pyrmont; admission free; ⊙ 9.30am-5pm

The maritime museum is a great place to learn about Australia's ongoing relationship with the sea. Entry to the permanent indoor collection is free; touring the vessels moored outside varies in cost depending on which and how many you visit. They include the submarine HMAS *Onslow*, and until May 2007, a replica of the *Endeavour*, James Cook's barque (which was worse than his bight – old nautical joke there). Inside, seven guided tours take place between 10am and 2pm daily, or make your own way through the numerous displays, videos and installations, which include a navy helicopter, a sailboat made of beer cans, and *Spirit of Australia*, the jet-propelled holder of the world speed record on water (510km/h!). Disabled access to the maritime museum is excellent.

AUSTRALIA'S NORTHERN TERRITORY & OUTBACK CENTRE Map pp228-9

☎ 9283 7477; 28 Darling Walk, 1-25 Harbour St; ⏱ 10am-6pm

Acting as both a tourist agency for the Northern Territory (NT) region and a retail outlet for authentic Aboriginal and Australiana-type goods, the centre has such objects of interest as woomeras (spear-throwers), *kalis* (jumbo-sized boomerangs), musical clap sticks and bullroarers (ceremonial musical instruments). The free 'Sounds of the Outback' performance takes place at the centre at 1pm, 3pm and 5pm daily.

CHINESE GARDEN OF FRIENDSHIP

Map pp228-9

☎ 9281 6863; adult/child/family $6/3/15; ⏱ 9.30am-5.30pm

This tranquil, traditional-style garden occupies a hectare of southeastern Darling Harbour. It was set up by Sydney's Chinese community to commemorate the Australian Bicentenary in 1988, and it was designed by landscape architects from Guangzhou (a sister city to Sydney). Its ponds, pavilions, waterfalls and lush plant life can make a refreshing break from hoofing it about the city on the hot pavement all day, especially if you finish your visit with a pick-me-up in the teahouse (⏱ 10am-4.30pm).

COCKLE BAY WHARF Map pp228-9

☎ 9264 4755; www.cocklebaywharf.com; Cockle Bay Wharf

Check out Cockle Bay, both for the large number of stylish places to eat and for its modern architecture softened by the use of timbers. The development helped pull Darling Harbour out of the financial dumps of the 1990s. Did we mention it holds Sydney's biggest nightclub, Home (p133)? Also check out the whale skeletons suspended from the roof in clear plastic bodies.

HARBOURSIDE Map pp228-9

☎ 9281 3999; Darling Dr; ⏱ 10am-9pm

Harbourside is not the comeliest structure around, but it's an enormous landmark of a shopping centre, with plenty of fashion buys, some souvenir shops and even a few

DARLING HARBOUR & CHINATOWN TOP FIVE

- Eating *yum cha* in Chinatown (p105)
- Exploring the Powerhouse Museum (below)
- Touring the Australian National Maritime Museum (opposite)
- Strolling the Chinese Garden of Friendship (left)
- Walking underwater at Sydney Aquarium (p74)

convenience stores selling refreshments and snacks at decent prices. Or if you prefer, take your chances at one of the several fancy restaurants.

KING ST WHARF Map pp228-9

☎ 9299 3513; Erskine St

Imagine Cockle Bay Wharf done up entirely in ultramodern metal, and you've got a picture of Darling Harbour's latest high-priced urban complex. All the luxury apartments in the $800 million development are sold, and the office space is completely leased out, but you can still get a taste of the high life by eating at Wagamama or one of the other trendy restaurants, and by hoisting a few ales or other concoctions at the bars.

POWERHOUSE MUSEUM Map pp228-9

☎ 9217 0111; www.powerhousemuseum.com; 500 Harris St, Ultimo; adult/child/concession/family $10/5/6/25; ⏱ 10am-5pm

It can be tough finding your way here, but the payoff is huge. As are some of the exhibits and the museum itself, occupying what was once the power station for Sydney's erstwhile tram system. Grab a map of the museum once you're inside; you'll need it!

The zillion exhibits at the Powerhouse are very well displayed and always engaging, covering everything from language to industrial design to musical instruments to robotics. There's plenty of interaction (via video or computer activities), or in some cases plain old action, as with the many demonstrations of steam machinery. You'll find that there's something here for the whole family, and occasional performances, demonstrations and films are offered. A variety of free tours are given, and entry for under fives and seniors is free. Special facilities available for visitors with a disability.

SYDNEY AQUARIUM Map pp228-9

☎ 8251 7800; sydneyaquarium.com.au; Aquarium Pier, Darling Harbour; adult/child/family $26/13.50/42-63; ☺ 9am-10pm
The aquarium is another one of Sydney's large places containing large things. The aquarium's three 'oceanariums' are enclosures that are actually moored in the harbour, and the main one holds some truly impressive sharks, rays and other big fish. You walk around and under them, inside transparent tunnels (just try to ignore the cheesy, piped-in music and whale sounds). Apart from those creatures, don't miss the Great Barrier Reef section – it has beautiful corals and tropical fish – and don't rush to get through the informative, well-presented exhibits of Australia's freshwater ecosystems (including the platypuses). Be sure to have a gander at the fairy penguins as well; they're the native penguins of the region. From Circular Quay you can obtain an aquarium pass (adult/child $29.10/14.50) which entitles you to the ferry ride as well as admission.

SYDNEY CONVENTION CENTRE & SYDNEY EXHIBITION CENTRE

Map pp228-9
☎ 9282 5000; www.scec.com.au; Darling Dr; ☺ varies
No, you're not in Texas. They like to do things big in Sydney too, like this behemoth on the western edge of Tumbalong Park. It was designed by Australian architect Philip Cox, who also did the aquarium and the maritime museum. The exhibition centre, on the south end of the complex, has steel masts from which its roofs are suspended. The convention centre is the rounder bit located nearer to the harbour. Check the website to find out about opening times and events; not all are open to the public.

TUMBALONG PARK Map pp228-9

Darling Harbour; ☺ 24hr
This friendly grassy area at Darling Harbour's south end has fountains with timed, acrobatic water jets, a delightful sculpture of sheep leaping into another dimen-

sion, and an amphitheatre that hosts free entertainment some lunchtimes and on weekends.

DARLINGHURST TO POTTS POINT

Eating p107; Drinking p122; Shopping p163; Sleeping p175

Darlinghurst is the inner-city mecca for groovy young hipsters, aspiring filmmakers and wannabe fashion stylists who are just desperate to be close to the action. There's no better way to soak up its ambience than to loiter at outdoors at a café and sip a good cup of coffee while eavesdropping on the conversation at the next table over.

The lifeblood of Darlinghurst (and Surry Hills and Paddington) is **Oxford St**, a strip of shops, cafés, bars and nightclubs. It is one of the more happening places for late-night action. Its flamboyance and spirit are largely attributed to its vibrant and vocal gay community, and the route of the Sydney Gay and Lesbian Mardi Gras parade passes through here. Darlinghurst also encompasses the block-long 'Little Italy' enclave on Stanley St.

Kings Cross is an eclectic cocktail of strip joints, prostitution, crime and drugs, peppered with fancy restaurants, designer cafés and upmarket hotels. It attracts an interesting mix of budget travellers, tourists, inner-city trendies, sailors and suburbanites, with a smattering of lowlifes thrown in for good measure.

The Cross has always had that raffishly larrikin spirit, from its early days as a centre of bohemian life to the Vietnam War era (when it became *the* sleaze centre of Australia). The 1970s and 1980s saw the Cross become the haunt of crooked cops and savvy underworld figures, but now times are changing. In the last couple of years the streets and footpaths have been spruced up, real-estate prices have risen and the neighbourhood is now hosting arts, food and wine festivals. However, you'll still find most budget accommodation in this area, and many backpackers begin and end their Australian travels here.

The suburb of **Woolloomooloo**, wedged between the city and the Cross and affectionately known as 'the loo', is one of

Sydney's older areas. It's crammed with narrow streets and, although it was run down in the early 1970s, has been given a face-lift and is now a pleasant place to explore.

Potts Point is the exclusive and stylish older sister of tarty Kings Cross. Despite coming from the same gene pool, she's kept herself nice, and offers some fabulous stately terraces from the Victorian-era building spree and wonderful Art Deco apartment blocks.

Orientation

Oxford St is Darlinghurst's major artery, starting at the wind tunnel of Whitlam Square and continuing past Darlinghurst's hub, Taylor Square.

Darlinghurst Rd branches north off Oxford St and is the colourful main drag of Kings Cross. It doglegs into Macleay St, which continues into the more exclusive suburb of Potts Point. Most hostels are on Victoria St, which diverges from Darlinghurst Rd north of William St near the iconic Coca Cola sign (which serves as a handy landmark).

DARLINGHURST

TAYLOR SQUARE Map pp232-3
At the junction of Oxford and Flinders and Bourke Sts, Taylor Square is the hub of social life in the Darlinghurst area. It's not exactly pretty, but it is charged with a certain energy, particularly late at night. Facing the square is Darlinghurst Courthouse (1842), and behind the courthouse is the Old Darlinghurst Gaol, where author Henry Lawson was incarcerated several times for debt

---

DARLINGHURST TO POTTS POINT & SURRY HILLS TOP FIVE

- Drinking, eating and promenading at **Finger Wharf** (p76)
- Downing a caffeine buzz in **Potts Point** (above)
- Hitting the night-time action in **Kings Cross** (opposite)
- Strolling your way down the gay mecca of **Oxford St** (opposite)
- Eating whatever nationality's food your palate craves on **Crown St** (p109)

TRANSPORT

Bus Numerous buses (including buses 378 and 390) run along Oxford St and through Taylor Square to/from the city; bus 311 runs from the city through Woolloomooloo, Potts Point and Darlinghurst; buses 324 and 325 run from the city through Kings Cross to Watsons Bay.

Train CityRail line to/from Bondi Junction stops at Kings Cross.

Parking This is a tricky area for parking, and theft can be a problem too; try the underground car park on Elizabeth Bay Rd (behind Fitzroy Gardens) in Kings Cross.

(he called the place 'Starvinghurst'). Today it houses the East Sydney TAFE College.

KINGS CROSS

EL ALAMEIN FOUNTAIN Map pp228-9
Fitzroy Gardens, Macleay St
One of the most notable landmarks in Kings Cross is the thistle-like fountain in the brick-paved Fitzroy Gardens (actually a rather grungy plaza). The fountain is known locally as 'the elephant douche'. Bunkered down behind the fountain is a fortresslike **police station** (☎ 8356 0099), where there are also some surprisingly safe public toilets, given that this area can be a little seedy. On Sundays a small flea market sets up in the plaza.

MCELHONE STAIRS Map pp228-9
Victoria St
These wonderful old stone stairs near Challis Ave connect Kings Cross and Woolloomooloo. The trip from Kings Cross is downhill and infinitely easier on the legs and lungs than the one from Woolloomooloo. Our walking tour on p98 incorporates these stairs.

WOOLLOOMOOLOO

ARTSPACE Map pp228-9
☎ 9368 1899; www.artspace.org.au; The Gunnery, 43-51 Cowper Wharf Rdwy; admission free; ✆ 11am-5pm Tue-Sat
This cutting-edge 'centre for experimentation' has changing, contemporary, avant-garde exhibitions that focus on

modern Australian life and culture. It's an admirable attempt to liven things up in Sydney's art scene, with sometimes disturbing ideas stretching across the borders that stifle expression. Interdisciplinary works are a speciality; disabled access is excellent.

FINGER WHARF Map pp228-9
Cowper Wharf Rdwy

A former wool and cargo dock, the Finger Wharf got a huge sprucing up in the late 1990s and has emerged as one of Sydney's most stellar eating, drinking and sleeping addresses. A slick five-star hotel, the W (p176), some marvellous eateries and stratosphere-priced apartments have transformed this bastion of working-class tough into a star-spotting paparazzi haunt. At the end of this wharf is Russell Crowe's penthouse, but don't expect to peek into his living room.

HARRY'S CAFÉ DE WHEELS Map pp228-9
☎ 9347 3074; Cowper Wharf Rdwy; pies $2.50-4; ✆ 9am-1am Mon-Wed, 9am-3am Thu, 9am-4am Fri & Sat, 9am-midnight Sun

Harry's is one of the few pie carts in the world to be a tourist attraction. It's been open since 1945, and photos prove that anyone and everyone comes to Harry's – even Pamela Anderson.

POTTS POINT
THE YELLOW HOUSE Map pp228-9
59 Macleay St

Once a sunflower-yellow symbol of all things bohemian, this former artists' residence housed cultural heroes such as Martin Sharp, Peter Weir, Brett Whiteley and George Gittoes. It fell into disrepair in the 1970s but has recently been renovated into a slick commercial gallery showcasing contemporary Australian and New Zealand art. All are welcome to have a peek around.

SURRY HILLS & EAST SYDNEY
Eating p109; Drinking p124; Shopping p164; Sleeping p177

Squeezed between the east side of Central Station and South Dowling St is multicultural Surry Hills, a former working-class neighbourhood that has been through hard times in the past, but recently has been undergoing a relentless gentrification. Originally the centre of Sydney's rag trade and print media, Surry Hills is now a wonderfully multicultural area that offers some of the best Indian, Lebanese, Chinese and Mod Oz food in town, and at great prices. There are also a handful of genuinely funky boutiques and some excellent record stores for stocking second-hand gems and the latest in electronica. Ignore the cheesy jokes about everyone having a piercing and being bisexual – you're more likely to find yuppies who can't afford Paddington and who spend a great deal of time complaining about the resident population of down-and-outers devaluing real-estate prices.

East Sydney connects the CBD with Darlinghurst, and has some delightful old homes and architecturally imposing new developments. If you fancy a good uphill walk, head from the city to the east, going up steep Liverpool St.

Orientation
Climbing uphill in an eastwards direction, East Sydney starts from the city's edge and melds with Kings Cross and Darlinghurst; its main strip is Liverpool St. To the south is Surry Hills, whose main streets of Crown, Riley and Bourke run parallel to each other. Both East Sydney and Surry Hills claim ownership of Oxford St, which cuts a separating swathe though both of them.

BRETT WHITELEY STUDIO Map pp232-3
☎ 9225 1740; www.brettwhiteley.com; 2 Raper St, Surry Hills; adult/concession $7/5; ✆ 10am-4pm Sat & Sun

One of Surry Hills' main attractions is down a small lane in a quiet part of the suburb. You'll be able to identify it by the two oversized matches (one burnt, one intact) at the door. The Brett Whiteley Studio is the former studio of this renowned modern Australian painter. It houses a selection of his paintings and drawings and has been 'preserved' to show just how the artist worked before his untimely death in the early 1990s. There are also tours, music and poetry at various times; call for details and bookings.

TRANSPORT

Bus Buses going up Oxford St get you close to some attractions in Surry Hills; buses taking Crown St are 301, 302 and 306.

Train Central is the nearest train station, although there's often a short walk involved. For some East Sydney locations, walking from Kings Cross train station is convenient.

Parking Difficult at times, although there is some metered parking available on the streets.

OBJECT GALLERY Map pp228-9
☎ 9361 4511; www.object.com.au; 417 Bourke St, Surry Hills; admission free; ⏰ 11am-6pm Tue-Sun
Also known as Australian Centre for Craft and Design, Object Gallery is a non-profit-making organisation which displays some of the most gorgeous homeware items in the city. Contemporary designs cover everything from furniture to fashion to typical household objects, with materials ranging from glass to metal to ceramic to plastic and wood. Occasional exhibitions are shown. They also have a store in The Rocks (p161).

SYDNEY JEWISH MUSEUM Map p235
☎ 9360 7999; www.sydneyjewishmuseum.com.au; 148 Darlinghurst Rd, East Sydney; adult/child/family $10/6/22; ⏰ 10am-4pm Sun-Thu, 10am-2pm Fri, closed Sat & Jewish holidays
This excellent and moving museum has guided tours and exhibits on the Shoah, presented by multilingual Holocaust survivors. There are fascinating and evocative displays on Australian Jewish history, from the First Fleet arrival to the present day, along with a sobering memorial to children killed during the Holocaust. Give yourself at least two hours to really soak up what you'll learn in this extraordinary place.

PADDINGTON & WOOLLAHRA
Eating p111; Drinking p124; Shopping p164; Sleeping p178

Pretty Paddington, 4km east of the city centre, is an inner-city residential area of leafy streets, tightly packed terrace houses and filthy-rich baby-boomers driving four-wheel behemoths or pushing prams while in jogging outfits. It was built for aspiring artisans in the later years of the Victorian era, but during the lemminglike rush to the dreary outer suburbs after WWII, the area became an overcrowded slum. A renewed interest in Victorian architecture, combined with a sudden recollection of the pleasures of inner-city life, led to the area's restoration from the 1960s on.

Paddington has since turned into a fascinating jumble of beautifully restored terrace homes (that's $1 million plus to you), elegant-yet-lively shops, cosy restaurants with five-star kitchens, sleek art galleries and cool bookshops – all tumbling down steep streets or lining fashionable Oxford St. But like any desirable place it has its detractors – the term 'Paddo trendy' is often used as an insult. Must be the sour grapes of not having scored a property when prices were low.

The best time to see Paddington at its liveliest is on Saturday, when the **Paddington Markets** and the surrounding fashion boutiques are in full swing.

In contrast to Paddington, Woollahra was never a slum, and it's this self-assured knowledge which, for a lot of residents, gives it the edge over its sister neighbour. A smattering of decent cafés, some great restaurants, lovely boutiques and a wealth of antique shops make it a good spot for a combined stroll/shopping spree. Put on your new-look trench coat, slip into some loafers and whack on the Jackie O shades to look the part.

www.lonelyplanet.com

Sights

PADDINGTON & WOOLLAHRA

Paddy's Markets (p159)

Orientation

Paddington's spine is Oxford St. If you're trying to find an address here be warned that tricky Oxford St street numbers restart a number of times: west of the junction with South Dowling and Victoria Sts, on the Darlinghurst/Paddington border; and again at Jersey Rd in Paddington, near the Light Brigade Hotel.

Ritzy Queen St, which is Woollahra's main artery, runs east of Oxford St near Centennial Park. Both suburbs are hilly.

PADDINGTON

AUSTRALIAN CENTRE FOR PHOTOGRAPHY Map pp232-3

☎ 9332 1455; www.acp.au.com; 257 Oxford St; admission free; ☷ 11am-6pm Tue-Sun
This non-profit-making centre has wonderful regular exhibitions plus its 'Project Wall', which highlights the work of up-and-coming artists. It's a good place to catch Sydney's photographic talent, and there are workshops and classes available (along with a darkroom, studios and a digital lab for hire). There's also a library and a stylish French bistro (see p111).

FOX STUDIOS Map pp232-3

☎ 9383 4333; Lang Rd, Moore Park; ☷ 10am-midnight
As well as a professional film studio (this is where *Moulin Rouge, The Matrix* movies and two *Star Wars* prequels were made), this giant entertainment complex also boasts a big Hoyts cinema, plenty of fashion and homewares shops, restaurants, live music and comedy venues, a market and sporting facilities. There's a monster car park to hold everyone's cars and disabled access is very good.

JUNIPER HALL Map pp232-3

248 Oxford St
This magnificently restored mansion on Oxford St, diagonally opposite Paddington Town Hall, was built by Robert Cooper as a family home in 1824 with profits from his gin business. He named it after the juniper berries from which he distilled his gin. It's owned by the National Trust and isn't open to the public, but is still worth a visit for a rest in the gardens or to admire its beautiful façade.

MOORE PARK Map pp232-3

☎ 9339 6699; www.cp.nsw.gov.au; Anzac Pde
This large utilitarian park, just south of Paddington, is a mecca for sporting activities. It comes complete with sports playing field, a walking, cycling and skating track, horse trails, a golf-driving range and grass skiing. The historic **Sydney Cricket Ground (SCG)** is also here. **Aussie Stadium Sportspace Tours** (☎ 9380 0383; adult/child/family $23.50/15.50/62.50; tours 10am & 1pm Mon-Fri) offers 1½-hour, behind-the-scenes guided tours of the facilities at Aussie Stadium and the SCG, which include historic displays featuring great players (and commentators) associated with sports played here.

PADDINGTON MARKETS Map pp232-3

☎ 9331 2923; www.paddingtonmarket.com.au; St John's Church, 395 Oxford St; ☷ 10am-4pm Sat
A cultural experience not to be missed, these quirky, long-running markets turn Saturdays in Paddington into pandemonium. Originating in the heady Whitlam era of the 1970s, Paddington Markets were a beacon

for larrikin artists and artisans, eastern-suburbs punks and skinheads, patchouli-scented hippies and fledgling fashion designers. It's a tad more mainstream now, but still worth checking out for its pricey cutting-edge fashions and vintage clothing, creative crafts, beautiful jewellery, tasty food and holistic treatments. Don't even think about finding a place to park – this is one for public transport.

VICTORIA BARRACKS Map pp232-3
☎ 9339 3000; cnr Oxford St & Greens Rd; admission free; ☺ 10am-12.30pm Thu (museum & barracks), 10am-3pm Sun (museum only)
There are free tours of the stately Victoria Barracks that include a performance by the military band (weather permitting). The Georgian buildings here have been called the British Empire's finest, and the museum is jam-packed with war paraphernalia. Disabled access is good.

WOOLLAHRA
CENTENNIAL PARK Map pp232-3
☎ 9399 6699; www.cp.nsw.gov.au; ☺ sunrise-sunset
Sydney's biggest park, Centennial Park is a leafy 220-hectare expanse popular with joggers, cyclists and horse riders; it also offers family entertainment with its barbeque sites, playgrounds and football grounds. You can hire bikes and inline skates from several places on Clovelly Rd, Randwick, near the southern edge of the park, or from places mentioned on p200. During summer, you can also catch the Moonlight Cinema here (see the boxed text, 'Outdoor Cinema', p133). Architecture worth noting here includes the Federation Pavilion, where Australia officially became a nation in the early 20th century. At the southern edge of the park is Royal Randwick Racecourse (p148), and south of there is the University of NSW.

QUEEN STREET Map pp232-3
Despite its status as the premier antique shopping strip in Australia, elegant Queen St retains a village atmosphere. It's a leafy tree-lined street with attractive boutiques that make for great window-shopping. Former prime minister Paul Keating owns a grand home here.

EASTERN SUBURBS
Eating p112; Drinking p125; Shopping p167; Sleeping p178

East of Kings Cross are some expensive and exclusive suburbs, where many multimillion-dollar mansions come with private drive-ways, high security and gorgeous harbour views. Local-lass-turned-movie-star Nicole Kidman owns a hideaway here.

Elizabeth Bay is a low-key millionaires' enclave that abuts Fitzroy Gardens on Macleay St and heads all the way down to the water's edge. Expect to see stunning Art Deco apartments and one of Australia's most expensive houses, Boomerang, on the corner of Billyard Ave and Ithaca Rd. Darling Point, on the eastern side of Rushcutters Bay, has astounding views and consequently was the place of choice for the city's first merchants when they were building mansions. Inland is the suburb of Edgecliff, centred on New South Head Rd and boasting one of the highest per capita incomes in Australia.

The wealthy (sense a theme here?) har-bourside suburb of Double Bay is further east. Double Bay's main shopping street is Bay St, which runs north off New South Head Rd and eventually leads to a quiet waterfront park and the ferry wharf. This suburb is worth a visit for its relaxing cafés and patisseries, and you can at least window-shop for some designer threads. There's a small beach near the ferry wharf and a saltwater pool to the east, near lovely Seven Shillings Beach. The latter is actually part of the Point Piper headland, which boasts waterside homes in the $10 million–plus range.

The next suburb over, Rose Bay has a pair of longer beaches visible at low tide, though people rarely swim (it's flat, grotty and filled with boats). On the harbour side of the peninsula is Vaucluse, probably the most exclusive suburb of all. You can walk from The Gap (at the southern end of Sydney Harbour National Park) to the tip of South Head, and back down to pretty Watsons Bay.

Orientation
The main road through this area is New South Head Rd, the continuation of William St. If you follow this east it eventually joins Old South Head Rd, which runs all the way to South Head.

ELIZABETH BAY HOUSE Map pp228-9

☎ 9356 3022; www.hht.nsw.gov.au; 7 Onslow Ave, Elizabeth Bay; adult/child/family $7/3/17; ⓨ 10am-4.30pm Tue-Sun (open Mon if public holiday)

Once known as 'the finest house in the colony', Elizabeth Bay House (1839) was meticulously restored by the HHT and has fine views of the harbour. It's been refurbished with early-19th-century furniture and the original colour scheme has been reproduced. The house was designed in English neoclassical revival style by the architect John Verge for then-colonial secretary of NSW Alexander Macleay (see St James' Church on p63 for Macleay's memorial tablet). The large original grounds of the house served as a sort of botanic garden for Macleay, who collected plants from around the world.

MACQUARIE LIGHTHOUSE Map pp226-7
South Head

Before this lighthouse was built a series of fires were lit along Sydney's headland to alert ships of the shore's whereabouts. It's believed that Francis Greenway designed this lighthouse, but it wasn't built until 1883, after his death. It's a pleasant spot to visit, with large surrounding grassy lawns and heavenly ocean views – best enjoyed while ambling along the Coastal Cliff Walk that passes the lighthouse.

NIELSEN PARK Map pp226-7
Sydney Harbour National Park, end of Greycliffe Ave, Vaucluse; ⓨ 5am-10pm

Nielsen Park is a beautiful bush area southwest of Vaucluse Point. Attractions include a decent netted beach, some lovely, gentle walking tracks and the well-regarded Nielsen Park Kiosk (which serves tasty food). The best time to come is on a weekday, when it's not too busy and the other layabouts are just mums, kids and oldies.

RUSHCUTTERS BAY PARK Map pp228-9

This delightful waterfront park is an ideal spot for a quiet walk or jog, surrounded by enormous Moreton Bay figs, luxury yachts and overly pampered pooches. In January, this is where you'll find the country's greatest yachties, as they prepare for the gruelling Sydney to Hobart race (p13).

TRANSPORT

Bus The 311 to/from Railway Square and Circular Quay passes through Elizabeth Bay. The 312 runs to/from St James train station to Taylor Sq in Darlinghurst via Elizabeth Bay. Buses 324 and 325 run from Circular Quay to Watsons Bay via Double Bay. The 326 connects Bondi Junction with Circular Quay via Double Bay. The less-frequent L82 goes between Watsons Bay and Circular Quay.

Ferry Services to/from Circular Quay's Wharf 4 to McKell Park, Darling Point (weekdays only); Bay St, Double Bay; Lyne Park, Rose Bay; and Military Rd, Watsons Bay.

Train Edgecliff train station is within walking distance of Double Bay. Bondi Junction train station has a few connecting bus services with the eastern suburbs.

Parking Street parking is not a huge problem in most areas, except on weekends; busy spots (such as Double Bay) have metered parking.

VAUCLUSE HOUSE Map pp226-7

☎ 9388 7922; www.hht.nsw.gov.au; Wentworth Rd, Vaucluse; adult/child/family $7/3/17; ⓨ 10am-4.30pm Tue-Sun

Vaucluse was a desirable address even in the colony's early days, so it's interesting to note that one of its finest mansions was built by William Wentworth, a prominent explorer, patriot and barrister who, as a result of his free thinking and vocal advocacy of self-government, suffered a sort of social ostracism.

Built in fine grounds in 1828, sumptuous Vaucluse House is an imposing, turreted example of 19th-century Gothic Revival and is easily one of Australia's finest mansions. It may not look special on the outside, but the interior is laden with beautiful period pieces from Europe, including Bohemian glass, Meissen china and – occasionally – a Venetian dining setting. Life may well have been privileged for the Wentworths, but it also had its share of sorrow, which you'll discover as you tour the house and read the fascinating signs that accompany the rooms (disabled access on ground floor only). The lush 10-hectare grounds are a delight too, and well worth a picnic.

WATSONS BAY Map pp226-7

This delightful part of Sydney is nestled on the harbour side of the peninsula as it narrows towards South Head. It was once a small fishing village, which is still evident today in some of the tiny heritage cottages that pepper the suburb's narrow streets (and fetch astronomical prices at auction today). On the ocean side of the peninsula is **The Gap**, a dramatic cliff-top lookout, while on the harbour side are the small beaches of **Camp Cove** and **Lady Bay** (nudist, but mostly male). At the tip is **South Head**, which offers great views across the harbour to North Head and Middle Head. While you're here, tradition demands that you sit on the sunny terrace and order some fish 'n' chips in the beer garden at the **Doyles Palace Hotel** (p178).

EASTERN BEACHES– BONDI TO COOGEE

Eating p113; Drinking p125; Shopping p167; Sleeping p178

The eastern beaches are really what make Sydney so damn glorious. Close to the city and the business end of things, this coastal slice of heaven is an outdoors-lover's paradise, with swimming, surfing, walking and alfresco dining easily available.

Although **Bondi** is Australia's most famous beach, things haven't always been glamorous here. Working-class roots still show here and there, and successive waves of migrants have shaped some aspects of the suburb. Recent years have seen Bondi upgraded to fashionable status, and consequently rents and land prices have skyrocketed. Today the area's unique flavour is a blend of old Jewish and European communities, dyed-in-the-wool Aussies, New Zealanders who never went home, Irish and British working travellers, devoted surfers and more models than you can poke a camera at. The main reason for coming here is to swim, surf, strut, sit at cafés or just chill out (but be sure to look good too).

South of Bondi, **Tamarama** (or 'Glamarama') is a lovely cove with notorious rips, so swim carefully. It's popular with Sydney's G-string-wearing 'beautiful people'.

Below Tamarama you'll find family-friendly **Bronte** and its pretty bowl-shaped

Surfing at Bondi (left)

park with picnic tables, barbeque pits and pleasant swimming pool. Lively cafés provide plenty of hustle and bustle with a casual atmosphere.

Further south is the shallow, protected lagoon of **Clovelly**, a small haven for families. Swimming is excellent, both from the beach and in the waterside pool, and there's a large concrete area for sun-worshipping. Cafés offer refreshments, and offshore waters host an abundance of marine life that attracts both snorkellers and divers.

Four kilometres south of Bondi is the lovely sweep of beach called **Coogee**. This resort almost seems like a miniaturised knock-off of Bondi but without the models or inflated airs and graces. There are plenty of green spaces for picnickers or sports-lovers and the nearby historic sea baths **Wylie's Baths** (p154) and **McIvers Baths** (p154) add to the charm.

Orientation

In Bondi, Campbell Pde is the main beachfront road where most shops, hotels and cafés are located. The main road to the beach is Bondi Rd, which branches off from Oxford St east of the mall in Bondi Junction. This is the same Oxford St that begins at Hyde Park and runs through Darlinghurst and Paddington.

Although Bondi Beach is usually referred to simply as Bondi, the suburb of Bondi is actually inland, between Bondi Junction and Bondi Beach. Tamarama is located on the spectacular coastal walk, or about a 10-minute walk down from the Fletcher St bus stop. Bronte and Clovelly are further down the coast and can be reached by bus.

In Coogee, the main beachfront street is Arden St, and the junction of Arden St

TRANSPORT

Bus Bondi 380, 389, L82; Coogee 313, 314, 372, 373, 374; Bronte 378; Clovelly 339; Maroubra 394.

Train Take the train to Bondi Junction station for Coogee (then bus 313 or 314), Bronte (then bus 378), Clovelly (then bus 360), or Bondi (then bus 380, 381 or 382).

Parking Meters at Bondi and Bronte; car parking areas at Clovelly and Coogee.

and Coogee Bay Rd is the commercial hub of the suburb.

ABORIGINAL ROCK ENGRAVINGS
Map p238
Bondi Golf Course, Military Rd, North Bondi
On the golf course in North Bondi, a short walk north (and uphill) from Bondi Beach, you'll find some good Aboriginal rock engravings. Look for the fenced areas about 20m southeast of the enormous chimney. The original carvings had to be regrooved by Waverley Council in the 1960s in order to preserve them, and some of the figures are a little hard to distinguish, though you should be able to make out the marine life and the figure of a man. There's also a great **lookout** at the end of Ramsgate Ave with stunning views back over Bondi Beach.

BONDI BEACH Map p238
Campbell Pde, Bondi
Sydney's (indeed, Australia's) most famous beach, Bondi Beach lures sun-lovers from around the world with its promise of sun, sand, surf and exposed skin, and all just 8km from the CBD. The average water temperature is a pleasant 21°C. If the ocean's too rough for swimming, there are saltwater swimming pools at either end, which are also suitable for young children. Watch

EASTERN BEACHES TOP FIVE
- Admiring views on the **Coastal Walk** (p95)
- People-watching at **Bondi Markets** (p159)
- Café-crawling in **Bronte** or **Coogee** (p113)
- Drinking or eating (or swimming!) at **Icebergs** (p113)
- Surfing waves at **Bondi Beach** (above)

out for rips and strong tides: every year, thousands of people are rescued by the lifesavers that patrol the beach, especially in summer, after Christmas Day and New Year's Eve. Drinking is forbidden on the beach, despite what you may have heard about the party scene. You can also start the blissful Bondi to Bronte (or Coogee) coastal walk from here (p95).

BONDI PAVILION Map p238
☎ 8362 3400; www.waverley.nsw.gov.au; Queen Elizabeth Dr, Bondi
'The Pav', just off the esplanade, is a 1929 Mediterranean–Georgian Revival–style edifice. It has changing rooms, lockers and showers, as well as a theatre and gallery hosting cultural and community events, holiday entertainment for children and a plethora of classes.

DUNNINGHAM PARK Map p238
Cnr Beach & Baden Sts, Coogee
This grassy park at Coogee Beach's northern end offers great ocean views, and has a delightful Eden-like rock pool (known as the Giles Baths). This same entrance now serves as a sobering shrine to locals killed in the Bali bombings of 12 October 2002. Coogee was hit hard by the bombings, with 20 locals killed out of a total of 89 Australians.

INNER WEST
Eating p114; Drinking p125; Shopping p168; Sleeping p180

Once a tough, working-class neighbourhood, **Balmain** first began attracting artists in the 1960s, and has since maintained its bohemian desirability and high real-estate prices. It rivals Paddington in Victorian-era trendiness, but there's nothing particularly special to do or see here other than wandering through backstreets, sitting outside at cafés and restaurants and shopping at the Saturday **Balmain Markets** (p159). Darling St, Balmain's spine, runs the length of the peninsula and hold most of the suburb's pubs, restaurants, antique shops, bakeries and boutiques.

William Balmain was a high achiever who arrived on the First Fleet and within a decade was the principal surgeon, a magistrate and a collector of customs. He was rewarded with several land grants, includ-

TRANSPORT

Bus Services 436, 437, 438, 440 and 470 run to/from Leichhardt and the city. For Newtown try 422, 423, 426 and 428. For Glebe and Balmain, catch 432, 433 and 434 which go along Glebe Point Rd, or 442 to East Balmain.

Ferry Balmain is connected to Circular Quay via ferries from wharves 4 and 5.

Train Newtown is served by CityRail trains on a regular basis.

MLR The Metro Light Rail runs through Glebe to Rozelle Bay and Lilyfield.

Parking Plenty of street parking is generally available, although Balmain, Glebe and Leichhardt can be tricky on weekends.

ing the 220 hectares of headland which bear his name. Most construction in Balmain occurred between 1855 and 1890, although there are colonial Georgian and early Victorian houses still standing.

The predominantly Italian suburb of **Leichhardt**, southwest of Glebe, is increasingly popular with students, lesbians and young professionals. Its Italian eateries on Norton St (the hip main drag) have a city-wide reputation as some of the best in Sydney.

Glebe is southwest of the city centre, close to the University of Sydney. It has been going steadily up the social scale in the last few decades but still has a hippie atmosphere that mixes well with Aboriginal locals, and holds more than its fair share of the city's judges (who can walk to court and avoid the traffic). The main thoroughfare, Glebe Point Rd, runs the length of the suburb from

Broadway to Glebe Point and offers affordable restaurants, interesting shops and the odd Internet café. There are several good places to stay, and its proximity to the city makes it a peaceful alternative to the Cross.

The area has been inhabited since the First Fleet's chaplain was granted the first church land (or glebe), covering an area of 160 hectares. Around 1826 the Church of England sold the land to wealthy settlers, who built mansions. After 1855 church land was leased for building downmarket housing and was subdivided, but a century later the estate had deteriorated into slums. In the mid-1970s the federal government bought the estate and rejuvenated the area for low-income families, many of whom had lived here for generations.

Bordering the southern edge of the University of Sydney, **Newtown** is a melting pot of semi-stoned students, social and sexual subcultures and spiffed-up home renovators. King St, the main drag, is packed with funky clothes shops, musty bookshops, cheap cafés and an inordinate number of Thai restaurants. The backstreets are full of aerosol graffiti art, the cafés full of creative types and the live-music venues full of grungy punters. While it's definitely moving up the social scale, Newtown comes with a healthy dose of eccentricity and political activism – which makes it a truly excellent place to walk around and check out.

Orientation

Most of this odd-shaped area is defined in the north by the water boundaries of Sydney Harbour and by Parramatta Rd and King St in its western and southern extremities. Both roads moonlight as major arterials like the Great Western and the Princes Hwys. Walking is not too difficult in the area, although traffic congestion hardly makes it an attractive prospect.

BALMAIN
ANZAC BRIDGE Map pp226-7
Completed in 1996, Sydney's newest eye-catching bridge spans Johnstons Bay, connecting Pyrmont and Balmain and replacing the old Glebe Island bridge. At 345m in length it's the longest cable bridge in Australia, and is pedestrian accessible, with great views as you stroll into the city from the inner west. Note the

Anzac Bridge (right)

Sights

INNER WEST

statue of the Anzac soldier on the left-hand side of the bridge as you come from the inner west.

ELKINGTON PARK Map pp226-7
Cnr Glassop & White Sts
This small, peaceful and hilly park on a waterfront escarpment was named in 1883 after a local politician. It has good views across the harbour. On its grounds is the oldest swimming club in Australia, which owns the murky saltwater **Dawn Fraser Baths** (☎ 9555 1903; adult/child $3.30/$2.20), named after Australia's greatest-ever swimmer and local-girl-turned-world-champion.

GLEBE
JUBILEE & BICENTENNIAL PARKS
Map pp236-7
Glebe Point Rd; MLR Jubilee Park
At the northern tip of Glebe Point Rd lie these two large parks with good views across the bay to Rozelle and back towards the city. Each park has walking paths, grassy picnic grounds and a rugby pitch. Fig and palm trees dot the landscape and mums and dads stroll along with their kiddies. It's a low-key, friendly atmosphere.

NICHOLSON MUSEUM Map pp236-7
☎ 9351 2812; Bldg A14, Main Quadrangle, University of Sydney; admission free; 🕑 10am-4.30pm Mon-Fri
Located near the University of Sydney's quad, this museum is a must-see venue for fans of prehistoric artefacts. The Nicholson Museum houses an impressive display of Greek, Cypriot, Egyptian, and Near Eastern antiquities, along with the mummified remains of a cat. It was founded in 1860 by Sir Charles Nicholson, who was an important figure in the founding of both the University of Sydney and the Australian Museum.

SYDNEY FISH MARKET Map pp236-7
☎ 9552 2180; www.sydneyfishmarket.com.au; cnr Pyrmont Bridge Rd & Bank St; 🕑 7am-4pm
With over 15 million kilograms of seafood sold and shifted out of here annually, this enormous fish market is the best place to get on first-name terms with a bewildering array of scaly critters. You can witness fish auctions happening in the early mornings, eat sushi or fish 'n' chips all day, attend seafood cooking classes (call for details and bookings), and buy the freshest seafood in town. To get here ride the Metro Light Rail (MLR) until you get to Fish Market station.

UNIVERSITY OF SYDNEY Map pp236-7
☎ 9351 2222; www.usyd.edu.au; Parramatta Rd
Australia's oldest tertiary institution, the University of Sydney was established in 1850, has over 30,000 students enrolled in its various faculties and even boasts its own postcode (2006). The main reason to make a trip here, however, is to see some of its fine architecture. The university's Great Hall, which features wooden ceilings and lovely stained-glass windows, sits on the charmingly proportioned Main Quadrangle, which is one of the greatest examples of Gothic Revival design that you'll see in Sydney. For information on the University of Sydney's excellent Nicholson Museum, see left.

LEICHHARDT
ITALIAN FORUM Map pp236-7
☎ 9518 3396; 23 Norton St
This recreation of an Italian piazza has had its fair share of criticism and compliments, and yes, it is a bit tacky (think Disneyworld's Italy), but the Italian Forum is also the best place to partake in fairly authentic Italian grub. Order a gelato or café latte, check everyone out and remember to say 'ciao' a lot. The Forum is also home to shops, cafés, restaurants and even a library.

INNER WEST TOP FIVE

- Browsing the hippie Saturday **Glebe Markets** (p159)
- Strolling Italian-themed **Leichhardt** (right)
- Shopping and nibbling your way down **King St, Newtown** (p83)
- Exploring the frangipani-filled backstreets of **Balmain** (p83)
- Checking out the catch at the **Sydney Fish Market** (right)

NEWTOWN

CAMPERDOWN CEMETERY Map pp236-7
☎ 9557 2043; 187 Church St; ☺ 6am-7pm
Take a self-guided tour beyond the monstrous fig tree (which dates from 1848) into this woodsy, spider-web-filled and eerily unkempt cemetery. Many famous Aussies were buried here between 1849 and 1942, including Eliza Donnithorne, the inspiration for Miss Havisham in Dickens' *Great Expectations*.

NORTH SHORE
Eating p117; Drinking p126; Sleeping p181

The suburbs north of the harbour are lumped together under the umbrella name of North Shore. It's a posh area with pretty bays and beaches, strips of bushland, million-dollar houses and cute shopping and dining clusters. Not all pockets of the North Shore are wealthy though – Chatswood is mainly a transport hub, and St Leonards and Crows Nest are little more than collections of offices and food joints catering to commuters.

North Sydney is just across the Harbour Bridge and is a less charming continuation of the CBD. Military Rd is the main artery and runs east of the Harbour Bridge through Neutral Bay, Cremorne and Mosman, which have some beautiful foreshore parks and walks. The beachside suburb of Balmoral faces Manly across Middle Harbour. It has three fine beaches and some good restaurants (p117).

TRANSPORT

Bus Wynyard Park has many buses to/from the city and the North Shore; the train or ferry can sometimes be faster.

Ferry Kirribilli, North Sydney, Neutral Bay (Hayes St), Kurraba Point, Cremorne Point and Mosman are serviced by ferries from Circular Quay's Wharf 4. For Valentia St, Woolwich, Milsons Point, and McMahons Point, ferries depart from Wharf 5. For Taronga Zoo, ferries depart from Wharf 2.

Train The North Shore Line connects to Parramatta via Central, Town Hall and Martin Place stations, with stops along the North Shore.

Parking Metered street parking all over the North Shore.

McMahons Point is a pleasant, sleepy suburb on the headland west of North Sydney. It's tipped by Blues Point Reserve, named after the Jamaican-born Billy Blue, who ferried people across from Dawes Point in the 1830s. Blues Point Tower was designed by the architect Harry Seidler and was one of the first high-rise buildings on the harbour; it's regarded by many Sydneysiders as an eyesore.

Orientation
Military Rd branches east off the Warringah Fwy near North Sydney, running east of the Harbour Bridge through Neutral Bay, Cremorne and Mosman. Another main road is the Pacific Hwy, which runs off the Bradfield Hwy (the Sydney Harbour Bridge) and up through the inland northern suburbs like North Sydney and Wahroonga.

BALLS HEAD RESERVE Map pp226-7
Balls Head Reserve not only has great views of the harbour and skyline, but also wonderful waterline and inland paths, ancient Aboriginal rock paintings and carvings (although they're not easily discernible) and barbecue facilities. It gives a great idea of how native Sydney used to be. From Waverton train station turn left and follow Bay Rd, which becomes Balls Head Rd (just before the harbour, turn right). It's a ten-minute walk.

CREMORNE POINT Map pp226-7
To the south of Neutral Bay is Kurraba Point. Off Bogota Ave you can pick up a footpath that runs from Kirribilli Point through bushy gardens to the end of Cremorne Point, which is an excellent spot to picnic on the grass reserve or go for a swim, with great views of the harbour. Cremorne Point is especially popular on Christmas Day and New Year's Eve as a vantage point for the annual fireworks. From here, you can continue up the other side to Mosman Bay and Taronga Zoo (see the walking tour, p94).

KIRRIBILLI POINT Map p239
The Sydney residences of the governor general and the prime minister are on Kirribilli Point, east of the Harbour Bridge. The prime minister (PM), John Howard, stays in the Gothic Revival–style Kirribilli House (1854), as opposed to The Lodge in Canberra where other PMs have lived (scandal!).

NORTH SHORE TOP FIVE

- Taking a walking tour along the **glorious shore-line** (p94)
- Admiring the views – and the animals – at **Taronga Zoo** (right)
- Dipping your toes in the **North Sydney Olympic Pool** (p154)
- Hiking through native bushland at **Balls Head Reserve** (p85)
- Relaxing in the beer garden at **The Oaks** (p126)

The governor general's digs are in **Admiralty House** (1846), the one nearer the bridge (and the one everyone dreams of living in if it came without the job). To the north of Kirribilli Point is the **Sydney Flying Squadron** (p151) headquarters for the Royal Yacht Squadron. Yachting has been popular on the harbour since the 1830s, and the Australian Yacht Club was formed in 1862.

LANE COVE NATIONAL PARK

Map pp226-7

☎ 9412 1811; Lady Game Dr, Chatswood; $7 per car; ☻ 9am-6pm (till 7pm in summer)

This 601-hectare park lies 10km northwest of Sydney's centre and is good for bushwalks. The Lane Cove River hosts rowing boats and kayaks, but swimming is inadvisable. You can cycle and camp, and wheelchair access is available in parts. Take bus 550 or 551 from Chatswood train station.

LUNA PARK Map p239

☎ 9922 6644; www.lunaparksydney.com; admission free; 1 Olympic Pl, Milsons Point; ☻ vary widely

A colourful landmark, this old-fashioned amusement park opened in 1935 and soon attracted thousands of people who flocked across the harbour on the new bridge. The park closed in the 1970s after a fatal fire on the Ghost Train and it has opened and closed a couple of times since, but in 2004 opened its toothy gates once again. Entry is free but rides cost a few dollars.

MARY MACKILLOP PLACE Map p239

☎ 8912 4878; www.marymackillopplace.org.au; 7 Mount St, North Sydney; adult/concession/family $7.50/5/15; ☻ 10am-4pm

This museum tells the life story of Australia's first hope for a saint, a dedicated and outspoken educator and pioneer who prevailed over conservative Catholic hierarchical ideals despite being excommunicated for six months. The building was blessed by Pope John Paul II on the day of MacKillop's beatification (19 January 1995). You'll find her tomb inside the still-functioning chapel.

NUTCOTE Map p239

☎ 9953 4453; www.maygibbs.com.au; 5 Wallaringa Ave, Neutral Bay; adult/concession/family $7/5/17; ☻ 11am-3pm Wed-Sun

Nutcote is the former home of well-known and much-loved Australian children's author May Gibbs (author of *Snugglepot and Cuddlepie*). It's now a museum, restored to its 1930s style, and has exhibits on her life and work. Volunteer guides can show you around and there are beautiful gardens, a tearoom and a gift shop. It's a five-minute walk from the wharf.

ROSE SEIDLER HOUSE Map pp224-5

☎ 9989 8020; www.hht.nsw.gov.au; 71 Clissold Rd, Wahroonga; adult/concession/family $7/3/17; ☻ 10am-5pm Sun

World-famous architect Harry Seidler designed this modest house (built 1948–50) for his mother and father, Rose and Max. It's a modernist construction and its interior reflects the style of the time, with plenty of open spaces, a muted colour scheme and the hippest furnishing of the era. Every year the Historic Houses Trust holds a Fifties Fair (usually in August) on the grounds of the house. Only 1950s architecture fans or true retro buffs need visit.

TARONGA ZOO Map pp226-7

☎ 9969 2777; www.zoo.nsw.gov.au; Bradleys Head Rd, Mosman; adult/child/family $27/14/61-70; ☻ 9am-5pm

A definite Sydney highlight, this exceptional zoo boasts a spectacular location with grand views from a hillside setting. Over 3000 furry, scaly and feathered critters (including a substantial number of Australian ones) call this place home. The animals are well looked after, and there are more natural open enclosures than cages. A zoo fave is the platypus habitat, in which day and night have been switched so that the nocturnal beasts are active during opening hours. The koala

Manly beach (below)

and giraffe display offers great photo ops ($3), and the seal and bird shows are also popular (so find a seat in advance). A new addition is the Asian elephant rainforest and exotic food court.

Ferries to the zoo depart from Circular Quay's Wharf 2 every half hour from 7.15am Monday to Friday, 8.45am Saturday and 9am Sunday. The zoo is on a steep hillside and it makes sense to work your way down if you plan to depart by ferry. A ZooPass (adult/child $33.50/14.50), sold at Circular Quay and elsewhere, includes return ferry rides and zoo admission. Parking ($10) is available for 500 cars. Disabled access is good, even for those who wish to come by ferry, and wheelchairs are available for hire.

MANLY
Eating p117; Drinking p126; Sleeping p181

The superstar of the northern beaches, Manly straddles a narrow peninsula that ends at the dramatic cliffs of North Head. It was one of the first places in Australia to be named by Europeans – Arthur Phillip tagged it after the 'manly' physique of the Aborigines he saw here in 1788.

This popular beach destination boasts a lively holiday-resort atmosphere along with a sense of community identity. Most of The Corso (Manly's cheeky pedestrian mall) is lined with touristy shops and mostly-mediocre cafés, but its brashness is a refreshing change from the prim upper-middle-class harbour enclaves nearby.

Make sure you get to Manly via the ferry: it's easily the best way to experience the harbour and drink in those views.

Orientation
Manly has both ocean and harbour beaches. The ferry wharf is on Manly Cove, on the harbour side, and The Corso runs from here to the ocean, where Manly Beach is lined with some wonderful Norfolk pines. The beachfront road is called North Steyne *and* South Steyne.

MANLY ART GALLERY & MUSEUM
Map p240
☎ 9949 1776; West Esplanade Reserve, Manly; adult/child/concession $3.60/free/1.20; ☽ 10am-5pm Tue-Sun
Next to Oceanworld on the Manly Cove foreshore, this small gallery focuses on Manly's special relationship with the beach. It has exhibitions on beachfront themes and the area's history (which are almost one and the same thing in Manly) and displays some fine Australian works. Admission free on Wednesdays.

MANLY QUARANTINE STATION Map
pp226-7
☎ 9247 5033; www.manlyquarantine.com; North Head; adult/child $11/7.70
This station was used as a quarantine area from 1828 to 1972, attempting to limit the spread of cholera, smallpox and bubonic plague. It was then used until 1984 to house illegal immigrants. To visit the station book a guided tour. The station is reputedly haunted and there are spooky three-hour adult ghost tours at night ($22 Wednesday, $27.50 Friday to Sunday). Kids' ghost tours are also available; bookings are essential.

NORTH HEAD Map pp226-7
North Head Scenic Dr
Spectacular North Head, at the Sydney Harbour entrance, about 3km south of Manly, offers grand views of the ocean, harbour and city skyline. The area is believed to have been used as a ceremonial site by the local Camaraigal Aborigines. The peninsula has the Manly Quarantine Station (see earlier entry), dramatic cliffs, and lookouts with views of the harbour and city centre; it would be great to explore on bike. Most of the headland is in the Sydney Harbour National Park; contact the National Parks and Wildlife Service office (NPWS; ☎ 9977 6522)

Sights

MANLY

near the Quarantine Station for information. Parking in the area costs $3.

OCEANWORLD Map p240
☎ 9949 2644; West Esplanade; adult/child/family
$17.50/9/30; ☼ 10am-5.30pm
Manly's tacky aquarium, whose big draw-
cards are the sharks and stingrays. Its
program includes various tours – check to
see what times you can view divers feeding
the sharks. The glass tunnel lets you feel as
though you really are walking underwater,
without the bother of getting wet or eaten.
There's reasonable access for wheelchairs
and prams too. After 3.30pm the admission
price drops 15%.

ST PATRICK'S COLLEGE Map p240
Darley Rd
The college (1889) is the large building on
the hill southeast of Manly's town centre. It
was a seminary for years and the first Catholic training college to be built in Australia;
you can read about it in author Thomas Keneally's early works. It's now a tourism and
hotel management school, and the recipi-
ent of a Unesco award for cultural heritage
conservation.

GREATER SYDNEY
Sleeping p182

Sydney's suburbs sprawl more than 50km
westward to the foothills of the Blue Mountains, and another 50km southwest to
Campbelltown. Give up the idea that every
Sydneysider has a harbour or beach view
off their front veranda – this is where the
majority of them live.

MANLY & GREATER SYDNEY TOP FIVE

- Taking the cheapest harbour cruise – the **Manly Ferry** (p69)
- Exploring the 10km **Manly Scenic Walkway** (p96)
- Checking out the 19th-century architecture in **Parramatta** (right)
- Hiking the natural wonderland of **Ku-ring-gai National Park** (opposite)
- Swimming, surfing and sunning your way through the **northern beaches** (p90)

TRANSPORT

Bus Numerous buses depart Wynyard Park or
Railway Square for the northern beaches. Bus 135
runs from outside Manly wharf to North Head and
the Quarantine Station.

Ferry STA ferries run from Circular Quay's Wharf 3,
while the Manly JetCat departs from Wharf 2. See opposite for thePalm Beach Ferry service and water taxis.

Parking In Manly parking can be found on metered
streets and in car parks. At North Head, there's
parking for $3 at the Quarantine Station. At the
various northern beaches, there's parking available
on the streets and beachfronts, but at weekends it's
very tricky.

The geographical heart of the city is Parramatta, 24km west of Sydney. It was the
second European settlement in Australia
and contains a number of historic buildings dating from early colonial days. When
Sydney proved to be a poor area for farming, Parramatta was selected for the first
farm. Now consumed by Sydney's westward
sprawl, Parramatta is a thriving commercial
centre, with some old architectural gems
nestled among the mostly forgettable modern developments.

North and south of the centre, suburbs
stretch for a good 25km to the beautiful national parks and beaches which mark the
end of the city and which some Sydneysiders
are lucky enough to call their backyard.

A string of ocean-front suburbs sweeps
along the coast from Manly up the 'In-
sular Peninsula', ending at beautiful **Palm
Beach** and the spectacular Barrenjoey Head.
Glorious beaches here include **Whale Beach**
and **Bilgola** (near Palm Beach), both with
dramatic, steep headlands. Several of the
northernmost beach suburbs also back onto
Pittwater, a lovely inlet off Broken Bay and a
favoured sailing spot for Sydney's yachties.
Ku-ring-gai Chase National Park lies on the western
side of Pittwater.

Orientation
Public transport to the northern beaches
area is limited; no trains run here, and bus
services seem to take hours. Exploration
by private car is best. However, there is
relatively good train service to the southern
national parks.

Sydney's western suburbs – where the bulk of the population lives – has good train service.

NORTH

BARRENJOEY LIGHTHOUSE
Map pp224-5

Located at the tip of the northern beaches peninsula (and in an annexe of Ku-ring-gai Chase National Park) is this historic lighthouse. You'll need to don sturdy shoes for the steep 40-minute hike (no toilets!), but superb views across Pittwater await. There are **weekend tours** (adult/child/family $10/6/30); call 9451 3479 or contact the Sydney Harbour National Parks Information Centre at **Cadmans Cottage** (p65) in The Rocks.

KU-RING-GAI CHASE NATIONAL PARK
Map pp224-5

Kalkari Visitors Centre ☎ 9457 9322; Ku-ring-gai Chase Rd; per car $11, adult/child entering by bus or taxi $4.40/2.20; ☽ sunrise-sunset
This 15,000-hectare national park is 24km north of the city centre and borders the southern edge of Broken Bay and the western shore of Pittwater. It has that classic Sydney mixture of sandstone, bushland and water vistas, plus walking tracks, horse-riding trails, picnic areas, Aboriginal rock engravings and spectacular views of Broken Bay. The park has over 100km of shoreline, several through-roads and four entrances. **Camping** (adult/child per night $10/5) is allowed only at the Basin (call ☎ 9974 1011 to book).

The **Kalkari Visitors Centre** is about 2.5km into the park from the Mt Colah entrance on Ku-ring-gai Chase Rd. It's staffed by friendly volunteers and has several taxidermy specimens, including stuffed koalas, an echidna, bandicoots and an eagle. The road descends from there to the picnic area at **Bobbin Head** on Cowan Creek, which also has a marina, an information centre, a café (serving hot meals, coffee and snacks) and a boardwalk leading through mangroves.

Elevated parts of the park offer superb views across inlets such as Cowan Creek and Pittwater, and from **West Head**, in particular, there's a fantastic view across Pittwater to Barrenjoey Head and Lion Island. You may also be lucky enough to see lyrebirds in this area during their May to July mating season.

West Head Rd offers access to some of the best places within the park to see **Aboriginal engravings and handprints**, listed here in order from east to west. Nearly at West Head itself is the Resolute picnic area, from which you can amble 100m to Red Hands Cave for a look at some very faint ochre handprints. About another 500m along Resolute Track (after a short steep section) is an engraving site. You can turn around or continue to one more site and make a 3.5km loop that takes in Resolute Beach.

Back on West Head Rd, just less than 2km west of the picnic area, is the Echidna Track, whose boardwalk provides good disabled access to engravings very near the road. Less than a kilometre up the road

Sights

GREATER SYDNEY

TRANSPORT

Bus Every hour on weekdays, **Shorelink Buses** (☎ 9457 8888; www.shorelink.com.au) runs bus 577 from Turramurra train station to the Ku-ring-gai Chase park entrance; one bus enters the park as far as Bobbin Head (on weekends fewer buses go to the entrance but more to Bobbin Head). Bus 156 runs from Manly to Church Point. From the city centre, E86 is a direct peak-hour service to Church Point, or catch L88, L90 or 190 from Wynyard Park as far as Warringah Mall and transfer to bus 156 from there.

Ferry The **Palm Beach Ferry Service** (☎ 9918 2747) runs to the Basin hourly from 9am to 5pm Monday to Thursday, 9am to 8pm Friday and 9am to 6pm Saturday, Sunday and public holidays (adult/concession $10/5). You can also use **Church Point Water Taxis** (☎ 0428 238 190) for the trip between Church Point and Palm Beach ($42 for up to six people; $6 surcharge from midnight to 6am).

Train To Turramurra, then Shorelink bus to Bobbin Head.

Driving & parking There are four road entrances to the park: Mt Colah, on the Pacific Hwy; Turramurra, in the southwest; and Terrey Hills and Church Point, in the southeast. Parking throughout the park is plentiful.

NORTHERN BEACHES

Avalon Beach (Map pp224–5; bus L88, L90) This medium-sized beach has challenging surf and tangerine sand. Great services like cafés, shops and picnic tables.

Bilgola (Map pp224–5; bus L88, L90) With its saltwater pool, this beach seems like a bit of a secret gem. Good swimming, and some services available.

Collaroy (Map pp224–5; bus L88, L90) A good spot to unwind, with a relaxed atmosphere that's good for families. Stretches for two suburbs, so there's room for everyone.

Curl Curl (Map pp224–5; ferry Manly, then bus 136 or 139) A well-balanced mix of family groups and experienced surfers, with lush lagoon nearby. Bring food and water.

Dee Why (Map pp224–5; bus 176) Big and popular with local families, and with a good reputation for surfing breaks. Near plenty of services.

Freshwater (Map pp224–5; ferry Manly, then bus 139) This is a nice sheltered beach with swimming pool, popular with local teenagers.

Narrabeen (Map pp224–5; bus L88, L90) This is surfing turf, so get experienced before trying the breaks here. Not the best for swimming, but there's a pool and lagoon.

Palm Beach (Map pp224–5; bus L90) The tip of Sydney and supremely blissful. Kids should stick to beach pools; cafés provide nourishment. Site of cheesy TV series *Home and Away*.

Whale Beach (Map pp224–5; bus L88 to Avalon, then bus 193) Heavenly and remote, this gorgeous beach is ideally sized and nontouristy. Good for surfers and families; no services.

from Echidna is the Basin Track, which makes an easy stroll to a good set of engravings.

Please note that it's unwise to swim in Broken Bay because of sharks, but if you're dying for a dip in waters that seem free of the usual hordes of tourists, there are safer netted swimming areas at Illawong Bay and the Basin.

SOUTH

BOTANY BAY NATIONAL PARK

Map pp224-5

Kurnell ☎ 9668 9111; per car $7; Discovery Centre ⏱ 11am-3pm Mon-Fri, 10am-4pm Sat & Sun; train Cronulla, then bus 987; La Perouse ☎ 9311 3379; adult/child $5.50/3.30; visitor centre ⏱ 10am-4pm Wed-Sun; bus 393, 394

Although many people think that Sydney was founded and built on the shores of Botany Bay, it is in fact centred on the harbour of Port Jackson, some 15km to the north. Today the city's suburbs have sprawled so far southward that they now almost completely encircle the bay. Botany Bay National Park comprises two locations (Kurnell and La Perouse) on either side of the bay's entrance.

Botany Bay is where Lieutenant Cook first stepped ashore in Australia. He wasn't well

received and didn't stay long, however. The bay was named by Joseph Banks, the expedition's naturalist, in honour of the many botanical specimens he found here. Cook's landing place is marked by monuments on the Monument Track, a 2km-long walk at Kurnell.

Bushwalks are possible on both sides of the park and offer visitors the chance to feel as though they are a million miles from busy Sydney.

The **Discovery Centre** in the Kurnell area of the park has material relating to Cook's life and expeditions, an exhibition about the first contact between Cook's *Endeavour* crew and the Aboriginal people of the area, and information on the surrounding wetlands. The park is open from 7am to 7.30pm.

La Perouse ('Laperouse' in French) is on the northern side of the bay entrance, at the spot where the French explorer of that name arrived in 1788, just six days after the arrival of the First Fleet. His arrival was utterly coincidental, and gave the Brits quite a scare – they weren't expecting the French to materialise in this part of the world quite so soon! Laperouse graciously conceded that he'd missed out on the chance to claim the area for France. He and his men camped at Botany Bay for a few weeks, then sailed off into the Pacific and vanished. Many years later the wrecks of their ships were discovered on a reef near Vanuatu.

The La Perouse area has strong links with the Aboriginal community. **Laperouse Museum & Visitor Centre** has an interesting Aboriginal gallery, as well as relics of the Laperouse expedition and antique maps. You can book guided tours on ☎ 9247 5033.

There's a monument at La Perouse commemorating the explorer, built in 1828 by French sailors searching for him.

BUNDEENA Map pp224-5
train Cronulla, then ferry to Bundeena
Bundeena is a quiet seaside village on scenic Port Hacking. There's not a lot to do here beyond swimming at Horderns Beach and walking the partially completed **Bundeena–Maianbar Heritage Walk**, which promises good coastal views and Aboriginal sites. If you'd like to spend the night, there are some B&Bs (see p182), and a couple of good cafés.

CRONULLA BEACH Map pp224-5
train Cronulla
Cronulla's got it all: great surf waves, sunbathing and sand dunes, and an atmosphere that couldn't be more relaxed without reaching the comatose level. In short, Cronulla is a top Sydney beach – maybe even the best. No wonder residents of 'The Shire' rarely leave the area.

ROYAL NATIONAL PARK Map pp224-5
Park Office ☎ 9542 0648; per car per day $11, free for cyclists & pedestrians; park office ⏰ 9.30am-4.30pm Mon-Fri, 8.30am-4.30pm Sat & Sun; train Loftus, then walk
Royal is the oldest gazetted national park in the world. Largely coastal, it holds dramatic cliffs, secluded beaches, scrub, lush rainforest and flocks of huge yellow-tailed black cockatoos. Royal begins at Port Hacking, just 30km south of Sydney, and stretches 20km further south. A road runs through the park with detours to the small township of **Bundeena** (see above) on Port Hacking, to the beautiful swimming beach at **Wattamolla**, and to the windswept surfers' paradise, **Garie Beach**.

The spectacular two-day, 28-km coastal walking trail running the length of the park is highly recommended. A walking and cycling trail follows the Hacking River south from Audley, and other walking tracks pass

tranquil, freshwater swimming holes. You can swim in the upper reaches of Kangaroo Creek but not the Hacking River. To do the coastal walks you'll need a permit ($3 per person per night). You can do car-based camping at Bonnie Vale for $8 per person per night. Be aware in any case that the park is home to tiger snakes, brown snakes, death adders and red-bellied black snakes, so watch your step.

The **visitors centre** is at the top of the hill at the park's main entrance, off the Princes Hwy near Audley. The friendly and knowledgable staff sell camping permits and help with any questions about bushwalking or other aspects of the park.

You can hire equipment at the **Audley Boat Shed** (☎ 9545 4967; Farnell Rd; ⏰ 9am-5pm; rowboats, canoes & kayaks $16/30 per hour/day, bicycles $14/30 per hour/day, aqua bikes $12 per 30min), 1km down the hill from the visitors centre.

The road through the park and the offshoot to Bundeena are always open, but the detours to the beaches are closed at 8.30pm.

If you're bringing a bike, the best route is by train to Cronulla then ferry across. Engadine, Heathcote, Waterfall and Otford train stations are all on the park boundary and have walking trails leading into the park.

Sights GREATER SYDNEY

TRANSPORT

Bus For La Perouse, bus 394 to/from Circular Quay or 393 to/from Railway Sq; for the Discovery Centre, take bus 987 after alighting from the train at Cronulla.

Ferry A scenic way to reach the Royal National Park and Bundeena is to take a train to Cronulla, then a **Cronulla National Park ferry** (☎ 9523 2990) to Bundeena. Ferries depart from Cronulla Wharf, just below the train station.

Train The Illawarra line connecting Sydney and Wollongong forms the western boundary of the park. For Cronulla, take Illawarra line from Bondi Junction or the city to Cronulla. The closest station is at Loftus, 4km from the park entrance and another 2km from the visitors centre.

Driving & Parking To get to the Botany Bay National Park, take the Princes Hwy, turning into Rocky Point Rd, then Captain Cook Dr. You can reach the Royal National Park from Sydney by taking the Princes Hwy and turning off south of Loftus. Parking is available at both parks.

WEST

PARRAMATTA Map pp224-5

The knowledgable **Parramatta Heritage & Visitors Centre** (☎ 8839 3311; 346A Church St; 🕑 9am-5pm) has lots of brochures and information. It's also a museum in its own right, with temporary exhibits by local artists, as well as a fine permanent exhibition on Parramatta's history and culture.

The site of the area's first farm, **Parramatta Park**, on the western edge of the city, contains the Old Government House (☎ 9635 8149; www.friendsofogh.com; adult/concession/family $8/5/18; 🕑 10am-4pm Mon-Fri, 10.30am-4pm Sat & Sun). The first structure here was built around 1790 and served as a country retreat for the early governors of NSW. It's the oldest remaining public building in Australia and now houses an interesting museum.

The area around **St John's Cathedral** (between Hunter St & Church St Mall) and the **Parramatta Town Hall** (Church St Mall) forms a pleasant civic centre. **St John's Cemetery** (O'Connell St), three blocks southwest of the cathedral, contains the graves of many of the first settlers.

East of the city centre is **Elizabeth Farm** (☎ 9635 9488; 70 Alice St, Rosehill; adult/child/family $7/3/17; 🕑 10am-5pm), the oldest surviving home in the country. John and Elizabeth Macarthur, the founders of Australia's wool industry, built the homestead in 1793; the only way to see the house is by guided tour. A block east is the exquisite **Experiment Farm Cottage** (☎ 9635 8149; 9 Ruse St, Harris Park; adult/concession/family $5.50/4/14; 🕑 10.30am-3.30pm Tue-Thu, 11am-3.30pm Sat & Sun), a beautiful colonial bungalow built on the site of the first land grant issued to a convict in Australia. Governor Phillip granted 12 hectares of land to James Ruse

TRANSPORT

Ferry/RiverCat For Sydney Olympic Park, take the RiverCat to Homebush Bay. You can also take the RiverCat to Parramatta. Both services depart from Circular Quay's Wharf 5.

Train For Parramatta, take the train ($4) to Parramatta train station. Sydney Olympic Park's train station is called Olympic Park – don't alight at Homebush station.

Driving & parking For Sydney Olympic Park and Parramatta, exit the city via Parramatta Rd and detour onto the Western Motorway tollway (M4; $2.20) at Strathfield. There's plenty of parking available at both places.

in gratitude for his successful agricultural efforts. Ruse continued to experiment with different farming techniques and these can still be seen today in the permanent exhibition.

SYDNEY OLYMPIC PARK Map pp224-5

☎ 9714 7888; www.sydneyolympicpark.com.au; 1 Herb Elliot Ave, Homebush Bay; 🕑 visitors centre 9am-5pm

Sydney Olympic Park, in the suburb of Homebush Bay, 14km west of the city centre, was the main venue for the spectacular 2000 Olympic Games. Other venues within the complex include the **Sydney Aquatic Centre** (p154) and the **Telstra Stadium**. Also here is the **Sydney Showground**, the home of the annual **Royal Easter Show** (p11).

A variety of tours of the area are available; contact the visitors centre or check the website for more details. The most scenic way to get to Olympic Park is to catch a RiverCat from Circular Quay to Olympic Park wharf.

Walking Tours

Walking Tours

Sydney's gorgeous harbour location, radiant weather and unpredictable layout make it a fabulous city for walking. These walks will guide you from shining waters to lush gardens to historic architecture, and we've thrown in walks for a rainy day and for shopping aficionados. If you prefer an organised guided tour, see p49 for details. Whatever you do, be prepared to puff your way up a few hills, wear comfortable shoes and sunscreen, pack a swimsuit and don't forget your camera!

Walkers on Bondi Beach

A NORTH SHORE HIKE

Some of Sydney's best vistas can be had on this excellent jaunt through lush coastline parks and pricey residential neighbourhoods. You'll see the city from a different vantage point – that is, from the *other* side of the bridge – and get a taste of where some of Sydney's luckiest inhabitants reside.

Start by hopping on a ferry to the **Neutral Bay wharf 1**. Head up Hayes St and turn right on Lower Wyncombe Rd and right again at Wallaringa Ave. Here you'll find **Nutcote 2** (p86), home to Australia's famous children's author, May Gibbs. At the end of the street jog left and take Hollowforth to Bogota via Shellcove and Honda Rds, reaching the entrance to **Cremorne Reserve 3**, a jungle-like strip of native shrubs and trees that lines Cremorne Point.

Stroll along the path and you'll soon come to the murky, saltwater **MacCallum pool 4**, founded by early Olympic swimmer

WALK FACTS

Start Ferry to Neutral Bay
End Taronga Zoo ferry back to Circular Quay
Distance 5.5km
Duration 3-3½ hours
Fuel Stop Mosman Rowing Club

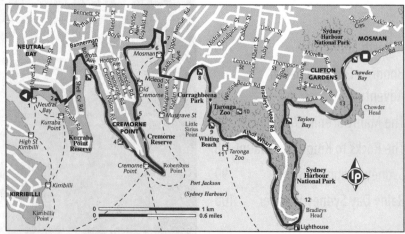

Fred Lane. At the tip of the Reserve are truly awesome views. Heading back the other side of the point you'll pass some well-tended plots of palms, ferns and philodendrons called **Lex and Ruby's garden 5**. Keep wandering along the path to **Mosman Rowing Club 6** (☎ 9953 7713); if you catch them open you can stop for a meal or drink.

After a refreshing break, amble around exclusive Mosman Bay (which used to be an old whaling cove). Note the historical stone building called **The Barn 7**, an early colonial structure that's now a scout hall. Just beyond is the Wharf Store; go up the stairs to Mosman St, following it up to McLeod St. Cross Musgrave St and take the stairs down to the other side, then across Raglan where you'll find more stairs that head down to the shore.

Wind around **Little Sirius Cove 8** and take the stone steps onto a shoreline path, which leads to the border of Taronga Zoo. To visit an isolated little sandy strip take the stairs down to **Whiting Beach 9** (look for the No Dogs sign). After heading further along this jungly path you'll finally reach the **Taronga Zoo 10** entrance and **ferry wharf 11**, where there's a stand selling drinks and quick snacks. If you can't stop walking, keep following the way to **Bradleys Head 12** and **Clifton Gardens 13**, where more beautiful paths and inspiring views await; if not, wait for the next ferry and head back to Circular Quay.

BONDI TO COOGEE COASTAL ADVENTURE

One of Sydney's most stunning walks is this coastal stroll from North Bondi to Coogee. You'll pass soft-sanded beaches with plenty of swimming opportunities, witness inspiring panoramic views and have loads of chances to stop for coffee or fresh juice.

Begin at the **Bondi Golf Club 1** (p155) to see the Aboriginal rock engravings (look for the

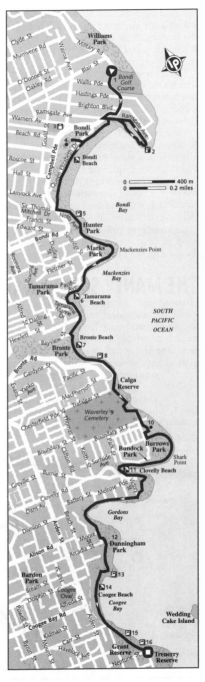

WALK FACTS

Start Buses 380, 389 or L82 to North Bondi
End Buses 314, 372, 373 or 374 from Coogee Beach
Distance 5km
Duration 2-2½ hours
Fuel stops Many along the way

tall chimney). Follow Military Rd south and turn left into Ramsgate Ave to reach the **lookout 2** for sweeping views of Bondi Beach. Head down to the beach and stroll along the boardwalk or on the sands; if it's a Sunday, check out the **Bondi markets 3** (p159) for hip beach gear. Otherwise, pop into the **Bondi Pavilion 4** (p82) in case there's an art show or musical performance happening.

Continue up the beach promenade to Notts Ave and the lavish **Icebergs 5** (p113) complex, which holds one of Sydney's hottest restaurants, two bars and a glorious swimming pool. Just beyond here starts the real path, which winds along sandstone cliffs and offers dramatic scenery. You'll soon reach pretty **Tamarama Beach 6** (p81) and peaceful **Bronte Beach 7** (p81), the latter with a host of wonderful cafés in case you need a break.

Continue past the **Bronte Baths 8**, and head south through the atmospheric **Waverley Cemetery 9**. When you reach the **Clovelly Bowling Club 10** (p153), you might be tempted to pop in for a beer with a view. From here, follow the path to sheltered **Clovelly Beach 11** (p81), a great beach for family picnics.

Take the footpath up through the car park, then head along Cliffbrook Pde and down the steps to small Gordons Bay. The parkland continues from here all the way to **Dunningham Park 12** (p82) and the ultracharming **Giles Baths rockpool 13**. There's also a sombre memorial here for Australian victims of the 2002 Bali bombings. A hop, skip and a jump down some steps puts you smack-bang on glorious **Coogee Beach 14** (p81). Beyond this stretch of sand, in Grant Reserve, are the historic seaside pools of **McIvers Baths 15** and **Wylie's Baths 16**. Take a dip, then turn around and head back to Coogee for a relaxing sit-down.

THE MANLY SCENIC WALKWAY

Hop on a ferry to Manly to enjoy this long, memorable walk, which offers good harbour views, peeks at pricey residential areas and a taste of pristine native bushland. You'll need comfortable shoes with decent traction, and water and snacks because supplies along the way are limited; there are several great places with views to stop for a nibble.

If you come by ferry you'll land at **Manly Cove 1**, where you can head over the peninsula to **Manly Beach 2** (p87). Walk down

WALK FACTS

Start Ferry Manly
End Spit Bridge bus 168 back to Milsons Point and the city
Distance 10km
Duration 3½-4 hours
Fuel stops None along the way; stock up in Manly

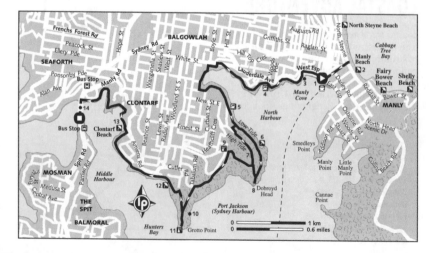

Walkers along Bondi Beach promenade.

The Corso, Manly's pedestrian party strip, while stocking up on supplies. Backtrack to Manly Cove and pop into the **Manly Visitors Information centre 3** (p211) for maps and advice. Head west along the shoreline past **Oceanworld** (p88) and the **Manly Art Gallery and Museum** (p87). After here the real walking begins.

Follow the well-marked shoreline path to **Fairlight Beach 4** and its lovely saltwater pool. After rounding the grassy park, go up the stairs and left on North Harbour Street, then left again at the curve in the road (you'll see a sign for The Spit). Soon you'll reach **Forty Baskets Reserve 5**, which has picnic tables, a fenced swimming area and small pools with oyster beds. Further on is pleasant **Reef Beach 6**; during high tide the path along this beach may be inaccessible, but a more inland detour path can be taken. You're now in the wonderfully native **Sydney Harbour National Park 7**. There are grand views from a lookout near **Dobroyd Head 8**, but the short path to it is unmarked so keep your eyes peeled.

> ### WHEELCHAIR ACCESS ON THE MANLY SCENIC WALKWAY
>
> A 1.5km path, starting at the Manly Pier Restaurant car park and finishing just past Fairlight Beach, is wheelchair accessible. It's known as the Fairlight Walk and is signposted. Other paths through the Manly Scenic Walkway do not offer wheelchair access.

Head back inland and, for more great views of Manly and North Head, detour 200 metres to a nearby loop road and **Arabanoo Lookout 9**. Double back down to the bushy path and keep walking until you spot some square logs on your left – these logs mark out ancient **Aboriginal rock carvings 10**. Back on the path and just beyond is **Grotto Point 11** and an old lighthouse which offers more glorious views.

Double back and stop at tiny **Castle Rock Beach 12**, admiring the large rock formations. Keep hiking along the shoreline, eventually reaching **Clontarf Beach 13** and its grassy picnic grounds. The walk ends at the iconic swing bridge, **Spit Bridge 14**, from where you can bus back to Manly or the city.

THE ROCKS TO KINGS CROSS JAUNT

This city walk joins together some of Sydney's biggest guns: The Rocks, Circular Quay, beautiful harbour views and Kings Cross. You'll have plenty of opportunities to pause for refreshments at each end.

Start your engines in the historic **Rocks neighbourhood 1** (p65). This area is best explored by simply wandering at your own pace amongst the atmospheric streets and alleyways; alternatively, visit the excellent **Visitors Centre 2** (p211). Don't miss going through **Argyle Cut 3** (p65) and climbing the hill to the **Sydney Observatory 4** (p67), from where you'll have good views over Millers Point and the harbour. The **Museum of Contemporary Art 5** (p66) is also a must-see and holds the wonderfully situated **MCA Café 6** (p104). If it's a weekend, you'll run into **The Rocks Market 7** (p159), where you can shop for crafts and souvenirs.

Now head south and east, walking along Circular Quay's stunning pedestrian boardwalk, enjoying the views and bustle of this very important transport hub. Along the way you'll pass **Customs House 8** (p68) and the **Justice and Police Museum 9**. Follow the water to the famed **Sydney Opera House 10** (p70). After the obligatory photo session, keep strolling along the waterline; you'll be edging the outstanding **Royal Botanic Gardens 11** (p68). Eventually you'll reach **Mrs Macquarie's Chair 12** (p68), a cut rock ledge originally built for governor Lachlan Macquarie's wife, Elizabeth. It's one of the city's best harbour vantage points.

Head south along the walking path until you see **Andrew 'Boy' Charlton Pool 13** (p154). You'll also notice elite **Finger Wharf 14** (p76) sticking out into Woolloomooloo Bay.

WALK FACTS

Start George St, The Rocks
End Train from Kings Cross
Distance 5km
Duration 3 hours
Fuel Stops MCA Café, The Bourbon

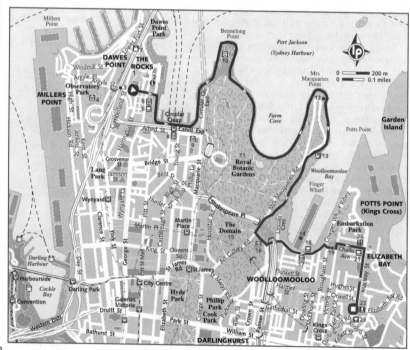

Work you way through **The Domain 15** (p61) to the **Art Gallery of NSW 16** (p60), worth a stop for its inspiring art. Afterwards take the path and stairs into Woolloomooloo, where **Artspace 17** (p75) and **Harry's Café de Wheels 18** (p76) are quirky attractions. Huff and puff your way up **McElhone Stairs 19** (p75) into Potts Point.

Jog left, then right onto Challis Ave and stop at **Fratelli Paradiso 20** (p108) or **Spring Espresso 21** (p109) for a well-earned coffee. If you need something stiffer, however, turn right onto Macleay St and head towards **El Alamein Fountain 22** (p75). Just beyond is **The Bourbon 23** (p122), one of the area's slickest drinking holes. Sit down and enjoy the view – soon Kings Cross' infamous nightlife will be starting up and waiting for you to join in.

SYDNEY SHOPPING STROLL

This shopping challenge (which *will* wear you out) is best done on weekends, when **The Rocks Markets 1** (p159) are open and in full swing. **Paddy's Markets** (p159) are only open Thursday to Sunday. Stores tend to have the shortest opening hours on Sunday (with some closing on this day). For more details on Sydney's shopping see p158.

Put on your comfortable shopping shoes in **The Rocks 2** (p65), where you'll find kitschy Australiana and souvenirs galore. Sunny weekends draw tourists and locals alike to The Rocks Markets and there's a festive feel to the air. You won't find the cheapest prices here, but the atmosphere can't be beat. After you're done poking around, head inland to the pleasantly pedestrian **Pitt St Mall 3** (p158). In this area you'll find a plethora of department stores, including **David Jones 4** (p160), **Myer 5** (p161) and the Sydney institution **Gowings 6** (p160). For a

WALK FACTS

Start The Rocks, train Circular Quay
End Oxford Street, bus 380 back to centre
Distance 3-5km
Duration As long as shopping all day takes
Fuel Stops Market City food court; Paddington Hotel

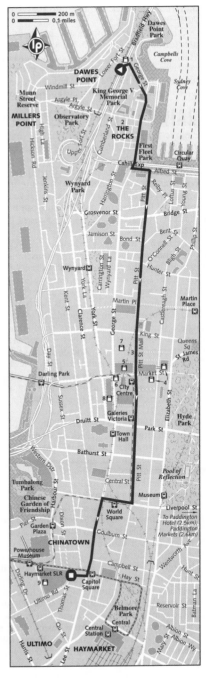

more old-time feel, wander into the classic **Strand Arcade 7** (p162) and plush **Queen Victoria Building 8** (p62).

Continue your shopping adventures by strolling south to Chinatown and Paddy's Markets (or take the Monorail, p203, which will get you directly there from Pitt St Mall). Here you'll find some of Sydney's best bargains on souvenirs, Australiana, electronics and whatever else you don't really need. Try your hand at bargaining, especially if you purchase a few items together. Paddy's Markets are on the ground floor; upstairs is **Market City 9** (p163), a large fashion mall with a cheap food court on the top floor with plenty of refreshments.

RAINY DAY SYDNEY WANDER

Despite being blessed with over 300 sunny days per year, Sydney does get some rain.

You're more likely to experience the heaviest downpours during the summer months, while autumn sees frequent but brief showers. This pleasant walk takes in some of Sydney's best indoor attractions, and if you don't feel like walking, many sights can be reached via Sydney's efficient **Monorail 1** (p203).

Begin your wet day at pedestrian-friendly **Darling Harbour 2** (p72). Attractive museums here include the **Australian National Maritime Museum 3** (p72), which boasts a hearty seafaring theme and a couple of docked vessels to explore. Another good choice is the **Powerhouse Museum 4** (p73), just a few blocks south, where you could spend hours wandering through the hands-on exhibits – especially entertaining for the kids! And don't miss the ever-popular **Sydney Aquarium 5** (p74), where you'll stay dry and the only wet animals will be the fish, seals and platypus. Feel like a movie? Check out the giant-screen **IMAX Cinema 6** (p132).

Darling Harbour also offers plenty of opportunities for shopping. Peek into **Harbourside 7** (p73), a modern shopping centre with choice fashion stores, souvenir stands and shiny restaurants. For didgeridoos, boomerangs and other Australiana, visit **Australia's Northern Territory & Outback Centre 8** (p73). If the sun does peek out for a little while, consider strolling the **Chinese Garden of Friendship 9** (p73) – if it sprinkles, you could at least sit indoors in their teahouse for a rest.

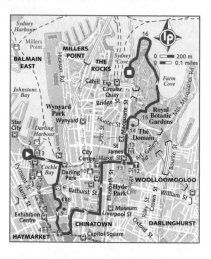

WALK FACTS

Start Monorail Harbourside; MLR and ferry Pyrmont Bay
End Sydney Opera House, train Circular Quay
Distance 5km
Duration 5-6 hours
Fuel Stop Myriad choices in Darling Harbour and Circular Quay

After exhausting your options at Darling Harbour, head to the closest Monorail station. Hop on for a few stops and get off at the City Centre station. Walk one block west to the Byzantine **Queen Victoria Building 10** (p62), an ex-fruit and vegetable market that's now the city's most beautiful shopping centre. Now take a quick walk east on Market St, cut through Hyde Park's northern end (noting the **Archibald Memorial Fountain 11**, p61), and enter **St Mary's Cathedral 12** (p63) for a quick look around. Just one block north is the **Hyde Park Barracks Museum 13** (p61), a well-presented museum showcasing a fascinating slice of Sydney's history. Keep wandering up Macquarie St past the **State Library of NSW 14** (p64). Soon you'll hit the lush **Royal Botanic Gardens 15** (p68). Take on some water as you head to the **Sydney Opera House 16** (p70), where you can stop at a covered bar or restaurant for a well-deserved break.

Eating ▪

Eating

Sydney is one of the world's great culinary centres. Innovative chefs, exceptional local produce and BYO (bring you own alcohol) licensing laws have all contributed to making this city a delightful place to eat out. Two f-words are the key to dining here – freshness and flavour. The locals wouldn't accept anything less! Another definite plus (and f-word) is Sydney's fine weather, making outside dining a very pleasant option at many restaurants and cafés.

Any taste can be catered to. You can greet the day with a heart-starting espresso and some ricotta hot cakes in the city centre; chow down the freshest catch of the day at a waterfront restaurant in The Rocks or Darling Harbour; stave off afternoon hunger pangs with tapas in Glebe; gobble a pie with sauce at an evening footy game at Aussie Stadium, or a pizza after a night on the tiles in Kings Cross; rise above it all with a glittering harbour view and the snazziest top-end cuisine in North Shore; or spend the wee hours revelling in a post-midnight supper at one of Chinatown's great-value eating dens.

As for fast-food options, you won't find a shortage in Sydney. Look for them on main streets and near train stations in most suburbs. In popular tourist areas such as Bondi, Manly and Kings Cross, you can't avoid them, so if you succumb, at least go for the great Aussie fish 'n' chips option. In recent times many Sydney fish'n'chippers have put up the stakes, offering alternatives to the fried flake (shark), such as grilled bream or trevally.

Many shopping centres also have a designated food floor, with budget eateries competing for customers. Cafés will often allow you to 'take away' your meal, which is a good idea if you're close to one of Sydney's vantage points, such as the Royal Botanic Gardens or, even better, any sandy stretch of beach.

Opening Hours

Cafés and restaurants generally open seven days a week, with many of the former serving food from 7am to 10pm. Sunday nights and Mondays are the usual closing days for those places that do close. Most restaurants open for lunch and dinner, while cafés and patisseries are best for breakfast.

Sydneysiders tend to have breakfast anywhere between 7am and 10am, although you'll find plenty of sunglasses-wearing sleepyheads taking advantage of 'all-day brekky' menus in the inner city and around the beach suburbs. The lunch hour takes place anywhere between noon and 3pm, with dinner between 6pm and 10pm.

How Much?

Eating in Sydney can be as thrifty as a $2.50 beef pie, a $7 bowl of Vietnamese *pho* (beef noodle soup) or a $12 Turkish pizza for two (see the Cheap Eats listings in each Neighbourhood section for budget options). At midrange restaurants you can expect to pay between $15 and $25 for a main course. At the city's top restaurants you can easily be looking at $30 to $50 for a main course, or about $70 for a degustation menu.

Booking Tables

Most restaurants take reservations for both lunch and dinner, so call ahead if you want to ensure a seat. Restaurants that don't take

TOP FIVE EAT STREETS

- **Crown St, Surry Hills** (p109) Indian, Turkish, Lebanese, Thai – hands down, the best, cheapest and most diverse cuisine in Sydney.
- **Chinatown, Haymarket** (p105) As good as Chinese food can get outside China, with great prices and long hours, too.
- **King St, Newtown** (p114) More restaurants, cafés and takeaway joints than you can count, especially Thai cuisine.
- **Norton St, Leichhardt** (p114) Sydney's Little Italy, complete with *gelato,* Italian coffees and reconstructed pastel-coloured plaza.
- **Victoria St, Darlinghurst** (p107) From cool bars with tasty tapas to nonpretentious Euro-cafés to upmarket Indian joints.

reservations often have a bar or arrangement with a nearby pub where you can wait for a table to become available. We've included reservation recommendations for the restaurants that frequently fill up fast.

Tipping

Waiting staff at cafés and restaurants are paid a living wage here in Sydney, so tipping is not at all compulsory. Some diners like to tip at the fanciest of eateries (provided the service is up to snuff, of course) so if you want to do this, think about leaving 10% to 15% of the bill.

Self Catering

Sydney's two big supermarkets are Coles and Woolworths, with branches in dozens of suburbs and throughout the city centre. Some are open 24 hours or until midnight. Paddy's Market in **Market City** (see p163) has a popular local produce market in the basement. Every suburb worth its weight will have a delicatessen that stocks cheeses, breads, olives and salted meats.

CITY CENTRE, THE ROCKS & CIRCULAR QUAY

There's no shortage of places for a snack or quick meal in the city centre, especially on weekdays when many restaurants cater to the business crowds. If you're looking for variety along with good value, snoop around for the food courts which are often hidden away in large buildings.

For a while The Rocks and Circular Quay were the centre of cheesy tourist-trade joints and themed restaurants, but in recent years the arrival of some big-name chefs and their cutting-edge restaurant design teams has rejuvenated the food scene. Finding the swish and sexy new places shouldn't be difficult – a run around Circular Quay (especially at the Overseas Passenger Terminal, p67) will turn up the goods.

See the boxed text on p59 for transport options to/from these areas.

TOP FIVE CITY CENTRE, THE ROCKS & CIRCULAR QUAY EATS

- **Tetsuya's** (p105)
- **Rockpool** (p104)
- **Sailor's Thai** (p104)
- **Guillaume at Bennelong** (p104)
- **MCA Café** (p104)

ARIA Map pp228-9 — Mod Oz

☎ 9252 2555; 1 Macquarie St, City; mains $42-49; ⏲ noon-2.30pm & 5.30-11.30pm Mon-Fri, 5.30-11.30pm Sat, 6-10pm Sun

A shining star in Sydney's eating establishment is this upmarket, European-influenced restaurant. Chef Matthew Moran whips up winning dishes like the crisp-skinned barramundi or poached lamb loin, and the stunning views of Circular Quay don't hurt one bit. A seven-course tasting menu ($135) is available; reservations recommended.

CASA ASTURIANA Map pp228-9 — Spanish

☎ 9264 1010; 77 Liverpool St, City; tapas $8-14, mains from $22; ⏲ noon-3pm & 5.30-11pm Mon-Sat, noon-10pm Sun

Located in Sydney's tiny 'Spanish Quarter,' this tapas joint reputedly serves the best tapas in town. Try the small platefuls of seafood or meat and vegetarian tidbits and order a fine Spanish wine, sangria or Austrian cider to help wash it all down. If you're in the mood for a *cazuela* (baked fish fillet), paella or even weekend flamenco, you're in luck.

DOYLES Map pp228-9 — Seafood

☎ 9252 3400; Overseas Passenger Terminal, West Circular Quay; mains $18-40; ⏲ 11.30am-3pm & 5.30-9.30pm Mon-Sat, 5.30-9.30pm Sun

Here is another slick, well-placed branch of the Doyles empire, offering outstanding views of the Sydney Opera House, the Harbour Bridge and Circular Quay in general. On a sunny day, snag a breezy promenade table under a white umbrella and enjoy the massive portions of fish 'n' chips (a hefty $32) – life doesn't get much better than this.

EST Map pp228-9 — Modern European

☎ 9240 3010; Level 1, Establishment Hotel, 252 George St, The Rocks; mains $38-42; ⏱ noon-3pm & 6-11pm Mon-Fri, 6-11pm Sat

Legendary Sydney chef Peter Doyle and sommelier Stuart Halliday keep the business crowds powering through deal-sealing corporate lunches at this slick eatery. Portions are small but high quality and the dining room more suited to groups than to intimate meals, but this classy place still exemplifies Sydney dining at its best. Thick wallet and fancy threads a must.

GUILLAUME AT BENNELONG

Map pp228-9 — Mod Oz

☎ 9250 7548; Sydney Opera House, Circular Quay; mains $39; ⏱ noon-3pm Thu & Fri, 5.30pm-midnight Mon-Sat

Start with some rock oysters or the braised oxtail, then delve into one of the heavenly seafood main dishes; you're located right at the Sydney Opera House and the building's airy architecture will accompany you the whole meal through. Award-winning chef Guillaume Brahmini's masterful style is evident in every divine dish, and the wine list certainly won't disappoint. Make a reservation.

HARBOUR KITCHEN & BAR

Map pp228-9 — Mod Oz

☎ 9256 1661; Park Hyatt, 7 Hickson Rd, The Rocks; mains $36-41; ⏱ 6.30-10.30am, 12-2.30pm & 6-10.30pm

Chef Danny Drinkwater offers up some of Sydney's finest cuisine, and the glass walls mean that stunning views of Circular Quay are guaranteed. Try the duck and beetroot tart or the salt-baked salmon *darne*, both his signature dishes. Lunch is decent value, with two courses going for $49; breakfast is also available.

MCA CAFÉ Map pp228-9 — Mod Oz

☎ 9241 4253; 140 George St, The Rocks; mains $16-27; ⏱ 10am-4pm

Wonderfully situated under the slick Museum of Contemporary Art, this trendy café's outside tables boast stunning views of Circular Quay and the Opera House. The simple menu offers café diners treats in the order of seared scallops with citrus *beurre blanc*, corn-fed chicken breast or beer-battered fish 'n' chips. Breakfast is also popular, and the service is right on the button.

ROCKPOOL Map pp228-9 — Mod Oz

☎ 9252 1888; 107 George St, The Rocks; mains $54-60; ⏱ 6-11pm Tue-Sat

Some of Sydney's finest food is produced at this sleekest of Neil Perry's restaurants, which for over 15 years has been tingling diners' culinary senses with such plates as roast pigeon with prawn-stuffed aubergine or grilled snapper with pomegranate salad. The award-winning seafood is exceptional, with filtered tanks keeping the critters fresh until the very last minute. Your bill will be astronomical, but a night of fine dining at Rockpool remains a quintessential Sydney experience. Reservations are crucial.

SAILOR'S THAI & SAILOR'S THAI CANTEEN Map pp228-9 — Thai

☎ 9251 2466; 106 George St, The Rocks; mains $25-36; ⏱ noon-10pm Mon-Sat

Sit yourself down at the long, communal table in the canteen (or snag yourself a balcony seat) and feast on some of the best Thai food this side of Bangkok. Consultant chef David Thompson whips up complex dishes fit for royalty, and you'll be sampling and discussing it with a mixture of artists, bureaucrats, politicians and tourists. For something more private and romantic, head downstairs to the fancy restaurant, where white tablecloths and upmarket attire rule the night (open noon to 3pm and 6pm to 10pm Monday to Saturday).

THE SUMMIT Map pp228-9 · Mod Oz

☎ 9247 9777; Level 47, Australia Sq, 264 George St, City; mains lunch $39-58, dinner $64-68; ⌚ noon-3pm Sun-Fri, 6-10pm Mon-Sun

Sure, it's not exactly cheap, but you're here for the supreme 360 degree views of Sydney. This high-rise restaurant rotates a full turn every hour and 45 minutes, giving you plenty of time to enjoy the chilli prawn tapas, seared rare tuna, wagyu beef rump or pepper crust snapper before the view starts repeating itself. And remember to dress up: they *won't* let you in wearing shorts.

SYDNEY COVE OYSTER BAR

Map pp228-9 · Seafood

☎ 9247 2937; East Circular Quay; mains $17-40; ⌚ 10am-late Mon-Sat, till 8pm Sun

Those seeking a sunny spot within spitting distance of the Opera House should snag a table at this outdoor-only eatery and enjoy the stunning views. As the name implies, oyster dishes are the speciality here (try the shots, $5.50) though other seafood temptations are also served. And while they may not be the best oysters in Sydney, you certainly can't beat the ambience!

TETSUYA'S Map pp228-9 · French-Japanese

☎ 9267 2900; www.tetsuyas.com; 529 Kent St, City; set menu only, $175 per person; ⌚ lunch from noon Sat, dinner from 6pm Tue-Sat

Tetsuya's has been ranked within the top five best restaurants in the *world*, and you must come here with a palate (and attitude) that seeks a culinary journey rather than a simple stuffed belly. The degustation menu offers ten courses of delightful, amazingly creative morsels of art (portions are very small) and tastes will be pure, refined and exhilarating. The infamous truffle butter, some say, is worth the price of admission. You'll need to book well in advance; bring your own wine ($18 corkage; check their website for menu) only if you're highly confident.

THE WHARF Map pp228-9 · Mod Oz

☎ 9250 1761; Pier 4, Hickson Rd, Walsh Bay; mains $33-35; ⌚ noon-3pm & 6-9.30pm Mon-Sat

Located above the Sydney Theatre Company wharf in Walsh Bay is this wonderfully airy restaurant set in a clean, converted warehouse space. Score a covered patio table and order the nashi pear salad with goat's cheese, following it with the roasted five-spice chicken and shallots. For dessert there's the quince terrine with white chocolate sabayon, or just sit back and enjoy the awesome bridge and harbour views.

Cheap Eats

BODHI Map pp228-9 · Asian Vegetarian

☎ 9360 2523; College St & Cook + Phillip Park, City; yum cha $5-8, mains $6-8; ⌚ 11am-10pm Tue-Sun, 11am-3pm Mon

Vegans need look no further than this flashy spot, located underneath the plaza in front of the cathedral. Lunch means tasty *yum cha,* and the simple, almost ascetic atmosphere will feed your soul, though the windy outdoor seating may bring you back to earth. There's another (much smaller) branch at Central Station (no *yum cha,* but try the veggie laksa soup for $7.50).

ZENERGY Map pp228-9 · Vegetarian

☎ 9261 5679; 68 Druitt St, City; mains $4-8; ⌚ 7am-4.30pm Mon-Fri

A true budget vegetarians' heaven, from *tempeh* burgers with chutney to rye bread, avocado and cheese sandwiches to tofu, sprouts and cabbage salads. From spinach and feta pies to brown rice *nori* rolls to veggie ratatouille to green Thai curries. And there are vegan pies, honey-free muffins and wheat-germ cookies for dessert – OK, aren't we going a bit far here?

DARLING HARBOUR & CHINATOWN

Chinatown has spilled out of Dixon St over into the Haymarket area, but luckily it offers some of the tastiest and best-value meals in Sydney. Penny-pinchers can venture into the various food courts, many at the top floors of shopping malls, while tasty *yum cha* (or dim sum) is so popular that on weekends you'll have to queue up. There's more than Chinese food too – Chinatown is also filled with the aromas of Japanese and Vietnamese cuisine.

Many of the eateries around Darling Harbour are aimed at the tourist trade, so don't come here searching for great deals or Sydney's finest cuisine. There's a large concentration of eateries at Cockle Bay Wharf,

TOP FIVE DARLING HARBOUR & CHINATOWN EATS

- **East Ocean** (right)
- **Zaaffran** (opposite)
- **Concrete** (right)
- **Chinta Ria** (right)
- **BBQ King** (below)

most with slick promenade views, white tablecloths and polished glass. Across the water at Harbourside are a handful of rejuvenated restaurants, also with water views and gleaming chrome. Further up towards Millers Point is the King St Wharf. There are many eateries here as well and most have menus posted outside, so you can wander along the water's edge and debate each kitchen's merits.

See the boxed text on p72 for transport options to/from these areas.

BBQ KING Map pp228-9 — Chinese
☎ 9267 2586; 18-20 Goulburn St, Haymarket; mains $12-24; ☻ 11am-2am
Vegetarians should give this place wide berth: the roast duck and barbecued pork are main attractions here, and they are deliciously decadent. It's an old-school eatery, with bustling service, generous pots of tea and a lack of fancy décor – everything an excellent Chinese restaurant should be. It's popular as a post-cinema haunt.

BLACKBIRD CAFÉ Map pp228-9 — Café
☎ 9283 7385; Level 2, Cockle Bay Wharf, Darling Harbour; mains $10-19; ☻ 8am-late
This large, popular restaurant is a good affordable option and offers good food for every taste. There are heaps of hot-stone pizzas, plenty of hot or cold salads, wok

Decorative Chinese lantern

stir-fries, a vegetarian list and staples like pasta and meat selections. The shady outdoor balcony is pleasant, as are the harbour views. A plus: it's open late; a minus: 10% surcharge on Sundays.

CHINTA RIA Map pp228-9 — Asian
☎ 9265 3211; Level 2, Cockle Bay Wharf, 201 Sussex St, Darling Harbour; mains $12-26; ☻ noon-2.30pm & 6-11pm
Despite its Malaysian-food-hawker-inspired menu it's not really cheap food, but the atmosphere more than makes up for it. An enormous Buddha greets you at the door of the giant pagoda dining room, while colourful plate settings, clanging dishes and efficient service only add to your enjoyment of the spicy chicken laksa. Look for Chinta Ria perched on a leafy rooftop at the northern end of Cockle Bay Wharf.

CONCRETE Map pp228-9 — Mod Oz
☎ 9518 9523; 224 Harris St, Pyrmont; breakfast $6-14, mains $15-19; ☻ 7am-4pm Mon-Fri, 8am-4pm Sat & Sun
This slick, minimalist joint boasts tasty offerings like buttermilk pancakes with grilled pineapple for breakfast, while lunch means eggplant and roasted almond ravioli or Mediterranean lamb skewers. Enjoy it all at a shady outdoor table. The location is a bit off the tourist path, just a few blocks from Darling Harbour.

EAST OCEAN Map pp232-3 — Chinese
☎ 9212 4198; 86-88 Dixon St, Haymarket; mains $10-22; ☻ 10am-2am Mon-Fri, from 9am Sat & Sun
Insanely popular on weekends for its *yum cha* (over 100 kinds), this massive Chinese restaurant can serve up to 1000 hungry folks – mostly discerning Asian diners – on a busy day. Popular dishes include the barbecue pork and roast duck, but don't miss the fresh seafood imported from Tasmania. Serves *yum cha* for both lunch and dinner.

GOLDEN CENTURY SEAFOOD RESTAURANT Map pp228-9 — Chinese/Seafood
☎ 9212 3901; 393-399 Sussex St, Haymarket; mains $12-22; ☻ noon-4am
This is the place for an upmarket Chinese dinner, especially if you like your seafood

fresh – it's sitting in nearby tanks (check out the abalone and giant crabs!). This is a favourite late-night eating spot for many of Sydney's chefs and hotel workers, who come for the exotic, engaging flavours, fast service and fancy Asian décor.

MARIGOLD CITYMARK Map pp232-3 Chinese

☎ 9281 3388; Levels 4 & 5, 683 George St, Haymarket; yum cha $2.50-5.25, mains $14-46; 🕑 10am-3pm & 5.30-11pm

This posh, 800-seat palace serves lunchtime *yum cha* daily and has an extensive menu of other dishes, so you're sure to find whatever you're looking for. Join the hordes. It's especially boisterous and interesting if you catch sight of a mammoth wedding banquet in full force.

ZAAFFRAN Map pp228-9 Indian

☎ 9211 8900; Level 2, 345 Harbourside, Darling Harbour; mains $17-26; 🕑 noon-2.30pm Mon-Sun, 6-9.30pm Sun-Thu, 6-10pm Fri & Sat

Indian food doesn't come fancier than this glassy-views, air-conditioned joint. Chef Vikrant Kapoor (of Singapore's Raffles fame) whips up both traditional and exotic selections. Try the tiger prawns with coconut and tamarind, or chicken biryani with mint. The menu offers good descriptions for easy selection, and includes some tasty vegetarian choices.

Cheap Eats

EMPEROR'S GARDEN BBQ & NOODLES Map pp232-3 Chinese

☎ 9281 9899; 213-215 Thomas St, Haymarket; mains $9-16; 🕑 9.30am-11pm

Here's a sizeable, busy eatery specialising in meat and poultry dishes. The little takeaway section out the front has many goodies, including some crimson-hued offerings hanging in the window; give the decadent roast duck and rice ($9) a try. There are plenty of vegetarian offerings as well, along with a healthy seafood list.

SEA BAY RESTAURANT

Map pp228-9 Chinese

☎ 9267 4855; 382 Pitt St, Haymarket; mains $8-12; 🕑 11.30am-10.30pm Mon-Sat

The tacky décor won't inspire you to write home, but the deliciously chewy home-

made noodles will. One steaming, slurpy bowl will fill you for less than $10, and there are steamed dumplings and wok-fried dishes to try too. Ask for the picture menu to make selecting your heavenly dish easier.

XIC LO Map pp232-3 Vietnamese

☎ 9280 1678; 213-215 Thomas St, Haymarket; mains $9-16; 🕑 11am-10.30pm Tue-Sat, till 10pm Sun & Mon

Sleek lines, stainless steel counters and muted earth colours translate into a hip Vietnamese restaurant, and the crowds drop in en masse during lunchtime. The crispy chicken with rice ($9) is a winner, but the *pho* (beef noodle soup) and rice rolls are also very popular with the folks who frequent Xic Lo.

DARLINGHURST TO POTTS POINT

Kitchens have spread like mushrooms in this neck of the woods, with snappy restaurant/bars and old-school budget eateries sharing real estate on strips like Victoria St, Challis Ave (Potts Point) and Darlinghurst Rd.

See the boxed text on p75 for transport options to/from these areas.

TOP FIVE DARLINGHURST TO POTTS POINT EATS

- **bills** (below)
- **Fratelli Paradiso** (p108)
- **Jimmy Lik's** (p108)
- **Otto** (p108)
- **Salt** (p108)

BILLS Map p235 Mod Oz

☎ 9360 9631; 433 Liverpool St, Darlinghurst; mains $18-23; 🕑 7am-10pm

Beautifully presented gourmet food. Gleaming open kitchen. Fresh flowers and fashion 'zines. Large communal table for conversations about your sweet corn frittata with bacon ($18.50) and his grilled Hiramasa kingfish with chickpea salad ($22.50). Unbearable weekend brunch crowds. The best scrambled eggs in town. Bill Granger (see p16).

FOODGAME Map pp232-3   Café
☎ 9380 8585; 185 Campbell St, Darlinghurst; mains $8-16; ☺ 10am-11pm

Whether you sit at the steel deli counter, in the plush lounge area, at the communal table or outside, you'll enjoy the salads (Thai to Caesar), burgers (Satay to steak) and pasta (ravioli to fettuccine). And don't even think about leaving without dessert (lemon tart, sticky date pudding, lime-infused coconut *panna cotta*…).

FRATELLI PARADISO Map pp228-9   Italian
☎ 9357 1744; 12 Challis Ave, Potts Point; mains $11-20; ☺ 7.30am-10pm Mon-Fri, 7am-6pm Sat & Sun

They serve lunch and dinner, and it's great, but what keeps us getting out of bed in the morning is the idea of breakfast here. The eggs are magnificent, the rice pudding superb, the coffee from God. Service is friendly and brisk, but just keep in the back of your mind that it closes at 6pm on weekends.

FU MANCHU Map p235   Chinese
☎ 9360 9424; 249 Victoria St, Darlinghurst; mains $9-20; ☺ 11.30am-3pm & 5.30-10.30pm

Think 21st-century Hong Kong slick chic, with chopsticks and elbows getting a work-out. Here you will find some of the best Asian eating in Darlinghurst, and it won't kill your wallet. Wrap your fingers around some steamed barbecue pork or ginger buns ($7.50) for a heavenly treat. Plenty of vegetarian options are also available.

JIMMY LIK'S Map p235   Modern Asian
☎ 8354 1400; 188 Victoria St, Kings Cross; mains $26-28; ☺ 6pm-midnight

A mirror image of its swanky bar next door, this upmarket eatery offers exotic Asian-inspired tapas like smoked eel in betel leaf ($3.50), while family-style main dishes include crispy pork hock, Vietnamese braised wagyu beef and salmon salad. There's usually a bit of a wait for restaurant seating, but with excellent bar snacks beckoning (the oysters *nam jim* are divine), you won't be in a hurry.

LURE Map pp232-3   Seafood
☎ 9361 3366; 381 Bourke St, Darlinghurst; mains $10-16; ☺ noon-10pm Fri & Sat, 5-11pm Sun-Thu

This small fish shop will make you look good eating fish 'n' chips and sipping organic coffee, right on Taylor Square. Its gleaming outdoor tables are airy and attractive, while a fancier back area offers privacy for the celebrity in you. Order the salmon teriyaki salad or salt 'n' pepper squid and feel even more special.

OTTO Map pp228-9   Italian
☎ 9368 7488; 8 Cowper Wharf Rdwy, Woolloomooloo; mains $24-38; ☺ noon-3pm & 6-10.30pm Mon-Sat, till 9pm Sun

One of Sydney's best restaurants, complete with water views and covered promenade seating. Chef James Kidman whips up a fine pasta selection (try the fresh egg *taglierini* with baby clams) and some truly gourmet meats (such as the braised wagyu beef cheeks with potato gnocchi, or roasted rack of lamb). Find it among a handful of other eateries; it'll be the most popular one.

SALT Map p235   Mod Oz
☎ 9332 2566; Kirketon Hotel, 229 Darlinghurst Rd, Darlinghurst; mains $40-46; ☺ noon-3pm Fri, 6-11pm Tue-Sat

Gourmet pleasure seekers will be in heaven as they dig into Chef Luke Mangan's blue-eye cod with Indian spices in pastry, or the mint-crusted pheasant with caramelised apple. A five- to seven-course tasting menu is also on offer ($125 without wine), and you'll be taking it all in among a simple mauve and chrome design.

SEL ET POIVRE Map p235   French
☎ 9361 6530; 263 Victoria St, Darlinghurst; mains $15-26.50; ☺ 6.30am-late Mon-Fri, 7.30am-late Sat & Sun

This casual bistro is perfect for homesick French expats; most of the staff speak French, the music is French, and the menu is available in French. Dishes like garlic snails, duck pâté and steak tartare are for the hard-core, so for something more mainstream order the delicious baguette sandwiches, roasted lamb loin or goats' cheese and walnut salad. *Bon appétit.*

UNA'S COFFEE LOUNGE

Map p235   European

☎ 9360 6885; 340 Victoria St, Darlinghurst; mains $12-19; ⏰ 7.30am-11pm Mon-Sat, 8am-1pm Sun
A true stayer, Una's has almost 30 years of experience in serving European comfort food and heavenly all-day fry-ups for brekky. Order your goulash, bratwurst, schnitzel or strudel, or steer towards the more mainstream omelettes and crepes, all the while enjoying your kitschy ski-lodge surroundings.

ZINC Map pp228-9   Mod Oz

☎ 9358 6777; 77 Macleay St, Potts Point; mains $14-25; ⏰ 7am-3pm Mon-Sun, 6.30-10pm Tue-Sun
Corner bistros don't come fancier than this joint, and if you score an outdoor table you'll be sitting among the prettiest people in Potts Point. Luxurious breakfasts (think pancakes with spiced plum sauce and crème fraîche, or poached-pear muesli) are served until 3pm weekends, when you'll fight for a spot. For a good lunch selection choose the bacon sandwich with beetroot, rocket and aïoli, and for dinner the roast Victorian lamb rump.

Cheap Eats

BAR COLUZZI Map p235   Café

☎ 9380 5420; 322 Victoria St, Darlinghurst; snacks $5-7.50; ⏰ 5am-7pm
The traditional Italian coffee served at this place attracts many of the city's Java-addicted residents; early on weekend mornings cyclists pedal in for their fix. Bar Coluzzi has achieved legendary status by making coffee for over 50 years, and it claims to be the heart and soul of Sydney's coffee world. Grab an outdoor stool and make them prove it.

DELECTICA Map p235   Café

☎ 9368 1390; 130 Victoria St, Kings Cross; mains $7-14; ⏰ 7.30am-3pm Mon-Fri, 8am-3pm Sat, 8.30am-3pm Sun
Breakfast is served all day, so get your blueberry pancakes with yogurt and honey for afternoon tea if you like. Or try the burger with beetroot or pumpkin salad with hummus dressing. There's plenty of other less fancy stuff, like omelettes, sandwiches and pasta, and if you're laid-back you'll be comfortable in the casual backpacker atmosphere.

HARRY'S CAFÉ DE WHEELS

Map pp228-9   Café

☎ 9347 3074; Cowper Wharf Rdwy, Woolloomooloo; pies $2.50-4; ⏰ 9am-1am Mon-Wed, 9am-3am Thu, 9am-4am Fri & Sat, 9am-midnight Sun
This pie cart and 'tourist attraction' serves decent pies and mash galore. See p76 for more information. As with many tourist attractions, the food's not that brilliant – but comes with million-dollar water views and gawking seagulls. After all, atmosphere is everything. There's another location on Hay St, next to the Capitol Theatre.

SPRING ESPRESSO Map pp228-9   Café

☎ 9331 0190; cnr Macleay St & Challis Ave, Potts Point; mains $8-12; ⏰ 7am-7pm Mon-Sat, 7.30am-6pm Sun
An old favourite in Potts Point, offering some of Sydney's best coffee along with some decent snacks and great atmosphere. It's a small place, so the gleaming outdoor tables are hot commodities during the morning rush, but the wait is worth it.

SURRY HILLS & EAST SYDNEY

From Modern French to fish 'n' chips to good-value Lebanese and Indian joints, this area has all the food bases covered, with rivers of excellent coffee filling the gaps. Crown St is the main thoroughfare in Surry Hills, but it's a long street and the restaurants occur in fits and starts. It's definitely worth a wander, however, and especially towards Cleveland St you'll find plenty of choice.

See the boxed text on p77 for transport options to/from these areas.

BÉCASSE Map pp232-3 — Modern French

☎ 9280 3202; 48 Albion St, Surry Hills; mains $32; ⏱ 6.30-10.30pm Wed-Sun

The muted, elegant décor at this under-stated restaurant is the perfect complement to chef Justin North's superbly created dishes. Try the degustation menu ($90); it's seven courses of gustatory heaven, with snapper, quail, barramundi and roasted wagyu beef dishes included in the package. The handful of regular main dishes should be equally memorable, however.

BILLS 2 Map pp232-3 — Mod Oz

☎ 9360 4762; 359 Crown St, Surry Hills; mains $19-28; ⏱ 7am-10pm

The loyal and eclectic crowd has followed Bill Granger's success from his Darling-hurst eatery to this shiny new upstart. This equally chic joint offers outdoor seating – a great place for a cup of tea from 4pm to 6pm. Tasty selections might be the roasted lamb rump with baked eggplant or black mussels with *romesco* sauce. Take it all in, and enjoy; your fellow diners certainly will. See p16 for more on Bill.

BILLY KWONG Map pp232-3 — Modern
CHINESE

☎ 9332 3300; 355 Crown St, Surry Hills; mains $16-39; ⏱ 6-10pm Sun-Thu, till 11pm Fri & Sat

Welcome to one of Sydney's hardest restaurants in which to snag a table – no reservations are taken except for one large table (choose from 6pm and 8pm seatings). If you do manage to sit down, you'll be treated to chef Kylie Kwong's wonderful seasonal menu – think silken tofu with mushrooms and ginger, crispy-skinned chicken with shallots, and spicy octopus salad with baby herbs. Ingredients are fresh and meats first-rate, so your lemon chicken *will* be memorable.

TOP FIVE SURRY HILLS & EAST SYDNEY EATS

- Billy Kwong (above)
- Longrain (right)
- Bécasse (above)
- Uchi Lounge (opposite)
- Red Lantern (opposite)

DRAGONFLY Map pp232-3 — Asian Fusion

☎ 9380 7333; 478 Bourke St, Surry Hills; mains $30-32; ⏱ 6-10pm Tue-Sat

This small but elegant restaurant is located in a cosy residential Surry Hills neighbourhood, so despite the crowds you'll feel like you're somewhere special. The half-dozen main dishes – including the delicious crispy-skinned duck and the slow-braised Mandarin pork neck – are delightful, or go for gold with the eight-course tasting menu ($80). Be sure to book and ask for a courtyard table.

IL BARETTO Map pp232-3 — Italian

☎ 9361 6163; 496 Bourke St, Surry Hills; mains $10-18; ⏱ 8am-3.30pm & 6-9.30pm Tue-Sat, 9am-3pm Sun

Packed to the rafters and dishing up some of the most heavenly pasta and gourmet sandwiches in Sydney, this tiny and chaotic restaurant offers fabulous food in local surroundings. You'll be waiting for sure, so head to the pub across the road; they'll come and get you. Try the *spaghetti alle vongole* (spaghetti with clams) or homemade gnocchi – 'yum!' is what you'll be thinking.

LONGRAIN Map pp232-3 — Modern Thai

☎ 9280 2888; 85 Commonwealth St, Surry Hills; mains $23-38; ⏱ noon-2.30pm Mon-Fri, 6-11pm Mon-Sat

It seems that all of Sydney's beautiful set are keen to graze on the superb Thai-inspired offerings here. They'll sit at the communal tables or long counter, so don't expect much privacy; try the caramelised pork hock with chilli vinegar, though, and you'll need to gush to nearby ears. Good service and an excellent bar are icing on the cake.

MOHR FISH Map pp232-3 — Seafood

☎ 9218 1326; 202 Devonshire St, Surry Hills; mains $7-18; ⏱ 10am-10pm

Don't expect to find yourself in a fancy eatery when you come to Mohr Fish – this small but popular place takes up a space that's about the size of your living room. It has a very casual atmosphere and only a short, simple menu of excellent fried seafood – can you say fish 'n' chips? Expect the locals in the know to join you at the crowded counter.

PRASIT'S NORTHSIDE THAI
TAKEAWAY Map pp232-3   Thai

☎ 9332 1792; 395 Crown St, Surry Hills; mains $12-20; ⏰ noon-3pm & 5.30-10pm

There's only a handful of tables at this purple-and-gold-painted eatery, so most folks come for the consistently good take-away. Try the young mango and crab salad or banana flower salad, and follow with the hot green peppercorn stir fry. Curries, soups and a good vegetarian selection are also pumped out at a fast and furious pace to keep up with the demanding masses.

RED LANTERN Map pp232-3   Vietnamese

☎ 9698 4355; 545 Crown St, Surry Hills; mains $12-20; ⏰ noon-3pm & 6-10pm Tue-Sun

Before anything else, call to make reservations – and ask for a front terrace table. This hot Vietnamese joint, headed by Mark Jensen and the brother and sister team of Luke and Pauline Nguyen, serves up some great shrimp rolls in rice paper ($9) and an exotic *muc rang muoi* (chilli salted squid), all the while softly glowing in atmospheric lighting.

TABOU Map pp232-3   French

☎ 9319 5682; 527 Crown St, Surry Hills; mains $22-29; ⏰ noon-2.30pm & 6-10pm

French right down to its lacy curtains, the flatteringly-lit Tabou is perfect for a low-key romantic dinner. Chef Jacob Brown whips out popular entrées like sautéed sweet-breads and cheese soufflés, along with main dishes like the black pudding and veal fillet. Service is typically Gallic, meaning you'll either be flirted with or barely acknowledged.

Cheap Eats
BILL & TONI'S Map pp228-9   Italian

☎ 9360 4702; 74 Stanley St, East Sydney; mains $13-15; ⏰ noon-2.30pm & 6-10.30pm

Folks come to Bill and Toni's – Sydney's most famous cheap pasta joint – because it's a traditional destination for basic Italian cuisine, and, in our opinion, a national treasure. Chicken plates, veal *parmigiana* and even liver and onions grace the menu, but the hard-core go for the incredibly affordable pasta. The service is lightning-fast, you still get your orange cordial for free and the café downstairs brews some of the best coffee in town.

MAH JONG Map pp232-3   Modern Chinese

☎ 9361 3985; 312 Crown St, Surry Hills; mains $15-24; ⏰ 6-10.30pm Mon-Sat

Siblings Billy To and Erika Chan offer up fresh, wholesome and creative Chinese cuisine at this atmospheric Surry Hills eatery. Choose one of the three cosy dining areas and dive into the steamed fish with ginger, crispy-skinned chicken or wok-fried lamb, and don't forget the Peking duck starter. In winter the mixed seafood hot pot is mandatory. Monthly mah jong classes are offered.

UCHI LOUNGE Map pp228-9   Japanese

☎ 9261 3524; 15 Brisbane St, Surry Hills; mains $14-17; ⏰ 6.30-11.30pm Mon-Sat

Dress up creatively – your server certainly will, and so will the décor around you. Blissful Japanese food takes centre stage, however; start with chilled *udon* with lime *ponzu* and follow with kingfish sashimi, seared tuna or tempura oysters. The raspberry, lychee or ginger sake goes down real smooth.

PADDINGTON & WOOLLAHRA

Woollahra and Paddington offer good eating that shies away from the aggressively modern tendencies of their neighbours. Here's where you'll find an appreciation of the just-so steak with the perfect wine, and subdued, well-mannered service to match.

See the boxed text on p78 for transport options to/from these areas.

BISTRO LULU Map pp232-3   French

☎ 9380 6888; 257 Oxford St, Paddington; mains $26-30; ⏰ noon-3pm Thu-Sat, 6-11pm Mon-Sat, 6-10pm Sun

How does blue-eye cod wrapped in prosciutto sound? And let's not forget the pan-fried gnocchi with cauliflower *polonaise* and truffle vinaigrette, followed with coconut and lemongrass *semi-freddo* for dessert. Add a prix fixe menu and decent wine list and you've got yourself a night to remember.

BISTRO MONCUR Map pp232-3   French/Mod Oz

☎ 9363 2519; Woollahra Hotel, 116 Queen Sts, Woollahra; mains $26-37; ⏰ noon-3pm & 6-10.30pm Tue-Sat, till 9pm Sun

With a striking mural running the length of one wall and highly regarded chef Damien

Pignolet creating marvels at the hot stove, Bistro Moncur has long been a local favourite. Order the marinated salmon or French onion soufflé, then go for the grilled sirloin with Café de Paris butter or roasted pork sausages and be in heaven.

GRAND NATIONAL HOTEL

Map pp232-3   Mod Oz

☎ 9363 4557; 161 Underwood St, Paddington; mains $23-29; ⏲ noon-3pm Fri-Sun, 6-10.30pm Tue-Sat, till 9pm Sun

It's located right next to its namesake drinking hole, but this is definitely *not* pub grub. A bright and elegant dining room offers inventive cuisine like duck breast with soused vegetables or roasted lamb with carrot purée. Well-chosen wine recommendations add even more punch, and the pear strudel with prune armagnac ice cream ends the night nicely indeed.

TOKO Map pp232-3   Japanese

☎ 9380 7001; 362 Oxford St, Paddington; sushi $2.50-5.50; ⏲ noon-10pm Tue-Sun

Great sushi, quick and easy, is on offer at this small but popular place. Warm up with a bowl of miso soup, then grab those rolls and *nigiri* morsels as they pass by. More substantial noodle soups, along with *gyoza, yakitori* and teriyaki, are also on the menu. End it all with dessert: tempura banana with green tea and vanilla-bean ice cream. Yum.

Cheap Eats

AND THE DISH RAN AWAY WITH THE SPOON Map pp232-3   Café

☎ 9361 6131; 226 Glenmore Rd, Paddington; mains $5-10; ⏲ 8am-10pm

Local yuppies cram into this charming little Paddington deli to lunch on great pasta, organic chicken and tofu burgers. It's a primo spot to pick up picnic fixings or

takeaway lunches and dinners, and breakfast is served all day. Try the low-fat 'skinny burger' ($8) – it tastes too good to be true.

JONES THE GROCER Map pp232-3   Deli

☎ 9362 1222; 68 Moncur St, Woollahra; mains $8-16; ⏲ 8am-6pm Mon-Fri, 9am-5.30pm Sat, 9am-5pm Sun

With the lovely food on display it's easy to see why this is one of Sydney's favourite places to stock up on fancy deli goods, such as Asian groceries, chutneys, cheese, olives and exotic teas and coffees. But it's also nice for the old coffee-and-cake break (check out the homemade fudge), and sitting at the slick communal table might just make you feel like a local.

EASTERN SUBURBS

Double Bay (jokingly referred to as 'Double Pay') has some nice low-key spots with tasty food, great for a break from all that high-class shopping you'll be doing in this neighbourhood. If you're looking for cheap dining options, however, this definitely isn't the place to be.

See the boxed text on p80 for transport options to/from this area.

BOTTICELLI Map pp226-7   Italian

☎ 9363 3266; 21 Bay St, Double Bay; mains $26-32; ⏲ 11am-10pm Mon-Fri, 5.30-10pm Sat

The Pacific oysters, char-grilled field mushrooms and Caprese salad make great appetisers, while the roast duck with Grand Marnier or veal scaloppine *lemone* fill the spaces left over. A darkish interior decked out in Italian murals and spartan décor keep attention focused on either the food or that engagement ring your lover just placed on your finger. It's that kind of place.

LIMONCELLO Map pp226-7   Italian

☎ 9363 3656; 29 Bay St, Double Bay; mains $23-25; ⏲ noon-3pm & 6-10pm Tue-Thu & Sun, 6-11pm Fri & Sat

Start with the antipasto or homemade *tagliani* with scampi, and proceed to main dishes like the grilled lamb fillet, stuffed calzone or one of 24 traditional and gourmet pizza choices. Flavours will take you straight to southern Italy, especially if you sit in the airy covered patio out the back or snag an outdoor seat up front.

EASTERN BEACHES

Sydney's eastern beaches are chock-full of cafés, restaurants and fast-food joints. The scene is popular, with plenty of bronzed, buff bodies grabbing 'skinny' (low-fat milk) café lattes throughout the day before putting on some sexy, expensive duds for a fancy dinner at the newest of the Mod Oz food temples.

Bondi has the most touristy eateries of all the eastern beaches, most stretching along the Campbell Pde seaside promenade, while fancier bistros can be found on side streets. Bronte's Bronte Rd hosts some quality cafés. Coogee has most of its food joints on inland Coogee Bay Rd, but again you're better off hitting the cafés on the side streets, which have healthier and better-value food. Cheap takeaway and an empty patch of sand are often your most atmospheric choices, however.

See the boxed text on p82 for transport options to/from these areas.

BARZURA Map p238   Café
☎ 9665 5546; 62 Carr St, Coogee; mains $17-24; ⏰ 7am-11pm
Airy and modern, this popular café offers pleasant meals any time of day. Breakfast means corn fritters with bacon, tomato and avocado; lunch could be an open salmon sandwich with capers; dinner tempts with grilled lamb liver with pancetta or the chorizo and saffron risotto. The specials board offers more interesting choices, and outdoor tables are pure gold.

GELBISON Map p238   Italian
☎ 9130 4042; 10 Lamrock Ave, Bondi; mains $12-18; ⏰ 5-11pm
This is an old favourite with many beach bums, film industry types and assorted gluttons coming here to look for great Italian staples. Gelbison never seems to

---

TOP FIVE EASTERN BEACHES EATS

- Sean's Panaroma (p114)
- Icebergs (right)
- Brown Sugar (p114)
- Hugo's (right)
- Gelbison (above)

---

change – and in Bondi that's a rare thing. There are pizzas galore (27 kinds), even more pastas and a few veal and risotto dishes. Outdoor tables within the ocean breezes' reach won't hurt your enjoyment of the casual atmosphere either.

HUGO'S Map p238   Mod Oz
☎ 9300 0900; 70 Campbell Pde, Bondi; mains $35-38; ⏰ 6pm-midnight Mon-Fri, 9am-3pm & 6pm-midnight Sat & Sun
The minute you take your seat at this well-known, swanky joint you'll notice that everything around you is pretty as a button, from the furnishings to the views to the food – even the staff look their best. Hit the jackpot by snagging an outdoor table at which to enjoy your seared scallops, duck omelette or sour-cherry soufflé. It's a bit of a scene, but after downing one of their sublime daiquiris you won't even notice.

ICEBERGS Map p238   Mod Oz
☎ 9365 9000; 1 Notts Ave, Bondi; mains $32-44; ⏰ noon-3pm & 6.30-10.30pm Tue-Sat, till 9pm Sun
Maurice Terzini's sleek celebrity magnet absolutely sizzles at its supreme cliff-top locale – you couldn't get better views from the moon. The chef laces the upmarket menu with entrees like sea scallops wrapped in pancetta, while mains run from Mandalong lamb rack to roasted barramundi with herbed chicken *caponata*. The only difficulty is getting a reservation – call way ahead and hope to luck out.

JACK & JILL'S FISH CAFÉ
Map p238   Seafood
☎ 9665 8429; 98 Beach St, Coogee; mains $14-20; ⏰ 5-9pm Tue-Sat, noon-8pm Sun
Up the hill and close to the north end of Coogee Beach, this simple, homely and nonpretentious place lies away from the maddening crowds. It's perfect for folks looking for good seafood dishes at reasonable prices. We recommend the Cajun-spiced barramundi with rice, but the tandoori perch is also worth a bite.

RICE Map p238   Thai
☎ 9664 6655; 100 Beach St, Coogee; mains $12-18; ⏰ noon-late
Stunning in its dark colour scheme, this fancy noodle joint serves up the Asian

goods to your specifications – choose your own combo of soup, noodles, sauce or curry. If you can't decide, pick specific dishes like steamed fish with ginger, beef salad, roast-duck stir fry or fried rice with egg and vegies. It's up the hill from the beach and right next to Jack & Jill's Fish Café.

SEAN'S PANAROMA Map p238   Mod Oz
☎ 9365 4924; 270 Campbell Pde, Bondi; mains $25-39; ☾ 6.30-10pm Wed-Fri, noon-3pm & 6.30-10pm Sat, noon-3pm Sun
You won't be disappointed in the always-evolving dishes at this modest eatery overlooking Bondi beach. Sean Moran and his team whip up preserved duck with potato cake, cabbage and pickled cherries, or just a simple *pici* (Tuscan pasta). Outdoor tables offer windy views, the ocean's roar and romantic charm, making your Barossa milk-fed lamb taste all the sweeter.

SWELL map p238   Mod Oz
☎ 9386 5001; 465 Bronte Rd, Bronte; mains $12-28; ☾ 7am-9.30pm
Swell is perfectly named, with an ideal Bronte location. A large front window lets the sunshine and the sea air right in to the Mod Oz décor that goes with the Mod Oz food. You can have lunch or dinner here, but something keeps us coming back – especially for the scrambled egg wrap ($10), which will see you through to lunch or assuage a post-surf hunger.

Cheap Eats
BROWN SUGAR Map p238   Café
☎ 9365 6262; 100 Brighton Blvd, North Bondi; mains $8-14; ☾ 7.30am-4pm Mon-Sat, 9am-4pm Sun
Finding an empty table here on weekends is a serious challenge, when Sydney's 'in' crowd floods the cramped spaces to test the staff's patience and chow down on tasty dishes like black-stone eggs. Weekdays are much less frantic, but the linguine with asparagus and rocket tastes just as good.

ERCIYES 2 Map p238   Turkish
☎ 9664 1913; 240 Coogee Bay Rd, Coogee; mains $8-13; ☾ 10am-11pm
The café up front serves quick takeaway meat pies and kebabs, along with some ex-

cellent dips – try the *jajik* (cucumber, yogurt and garlic). If it's good Turkish pizza you're after, you won't go away hungry. For something fancier, come at night, when the BYO restaurant does similar fare but with belly dancing as well (Friday and Saturday only).

A FISH CALLED COOGEE Map p238 Seafood
☎ 9664 7700; 229 Coogee Bay Rd, Coogee; mains $5-8; ☾ 11.30am-9pm
This busy little fishmonger sells fresh seafood cooked many different ways. Grab some great takeaway fish 'n' chips, crumbed calamari or battered prawns and sit on the beach, 'cause you probably won't be able to snag one of those gleaming outdoor tables – and with the sands so close by, you won't want to.

FISHFACE Map p238   Seafood
☎ 9332 4803; Bronte Rd, Bronte; mains $7-10; ☾ 11am-8pm
A great place for beachside fish 'n' chips and seafood combos, with big portions and tasty morsels. It's take away only, so grab your bag and head to the beach; you'll be fighting off long lines on the weekends, and the seagulls will always be watching.

LA PLAGE Map p238   Café
☎ 9389 3527; 481 Bronte Rd, Bronte; mains $8-12; ☾ 7.30am-5.30pm
Especially popular for weekend brunch is this small, airy and casual eatery on Bronte's beach eating strip. Snag an outside table and enjoy the grilled burgers, toasted sandwiches and tortilla wraps, though of course breakfast foods are whipped up as well. Plenty of good coffee is also available to get your morning going.

INNER WEST
Four main streets offer the best cuisine in this region – Glebe Point Rd, Glebe; King St, Newtown; Darling St, Balmain; and Norton St, Leichhardt. Glebe Point Rd was Sydney's original 'eat street' but what it lacks in cutting-edge dining experiences it retains in laid-back, unpretentious atmosphere, good-value food and convivial service. A swag of funky cafés and restaurants lining Newtown's King St offer an interesting introduction to the suburb's community life – many cater to university students.

TOP FIVE BREAKFASTS

- **Barzura**, Coogee (p113)
- **bills**, Darlinghurst (p107)
- **Brown Sugar**, Bondi (opposite)
- **Concrete**, Darling Harbour (p106)
- **Fratelli Paradiso**, Potts Point (p108)

Balmain's Darling St has plenty of trendy yet still mostly casual dining among well-heeled yuppies and families. You can still get a cheap spaghetti *puttanesca* on Norton St, Leichhardt, but the classic bistros are now rubbing shoulders with the classy restaurants, plus a few Greek, Chinese and Thai interlopers.

See the boxed text on p83 for transport options to/from these areas.

BALMAIN EATING HOUSE

Map pp226-7   French/Mod Oz
☎ 9810 3415; 359 Darling St, Balmain; mains $14.50-25; ☽ 9am-3pm & 6.30-11pm Mon-Fri, from 8am Sat, 8am-3pm Sun
Breakfast is a treat at this French eatery, with the farmhouse breakfast (poached free-range eggs, provolone and pork sausage and oven-roasted tomatoes) competing with the mustard-scrambled eggs (with oven-baked ham, roasted mushrooms, and spinach on Turkish toast) for your favour. Dinner mains are equally tempting, and the rustic wooden furniture adds classy but casual atmosphere.

BOATHOUSE BLACKWATTLE BAY

Map pp236-7   Seafood
☎ 9518 9011; Ferry Rd, Glebe; mains $38-43; ☽ noon-3pm & 6.30-10.30pm Tue-Sun
One of Sydney's best, with 9 kinds of oysters, fresh crab and lobster and an incredible snapper pie that will zoom to the top of your favourite dish list. Other delec-table things to try include the slow-roasted Tasmanian salmon with caviar lentils or the roasted blue-eye with scallop and *wasabi* vinaigrette. And yep, there's a view of the bridge – only this time it's the Anzac Bridge. Reservations recommended.

ELIO Map pp236-7   Italian
☎ 9560 9129; 159 Norton St, Leichhardt; mains $22-30; ☽ 6-11pm
Personal attention and informed service are a hallmark at this no-nonsense Italian institution, and the food's not too bad either. Try the homemade gnocchi with creamed pumpkin, portobello mushroom risotto or black Spring Bay mussels with dill. In winter, the rabbit and olive pie with roast parsnips and green peas will warm you right up.

GRAPPA Map pp236-7   Italian
☎ 9560 6090; Shop 1, 267-277 Norton St, Leichhardt; mains $23-38; ☽ 6-10pm Mon, noon-3pm & 6-10pm Tue-Fri, 6-11pm Sat, 6-9.30pm Sun
Oddly located above a parking garage, this spacious eatery looks better on the inside; its open kitchen, snazzy bar and elegant décor will impress your picky date. Tasty mains include snapper in rock salt, buffalo *bocconcini* and tuna *carpaccio*, or go for pure excess with the ½ roast duck or 450g T-bone steak. An award-winning wine list only adds to the appeal.

ROSALINA'S Map pp236-7   Italian
☎ 9516 1429; 30 King St, Newtown; mains $14-18; ☽ 6-10.30pm Tue-Sun
On King St's less lively section lies homely Rosalina's, offering tasty traditional dishes like chicken cacciatore, veal *parmigiana* and scaloppine, plus of course heaps of spaghetti varieties. Service is charming and the wine's not bad, making it a popular stop on weekends (be sure to book).

TOP FIVE INNER WEST EATS

- **Boathouse Blackwattle Bay** (above)
- **Grappa** (right)
- **Iku Wholefoods** (p117)
- **Thai Pothong** (p116)
- **Bar Italia** (p116)

SPANISH TAPAS Map pp236-7   Spanish
☎ 9571 9005; 28 Glebe Point Rd, Glebe; tapas $8-14; ☽ 6-11pm
Those in search of tapas need look no further, as this fancier joint offers those little Spanish dishes that range from good to great. Sample the mussels in tomato, tuna croquettes, garlic mushrooms or spinach and onion omelettes. The low lights, music and convivial diners add to the festive atmosphere.

Eating

INNER WEST

TANJORE Map pp236-7 — Indian
☎ 9660 6332; 34 Glebe Point Rd, Glebe; mains $8-18; ⊙ 6-11pm
A pioneer of South Indian food in Australia, Tanjore attracts a range of locals, Indian-food lovers and celebrities to its cosy, dark dining room. Worthy dishes include the tandoori prawns, mango chicken and lamb *saag* (lamb with spinach). And don't forget the garlic naan, along with a mango lassi to wash it all down.

THAI POTHONG Map pp236-7 — Thai
☎ 9550 6277; 294 King St, Newtown; mains $8-26; ⊙ noon-3pm Tue-Sun, 6-10.30pm Sun-Thu, till 11pm Fri & Sat
Still flush from their 2002 'best Thai restaurant in Sydney' trophy, this large and hugely popular restaurant serves up an interesting and delicious range of vegie dishes, seafood, curries and salads. For a special treat, check out their green mango barramundi salad or pumpkin curry, or go for the attention-grabbing seafood flambé.

Cheap Eats

BACIGALUPO Map pp236-7 — Italian
☎ 9565 5238; 284 King St, Newtown; mains $11-16; ⊙ 8am-10pm
This airy and casual place will satisfy your rumbling tummy with more choices you can shake a breadstick at. Hearty breakfast selections tempt with three-egg omelettes, muesli and corn bread with braised tomato, while light meals include risotto with egg-plant and grilled octopus salad. End things with a satisfying caffeine hit – try their mocha or flat white.

BADDE MANORS Map pp236-7 — Café
☎ 9660 3797; 37 Francis St, Glebe; mains $8-13; ⊙ 8am-midnight Mon-Thu, 8-1am Fri & Sat, 9-midnight Sun
This long-established corner haunt is especially hectic on market day, when footpath tables are the holy grail. There are plenty of choices to make; lentil or tofu burgers, focaccias, bagels, frappés, smoothies, cakes, gelato and sticky date fig ginger pudding, among many other things. Just don't expect great service – they seem to revel in their name.

Badde Manors Café, Glebe (left)

BAR ITALIA Map pp236-7 — Italian
☎ 9560 9981; 169-171 Norton St, Leichhardt; mains $10-17; ⊙ 9am-midnight Mon-Thu, 10-1am Fri & Sat
This popular family-style restaurant, café and gelateria offers all the traditional pastas and sauces, along with salads, focaccia and – for those who can take it – plenty of veal. During the day outdoor tables fill with appreciative diners, while at night seafood like garlic prawns and fish 'n' chips are a big draw. Their famous gelato is a must-have accessory for a Norton St stroll.

GREEN GOURMET
Map pp236-7 — Asian Vegetarian
☎ 9519 5330; 115 King St, Newtown; mains $11-15; ⊙ noon-3pm & 6-10pm
A peaceful Zen-like atmosphere greets you at the door, and along with the soothing music and simple aesthetics make the tofu dishes and soups go down easy. Great Chinese-Malaysian vegetarian food is the speciality here, with *yum cha* livening up weekend lunch. Come enjoy it all – your spirit chakra will thank you later.

GRIND Map pp236-7 — Café
☎ 9568 5535; 151 Norton St, Leichhardt; mains $9-15; ⊙ 7am-3pm Mon-Fri, 7am-3.30pm Sat & Sun
Try the delicious pasta dishes or go for the focaccia sandwiches – how does roast beef, aïoli, *arugula* and tomato chutney sound? Or perhaps the lamb skewers with Greek salad rings truer? Either way you'll be golden, and if you scored a table on the balcony above, you can even smoke afterwards. An espresso bar ices the cake.

IKU WHOLEFOODS

Map pp236-7   Macrobiotic/Vegetarian

☎ 9692 8720; 25A Glebe Point Rd, Glebe; mains $3-9; ☺ 11.30am-9pm Mon-Fri, 11.30am-8pm Sat, 12.30-7.30pm Sun

Here's one of the best vegan places in town, offering cheap and healthy takeaway treats (mostly organic). Order the miso soup, tofu fritters and Japanese rolls and go picnic at nearby Victoria Park. Just note that it closes relatively early on weekends.

NORTH SHORE

Having well and truly ditched a reputation for having nowhere decent to eat, the North Shore has a different perspective on Sydney Harbour. On weekends, however, it'll feel like everyone else has the same idea.

See the boxed text on p85 for transport options to/from this area.

AQUA DINING Map p239   Mod Oz

☎ 9964 9998; cnr Paul & Northcliff Sts, Milsons Point; mains $30-42; ☺ noon-2.30pm Mon-Fri & Sun, 6.30-10pm Sun-Fri, 6-10pm Sat

You'll be hard pressed to find a flashier restaurant design, but it's the astounding view of the bridge and Opera House (plus the Olympic swimming pool below) that will take your breath away. Expect sterling service and fancy food (the hickory-smoked Yamba prawns are especially good, though the meat dishes can have overwhelming sauces), plus worthy wine list. Reservations recommended.

AWABA CAFÉ Map pp226-7   Café

☎ 9969 2104; 67 The Esplanade, Balmoral; mains $10-29; 7.30am-4pm Mon-Wed, 7.30am-10pm Thu-Sat, 7.30am-5pm Sun

This big, white, airy corner café works well in pretty Balmoral, feeding the beach-going masses. For something memorable order the lamb rump with roasted vegetables or the beetroot and avocado salad with goats' cheese and basil – and be prepared to line up on weekends.

RIPPLES Map p239   Mod Oz

☎ 9929 7722; Olympic Dr, Milsons Point; mains $20-28; ☺ 7am-11pm

With killer views of the Harbour Bridge and Opera House, this mostly outdoor eatery offers Mod Oz cuisine with European and Asian influences. The chef-recommended prawn noodle salad and tempura garfish promise to be great choices. Look for it under North Sydney's Olympic Pool.

WATERMARK Map pp226-7   Mod Oz

☎ 9968 3433; 2A The Esplanade, Balmoral; mains $30-38; ☺ 8am-10.30am, noon-3pm & 6.30-10.30pm Mon-Fri, 8am-10.30am, 12.30-3.30pm & 6.30-10.30pm Sat & Sun

Start with the natural, steamed or smoked oysters, then head right into the sautéed Queensland king prawns or muscovy duck with cream-chilled lychees. Watermark's beachside location and wonderful views will only add to your dining enjoyment, especially if you score a table on the airy wood deck in front.

Cheap Eats
DON ADÁN COFFEE HOUSE

Map pp226-7   Café

☎ 9968 2828; 5 Spit Rd, Mosman; mains $8-12; ☺ 9.30am-8.30pm Mon-Fri, till 9pm Sat

For fair-wage coffee, high-quality Arabica beans and a multi-award-winning brew, stop in at this cosy café during your North Shore travels. A mind-boggling espresso list makes caffeine choices difficult, but you can't go wrong with the sandwiches or omelettes. Expect a few small tables, painted murals on the ceiling and a funky vibe throughout. Loose-leaf teas also available.

NEUTRAL BAY SEAFOOD

Map pp226-7   Seafood

☎ 9953 2767; 163 Wycombe Rd; mains $8-12; ☺ 9.30am-8.30pm, till 9pm Sat

If you ever find yourself in Neutral Bay, madly craving fish 'n' chips, then this is the place. Choose between white fish or barramundi, and add a few calamari rings for good measure (80 cents each). Tasmanian scallops, battered oysters and pineapple fritters can also be had, but you'll have to find a good bench to enjoy it all.

MANLY

The ocean end of The Corso (Manly's pedestrian mall) is jam-packed with takeaway places and outside tables. Manly Wharf and South Steyne have plenty of

TOP FIVE NORTH SHORE & MANLY EATS

- **Ripples** (p117)
- **Awaba Café** (p117)
- **Neutral Bay Seafood** (p117)
- **Alhambra** (below)
- **Blue Water Café** (right)

airy eateries that catch the sea breeze and bustle on sunny days. Note that weekends see restaurant surcharges of 10%.

See the boxed text on p88 for transport options to/from this area.

ALHAMBRA Map p240   Spanish
☎ 9976 2975; 54A West Esplanade, Manly; mains $19-25; ⊗ noon-3pm & 6-10.30pm Mon-Fri, noon-5pm & 6-10.30pm Sat & Sun
We love coming to Manly, because it means we can make sure Alhambra has maintained its high standards. The Spanish- and Moroccan-inspired dishes (including tapas) are excellent – try the grilled octopus, lamb salad with couscous or potato *alioli*. Choose the covered outdoor tables, or admire the Moorish décor inside.

BARKING FROG Map p240   Café
☎ 9977 6307; 48 North Steyne, Manly; mains $12-16 lunch, $19-29 dinner; ⊗ 8am-midnight Mon-Sat, 8am-5pm Tue, 8am-10pm Sun
Right off the beach, this attractive place does good lunchtime fare (think pasta and burgers), while the evenings are more loungey and Mod Oz – things like Sumac-crusted lamb on fig couscous or grilled

wild barramundi with braised leek and fennel. There's even a DJ on weekends.

BLUE WATER CAFÉ Map p240   Café
☎ 9976 2051; 28 South Steyne, Manly; mains $16-27; ⊗ 7.30am-10pm Mon-Fri, 7.30am-10.30pm Sat & Sun
The huge portions are a major draw at this bustling, popular beach café. The whopping lemon chicken burger ($14) or crispy-skinned ocean trout with cherry tomatoes will really satisfy a post-surf hunger, although the boards on the wall will remind you to get back into the foam.

Cheap Eats

BEANRUSH Map p240   Café
☎ 9977 2236; 7 Whistler St, Manly; coffees $2.50-4, mains $7-10; ⊗ 6.30am-5pm Mon-Fri, 7am-4pm Sat
A small hole-in-the-wall café with great coffee made from wonderfully exotic, organic beans (think Sumatran or Nicaraguan); and the snacks are mighty fine, too. Worth a visit if your engine needs revving, but keep in mind it closes at 5.30pm.

MANLY FISH MARKET Map p240   Seafood
☎ 9976 3777; Shop 1, Wentworth St, Manly; mains $9-13; ⊗ 8am-8pm
Here's a tiny fish shop with just two tables, though with the beach so near most folks grab the delicious (and generous) fish 'n' chips bag and head to the water. If you want to be fancy, however, there are the prawn cutlets or mixed seafood boxes, or just swing next door to their upmarket restaurant.

Drinking ▪

Drinking

Pubs are a quintessential part of your Sydney experience, and fortunately you'll have plenty of ways to get experienced. These drinking holes range from traditional affairs with elaborate 19th-century detail and pressed tin ceilings to cavernous Art Deco joints with tiled walls to the modern and minimalist. During the week they often have a totally different atmosphere from that on weekends, when the roving hordes (or, God forbid, bucks' or hens' nights) are out on the town. See the Entertainment chapter (p128) for details on pubs with music.

Bars have a classier feel to them, and though most are swankier than your typical pub, they don't all fall into this category. Some offer the odd bit of entertainment, but that doesn't mean you'll be dancing the night away. Many bars located in the CBD are geared towards well-to-do businesspeople blowing off steam after work, so you'll probably feel more comfortable in fancier duds (and some may require smart casual-wear anyway).

Oddly enough, Bondi doesn't have a surfeit of pubs and bars, and neither does breezy Coogee, but the beachside beer barns they do have (such as the Coogee Bay Hotel) do a roaring trade with sun-kissed locals and sun-burned travellers alike.

There are some atmospheric old pubs in The Rocks, which attract a good share of the tourist trade. There are also plenty of notorious boozers, who mainly hydrate rowdy crowds of young men and women, especially on weekends and St Patrick's Day (17 March). The main drag in this area, George St, is where the action is, but also try Lower Fort St or Cumberland St. For infinitely more stylish surrounds, some great views and long cocktail lists, Circular Quay is definitely the best place to sit back with a drink in your hand. It's popular with a smart after-work crowd, particularly on Friday night.

> ## TOP FIVE BARS IN SYDNEY
>
> Sure this list is biased and everyone's got their own personal fave, but you won't go wrong stepping into these places for a refreshing drink.
>
> - **Hero of Waterloo, The Rocks** (opposite) One of Sydney's oldest bars, atmospheric and friendly.
> - **Darlo Bar, Darlinghurst** (p122) Tight, local and sporting a great feel. Cool furniture, too.
> - **Bank Hotel, Newtown** (p125) Best for its large balmy beer garden, and the Thai food's not bad.
> - **London Hotel, Balmain** (p126) Gorgeously restored, with breezy stools out the front a highlight.
> - **Icebergs Bar, Bondi** (p125) Ultra chic, ultra slick joint with views that can't be beat. Dress well.

There is also a cluster of slick drinking holes in Darling Harbour, complete with water views and airy atmosphere. These cater to tourists as well as locals, and tend to be up-market productions with plenty of people-watching opportunities.

Twenty-four-hour party-seekers head to Oxford St in Darlinghurst, or Kings Cross. The Cross' neon-lit main drag, Darlinghurst Rd, has plenty of drinking and stripping options, although there are some very stylish spots to imbibe here too. Fashionable types can find popular pubs in neighbouring suburbs like Paddington (Oxford St) and Surry Hills. The inner west is great for a low-key schooner, with suburbs like Balmain featuring plenty of pubs along Darling St alone.

All places listed in this chapter have free entry unless otherwise indicated.

CITY CENTRE, THE ROCKS & CIRCULAR QUAY

See the boxed text on p59 for transport options to/from these areas.

AQUA LUNA Map pp228-9

☎ 9251 0311; 2 Macquarie St, East Circular Quay; ☻ noon-midnight Mon-Thu, noon-1am Fri & Sat, noon-9pm Sun

This modern joint is right on the promenade, along with plenty of other restaurant/bars. Place yourself at a breezy table and take in the swell harbour views, order a $15 cocktail or passionfruit-infused vodka ($7) and just relax to the cruisy DJ sounds. With all that black and chrome going on under those white umbrellas you'll be sure to look good.

ARTHOUSE HOTEL Map pp228-9

☎ 9284 1200; 275 Pitt St; ☻ 11am-midnight Mon-Tue, till 1am Wed & Thu, till 3am Fri, 5pm-6am Sat

This gorgeous ex-School of Arts (1836) now contains three upmarket bars and an elegant restaurant lounge. Downstairs is the Gallery bar, which often displays good artwork, and the high-ceilinged Verge bar, once a chapel (of all things). Upstairs is the Dome restaurant, with live jazz from 6pm to 9pm on Saturdays, and the eclectic fat-cat Attic bar. A visit is definitely worthwhile.

AUSTRALIAN HOTEL Map pp228-9

☎ 9247 2229; 100 Cumberland St, The Rocks; ☻ 10am-midnight Mon-Sat, 10am-10pm Sun

Grab a pleasant outdoor table at this classic corner pub and order a Scharer's lager on draught – it's got a cult following here in Sydney. Exotic gourmet pizzas (try the crocodile, emu and roo toppings) help fill the time between drinks. Good affordable rooms are also available (see p170).

BRIDGE BAR Map pp228-9

☎ 9252 6800; Level 10, Opera Quays, 2 East Circular Quay; ☻ 11am-midnight Sun-Thu, till 2am Fri & Sat

Hanging high as a connecting bridge between two Circular Quay buildings is this dark and loungey bar with good music and killer views of the harbour. Herbed drinks and award-winning cocktails are a draw; try their raspberry kamikaze shot, or Casablanca martini with gin and vanilla. Take the elevator to the right of the Dendy cinemas up to the 10th floor.

ESTABLISHMENT Map pp228-9

☎ 9240 3000; 252 George St, City; ☻ 11am-late Mon-Fri, 6pm-late Sat

Flashier than greased lightning is this upmarket yuppie bar that brings white columns, marble bars, leather sofas and dressed-up crowds together. The patio garden out the back is a fine place to enjoy the Aussie and Thai tapas, and the music is downright slick. For the swankiest rooms in town stay here (see p171).

HEMMESPHERE Map pp228-9

☎ 9240 3040; Level 4, 252 George St, City; ☻ noon-3pm Thu & Fri, 6pm-late Tue-Sat

It feels like an exclusive lounge, with low sofas everywhere like in a giant living room. Cocktails are big here (try the 'Hemmesphere': Grand Marnier, Hennessy cognac and peach liqueur with guava and lime, $18) as are the flavoured martinis and Belvedere vodkas. Weekdays for lunch there is sushi finger food, while weekends see celebrities and after-party hipsters. Reservations advised.

HERO OF WATERLOO Map pp228-9

☎ 9252 4553; 81 Lower Fort St, The Rocks; ☻ 11am-midnight Mon-Sat, noon-10pm Sun

Enter into the wonderful stone interior, meet some of the boisterous locals here for a laugh and enjoy the nightly music (piano, folk, jazz or Irish tunes) of this historic, old-time bar. Downstairs is an original dungeon, where drinkers would sleep off a heavy night before being shanghaied to the high seas.

LORD NELSON BREWERY HOTEL
Map pp228-9

☎ 9251 4044; 19 Kent St, The Rocks; ☻ 11am-11pm Mon-Sat, noon-10pm Sun

The Lord Nelson is an atmospheric old pub that claims to be the 'oldest pub' in town, although others do, too! It brews its own beers (Quayle Ale, Trafalgar Pale Ale, Victory Bitter, Three Sheets, Old Admiral and Nelsons Blood) and you can try them all, especially if you stay here. After all it's only a short stumble up the stairs (see p172).

MARS LOUNGE Map pp228-9

☎ 9267 6440; 16 Wentworth Ave, City; ⏰ 5pm-midnight Tue, Wed & Sun, 5pm-3am Thu-Sat
This futuristic-looking drinking hole doesn't quite fit in at its location, but if you feel the urge to while away some hours sitting at a modern booth with red-tinged atmosphere and listening to sometimes deafening music, you could do worse than here.

TANK STREAM BAR Map pp228-9

☎ 9240 3109; 1 Tank Stream Way, Circular Quay; ⏰ 4pm-midnight Mon-Thu, noon-midnight Fri
Tucked away behind the swanky Establishment Hotel and down a dark alley is this upmarket and nicely lit bar. It's a great place to unwind after the hard working day. Flashes of steel and high stools add elegance – an interesting blend of original features and new flourishes, with plenty of ventilation.

DARLING HARBOUR

See the boxed text on p72 for transport options to/from these areas.

CARGO BAR Map pp228-9

☎ 9262 1777; 52-60 The Promenade, King St Wharf, Darling Harbour; ⏰ 11am-midnight Sun-Wed, till 3am Thu & Fri, till 4am Sat
A nice paradise for the smooth set, which sees them relaxing on the smooth wood benches or leather sofas while enjoying the wonderful views of the water. The seating located along the promenade is the best; plant yourself under a white umbrella, amongst the preeners and the romantics, to take in the airy breezes and sweet cocktails.

PONTOON Map pp228-9

☎ 9267 7099; Cockle Bay Wharf, 201 Sussex St, Darling Harbour; ⏰ 11am-midnight Mon-Wed & Sun, till 3am Thu-Sat
One of the most popular drinking dens at Darling Harbour, offering water breezes, high-tech atmosphere and cool sounds. There's plenty of dancing on weekends, when DJs bring out the R&B and hip-hop,

and live jazz fills the air on Sunday afternoons. Meals can also be had and are well priced.

SLIP INN Map pp228-9

☎ 8297 9999; 111 Sussex St, City; ⏰ noon-late Mon-Fri, 6pm-late Sat
Plenty of choice if you're looking for bars and dancing. See under clubs, p134.

DARLINGHURST TO POTTS POINT

See the boxed text on p75 for transport options to/from these areas.

ARCARDI Map pp228-9

☎ 9380 2121; 1A Burton St, Darlinghurst; ⏰ 5pm-midnight Wed-Sat, noon-midnight Sun
Not for the grungy among us, this sleek Oxford St bar offers some of the coolest cocktails in Darlinghurst, along with a selection of 70 Russian vodkas. Décor is red-hued and artsy, and meant for the likes of Cate Blanchett and Anna Nicole Smith, who've been known to frequent. DJs spin on weekends, and there's a smooth restaurant too.

THE BOURBON Map p235

☎ 9358 1144; 24 Darlinghurst Rd, Kings Cross; ⏰ 10am-3am Mon-Thu, till 6am Fri-Sun
Flash to the max and attracting young, hip and upper-crust crowds that come to lounge in booths, sit back on sofas or overlook the park and bustling sidewalk. Hip music, mod lighting and swanky service are included, there's a cool nightclub upstairs, and late-night drinkers will love the hours: it's open until 6am on weekends.

DARLO BAR Map p235

☎ 9331 3672; cnr Liverpool St & Darlinghurst Rd, Darlinghurst; ⏰ 10am-midnight Mon-Sat, noon-10pm Sun
Darlo's great vibe attracts a boisterous crowd on weekends, and its hip music doesn't hurt one bit. Service is friendly, furniture is retro and creative lighting makes things bright and cosy. Add an interesting neighbourhood and you've got a winner.

EMPIRE BAR Map p235
☎ 9360 7531; cnr Darlinghurst Rd & Roslyn St, Kings Cross; ☾ 24hr

This place is hard to miss, with airy open windows offering great views of one of the Cross' busiest intersections. Inside marble details and a cosy, classy feel welcome you, as do the daily drink specials. Ry Cooder might serenade you from the speakers, but if you need more action there's pool going on upstairs.

GREEN PARK HOTEL Map p235
☎ 9380 5311; 360 Victoria St, Darlinghurst; ☾ 10am-1am Mon-Sat, noon-midnight Sun

Mostly locals come to the good old Green Park, with its tiled walls and bar; it's also a popular hang-out for pool-shooters (Wednesday night means comps). Loungey seating, hip-hop music, good draught beer and outdoor tables are pretty darn cool too.

JIMMY LIK'S Map p235
☎ 8354 1400; 188 Victoria St, Kings Cross; ☾ 6pm-midnight

Long benches and a longer cocktail list (try the Japanese pear with lemon juice, sake and vodka) fit the highfalutin atmosphere, a welcome sight to yuppie eyes in Kings Cross. It's a great place to wait for a table at their snappy restaurant right next door.

KINSELAS Map pp232-3
☎ 9331 3100; 383 Bourke St, Darlinghurst; ☾ 10am-4am Sun-Thu, till 6am Fri & Sat

In what used to be a funeral parlour, this darkish place has come back from the dead more times than we can recall. The downstairs part is poker machines and bad carpet, but the bar upstairs is stylish, modern and incredibly popular with the bright young things. The cocktails are very good too. On hot summer nights, hanging on the minuscule balcony is *de rigueur*.

SOHO BAR & LOUNGE Map p235
☎ 9326 0333; 171 Victoria St, Kings Cross; ☾ 10am-4am Sun-Thu, 7pm-5.30am Fri & Sat

In an old Art Deco pub, the revamped ground floor bar hosts numerous Sydneysiders' social lives. It's a dark, relaxed drinking lounge with smooth leather chairs and sofas, so you'll want to wear

your sleekest. Happy hour sees two-for-one cocktails.

STONEWALL Map pp232-3
☎ 9360 1963; 175 Oxford St, Darlinghurst; admission free; ☾ noon-2am Sun-Thu, noon-5am Fri & Sat

The nightly drag shows and good vibe make this a popular choice out of the Sydney gay institutions (see p135 for others), and the nice airy location also helps. In recent times, the ceiling has collapsed here, causing one DJ to proclaim 'I finally brought the house down!'

TAXI CLUB Map pp232-3
☎ 9331 4256; 40-42 Flinders St, Darlinghurst; ☾ 9am-6am

Bring ID, because you'll have to present it to 'reception' at the door – this is a club of sorts, but all are welcome. Head on upstairs to the small but casual and comfy areas (which have too many pokies for our taste). At least happy hour sees $2 draught beers and $3.50 spirits, and there's bingo on Monday nights. Taxi Club is popular with cross-dressers and gets most boisterous after midnight. See p135 for other gay-oriented venues.

WATER BAR Map pp228-9
☎ 9331 9000; W Hotel Sydney, 6 Cowper Wharf Rdwy, Woolloomooloo; ☾ 4-10pm Sun-Thu, 4pm-midnight Fri & Sat

This stylish bar, in the luxurious W Hotel at Finger Wharf, is located in the ultimate warehouse space. The cocktail list is long, the ceilings are high and the sofas are so comfy you may well find yourself horizontal in record time. Try the 'W' martini (made with a touch of absinthe) and sit back to enjoy the loftiness and elegance of your surroundings.

WORLD BAR Map p235
☎ 9357 7700; 24 Bayswater Rd, Kings Cross; ☾ 1pm-2.30am Sun-Thu, till 7am Fri & Sat

Three floors of cool spaces attract the backpacking crowd (especially on Tuesday), and happy hour's $2.50 schooners keep them rockin'. There's an airy tropical terrace out the front, free pool until 6pm and DJs nightly; on weekends a live Latin band performs. It's easy to see how this place used to be Australia's best bordello.

SURRY HILLS & EAST SYDNEY

See the boxed text on p77 for transport options to/from these areas.

THE CLOCK Map pp232-3

☎ 9331 5333; 470 Crown St, Surry Hills;
🕒 11.30am-midnight

Slick as all get-out is this refurbished pub, which boasts three bars and a restaurant in gentrifying Surry Hills. Slip a coin into the jukebox, play some pool, watch video clips or check the time back home (there are 11 clocks with international times). The outdoor tables are nice and airy, and the late afternoon 'tini time (martinis half-off) or happy-hour spirits are sure to please. Amateur films shown monthly.

COLOMBIAN Map pp232-3

☎ 9360 2151; cnr Oxford & Crown Sts, Surry Hills;
🕒 10am-4am

Insanely popular, this (mostly gay) swanky drinking spot offers an intoxicating mix of cute guys, thumping music and heady drinks. The décor is to die for and the street-facing counter makes it oh so easy to check out the boisterous street scene. Women and handlebar moustaches welcome. See p135 for other popular gay nightspots.

CRICKETERS ARMS HOTEL Map pp232-3

☎ 9331 3301; 106 Fitzroy St, Surry Hills; 🕒 noon-midnight Mon-Sat, noon-10pm Sun

A cosy vibe fills this friendly pub with friendly locals (many gathered at the wraparound bar) and those appreciative of the good DJ skills displayed from Thursday to Sunday. There's also tapas, a small beer-garden patio with wooden benches and an intimate upstairs area.

HOLLYWOOD HOTEL Map pp232-3

☎ 9281 2765; 2 Foster St, Surry Hills; 🕒 10am-midnight Mon-Sat, 10am-10pm Sun

This Art Deco pub looks nondescript from the outside, but its dark intimate inside reveals a somewhat bohemian crowd happy to start the weekend with gusto. Eclectic live music is played Monday through Wednesday nights.

HOPETOUN HOTEL Map pp232-3

☎ 9361 5257; 416 Bourke St, Surry Hills; 🕒 noon-midnight Mon-Sat, noon-10pm Sun

Great little venue with an array of live music. See p136 for details.

PADDINGTON & WOOLLAHRA

See the boxed text on p78 for transport options to/from these areas.

LIGHT BRIGADE HOTEL Map pp232-3

☎ 9331 2930; 2A Oxford St, Woollahra;
🕒 noon-1am

This glorious Art Deco pub offers patrons a relaxed ground-floor bar with gourmet bar menu, pool table and snazzy sofa lounges; practise your backhand spin and show up on Tuesday night for the table tennis competition. Upstairs is a damn fine restaurant and two wonderful cocktail lounges with a good selection of imported beers; check out the ladies' toilets too (if you're a lady).

LORD DUDLEY HOTEL Map pp232-3

☎ 9327 5399; 236 Jersey Rd, Woollahra; 🕒 10am-midnight Mon-Sat, 10am-10pm Sun

The Lord Dudley is as close as Sydney really gets to an English pub atmosphere, with dark wood details and good beer (36 on tap!) in pint glasses. It gets packed with a noisy crowd, including Rugby Union fans (plenty of sport on the TV screens) and there's good food served downstairs. Needless to say, it draws a good share of Sydney's English expats.

PADDINGTON INN HOTEL Map pp232-3

☎ 9380 5277; 338 Oxford St, Paddington;
🕒 noon-midnight Mon-Wed & Sun, noon-1am Thu-Sat

On the outside, this pub is large, popular and pretty – but it's surprisingly swanky on the inside. The airy window seats are gold, especially on weekend afternoons when the nearby Paddington market is in full swing. The food is fancy and the cocktails elaborate, while funky music helps it all go down easy. And if you need a change of pace, Oxford street's more rowdy (read: gay) bars are a stone's throw west.

EASTERN BEACHES

See the boxed text on p82 for transport options to/from these areas.

BEACH ROAD HOTEL Map p238
☎ 9130 7247; 71 Beach Rd, North Bondi;
🕑 10am-12.30pm Mon-Sat, noon-10.30pm Sun
Reputedly 'the' pub in Bondi, though it's well inland. This huge, beautiful place offers snazzy atmosphere, a large and pleasant beer garden and a swanky cocktail bar upstairs with live music. Wednesday nights are especially popular with backpackers. See p136 for more.

ICEBERGS BAR Map p238
☎ 9365 9000; 1 Notts Ave, Bondi; 🕑 noon-midnight Tue-Sat, noon-10pm Sun
You can't get more modern and trendy than this classy spot, which shares the same space as the famous Icebergs restaurant. The hanging chairs, colourful sofas and elegant cocktails are just fine, but the view's the absolute killer. Make sure your bank account's up to snuff.

BONDI ICEBERGS CLUB Map p238
☎ 9130 3120; 1 Notts Ave, Bondi; 🕑 10am-11pm Mon-Thu & Sun, till midnight Fri & Sat
Located just below the Icebergs Bar, this is a more affordable and laid-back place but with practically the same views. Order café food (pizzas and burgers) and $3.50 beers. Bring ID, since if you're not a member you need to prove you live at least 5km away.

COOGEE BAY HOTEL Map p238
☎ 9665 0000; cnr Coogee Bay Rd & Arden St;
🕑 9am-1am summer, less in winter
Four bars live on the premises here, so think about whether you want breezy (water view), casual (beer garden), classy (balcony) or sporty (TV screens). Whichever way you choose, you'll be drinking up with the popular crowd in the heart of Coogee.

RAVESI'S Map p238
☎ 9365 4422; cnr Campbell Pde & Hall St, Bondi; 🕑 11am-midnight Mon-Sat, 10.30am-10pm Sun
Bondi's fanciest drinking spot with floor-to-ceiling views of the ocean scenery and the hip crowds strutting by. Low black leather sofas and high chrome stools mean the martinis won't come cheap, but this mini-

DOYLES AT WATSONS BAY
Also known as the Watsons Bay Hotel, the large establishment **Doyles** (Map pp228–9; ☎ 9337 5444; 10 Marine Pde, Watsons Bay; 🕑 10am-midnight Wed-Sat, 10am-10pm Sun-Tue) includes pricey seafood restaurants, a lovely boutique hotel and some very pleasant outdoor seating. Grab a jug of beer, order one of the gargantuan portions of fish 'n' chips and settle on the terrace to enjoy a superlative view of Sydney Harbour. Doyles is a time-honoured tradition that every traveller should experience, but avoid sunny weekends unless you like ridiculously heavy crowds. See the boxed text on p80 for transport options to/from the eastern suburbs area.

malist swagger pretty much guarantees a good-looking body perched on the seat next to you.

INNER WEST

See the boxed text on p83 for transport options to/from these areas.

BANK HOTEL Map pp236-7
☎ 9557 1692; 324 King St, Newtown; 🕑 noon-midnight Sun-Thu, noon-3am Fri & Sat, noon-midnight Sun
High in the esteem of gay people, sports fans, students and just about everyone else, this trendy institution boasts great lounge spaces, pool tables and an elegant cocktail bar. However, the highlight of the venue is its tropical beer garden, which offers drinkers plenty of fresh air, bamboo accents and a Thai restaurant. Grab a Cooper's jug ($10) to help you whittle the night away.

CAT & FIDDLE Map pp226-7
☎ 9810 7931; 456 Darling St, Balmain; 🕑 noon-midnight Mon-Sat, noon-10pm Sun
Mostly a music venue, but good for local drinking also. See the Entertainment chapter (p136) for more details.

FRIEND IN HAND HOTEL Map pp236-7
☎ 9660 2326; 58 Cowper St, Glebe; 🕑 10am-midnight Mon-Sat, noon-10pm Sun
It's hardly yuppie and not very relaxing (what with all that betting going on), but you can enjoy the poetry slams on Tuesdays, hermit crab races on Wednesdays or comedy gigs on Thursdays. Or just grab an

eyeful of the bric-a-brac around you, and say 'hi' to the cockatoo.

IMPERIAL HOTEL Map pp226-7
☎ 9519 9899; 35 Erskineville Rd, Erskineville; 🕙 3pm-midnight Mon, till 1am Tue, till 2am Wed, 3pm-3am Thu, 3pm-late Fri & Sat, 1pm-midnight Sun

With nightly drag and long opening hours, this is *the* place for gay partying. See the Entertainment chapter (p136) for details.

LANSDOWNE HOTEL Map pp236-7
☎ 9211 2325; 2 City Rd, Chippendale; 🕙 10am-11pm Mon & Tue, till 3am Wed-Sat, noon-10pm Sun

Live music and DJs on most nights. See the Entertainment chapter (p137) for details.

LONDON HOTEL Map pp226-7
☎ 9555 1377; 234 Darling St, Balmain; 🕙 11am-midnight Mon-Sat, noon-10pm Sun

Snag an outside counter stool at this lively pub, located in a beautifully restored historical building. It's a good place for a cleansing ale (12 beers on tap, including Cooper's, Stella and Redback), especially after a trawl through the nearby Saturday market; there's also a fancy restaurant. Sundays are good locals' days, when live music plays.

NEWTOWN HOTEL Map pp236-7
☎ 9517 1728; 174 King St, Newtown; 🕙 11am-midnight Mon-Fri, 10am-midnight Sat, 10am-10pm Sun

A good place for a gossip, a drink, and great drag acts. A fave with the local gay community. See p137 for details.

NORTH SHORE
See the boxed text on p85 for transport options to/from this area.

GREENWOOD HOTEL Map p239
☎ 9964 9477; 36 Blue St, North Sydney; 🕙 10am-midnight Mon-Sat, noon-10pm Sun

This charming, 19th-century sandstone building looks out of place among the shiny high-rises, but it's a slick modern pub with great outdoor seating and a popular Friday afternoon ladies' hour, when females get all the free bubbly they can drink (!). Look for it upstairs in Greenwood Plaza.

THE OAKS Map p239
☎ 9953 5515; 118 Military Rd, Neutral Bay; 🕙 10am-midnight Sun-Wed, till 1am Thu, till 1.30am Fri & Sat

An institution, The Oaks empire encompasses five bars (with pool tables, piano lounge and plenty of pub fare) on two floors. The large beer garden – complete with giant oak tree – is the highlight, however. Grab a table, cold beer and spot on the grill at the massive barbecue to begin your North Shore rite of passage.

MANLY
See the boxed text on p88 for transport options to/from this area.

CERUTI'S Map p240
☎ 9977 7600; 15 Sydney Rd; 🕙 noon-10.30pm Mon-Sat, till 9pm Sun

Weekends rock here, when the restaurant becomes part of the bar party and DJs fire up the youthful crowd with spinning house beats. Weekdays offer happy hour from 4pm to 7pm – a good time to try their specialty cocktail called '42 below', made with New Zealand vodka.

NEW BRIGHTON HOTEL Map p240
☎ 9977 3305; 71 The Corso; 🕙 10am-3am Mon-Sat, noon-midnight Sun

This bar/nightclub's best feature is probably the upstairs wraparound balcony, offering primo views of The Corso and the ocean. Head inside and spin to DJs Captain Kirk and White Brothers, or play on the purple-felted pool tables. For quieter conversation stick to the crimson-hued bar the with elegant leather sofas downstairs; there's live music on Friday.

STEYNE HOTEL Map p240
☎ 9977 4977; The Corso & Ocean Beach; 🕙 10am-midnight Sun-Thu, till 3am Fri & Sat

Boasting 9 bars on two levels, this place has a spot for everyone. Sports fanatics can glue themselves to the seven big-screen TVs at Harry's sports bar, while outdoors enthusiasts can check out the beer garden. Smoke-free Kelly's bar overlooks the beach, while Redheads bar offers cigar aficionados a place to light up. There's more, but you get the picture.

Entertainment

Entertainment

Sydney is a thriving metropolis blessed with a broad array of cultural and artistic diversions. You can watch avant-garde dance, stately musical performances, moving classical opera and a plethora of blockbuster and independent movies. And there's no shortage of nightlife, either – after-hours entertainment runs the gamut from pub rock bands to elegant jazz gigs to throbbing gay dance clubs to booze-soaked comedy nights. You can even gamble to the last threads of your wallet, at either the races or the many 'pokies' (poker machines) in town. No matter what your cultural interests, your days and nights won't be boring in Sydney.

Sydneysiders are often accused of hedonism and anti-intellectualism, mostly due to the fact that they seem to prefer going to the beach and playing sport over enriching their minds with culture. There is some truth in this, as it's hard to stay indoors and enjoy cultural pursuits when it's so beautifully warm and happening outside, and for this reason many of the larger arts companies tend towards more easily digestible works.

One of the best sources of 'what's on' information is Friday's Metro section in the *Sydney Morning Herald*. It lists events for the week ahead and includes gallery listings, film reviews, and music and theatre interviews. *The Daily Telegraph*'s SLM lift-out (published on Wednesday) is also good. For specialised music listings, pick up one of the free and widely available weekly papers, such as *Drum Media, Revolver* or *3D World*.

TICKETS & RESERVATIONS

HALFTIX Map pp228-9
☎ 1300 668 413; www.halftix.com.au; 91 York St, City; ❂ 9.30am-5.30pm Tue-Fri, 10am-3.30pm Sat
This agency sells discounted tickets, though choices are limited. Phone and Internet bookings available.

TICKETEK Map pp228-9
☎ 9266 4800; www.ticketek.com.au; 195 Elizabeth St, City; ❂ 9am-7pm Mon-Fri, 9am-4pm Sat
The main booking agency for theatre, concerts and sport. Book by phone, Internet or agencies around town.

PERFORMING ARTS VENUES

CAPITOL THEATRE Map pp228-9
☎ 9320 5000; www.capitoltheatre.com.au; 13 Campbell St, Haymarket; monorail Powerhouse Museum, MLR Haymarket, train Central
Lavishly restored, this big theatre is home to big-name concerts (Sting, Natalie Merchant) and long-running musicals (*Chicago, the Musical; The Lion King*).

CITY RECITAL HALL Map pp228-9
☎ 8256 2222; www.cityrecitalhall.com; 2 Angel Pl, City; train Martin Place
This is a world-class, 1200-seat performance venue with wonderful acoustics, hosting live music performances. Its architecture is based on the 19th-century European blueprint, and it's an excellent place to hear the Australian Brandenburg Orchestra and Australian String Quartet, among others.

EUGENE GOOSSENS HALL Map pp232-3
☎ 9333 1500; 700 Harris St, Ultimo; train Central
The ABC's intimate Eugene Goossens Hall often has good classical recitals that are broadcast live. It seats up to 500 on a good day, and is not the place to come with a cough. It's located in the ABC Ultimo Centre.

LYRIC THEATRE Map pp228-9
☎ 9657 9657; Star City, 80 Pyrmont Rd, Darling Harbour; MLR Star City, bus 888, ferry Pyrmont Bay
The large Lyric stages flashy musical extravaganzas and has good acoustics. It's in the Star City Casino complex, so if you get bored with the musical you can walk out and gamble your money away nearby.

STATE THEATRE Map pp228-9
☎ 9376 6861; www.statetheatre.com.au; 49 Market St, City; train Town Hall or St James
The beautiful, 2000-seat State Theatre is a lavish, gilt-laden, chandelier-dangling palace from 1929. It hosts the Sydney Film Festival, concerts and performances and the odd musical. For more details see p64.

SYDNEY CONSERVATORIUM OF MUSIC Map pp228-9

☎ 9351 1222; www.usyd.edu.au/su/conmusic/; Macquarie St, City; train Martin Place or Circular Quay
Located in the Botanic Gardens, this historic music venue showcases the talents of its students and their teachers. Choral, jazz, operatic and chamber concerts are held here from March to September, along with a range of free lunch-time recitals Wednesdays at 1pm (March to November).

SYDNEY OPERA HOUSE Map pp228-9

☎ 9250 7777; www.sydneyoperahouse.com; Bennelong Point, East Circular Quay; bus, train, ferry Circular Quay
The heart of performance in Australia, with the Concert Hall and Opera Hall holding about 2600 and 1500 people respectively. Witness theatre, comedy, music, dance and ballet, but it's opera that really shines. Box office hours are 9am to 8.30pm Monday to Saturday and 2 hours before a Sunday performance. Don't be late or you'll be shut out till intermission! See p71 for details on tickets and reservations.

SYDNEY SUPERDOME Map pp224-5

☎ 9250 7777; www.superdome.com.au; Olympic Blvd, Sydney Olympic Park; train or RiverCat Olympic Park or Homebush Bay
Housed within the Sydney Olympic Park complex, this is Australia's largest indoor entertainment and sporting venue (21,000 seats). Everything from dance parties to conventions to musicals to off-road-vehicle

shows are hosted here, and Pavarotti and Alanis Morissette have graced its dressing rooms. Disabled access is excellent. See p92 for other venues located at Sydney Olympic Park.

SYDNEY THEATRE Map pp228-9

☎ 9250 1999; www.sydneytheatre.org.au; 22 Hickson Rd, Walsh Bay; bus, train, ferry Circular Quay
Opened in 2004, this new venue is the most significant theatre built since the Sydney Opera House 30 years ago. It's also the centrepiece in Walsh Bay's face-lift – it was once a warehouse. The state-of-the-art theatre seats 850 and is managed by Australia's largest theatre company, Sydney Theatre Company. Expect the best in ambitious and artistic drama and dance performances.

WHARF THEATRE Map pp228-9

☎ 9250 1700; www.sydneytheatre.com.au; Pier 4, Hickson Rd, Walsh Bay; bus, train, ferry Circular Quay
The Sydney Theatre Company (STC), the city's top theatre company, has its own venue here. It's also home to the **Bangarra Dance Theatre** (p131) and the **Sydney Dance Company** (p131). A restaurant on the premises called **The Wharf** (p105) delivers much better than average pre- and post-show fare.

THEATRE

There's no distinct theatre district in Sydney, but that hardly means theatre-lovers suffer. The city offers a vigorous calendar of productions at its numerous theatres spread out in various locations. Offerings range from Broadway and West End shows at mainstream theatres to experimental theatre at smaller inner-suburban venues. Most tickets cost from around \$20 to \$70, but last-minute specials can be found (see opposite), and there are generally concession prices available to students and seniors. The following are some local theatre companies worth checking out.

BELVOIR ST THEATRE Map pp232-3

☎ 9699 3444; www.belvoir.com.au; 25 Belvoir St, Surry Hills; tickets \$27-45; train Central
Located in a residential neighbourhood and sporting a cute café, this intimate venue hosts the wonderful experimental production team Company B. Shows are often twists on original productions, and

sometimes sport big names like Geoffrey Rush and Cate Blanchett.

ENSEMBLE THEATRE Map p239

☎ 9929 0644; www.ensemble.com.au; 78 McDougall St, Kirribilli; train Milsons Point, ferry Kirribilli
Located on the waterfront at Careening Cove (North Shore), the small, non-profit-making and long-running Ensemble Theatre presents just eight or nine mainstream productions per season. Playwrights can be Australian (think David Williamson, Nick Enright) or international, and well-known Australian actors are generally featured. It caters to a mature, sophisticated crowd.

GRIFFIN THEATRE COMPANY Map p235

☎ 1300 306 776; www.griffintheatre.com.au; 10 Nimrod St, Kings Cross; train Kings Cross
Stables Theatre is the home of the Griffin Theatre Company, a proud and independent group dedicated to the production of new Australian works (such as playwright Katherine Thomson's *Wonderland*). It has staged Australian works since 1970, and is often referred to as 'the writers' theatre'.

NATIONAL INSTITUTE OF DRAMATIC ART (NIDA)

☎ 9697 7600; www.nida.edu.au; 215 Anzac Pde, Kensington; bus 393-4
Former stomping ground of Mel Gibson, Cate Blanchett and Geoffrey Rush, NIDA is a good place to see 'stars of the future'. Student and graduate plays are presented throughout the year at its attractive 725-seat theatre or intimate 120-seat studio.

NEW THEATRE Map pp236-7

☎ 9519 8958; 542 King St, Newtown; train Newtown
Australia's oldest continuously performing theatre), the eclectic New Theatre produces cutting-edge drama in addition to traditional pieces. The on-site theatre seats a tad more than 150 people. Special summer tickets run as low as $15.

OLD FITZROY HOTEL Map p235

☎ 9356 3848; 129 Dowling St, Woolloomooloo; ⏲ noon-midnight Mon-Sat, 3-10pm Sun; bus 311, train Kings Cross
Is it a pub? A theatre? A bistro? Actually it's all three. Grab a bowl of laksa, see the acting

stars of tomorrow and wash it all down with a beer, for about $30. The little balcony is unbeatable on a hot, steamy night, though there are also airy outdoor tables.

SYDNEY THEATRE COMPANY

Map pp228-9

☎ 9250 1777; www.sydneytheatre.com.au; level 2, Pier 4, Hickson Rd, Walsh Bay; bus, train, ferry Circular Quay
Established in 1978, the STC has had three powerful and influential artistic directors: Richard Wherrett, Wayne Harrison and, most recently, Robyn Nevin. Collaborations with national and international artists and companies bring about fairly safe but meticulously crafted works that appeal to mainstream sensibilities while still managing to push a few buttons.

DANCE

With its adoration of the body beautiful, it seems only logical that Sydney has a vital dance culture. Performances range from straight-down-the-line traditional ballet with tutus and packed-lunchbox tights to edgy, liberating 'physical theatre'. Australian dancers have a reputation for fearlessness in performance, resulting in some breathtaking displays of physical skill and bravado (and sometimes a lack of costume).

AUSTRALIAN BALLET

☎ 1300 369 741; www.australianballet.com.au
Going strong for over 40 years, the Australian Ballet (which is actually based in Melbourne) performs a wide repertoire of classic as well as contemporary works. It's shaken off some of the controversy and behind-the-scenes political skulduggery that has dogged it over the last few years, and Sydney productions have been positively received. See them perform at the Sydney Opera House.

PERFORMANCE SPACE Map pp232-3

☎ 9698 7235; www.performancespace.com.au, 199 Cleveland St, Redfern; train Redfern
This dynamic company features young choreographers and dancers working on new, contemporary and challenging Australian works, including retrospectives, and also offers dance and film workshops. It sports a main theatre, a studio and two gallery

spaces, and puts on more than 50 public events annually.

SYDNEY DANCE COMPANY

Map pp228-9

☎ 9221 4811; www.sydneydancecompany.com
.au; Pier 4, Hickson Rd, Walsh Bay; bus, train, ferry
Circular Quay

Headed since 1976 by the extraordinary creative team of Graeme Murphy and Janet Vernon, this is easily Australia's best dance company, with innovative choreography, spellbinding performances, great production values and the sexiest dancers. Catch anything you can, anywhere you can – it'll be a highlight. Dance classes, for all levels, are also available on a casual basis.

ABORIGINAL PERFORMANCE

BANGARRA DANCE THEATRE

Map pp228-9

☎ 9251 5333; www.bangarra.com.au; Wharf
Theatre, Pier 4, Hickson Rd, Walsh Bay; bus, train,
ferry Circular Quay

Widely regarded as one of Australia's finest dance companies, Bangarra regularly performs in Sydney and around Australia. Artistic director and national treasure Stephen Page creates a fusion of contemporary and traditional influences, blending indigenous and Western dance techniques.

CINEMAS

The cinema strip in the city is on George St, near the Town Hall train station. Other mainstream cinemas can be found in various suburbs and in shopping centres, while art-house cinemas abound in the inner city. Movie listings can be found in Sydney's daily newspapers.

ACADEMY TWIN CINEMA Map pp232-3

☎ 9331 3457; 3A Oxford St, Paddington; adult/
concession $14.50/10.50; ☽ 11am-9.30pm; bus
378, 380

The Academy Twin is a smaller cinema that's seen better days, but the choice of art-house and independent films certainly can't be faulted. Mondays are bargain days, when all film screenings cost $9.50.

CREMORNE HAYDEN ORPHEUM

Map pp226-7

☎ 9908 4344; 380 Military Rd, Cremorne; adult/
concession $15.50/11.50; ☽ noon-9.30pm; bus
151, 176, 178, 180

At the junction of Military and Cremorne Rds is this fabulous Art Deco gem, complete with original organ and a bar. Go for the movie/lunch and coffee ($11) – unfortunately it's only once a month (call ahead for date). Tuesday is bargain day; movies cost $10.50.

DENDY NEWTOWN Map pp236-7

☎ 9550 5699; www.dendy.com.au; 261 King St,
Newtown; adult/child $14/9.50; ☽ 11am-9.30pm;
train Newtown

This cinema is handy for those wishing to see art-house films close to the inner west, saving a trip into town. There's a good bookshop and café handy to the premises too. Discount nights are on Mondays, with movies $9.

DENDY OPERA QUAYS Map pp228-9

☎ 9247 3800; www.dendy.com.au; Shop 9, 2
Circular Quay East; adult/child $14/9.50; ☽ 11am-
9.30pm; bus, train, ferry Circular Quay

This lavish cinema screens first-run or independent films, and lies within spitting distance of the Opera House. Great bar for ticketholders only. On Mondays movies cost $9 for everyone

FOX STUDIOS Map pp232-3

☎ 9383 4000; www.foxstudios.com.au; Bent St,
Moore Park; adult/child $14/9; ☽ 10am-9.30pm;
bus 339, 371-8, 380, 382, 392-9

This huge film and entertainment complex has more than a dozen cinemas. These include La Premiere, which offers a more luxurious cinematic experience – think reclining lounges, glasses of wine and cheese platters – and the price is also luxurious at $28 per person.

GREATER UNION HOYTS VILLAGE COMPLEX Map pp228-9

☎ 9273 7431; 505 George St, City; adult/child
$14.50/9; ☽ 10am-9.30pm Sun-Thu, 10am-
11.30pm Fri & Sat; train Town Hall

This monster-sized movie palace comes with 17 screens, plenty of eateries and a few youth-oriented distractions. It's an orgy of popcorn-fuelled mainstream entertainment, and disabled access is good.

GOVINDA'S Map p235

☎ 9380 5155; www.govindas.com.au; 112 Darlinghurst Rd, Darlinghurst; dinner & movie $20, movie only $11; ☽ 6pm-10.30pm nightly; train Kings Cross

Just south of Kings Cross is the Hare Krishna–run Govinda's, an all-you-can-gobble vegetarian smorgasbord that has its fans. The cinema upstairs shows mainstream blockbusters, art-house fare and old favourites, and plenty of floor cushions add atmosphere. There's incense in the air and yoga classes are available too.

IMAX CINEMA Map pp228-9

☎ 9281 3300; Southern Promenade, Cockle Bay; adult/child $17/12; ☽ 10am-10pm; monorail Darling Park

IMAX uses the world's biggest movie screens. If you're into being wowed (or made motion-sick) by massive images, some in 3D, then the IMAX is for you. Movies shown tend to be either thrill-fests or nature documentaries.

VERONA CINEMA Map pp232-3

☎ 9360 6296; www.palace.net.au; level 1, 17 Oxford St, Paddington; adult/concession $14.50/11; ☽ 11.15am-9.30pm; bus 378, 380

This cinema also has a café and bar, so you can discuss the good (invariably nonmainstream) flick you've just seen. Mondays are bargain days with $9.50 tickets.

Imax Cinema (above), Darling Harbour

FILM FESTIVALS

Sydney plays host to several film festivals, including the well-regarded Flickerfest (p10), the Sydney Film Festival (p12), and the biggest short-film festival in the world, Tropfest (p10).

COMEDY

Perhaps a reason for the paucity of Sydney's comedy scene can be found in the great weather that Sydney enjoys. Why sit indoors making cynical, cutting quips when you can be out in the sunshine?

SYDNEY COMEDY STORE Map pp232-3

☎ 9357 1419; www.comedystore.com.au; Fox Studios, Driver Ave, Moore Park; tickets $15-30; shows ☽ 8.30pm Mon-Fri, 8pm Sat; bus 339, 371-8, 380, 382, 392-9

In its purpose-built home in the Fox Studios, this comedy venue has stand-up and open-mike nights; acts have included international jokesters Arj Barker and Doug Stanhope, and local comedians Jimeoin, Scared Weird Little Guys, Wil Anderson and Peter Berner.

CLUBBING

Sydney's dance-club scene is very much alive and kicking, with local and international DJs helping thousands of people swing and grind their hips every weekend. Some places have strict door policies and a lot of attitude, while others are more casual and great places to catch up with friends, or meet new ones. Note however that Sydney's clubs are fickle things, with exclusive clubs or specific nights popping up and vanishing in the blink of an eye. Check the street press (p128) and fliers in record stores, for up-to-the-minute information.

ARQ Map pp232-3

☎ 9380 8700; 16 Flinders St, Darlinghurst; admission free-$20; ☽ 5pm-7am Thu, 5pm-9am Fri, 24hr Sat & Sun; bus 378, 380

Downstairs is cool and loungey, with amoeba-shaped sofas and pool tables. Upstairs you'll find the cutting-edge light and sound system, along with drag shows and good DJs. This large club has it all, and is a popular place to 'recover' on Sundays.

CAVE Map pp228-9

☎ 9566 4755; Star City Casino, Pirrama Rd, Pyrmont; admission $10-25; ☯ 9pm-3am Wed & Thu, 9pm-5am Fri-Sun; MLR Star City, ferry Pyrmont Bay
This flashy, fleshy joint, located in Sydney's largest casino, hits the spot for those who like their state-of-the-art dance music all lit up and dynamic sounding. The dress code is geared more towards labels and sex appeal rather than comfort, attracting J-Lo wannabes and the gambling men who love 'em.

EXCHANGE HOTEL Map pp228-9

☎ 9331 1936; 34 Oxford St, Darlinghurst; admission free; ☯ 9pm-6am Thu-Sat, 9pm-noon Sun & Mon; bus 378, 380
You get four-in-one at this long-running temple of drinking and dancing. Choose from the Palace Lounge, a small and hip bar; Spectrum, a nightclub with DJs and live bands; and Q Bar and Phoenix, both gay magnets. Good, rowdy fun on weekends.

GAS Map pp232-3

☎ 9211 3088; 477 Pitt St, City; admission $15-30; ☯ 10pm-4am Thu, 10pm-6am Fri & Sat
Hit the hip bullseye at this large dancing mecca, located in the basement of Sydney's old gas-production building. Premier perks include two dance floors, three bars, a stylish chill-out zone and a state-of-the-art lightshow. DJs bring on cutting edge dance music, which ranges from hip-hop, R&B and soul to house and trance. Dress well.

GOODBAR Map pp232-3

☎ 9360 6759; 11A Oxford St, Paddington; admission $10; ☯ 9pm-3am Wed-Sat; bus 378, 380
Two-level and trendy, this popular, intimately sized club is still attracting crowds of the pretty people. It boasts funk, R&B, hip-hop and soul, plus a chance at celeb-spotting. The best nights to shake things up with the taut crowds are on Wednesdays and Saturdays.

HOME Map pp228-9

☎ 9266 0600; Cockle Bay Wharf, 101 Wheat Rd, Darling Harbour; admission $20-25; ☯ 10pm-7am Fri & Sat, 6pm-midnight Sun; monorail Darling Park, train Town Hall
With gorgeous views of Darling Harbour, this monster-sized pleasure dome offers

stupendous sound systems on three levels. Speciality nights are 'Together' on Saturdays (funky house music) or 'Queer Nation' on the Sundays of 3-day weekends. Drinks from the Mobo Bar, along with the views, help keep the masses satisfied.

HUGO'S LOUNGE Map p235

☎ 9357 4411; Level 1, 33 Bayswater Rd, Kings Cross; admission free-$10; ☯ 6pm-3am Wed-Sun; train Kings Cross
Hugo's reflects the changing face of Kings Cross, bringing the area a well-needed touch of class. The atmosphere is slick, the spaces contemporary and the outside lounge booths pure heaven. Order their signature drink, a mango daiquiri ($15), which will help you swing to the DJs on weekends. And remember to dress well; clientele are sophisticated and even include celebrities. Look for their white awning on the first floor in the plaza; their café is at street level.

MIDNIGHT SHIFT Map pp232-3

☎ 9360 4319; 85 Oxford St, Darlinghurst; admission free; ☯ noon-4am Mon-Wed, noon-6am Thu-Sun; bus 378, 380
The ground floor is quite pubby despite the disco balls, but upstairs it's a licence to booze and cruise with less conversation. We like the fact that a range of gay men shows up here – it's especially popular with Asians and older men. 'Retro' nights add interest.

OUTDOOR CINEMA

Summer means getting outdoors, even to watch movies. There's nothing quite like seeing a flick in fresh air, with the wind cooling your skin and the stars (those in the sky, that is) lending their light. It's practically become a tradition.

Moonlight Cinema (Ticketek ☎ 9266 4800; Centennial Park Amphitheatre) shows flicks with an art-house bent in Centennial Park from early December to late February. OpenAir Cinema (☎ 1300 366 649; www.stgeorge.com.au/openair; Mrs Macquaries Point, The Domain) is the same sort of thing, running from early January to mid-February, but here you'll catch the sea breezes coming off Sydney Harbour. Tickets for both venues (about $16-18) sell out quickly, especially on weekends.

OXFORD HOTEL Map pp232-3

☎ 9331 3871; 134 Oxford St, Darlinghurst; admission free; ⏱ 24 hrs; bus 378, 380

The bustling corner locale can't be beat, especially if you land a patio table on the square. Downstairs it's the hard-core manly gay bunch, while on the second floor Gilligan's cocktail bar attracts a fancy mixed crowd of bohemians. The top floor is open weekends only, and definitely worth a stop.

PLAN B Map p235

☎ 9358 1144; 24 Darlinghurst Rd, Kings Cross; admission $5-20; ⏱ 11pm-6am Fri-Sun; train Kings Cross

So hot and new the bouncers are working overtime, this classy disco sports a glowing pink bar, a lounge area for wallflowers and of course the hoppin' dance floor. Wear your best and get ready for slammin' house and funk music. Friday night is ladies' night, complete with male strippers. It's located above the snazzy Bourbon bar.

Q BAR Map pp228-9

☎ 9360 1375; level 2, 44 Oxford St, Darlinghurst; Fri & Sat admission $15-20; ⏱ 7pm-5am Mon-Thu, 7pm-9am Fri & Sat, 7pm-6am Sun; bus 378, 380

With more reincarnations than Cleopatra, this funky and eclectic joint (located in the Exchange Hotel) has DJs playing nightly. Weekends means house and dance music, but if you're not into that there's always the pool table and cocktail bar.

SLIP INN Map pp228-9

☎ 8295 9999; 111 Sussex St, City; admission $15-18; ⏱ 11pm-4am Fri, 10pm-4am Sat; monorail Darling Park, train Town Hall

Warrenlike and sporting three different lounges (and themes), this place struggles with a multiple personality disorder, but that doesn't stop the cool kids from enjoying the funky house and hip-hop breaks on the turn table. The actual nightclub is called Chinese Laundry; there are several bars with separate names to sort out also.

TANK Map pp228-9

☎ 9240 3000; 5 Bridge Lane, City; admission $15-20; ⏱ 10pm-6am Fri & Sat

Basement spaces never looked so good. Dress up as fine as you're able, pretend you're a movie star and crash the VIP room; you might just run into someone famous. The corporate types here are young and thin, and gyrate to the funky house music whipped up by some of Sydney's best spinners.

YU Map p235

☎ 9326 0333; 171 Victoria St, Kings Cross; admission $10-20; ⏱ 10pm-6am Fri-Sun; train Kings Cross

Yu wants you to get down to the best of house and funk, played by some of Sydney's most venerable DJs. We love After Ours, which solves the dilemma of what to do on a Sunday night. The club itself is slick-looking and attached to fancy Soho bar.

ROCK, FOLK & POP MUSIC

The live rock and pop scene has seen something of a revival within the last few years, as venues once infested with pokie machines have been brought back to their more musical traditions. The fact that Sydney plays host to most of the country's record companies certainly has helped the genre as well, and the revered ARIA (Australian Record Industry Association) awards are handed out here too.

LARGE VENUES

Sydneysiders enjoy hearing performances by a wide range of talent at a number of city venues, both big and small. The following venues cater to larger crowds; for more intimate shows seek out key pubs (opposite). There's sometimes no charge to see young local bands, while between $5 and $20 is charged for well-known local acts, and at least $60 for international performers.

ENMORE THEATRE Map pp236-7

☎ 9550 3666; www.enmoretheatre.com.au; 130 Enmore Rd, Newtown; tickets $15-120; train Newtown

The Enmore plays host to a lot of major Australian and overseas acts like Kiss, Oasis, Alicia Keyes and David Byrne, plus comedy and jazz. The Rolling Stones showed up and played a brilliant 'intimate' concert here in early 2003.

OUT & ABOUT IN GAY & LESBIAN SYDNEY

The gay and lesbian scene is alive, healthy, well-organised and looking fabulous in tolerant Sydney, forming a vibrant and colourful part of the city's culture. Sydney's annual **Gay & Lesbian Mardi Gras** (see p10) has become Australia's biggest tourist event, drawing over half a million revellers. And in 2002 Sydney made history by hosting the best-dressed Olympics ever – the Gay Games.

One weekend night on Oxford Street, the city's gay heartland, will give you a good idea of how boisterous all things gay can become. The following represent a mix of old favourites and newer club nights that cover both low-key and 'out there' bases. For a more complete list look in local gay publications such as the **Sydney Star Observer** (www.ssonet .com.au) or **Lesbians on the Loose** (www.lotl.com).

ARQ (p132) Still hugely popular for its great sound system and raucous drag shows.

Colombian (p124) Crowded up to your handlebar moustache with buff bods and swank.

Exchange Hotel (p133) Multi-venue of intimate bars and clubs with staying power.

Midnight Shift (p133) Your stereotypical gay magnet, with flashing lights and thumping heartbeats.

Newtown Hotel (p137) Newtown's gay core, offering bars, drag shows and themed nights.

Oxford Hotel (opposite) Three floors of gay excess, smack bang on lively Taylor Square.

Stonewall (p123) Full of pretty boys lined up at the bar or peeking onto bustling Oxford St.

Taxi Club (p123) Stuffy but not sniffy, with cheap drinks and a casual atmosphere.

HORDERN PAVILION Map pp232-3
☎ 9383 4063; www.playbillvenues.com; Fox Studios, Driver Ave, Moore Park; bus 339, 371-8, 380, 382, 392-9

The 80-year-old Hordern (which seats just over 4200 people) has hosted distinguished and hot international acts such as Santana, Beastie Boys, Chemical Brothers and Nine Inch Nails along with the legendary Frank Sinatra. It's on the grounds of Fox Studios.

METRO THEATRE Map pp228-9
☎ 9287 2000; www.metrotheatre.com.au; 624 George St, City; tickets $10-75; train Town Hall

Easily the best place to see well-chosen local and alternative international acts (plus the odd DJ) in well-ventilated comfort. Before and after gigs, you can hang out in the Transit Lounge, where beer, wine or spirits will only set you back $3. Other offerings include comedy, cabaret, music and theatre.

HIBISCUS LOUNGE Map p238
☎ 9665 0000; www.coogeebayhotel.com.au; Coogee Bay Hotel, cnr Coogee Bay Rd & Arden St, Coogee; cover charge $10-50; bus 314, 272-4

Part of the Coogee Bay Hotel's entertainment complex (with plenty of bars catering to everyone) is this club which, on weekends, offers top Australian and inter-national bands under its umbrella theme 'Coogee Bay Live'. Midnight Oil has played here in the past. Expect loud music and a younger mixed crowd of locals and English backpackers.

SYDNEY ENTERTAINMENT CENTRE Map pp228-9
☎ 136 100; Harbour St, Haymarket; monorail Powerhouse Museum, MLR Haymarket

This big concrete box has hosted superstars like Mark Knopfler, Bryan Adams, REM, Elton John and Cher. It seats just over 12,000 and despite being purpose-built for these bigger gigs, the sound quality is only adequate at best. Sport is played here too.

PUBS

Pubs and bars are still the venues of choice for Sydney's most social scenes, and those with mighty thirsts will find plenty of drinking holes in which to hydrate and chat up their seatmates. Lively music is often thrown into the entertainment mix (canvassing acoustic, folk and traditional pub-rock music along with DJ-spun sounds), especially on weekends. Good gig guides can be found in the Friday Metro section of the *Sydney Morning Herald*, and the street press (p128) is always good for finding out what's on. Many pubs have succumbed to the lure of making money rather than music, though, so you'll often find a bank of pokies in the place of a stage or dance floor – good for those who like a quick gamble with their $3 happy-hour schooner.

ANNANDALE HOTEL Map pp236-7
☎ 9550 1078; www.annandalehotel.com; 17 Parramatta Rd, Annandale; admission free-$30; ⏰ 11am-midnight Mon-Sat, 4-10pm Sun; bus 413, 436-8, 440, 461, 483
This venue plays host to a sometimes eclectic assortment of local and international alternative music acts. Loud rock, heavy metal, dance and acoustic gigs jam nightly from Tuesday to Sunday (tickets $8 to $30), while cult movies (!) play Monday nights.

BEACH ROAD HOTEL Map p238
☎ 9130 7247; 71 Beach Rd, North Bondi; admission free; ⏰ 10am-12.30pm Mon-Sat, noon-10.30pm Sun; bus 380, 389
A virtual multilevel fortress of fun, with two classy upstairs bars hosting live music and some good local DJs. Wednesday and Sunday the place gets crowded, as do the banks of pool tables. Behold the sight of the beautiful, bronzed and boozed-up at play.

CAT & FIDDLE Map pp226-7
☎ 9810 7931; 456 Darling St, Balmain; admission $8-10; ⏰ 10am-midnight Mon-Sat, noon-9pm Sun; bus 440
Nightly live music runs from 8pm, with local folk and acoustic bands providing the energy at this smoky venue. Tall stools and tables seat the crowd, happy hour runs

Newtown Hotel (opposite)

from 4pm to 6pm weekdays (Saturdays from 10am-4pm) and there's even a small theatre on the premises (about 35 seats).

CIVIC HOTEL Map pp228-9
☎ 8267 3186; 388 Pitt St, City; admission fee varies; ⏰ 11am-midnight Mon, 11am-1am Tue & Wed, 11am-2am Thu, 11am-3am Fri, 11am-4am Sat; monorail World Square, train Central Station or Museum
This three-storey Art Deco hotel is a bit of a 'world of entertainment'. Sure, there's drinking at the smooth and snappy lounge, but there are also great DJs on weekends, live jazz and rock music, and even a theatre in the basement (which turns into a nightclub on Friday and Saturday nights). And of course there's an upmarket restaurant as well.

EXCELSIOR Map pp232-3
☎ 9211 4945; 64 Foveaux St, Surry Hills; admission free-$10; ⏰ 10am-midnight Mon-Sat, 4-10pm Sun; train Central
'The alternative to alternative' is the claim, and also that the band Cog got its start here. This casual, lively and even grungy joint has been attracting an eclectic crowd for 25 years with its nightly live music. Jazz bands swing Tuesdays, young grass-roots bands liven up Wednesdays and regulars (always original Aussie bands) blast the weekends. Bistro food available.

HOPETOUN HOTEL Map pp232-3
☎ 9361 5257; 416 Bourke St, Surry Hills; admission $6-12; ⏰ 3pm-midnight; train Central
This great little venue offers flexibility for artists and patrons alike and features an array of modern musical styles from folk to rap to DJs. Big-name bands that have played here include Spiderbait, Tex Perkins and You Am I.

IMPERIAL HOTEL Map pp236-7
☎ 9519 9899; 35 Erskineville Rd, Erskineville; admission Mon-Fri free, Fri & Sat $5; ⏰ 3pm-midnight Mon, 3pm-1am Tue, 3pm-2am Wed, 3pm-3am Thu, 3pm-late Fri & Sat, 1pm-midnight Sun
The film Priscilla – Queen of the Desert was inspired by these nightly drag acts, which are world class. For the ladies there's Go Girl on Thursday. Long hours makes this a bastion of gay partying in the inner west.

LANSDOWNE HOTEL Map pp236-7

☎ 9211 2325; 2 City Rd, Chippendale; admission free; ◷ 10am-3am Mon-Sat; train Central

Right near the University of Sydney is this casual pub with karaoke at 9pm Thursday, rock bands from Thursday to Sunday, and DJ tunes almost nightly. Upstairs the restaurant serves pub meals for either $5 or $10.

NEWTOWN HOTEL Map pp236-7

☎ 9517 1728; 174 King St, Newtown; admission free; ◷ 10am-midnight Mon-Sat, 10am-10pm Sun; train Newtown

In Sydney's other gay enclave, the Newtown does a roaring trade with gay folk looking for Tuesday pool competitions, Wednesday night trivia, and DJs (or 'eclectic fetish' shows) on Thursdays. Friday nights are girls' (lesbians') nights, and good drag acts liven up the crowds all through the weekend.

SANDRINGHAM HOTEL Map pp236-7

☎ 9557 1254; 387 King St, Newtown; admission $6-15; ◷ noon-midnight Mon-Sat, noon-10pm Sun; train Newtown

You can still pay a minimal amount of money at this intimate, 150-seat venue to get your earwax blasted out while munching on tapas. Acts play mostly on weekends (alongside pool competitions) and you can mostly expect local rock and pop bands; occasional names like Diesel and Jon Stevens show up.

JAZZ & BLUES

Despite an up-and-down history of renaissances come and gone, Sydney's jazz scene is currently alive and healthy. Innovative new musicians bring fresh experimentations, keeping the older, more experienced players from resting on their laurels, but often they'll join together to really kick out the jams. Key figures to look out for include Bernie McGann, alto sax veteran extraordinaire; Mike Nock, jazz piano guru; Jackie Orszaczky, alternative bassist; Tina Harrod, once described as 'Australia's Aretha Franklin'; and award-winning, sultry-jazz clarinet player Don Burrows. For those looking to catch some gravelly blues, there are still a couple of venues showcasing great blues artists at work.

Jazz celebrations in Sydney include October's **Manly International Jazz Festival** (see p13) and January's Jazz in the Domain, which is tied to the popular Sydney Festival. Check www.jazzscene.com.au for more info on current gigs and schedules.

BASEMENT Map pp228-9

☎ 9251 2797; 29 Reiby Pl, Circular Quay; admission $12-50; ◷ noon-1.30am Mon-Thu, noon-2.30am Fri, 7.30pm-3am Sat, 7pm-1am Sun; bus, train, ferry Circular Quay

This subterranean place has decent food, good music (plus the odd spoken-word and comedy gig) and some big international names occasionally dropping by, making cover charges skyrocket. Exotic notes come with the monthly Indian and African gigs.

BRIDGE HOTEL Map pp226-7

☎ 9810 1260; 135 Victoria Rd, Rozelle; admission $5-40; ◷ 24hr (closed Sun night); bus 500, 501

Way out in Rozelle is this smoky, grungy drinking hole, one of Sydney's last original bastions of pub entertainment. It's a working class neighbourhood so don't expect fancy cocktails or pretty people, just good live rock and blues with names like Mark Seymour and James Reyne. It attracts a late night crowd from the inner west; DJs entertain on weekend nights after midnight.

CAFÉ SYDNEY Map pp228-9

☎ 9251 8683; Level 5, Customs House, 31 Alfred St, Circular Quay; ◷ noon-midnight Mon-Sat, noon-5pm Sun; bus, train, ferry Circular Quay

You'll need a lunch table to catch their Sunday afternoon jazz session (starting at 1.30pm), but it'll be worth it to see bass player Jonathan Zwartz or the drummer-led Felix Bloxum Trio. Sit back with an elegant cocktail and enjoy the balcony breezes and stunning harbour views.

EMPIRE HOTEL Map pp236-7

☎ 9557 1701; www.empirelive.com.au; 103 Parramatta Rd, Annandale; Fri & Sat admission $5-15; ◷ 10am-midnight Mon & Tue, 10am-3am Wed-Sat, 10am-10pm Sun; bus 438, 440, 461

Blues (along with ska, pop and rockabilly) buffs should investigate the Empire for live acts, aided by a very good sound system. They're trying to diversify here, with Tuesday nights seeing free swing dance lessons.

STRAWBERRY HILLS HOTEL Map pp232-3
☎ 9698 2997; 453 Elizabeth St, Surry Hills; admission free; ⏰ 24 hrs; train Central
This refurbished pub features the live jazz of the Eclipse Alley Five from 4pm to 7pm on Saturday, and Bill Dudley & the New Orleanians from 5pm to 8pm on Sunday. Plus there's happy hour from 2pm-6pm, so throw down some $3 schooners before the show.

WINE BANQ Map pp228-9
☎ 9222 1919; 53 Martin Pl, City; admission $10; ⏰ noon-3pm & 5pm-late; train Martin Place
Hands down, this is the sexiest place to hear live jazz in Sydney. The whole place looks like it was carved out of an architect's dream bunker, and a brilliant wine list only adds to the appeal. Past performers here have included Wynton Marsalis, Barbara Morrison and Harry Connick Jr.

OPERA & CLASSICAL MUSIC

OPERA

Despite its relatively small population, Australia has produced a large share of the world's most magnificent opera singers, including Dames Nellie Melba and Joan Sutherland. Sydney has attached itself to this elegant art genre by making its opera house a symbol of the city – bad acoustics notwithstanding. Supporting such a cost-heavy art form, however, is a difficult prospect in a country with such enormous distances between its cities.

World-renowned conductor Simone Young was brought in as Opera Australia's artistic and musical director in a millennial move to heighten the quality and scope of OA's productions. Improvements were made, but differences in artistic vision eventually led to her departure in 2003. Englishman Richard Hickox, former principal conductor of the BBC National Orchestra of Wales, is Opera Australia's current musical director.

The Sydney opera season lasts from January to March and then June to November, and performances take place in the Sydney Opera House, the Capital Theatre and the City Recital Hall.

OPERA AUSTRALIA
☎ 9699 1099; www.opera-australia.org.au
Opera Australia is a big player on the Sydney arts scene. Visit the website to access details and buy tickets.

PINCHGUT OPERA
☎ 9518 1082; www.pinchgutopera.com.au
This relative newcomer on Sydney's opera scene specialises in more intimate 'chamber' operas, performing neglected works without the hype and fanfare (or behind-the-scenes woes!) that are associated with Opera Australia's productions. Music and its impact with the audience is a key concept here.

CLASSICAL MUSIC

Sydneysiders live with an image of being self-absorbed, sports-crazed outdoor fanatics, but they can also be surprisingly open to such arts as classical music. While Sydney's relative youth means there's no confusion as to whether you're in Old Europe or Sin City, you will find a surprising number of musical performances happening all year round, especially at the Sydney Opera House.

The following companies have excellent local (and often international) reputations for classical music performances. Broadcasts (live and prerecorded) of major concerts can be heard on the ABC's radio network (ABC Classic FM 92.9). Check the Guide in the *Sydney Morning Herald* on Monday for details.

AUSTRALIAN BRANDENBURG ORCHESTRA
ABO; ☎ 9328 7581; www.brandenburg.com.au
In less than 15 years the ABO has become a distinguished part of Australia's artistic landscape, and this wonderful orchestra plays baroque and classical music on instruments of those periods. Leading international guest artists appear frequently. Performances are held at City Recital Hall and various local churches – check the website for details.

AUSTRALIAN CHAMBER ORCHESTRA
ACO; ☎ 8274 3800; www.aco.com.au
Since 1975 the ACO has been making chamber music sexy and adventurous, especially

(Continued on page 147)

Entertainment

OPERA & CLASSICAL MUSIC

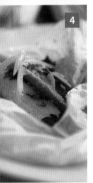

1 *Fruit slice at Fratelli Paradiso (p108)* 2 *The Summit (p105), a revolving restaurant at level 47, Australia Square* 3 *Roasted ducks in Chinatown (p72)* 4 *Fine dining (pp15-17) on papillote of ocean trout*

1 *Grilled salmon with capers and wasabi at Uchi Lounge (p111)* 2 *Croissant and coffee at Circular Quay (p59)* 3 *Sign to an eatery at the Sydney Fish Market (p84)* 4 *Baguettes at Fratelli Paradiso (p108)*

1 *After-work drinks at the Civic Hotel (p136)* **2** *City lights* **3** *Bar at Pontoon (p122), Darling Harbour* **4** *Mineral water at bills (pp106-7)*

1 *The Lyric Theatre (p128) at the Star City Casino, Pyrmont* **2** *Bar at Aqua Luna (p121), Circular Quay* **3** *Live music in The Rocks (p50)* **4** *A cold beer*

1 Modern architecture (p38) at Circular Quay 2 Sydney Tower (p64) behind the MLC Building 3 A welcoming face at the Sydney Fish Market (p84) 4 Cahill Expressway (p59), Circular Quay

1 Fresh lobsters for sale at the Sydney Fish Market (p84) 2 Book shop in Glebe (p83) 3 Alannah Hill store (pp159-60), Strand Arcade 4 Mambo cap and badge (p166)

1 *Cycling in Centennial Park (p79)*
2 *Surfers hit the waves at Bondi Beach (p82)* 3 *Lunchtime rugby match (p18) in The Domain (p61)*
4 *Flymotion amusement ride at Fox Studios (p131)*

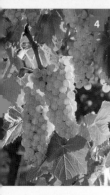

1 *Rose Cottage at Hawkesbury (pp194-5)* **2** *Blue-gum forest in Grose Valley (p188), Blue Mountains National Park* **3** *Temperate rainforest in the NSW's Blue Mountains National Park (p188)* **4** *Chardonnay grapes on the vine (p12)*

(Continued from page 138)

under the tutelage of artistic director and lead violinist Richard Tognetti. Musicians play standing up (a common practice in the early centuries) and there is a warm cohesion not regularly found outside small chamber groups. Innovative and versatile concerts are staged throughout the year at both the Sydney Opera House and the City Recital Hall.

MUSICA VIVA AUSTRALIA
☎ 8394 6666; www.mva.org.au
Musica Viva is the largest organisation of its type in the world, and provides some 2,500 concerts (small and large ensembles) around Australia in a number of musical styles (including chamber music, a cappella, experimental and jazz). In 2005 it celebrated its 60th anniversary.

SYDNEY PHILHARMONIA CHOIRS
☎ 9251 2024; www.sydneyphilharmonia.com.au
If you want your world rocked by 450 enthusiastic voices, this is your choir. They also have a 100-voice symphonic choir, 32-voice motet choir and a youth-based choir. Internationally renowned, and deservedly so, you can generally find them at the Sydney Opera House, City Recital Hall and St Andrew's Cathedral.

SYDNEY SYMPHONY ORCHESTRA
SSO; ☎ 8215 4600; www.symphony.org.au
The biggest orchestra in Australia, the SSO is now blessed with chief conductor and

Poker machine (below) at Bondi Icebergs Club (p125)

artistic director Gianluigi Gelmetti and plays with excellent local and international musicians. Catch them at the Sydney Opera House or City Recital Hall.

GAMBLING
Australians love to gamble, and Sydney provides plenty of opportunities for punters to be separated from their cash (many drinking establishments, for instance, have a pokie room). Indeed, it's been estimated that an average of $1000 per year is spent by each Australian in the pursuit of 'striking it lucky', whether it be at the track, at the casino or at the pub. Gamblers Anonymous has a 24-hour helpline (☎ 9564 1574; www.gamblersanonymous .org.au) for compulsive gamblers and their friends and families.

POKIES
Poker machines, also known by their cute name 'pokies', are insanely common in Sydney's bars, pubs and clubs. Australians are some of the world's biggest gamblers, and NSW itself has 10% of the world's pokies – almost 100,000 of them.

One reason there are so many machines in Sydney is that buying an existing liquor licence here can be prohibitively expensive. This keeps the number of pubs down, while forcing them to bring in a heavy cash flow. Pokies do this; one machine can make tens of thousands of dollars per year. Many of Sydney's music venues have closed down their stages and put up a row of pokies, simply because they rake in more money than live music (though, to an extent, this trend is starting to reverse).

Sydneysiders are realising the gambling problems these ubiquitous pokies bring with them, however. Laws have been passed which ban free drinks from being served to gamblers, and ATMs have to be located outside pokie rooms. Even messages are being flashed across pokie screens, reminding patrons how long they've been playing, and gambling hotlines have been advertised heavily. This pokie phenomenon doesn't look to be going away soon, but at least folks are slowly coming to terms with the dangers and cultural losses they bring about.

Horse racing alternates between tracks throughout the year. However, it's more colourful and exciting during the spring and autumn carnivals, when major events like the Golden Slipper at Rosehill or the Sydney Cup at Randwick take place. A little down the social scale, but with a die-hard following, are trotting/pacing (harness racing) meetings and greyhound racing.

The RSL (Returned Services League) is an Aussie institution, giving returned servicemen and women a place to gather socially. In reality, the cheap beer and the walls of pokies attract anyone and everyone. It's best to show a bit of respect and not look too shabby (singlets and no shoes are a definite insult), and never, ever, fail to show respect for the various traditions and rituals of the RSL.

HAROLD PARK PACEWAY Map pp236-7

☎ 9660 3688; www.haroldpark.com.au; Ross St, Glebe; free Tue, adult/concession $8/2 Fri; ⏱ 1.30-5.30pm Tue, 7-10.30pm Fri; MLR Jubilee Park,bus 432-4

Close to the city, the Harold Park trots are easy to get to, and are a great way to watch all the pretty horses without having to get very dressed up. Friday night meets are the most fun, with a mix of people and an inner city location handy for partying afterwards. There's bingo Mondays and Thursdays.

NORTH BONDI RSL CLUB Map p238

☎ 9130 8770; 120 Ramsgate Ave, North Bondi; admission free; ⏱ noon-midnight Mon-Fri, 10am-midnight Sat & Sun; bus 380, 389

One of our favourite Sydney RSLs – big with visitors and locals alike – is the North Bondi RSL, more commonly referred to as the 'Rissole'. Cheap drinks on offer and a balcony overlooking the lovely stretch of Bondi Beach are reasons for its popularity, but don't come expecting fancy décor. Bring ID, as you need to prove you live at least 5km away to justify your lack of a membership.

ROSEHILL GARDENS Map pp224-5

☎ 9930 4000; www.theraces.com.au; James Ruse Dr, Rosehill; admission $11; train Rosehill

Rosehill Gardens is located about 20km west of the city centre (near Parramatta) and is one of Sydney's most famous racecourses. Its premier event is the Golden Slipper (a race for two-year-old horses), which takes place in March or April of each year.

ROYAL RANDWICK RACECOURSE

Map pp226-7

☎ 9663 8400; www.ajc.org.au; Alison Rd, Randwick; admission $10-25; bus 372-4

The closest horse-racing venue to the city, Royal Randwick is near Centennial Park and attracts some glamorous types, plus the usual array of 'colourful' racing identities. Races are usually on Monday, Wednesday and Saturday, with gates generally opening at 11am, and the last race at around 5pm.

STAR CITY CASINO Map pp228-9

☎ 9777 9000; www.starcity.com.au; 80 Pyrmont St, Pyrmont; ⏱ 24hr; MLR Star City, ferry Pyrmont Bay

This large and smoky casino complex includes a major theatre, retail stores, restaurants, bars and a luxury hotel. It's located on the waterfront in Pyrmont, on the northeastern headland of Darling Harbour. The décor is best described as 'Disney-meets-Outback', complete with lagoon bar (think indoor waterfall), fake palm trees and flashy lights all over the place.

WENTWORTH PARK Map pp236-7

☎ 9660 4308; www.wentworthparksport.com.au; Wentworth Park Rd, Glebe; admission $5.50; ⏱ 6-10.30pm Mon & Sat; MLR Wentworth Park

Wentworth Park is Australia's premier greyhound-racing complex, with skinny, fast dogs salivating madly after tin hares every Saturday and Monday evening. Races have been held at these grounds since 1932 and the grounds hold a café, some bars and a bistro. There's a lovely old-fashioned feel about the place, like something from another era.

Activities ▪

Activities

After a few days in Sydney you may notice something about its inhabitants. They do their damnedest to look good, and take every opportunity to show off their shiny, hard bodies. How do they get this way? Exercise.

Sydney's glorious sunshine, lush parks, long winding trails and an absolute need to look good conspire to make this a delightful city for staying fit or watching sport. If you like to watch, have a credit card handy and book tickets to a variety of sporting events, big and small. If you're the one being sporty, it can be as simple as putting on some jogging shoes and picking up a racquet or slipping into some laps at a beachside pool. It can also be as tricky as getting in a golf game on a warm, sunny weekend, but any which way you'll be out in the open enjoying Sydney's famously great weather.

WATCHING SPORT

Tickets & Reservations

TICKETEK Map pp228-9

☎ 9266 4800; www.ticketek.com.au; 195 Elizabeth St, City; ◷ 9am-7pm Mon-Fri, 9am-4pm Sat

The city's main booking agency for theatre, concerts, sport and other events. Book by phone or Internet or via agencies around town.

FOOTBALL

Sydney is one of **rugby league's** world capitals. The main local competition is the National Rugby League's (NRL) Telstra Premiership, with games played at various grounds around Sydney (around $20 a ticket from Ticketek). Sell-out finals can be seen at either the Telstra Stadium (Sydney Olympic Park) or Aussie Stadium (Moore Park).

The other big rugby league series is the annual State of Origin comp, when Queensland battles New South Wales (NSW) three times a year and passions run high between the Cane Toads and the Cockroaches. When games are played in Sydney, they're generally at the Telstra Stadium.

Rugby union, which has a more upper-class reputation, despite its biff content, has a less fanatical following, but Australia's team, the Wallabies, is one of the world's best and the 2003 Rugby World Cup was staged in Australia. The Waratahs are NSW's team. Visit www.rugby.com.au to find out when matches are being played, and where.

Aussie Rules, more formally known as Australian Rules Football (AFL; www.afl.com.au), has the sometimes high-flying Sydney Swans (www.sydneyswans.com.au) playing for the harbour city. Catch them at the Sydney Cricket Ground (SCG), where a ticket will set you back around $20 to $60, though 'gold' (front row) seats can cost double. Matches are played between March and September.

Soccer is technically Australia's most popular sport, although it's given relatively little coverage in the media when compared with the other football codes. It has a semiprofessional national league in Australia; contact **Soccer Australia** (☎ 9267 0799) for information on catching a game.

TOP FIVE BEACHES

Sydney, lucky soul that it is, comes blessed with more than its fair share of beaches. Many are only a quick stroll or bus or ferry ride away from the city centre. Following is a list of favourites that keep the locals kicking back and sporting that sun-kissed look.

- **Bondi** (Map p238) Closest to Sydney's centre and the most famous slice of sand around.
- **Dee Why** (Map pp224–5) Great for surfers, families and tourists, with plenty of services nearby.
- **Manly** (Map p240) Close to the surfing action, as well as to restaurants, cafés and shops.
- **Parsley Bay** (Map pp226–7) A hidden harbour gem, best for grassy picnics and peaceful swims.
- **Whale Beach** (Map pp224–5) Isolated, non-touristy and no services to speak of; in other words, paradise.

CRICKET
SYDNEY CRICKET GROUND
Map pp232-3

☎ 9360 6601; Moore Park Rd, Paddington; bus 339, 371-8, 380, 382, 392-9

The Sydney Cricket Ground (SCG) is the venue for sparsely attended Pura Cup (interstate) matches, well-attended (international) test matches that can last for five days, and sell-out World Series Cup (one-day international) matches. The cricket season lasts from October to March.

TENNIS
SYDNEY INTERNATIONAL TENNIS CENTRE Map pp224-5

☎ 8746 0777; www.sydneytennis.com.au; Homebush Bay Dr, Homebush Bay; train Olympic Park

The Medibank International Tennis tournament is held at this tennis centre in Sydney Olympic Park in the second week of January. It's a prelude to the Australian Open in Melbourne and it attracts some big tennis names. The Davis Cup is also held here in mid-July. Book through Ticketek.

YACHTING
On weekends, hundreds of yachts weave around ferries and ships on Sydney Harbour. The most spectacular are the 18-foot racers. The yachting season runs from mid-September to April and the Sydney to Hobart Yacht Race (p13) leaves from here on Boxing Day.

SYDNEY FLYING SQUADRON Map p239

☎ 9955 8350; 76 McDougall St, Milsons Point; train Milsons Point, ferry Kirribilli

You can organise to see a race with this club. Ferries depart from here to watch skiff racing from 2pm to 4pm on Saturdays during the yachting season (adult/child $15/5.50). Ferries are also provided for occasional special shows.

SURF LIFE-SAVING CARNIVALS
The volunteer surf life-saver is one of the country's icons, and Australia was one of the first places in the world to have surf life-saving clubs. Despite the macho image often associated with this profession, many surf life-savers are women. You can see these dedicated athletes in action each summer at surf carnivals held all along the coast. Check at a local surf life-saving club for dates or contact Surf Life Saving NSW (☎ 9984 7188; www.surflifesaving.com.au).

OUTDOOR ACTIVITIES
SURFING
South of the Heads, the best spots are Bondi, Tamarama, Coogee and Maroubra. Cronulla, south of Botany Bay, is also a serious surfing spot. To the north, the best beaches are Manly, Curl Curl, Dee Why, North Narrabeen, Mona Vale, Newport Reef, North Avalon and Palm Beach. For current wave activity check www.wavecam .com.au.

ALOHA SURF Map p240

☎ 9977 3777; www.aloha.com.au; 44 Pittwater Rd, Manly; board hire half/full day $25/50; ferry Manly

If you're on the North side and you just want to hire a board, pop into this friendly, easy-going place. It also sells and trades equipment.

WAVES SURF SCHOOL map p238

☎ 9369 3010; 192 Bronte Rd, Waverley; surf trips from $69; bus 378

This popular surf school has been doing outings to Byron Bay and Royal National Parks for more than six years. Adventure trips and surf camps from one to five days are available.

LET'S GO SURFING Map p238

☎ 9365 1800; www.letsgosurfing.com.au; 128 Ramsgate Ave, Bondi; bus 380, 389

Learn to catch waves with this outfit (private lessons from $95), which caters to practically everyone with kids' classes, women-only classes and safety instruction. Board and wetsuit rental is $20 per hour.

SAILING
With such a glamorous harbour, Sydney has a large share of sailing schools. Even if you're not serious about 'learning the ropes', an introductory lesson can be a fun

way of getting out on the harbour (though it's not for the budget-conscious).

EASTSAIL SAILING SCHOOL
Map pp228-9

☎ 9327 1166; www.eastsail.com.au; d'Albora Marina, New Beach Rd, Rushcutters Bay; from $465; bus 324-5, 327

Charters, cruises, corporate events and overnight packages. Plenty of boats and you'll need big bucks. From introductory to racing-level courses.

SYDNEY BY SAIL Map pp228-9

☎ 9280 1110; www.sydneybysail.com; Australian National Maritime Museum; monorail Harbourside

Departing daily from the Australian National Maritime Museum in Darling Harbour, Sydney by Sail offers plenty of courses, including a weekend introductory sail course for $425.

CANOEING & KAYAKING

The obvious choice for a kayaking experience in Sydney is on lovely Sydney Harbour – but be warned that the harbour is both big and busy, and especially challenging if you're a novice.

NATURAL WANDERS

☎ 9899 1001; www.kayaksydney.com.au; $90 per half-day tour

Natural Wanders has exhilarating kayak tours of the harbour which pass under the bridge and stop in secluded islands and bays.

Sailing (p151) on Sydney Harbour

NEW SOUTH WALES CANOEING ASSOCIATION

☎ 9660 4597; www.nswcanoe.org.au

This association has information on canoe courses and hire around Sydney.

SYDNEY HARBOUR KAYAKS

☎ 9960 4389; www.sydneyharbourkayaks.com.au

Offered are lessons, sales and rentals, along with tours to Shark Island, Middle Harbour and eco-destinations like Garrigal National Park (most from $99).

DIVING

The best shore dives in Sydney are the Gordons Bay Underwater Nature Trail, north of Coogee; Shark Point, Clovelly; and Ship Rock, Cronulla. Popular boat dive sites are Wedding Cake Island, off Coogee; around the Sydney Heads; and off the Royal National Park. In Manly, you can make beach dives from Shelly Beach.

DIVE CENTRE MANLY Map p240

☎ 9977 4355; www.divesydney.com; 10 Belgrave St, Manly; ferry Manly

One of the largest dive shops in Sydney. Shore dives with gear start at $100, boat dives at $130. An open-water Professional Association of Diving Instructors (PADI) course costs $350. Full- and part-time courses available. Another branch can be found at 192 Bondi Rd, Bondi (☎ 9369 3855).

PRO DIVE Map pp228-9

☎ 9264 6177; www.prodive.com.au; 478 George St, City; train Town Hall

Offers shore dives with gear for $85, boat dives with/without gear for $169/109 and diving courses from $295 to $495. The main office is conveniently located in the centre, though there are several outlets in and around Sydney.

LAWN BOWLS

Generally the pastime of old-age pensioners, lawn bowls has experienced something of a revival in recent years. Young folks are playing and becoming seriously hooked, thanks to the sports' qualities of affordability, accessibility to all fitness levels and the tradition of drinking and smoking while balls are rolling. A certain retro-kitsch vibe doesn't hurt. Following are the pick of the bunch.

CAMPERDOWN BOWLING CLUB
☎ 9519 7961; Mallett St near Parramatta Rd, Camperdown; ⏰ noon-8pm Monday, 11am-8pm Tue-Thu, till midnight Fri, 9.30am-10pm Sat, 9am-8pm Sun; bus 436-8, 440, 480, 483

The CBC is as much a social scene as a bowling venue. The beer prices seem to get cheaper the longer a game wears on. The $10 bowling fee includes two hours of play time and coaching. There's a bar and bistro on the premises, and live music on Friday nights.

CLOVELLY BOWLING CLUB Map p238
☎ 9665 1507; cnr Ocean & Boundary Sts, Clovelly; ⏰ 3.30-6.30pm Mon, noon-6.30pm Tue-Thu, till 7.30pm Fri, 11am-6.30pm Sat, 9am-6.30pm Sun

Located in a prime spot right near the ocean, this club offers glorious views of the Pacific Ocean and something of a hipster scene on weekends. Being right on the Bondi to Coogee walk (see p95) means many folks pop in for a refreshing drink, but if you want to bowl it'll cost you $10 (be sure to book). There's free coaching for beginners; call for more information.

HORSE RIDING
CENTENNIAL PARKLANDS EQUESTRIAN CENTRE Map pp232-3
☎ 9332 2809; cnr Cook & Lang Rds, Paddington; per hr $50; bus 355, 380

Those seeking equestrian delights will enjoy the large indoor arena and 3km of tracks at this world-class centre, along with some historical and traditional atmosphere. It can be found near Fox Studios in Sydney's Moore Park.

HEALTH & FITNESS
GYMS
Most large hotels have a gym and pool for guests' use, and often these facilities are made available to nonguests for a fee. Sydney also has plenty of independent gyms throughout town, including one at Cook + Phillip Park (see p154).

CITY GYM Map pp228-9
☎ 9360 6247; www.citygym.com.au; 107 Crown St, East Sydney; ⏰ 24hr from 5am Mon to 10pm Sat, 8am-10pm Sun; $16; bus 311, 324-5, train Kings Cross

Gay friendly to the max, this sweaty gym has been pumping hard bodies for over 30 years (which says it all). A dozen classes, including aerobics, pilates and yoga, are available, along with massage, chiro and spray tan services. The bravest can tackle the steam room.

JOGGING
The foreshore from Circular Quay around Farm Cove to Woolloomooloo Bay and through the Royal Botanic Gardens and the Domain is very popular with joggers. Running across the Harbour Bridge is a popular way for North Shore residents to commute to work in the city. Another good bridge for jogging is the Anzac Bridge.

Centennial Park and the promenades at Bondi Beach and Manly are the city's best jogging spots, while the cliff trail between Bondi Beach and Bronte is also good. If it's steep challenges that you're after, suburbs like Paddington, Rushcutters Bay, Darling Point and Vaucluse will get your heart pounding. For a serious running club, contact Sydney Striders (www.sydneystriders .org.au); they'll often have details on current races.

See the City Calendar (p12) in this book for information on August's 14km City to Surf Run.

SWIMMING
Sydney's harbour beaches offer sheltered swimming spots. Just remember that after heavy rains excess water gets washed into the harbour from city streets, so keep out.

If you want to frolic in real ocean waves, stay within the flagged areas patrolled by lifeguards. There are some notorious but clearly signposted rips, even at Sydney's most popular beaches, so don't underestimate the surf just because it looks safe.

As for public swimming holes, Sydney boasts over 100 within the city limits; some are set into the beach or overlook Sydney Harbour. Many outdoor pools close at the end of April for the cooler months and re-open in early October.

ANDREW 'BOY' CHARLTON POOL

Map pp228-9

☎ 9358 6686; Mrs Macquaries Rd, The Domain, City; adult/child $5/3.50; ⏲ 6am-8pm Oct-Apr; train Martin Place or St James

Sydney's best pool, with saltwater, smack-bang next to the harbour and a magnet for water-loving gays, straights, mums and fashionistas. It's more for serious lap-swimmers than for those wishing to splash around for fun, so keep to your lane if you're a leisurely swimmer. Worth it for its five-star change rooms alone. Wheelchair accessible.

BONDI ICEBERGS SWIMMING CLUB

Map p238

☎ 9130 4804; 1 Notts Ave, Bondi; adult/child $4/2.50; ⏲ 6am-8pm Mon-Fri, 6.30am-8pm Sat & Sun; bus 380

With supreme views of Bondi Beach, this place is an institution (with membership hard to get). Casual swimming is open to all, however, and available year-round. There's also a gym on the premises ($15 day use includes pool entry) and you can get a massage or sauna too. Winter hours are shorter.

COOK + PHILLIP PARK Map pp228-9

☎ 9326 0444; www.cookandphillip.com.au; cnr College & William Sts, City; adult/child $5.80/4.20; ⏲ 6am-10pm Mon-Fri, 7am-8pm Sat & Sun; train St James

This Olympic-sized underground indoor pool also has a hydrotherapy area and gym ($16 with pool use). Also available are massage services, acupuncture, a basketball court, Ashtanga yoga and swimming lessons.

MCIVERS BATHS Map p238

Grant Reserve, Coogee; $0.20; ⏲ noon-5pm; bus 314, 372-4

For women and kids only, McIvers is a wonderful outdoor saltwater escape. No topless bathing; entry is via the honesty/donation system. It's a popular spot with lesbians.

NORTH SYDNEY OLYMPIC POOL

Map p239

☎ 9955 2309; Alfred St South, Milsons Point; adult/child $4.70/2.30; ⏲ 5.30am-9pm Mon-Fri, 7am-7pm Sat & Sun; train Milsons Point

On the north shore and right near Luna Park are these beautifully-situated pools – you'll

find an Olympic-sized outdoor pool, a 25m indoor one and some kids' splash zones. The views of the Harbour Bridge are unbelievable, and nearby **Ripples** (p117) offers upmarket after-swim treats.

SYDNEY AQUATIC CENTRE Map pp224-5

☎ 9752 3699; www.sydneyaquaticcentre.com; Olympic Blvd, Sydney Olympic Park, Homebush Bay; adult/child $6/4.90; ⏲ 5am-8.45pm Mon-Fri, 6am-6.45pm Sat & Sun; train Olympic Park

A variety of leisure and exercise pools on offer here in Sydney Olympic Park, including the competition pool where records were smashed during the 2000 Sydney Olympics. Other perks include a state-of-the-art gym, large outdoor patio area, café, and swim shop; childcare and massage services also available. Wheelchair accessible.

WYLIE'S BATHS Map p238

☎ 9665 2838; Neptune St, Coogee; adult/child $3/0.50; ⏲ 7am-6pm; bus 314, 372-4

The waves wash in, but the sharks don't. It's like swimming in the ocean, but you're in a saltwater pool. Freezing in winter, but delightful in summer.

CYCLING

Sydney's steep hills, narrow streets and busy traffic don't help to qualify Sydney as a bike-riders' haven, but a few adventurous spoke-loving souls get about on their wheeled mounts. Look for roads with designated cycle lanes and stay aware of parked cars and moving traffic. With less-hectic traffic and long cycle paths, both Manly and Centennial Park are popular pedalling spots.

Bicycles can travel on suburban trains for concession rates during peak hours, and for free outside peak times. Cycling is prohibited in Darling Harbour and Martin Pl. See p200 for details on where to hire bicycles.

BICYCLE NSW

☎ 9281 4099; www.bicyclensw.org.au

Publishes a handy book called *Cycling Around Sydney*, detailing routes and cycle paths in and around the city.

ROAD TRANSPORT AUTHORITY (RTA)

☎ 1800 060 607; www.rta.nsw.gov.au

The RTA issues maps of metropolitan Sydney's cycle path network. You can pick them up at bicycle retailers or download them from the website.

TENNIS

There are tennis courts for hire all over the city. Tennis NSW (☎ 9763 7644; www.tennisnsw.com.au) can provide you with details of facilities available.

MILLER'S POINT TENNIS COURT
Map pp228-9
☎ 9256 2222; Kent St, The Rocks; per hr $25; ⏱ 8am-10.30pm; bus, train, ferry Circular Quay
This synthetic-surface, old-school court has a charming, secret-location feeling. Call ahead or reserve through the concierge at the Observatory Hotel. It's close to The Rocks for cold beers after a hard game.

RUSHCUTTERS BAY PARK TENNIS
Map pp228-9
☎ 9357 1675; Rushcutters Bay Park; per hr $20-24; ⏱ 7am-11pm; train Kings Cross
The courts here are open to all members of the public, with the cheapest rates available before 4pm weekdays. It's a relaxed place for a game, and racket hire is available ($3).

SYDNEY INTERNATIONAL TENNIS CENTRE
☎ 8746 0777; Homebush Bay Dr, Homebush Bay; per hr $20-24; ⏱ 8am-11pm; train Olympic Park
Far from centre, but the big stars play here. Rates go up after 5pm and on weekends.

GOLF

MOORE PARK GOLF CLUB Map pp232-3
☎ 9663 1064; Centennial Ave, Paddington; 18 holes $45 Mon-Fri, $50 Sat & Sun; bus 391-399
Moore Park is the most central of Sydney's 40-odd public golf courses, with 18 holes and par 70.

BONDI GOLF CLUB Map p238
☎ 9130 1981; www.bondigolf.com.au; 5 Military Rd, North Bondi; unlimited golf $18.50; bus 380, 389
Another public course (spectacularly located) which has the added bonus of wonderful ocean views and intriguing Aboriginal rock engravings (see p82).

YOGA

Always seeking physical enlightenment, Sydney's locals have long taken to yoga with a serious fervour. In recent years it's faced some stiff competition from Pilates as the exercise *du jour*, but it still holds firm (and so do its buff, flexible adherents), with some very snazzy classes available. For something different check out Govinda's (p132). Call ahead for schedules.

SYDNEY YOGA SPACE Map pp228-9
☎ 9360 0577; www.sydneyyogaspace.com; Level 3, 63 William St, Potts Point; per class $10-20
Plenty of yoga classes (covering three skill levels) are offered at this large studio. The teachings of Indian guru BKS Iyengar (which emphasise standing asanas and precision alignment) are used, and introductory workshops, intensives and retreats can be had for the more dedicated bodybenders.

ASHTANGA YOGA SPACE Map pp232-3
☎ 9360 7602; www.ashtangayogaspace.com.au; Verona Cinema Bldg, 17 Oxford St, Paddington; per class $17; bus 378, 380
Ashtanga Yoga Space adheres to Ashtanga and offers wonderful Mysore-style classes that'll make your muscles sing. Find nirvana at their spacious, wood-floored studio in the lane between the Verona Cinema and Berkelouw's, and follow the smell of incense up the stairs. Five- and ten-class packages offer a small discount.

Yoga (above) in The Domain

INLINE SKATING

The beach promenades at Bondi and Manly are the favoured spots for skating, but Coogee and Bronte are becoming popular too. Centennial Park is a sensible choice for novice inline skaters, as the traffic is slow and one way.

MANLY BLADES Map p240

☎ 9976 3833; 49 North Steyne, Manly; ferry Manly
This busy place will get you sorted for blade hire ($15/hour). For the adventurous there are skateboards (from $10/hour) and scooters (from $7/hour)

TOTAL SKATE Map pp232-3

☎ 9380 6356; 36 Oxford St, Woollahra; 1st hr $10, per hr thereafter $5; bus 378, 380, 382, L82
Perfectly positioned near Centennial Park, this outfit rents out the goods and includes protective gear like helmets and knee pads. Very popular on weekends, you may want to get in early to avoid a stock run-out.

ALTERNATIVE THERAPIES

With narcissism and relaxation among the favourite activities of Sydneysiders, alternative therapies are enormously popular with everyone – from the stressed-out socialite who needs to detox, to the bricklayer who wants his back rubbed right.

GINSENG BATHHOUSE Map p235

☎ 9356 6680; Level 1, Crest Hotel, 111 Darlinghurst Rd, Kings Cross; adult/child from $25/11; ⏰ 9.30am-9.30pm Mon-Fri, 9am-9.30pm Sat & Sun; train Kings Cross
Korea comes to Sydney in this marvellous bathhouse, which will eliminate your toxins and have your circulation firing in no time. Separate men's and women's facilities have ginseng spas, hot/cold baths and wet/dry saunas. Pay extra for various massages or be scrubbed to within an inch of your skin's life and emerge on the mean streets of the Cross as smooth as a baby's bottom.

NATURAL HEALTH CARE CENTRE Map pp236-7

☎ 9660 0677; 20 Glebe Point Rd, Glebe; treatments $30-100; ⏰ 9am-5pm Mon, Wed, Fri & Sat, 9am-8pm Tue & Thu, 10am-5pm Sun; bus 431-4
Students of the Australian College of Natural Therapies fulfil practical components of their various courses for members of the public, at a substantially reduced rate. You can get treatments such as remedial massage, aromatherapy, naturopathy, reflexology and even ear candling.

Shopping

Shopping

Sydney's residents exhibit a brash hedonism that carries well over into their social life, definitely influencing their shopping habits. They work hard, play hard and most especially love to *shop* hard. Many locals even see it as a recreational activity, and in some cases as a competitive sport or a full-time job. The proliferation of weekend markets (see opposite) is a good example of this, and the increasing flexibility of opening hours has enabled Sydneysiders to burn holes in their pockets every single day of the week. Shopping in Sydney can be fun, frantic and frivolous, and service is generally reasonable, although travellers from overseas may find the customer service a bit laid-back at times.

The Central Business District (CBD) is cramped to the brim with department stores, pedestrian-friendly shopping strips (such as Pitt St Mall), shopping centres (many with food courts), chain stores, small boutiques and the lion's share of international luxury brands. For a much more relaxed experience, head to the fashionable inner-city shopping strips like Paddington (although Saturday is crazy), Glebe and Newtown, which offer a pleasing variety of cafés, boutiques, pubs and cinemas.

If it's Australia-specific goods and top-end souvenirs you're after, then the historic Rocks district is the most obvious – and expensive – choice. You can find everything here: Aboriginal art, opals, footwear, tea towels, clothes and trinkets – and there's a market held every weekend (for the cheapest 'Australiana', however, head to **Paddy's Markets**, opposite). Looking for vintage clothes or CDs? Then Crown St in Surry Hills and King St in Newtown are hard to beat, and Woollahra's Queen St is the holy grail for pricey antiques and discreet service. Double Bay (jokingly referred to as 'Double Pay') is peppered with smart shops catering to wealthy trophy wives. The Eastern Beaches are good spots to search for surfwear, swimwear and the sort of casual gear that looks great in a beer-garden setting.

Opening Hours

Most stores are open from 9.30am to 6pm Monday to Wednesday, Friday and Saturday, and until 9pm Thursday. Sunday trading is increasingly popular, but expect shorter hours, such as noon to 4pm or 5pm.

Consumer Taxes

A 10% federal tax on goods and services (GST) is automatically added to pretty much everything you buy in Australia. Visitors to Australia are entitled to a refund of any GST paid on items over $300 from one supplier within 30 days of departure from Australia. You can get a cheque refund at the designated booth located past customs at Sydney airport, or contact the **Australian Taxation Office** (ATO; ☎ 13 28 61).

Bargaining

Sydney's shops are not a place to bargain, though you could try your skills at some of the grungier markets around the city. Some vendors at Paddy's Markets might be open to bargaining, especially if you're buying in volume. Sales are usually held in early January and July.

TOP FIVE SHOPPING STRIPS

- **Oxford St** (p74) Boutiques, chain stores and plenty of cafés to keep the fashionistas buzzing.
- **King St, Newtown** (p83) An endless procession of the grungy, cool and funky – with vintage ruling the day.
- **Pitt St Mall, City** (opposite) A pedestrian frenzy of upmarket department stores.
- **Crown St, Surry Hills** (p109) Second-hand records, retro home furnishings and old-style fashions.
- **Queen St, Woollahra** (p79) For thick wallets full of cashed-up credit cards: these antiques and art aren't cheap.

CITY CENTRE, THE ROCKS & CIRCULAR QUAY

See the boxed text on p59 for transport options to/from these areas.

ABORIGINAL & TRIBAL ART CENTRE

Map pp228-9   Indigenous

☎ 9247 9625; 117 George St, The Rocks; ⊗ 10am-5.30pm

This gallery has a small but good quality range of crafts for sale; look for bark paintings, didgeridoos, boomerangs and weavings. Free exhibitions are often on display in the open space. Overseas packing and shipping available.

ALANNAH HILL

Map pp228-9   Clothing & Accessories

☎ 9221 1251; Shop 50, Strand Arcade, Pitt St Mall, City; ⊗ 9.30am-5pm Mon-Wed & Fri & Sat, 9.30am-9pm Thu, 10am-5pm Sun

Step into this fun, fruity palace of fancy, with flirty, frilly, flimsy fabrics made into

---

To Market, to Market

Sydney's markets probably offer the city's most fun way to shop, and the wide range of goods available will suit a variety of tastes. While some are quite touristy, there are also a few where you'll definitely feel the local vibe – it'll run the gamut from groovy to sniffy-nosed boutique-y.

Balmain Markets (Map pp226–7; ☎ 0418 765 736; St Andrew's Church, 223 Darling St, Balmain; ⊗ 8.30am-4pm Sat; bus 433,434, 442) This small but delightful local market offers high-quality creative crafts like handmade candles, soaps, funky jewellery, exotic textiles, artwork and used clothing and books. The feel is friendly, social and low-key, and there are some great Asian stalls to try.

Bondi Markets (Map p238; ☎ 9315 8988; Bondi Beach Public School, cnr Campbell Pde & Warners Ave, Bondi; ⊗ 9am-4pm Sun; bus 380) Sitting across from the beach at the northern end of Campbell Pde, this small market is good for hip clothing, exotic imports, jewellery, fashion accessories, knick-knacks and skimpily-dressed-people watching.

Glebe Markets (Map pp236–7; ☎ 4237 7499; Glebe Public School, cnr Glebe Point Rd & Derby Pl, Glebe; ⊗ 10am-4pm Sat; bus 431-4) This large and slightly grungy market hawks a wide assortment of books, vintage clothes, glassware, leather goods, herbal teas, hippie crafts, oddities and curios. It takes over the neighborhood on Saturdays, so crowds will be heavy everywhere.

Kirribilli Markets (Map p239; ☎ 9922 4428; Bradfield Park North, Milsons Point; ⊗ 7am-3pm 4th Sat every month; train Milsons Point, ferry Kirribilli) A wonderful monthly market offering everything from vintage clothes to real (and faux) antiques to kids' gear to all kinds of jewellery. Plenty of exotic foods too, and great lively atmosphere.

Paddington Markets (Map pp232–3; ☎ 9331 2923; www.paddingtonmarkets.com.au; St John's Church, 395 Oxford St, Paddington; ⊗ 10am-5pm Sat; bus 378, 380) Very popular, upmarket and pricey, with vintage clothing, creative crafts, beautiful jewellery, tasty food and holistic treatments. Some fledgling designers get their start here. Don't even think about finding a place to park – this is one for public transport.

Paddy's Markets (Map pp228–9; ☎ 1300 361 589; www.paddysmarkets.com.au; Market City, cnr Hay & Thomas Sts, Haymarket; ⊗ 9am-5pm Thu-Sun; monorail Powerhouse Museum, MLR Haymarket) In the heart of Chinatown, this Sydney institution is a great place to find cheap souvenirs, clothing, wigs, electronics, sheepskin rugs, cosmetics, mobile phones and plenty of knick-knacks. In the basement there's a good selection of fresh fruit, vegetables and seafood. Paddy's Markets in Flemington, on Parramatta Rd near Sydney Olympic Park, operates (along with the huge Sydney fruit and vegetable market) on Friday and Sunday.

The Rocks Market (Map pp228–9; ☎ 9240-8717; www.therocksmarket.com; George St, The Rocks; ⊗ 10am-5pm Sat & Sun; ferry Circular Quay) Held weekends only at the top end of George St, this market is definitely on the touristy side, but still fun for a browse. Crafts made of metal, ceramic, stone, leather and glass abound, while souvenirs (including 'roo balls) are also available. It's close to many pubs and cafés, so your nonshopping partner can sit, drink and wait it out.

Rozelle Markets (Map pp226–7; ☎ 9818 5373; cnr Darling & National Sts, Rozelle; ⊗ 9am-4pm Sat & Sun) This is one of Sydney's best markets for bargain hunters, and you're unlikely to run into fellow tourists. Hippie jewellery, vintage (or just recycled) clothes, plants, books, knick-knacks, live folk music, palm readings, exotic food stalls and some basic junk can be sifted through. It's lots of fun.

chocolate-box dresses and bordello-style boudoir ornaments. Loud music helps the fluffy chicks forget about their credit card bills as temptation finds no boundaries…

AUSTRALIAN WINE CENTRE

Map pp228-9   Food & Drink

☎ 9247 2755; Goldfields House, 1 Alfred St, Circular Quay; ⏰ 9.30am-6.30pm Mon-Sat, 11am-5pm Sun

Look for this place under the Goldfields House, behind Circular Quay. Here you'll find wines from every Australian wine-growing region. The centre will package and send wine overseas, and of course you're welcome to sample a few drops.

COUNTRY ROAD

Map pp228-9   Clothing & Accessories

☎ 9394 1818; 142 Pitt St Mall, City; ⏰ 9am-6pm Mon-Wed, 9am-9pm Thu, 9am-6pm Fri & Sat, 11am-5pm Sun

Hip designer Sophie Holt's new Country Road products make a welcome youthful statement alongside those old traditional lines. All ages and both sexes are catered to; plenty of CR branches dot the city.

DAVID JONES

Map pp228-9   Department Store

☎ 9266 5544; cnr Elizabeth & Market Sts, City; ⏰ 9.30am-6pm Mon-Wed & Fri, 9.30am-9pm Thu, 9am-6pm Sat, 11am-5pm Sun

Bright and sparkling, this is considered the city's premier department store, and boasts two locations in the centre. The one on the corner of Castlereagh and Market Sts has menswear and electrical goods, along with a food hall with luxury food items. The Elizabeth St store sells women's and children's goods and has a concierge who can book city tours and tickets. David Jones also has suburban stores.

DONE ART & DESIGN

Map pp228-9   Australiana

☎ 9251 6099; 125 George St, The Rocks; ⏰ 10am-6pm

Ken Done's bright, sunny and cartoonish images adorn T-shirts, shorts, towels, bathing suits, robes, dresses and any other kind of resort item you can think of. He's been an artist for over 25 years and his colourful style may remind you of Matisse on Prozac;

if you want more, check out his gallery nearby at 1 Hickson Rd.

DYMOCKS Map pp228-9   Books

☎ 9235 0155; 424 George St, City; ⏰ 9am-6.30pm Mon-Wed & Fri, 9am-9pm Thu, 9am-6pm Sat, 10am-5.30pm Sun

Sydney's huge bookstore, with more than 250,000 titles spread over three floors; look for the Lonely Planet aisle! Great for almost every kind of book you're looking for, plus there's a café. Has several other branches in town.

GOWINGS

Map pp228-9   Department Store

☎ 9287 6394; 45 Market St, City; ⏰ 8.30am-6pm Mon-Wed & Fri, 8.30am-9pm Thu, 9am-6pm Sat, 10am-5pm Sun

One of the most eccentric department stores you'll ever set foot in, this large Aussie-themed store offers five floors of dress shirts, outdoor gear, gag gifts (vibrating soap anyone?), Speedos, rubber chickens, luggage, jester hats and flip-flops. You're bound to find something you like, and plenty you don't.

JURLIQUE

Map pp228-9   Cosmetics & Skincare

☎ 9231 0626; Shop 33, Strand Arcade, Pitt St, City; ⏰ 9am-6pm Mon-Wed & Fri & Sat, 9am-9pm Thu, 11am-5pm Sun

With many branches, this highly regarded Australian skin-care brand offers its customers hypoallergenic and PH-balanced products made from organic herbs (grown at their own farms). Nothing is tested on animals. A spa on the premises pampers clients – both men and women – with facials, body treatments and hydrotherapy. Also at 352 Oxford St in Paddington (Map pp232–3).

KINOKUNIYA Map pp228-9   Bookstore

☎ 9262 7996; level 2, 500 George St, City; ⏰ 10am-7pm Mon-Wed, Fri & Sat, 10am-9pm Thu, 10am-6pm Sun

Located in the Galeries Victoria is this large Japanese bookstore with great book sections including art and design, travel and children's books. Also plenty of magazine, stationery and Japanese language selections.

LEONA EDMISTON

Map pp228-9   Clothing & Accessories
☎ 9230 0322; Chifley Plaza, 2 Chifley Sq, City;
🕒 10am-6pm Mon-Fri, 10am-4pm Sat
Queen of Oz frocks Leona Edmiston knows what girls want – the perfect dress, whether of the little and black variety, whimsically floral or all-out sexy. A new line of accessories includes cute red satin shoes and polka-dot handbags, with exotic Asian fabrics thrown in for good measure. Also at 88 William St, Paddington (Map pp232–3).

MARCS

Map pp228-9   Clothing & Accessories
☎ 9221 5575; Mid City Centre, 197 Pitt St Mall, City; 🕒 9.30am-6pm Mon-Wed & Fri & Sat, 9.30am-9pm Thu, 11am-5pm Sun
Sydney's trendiest young hipsters flock to this streetwear shop to try on the high-quality jeans, chinos, sweaters, shirts and dresses. Source the good stuff from Europe with labels like Paul Smith and Diesel, or ferret through the great youth label Baby Doll for hipsters, tiny T-shirts and denim jackets. Also at 270 Oxford St, Paddington (Map pp232–3) and at 11B Campbell Pde in Bondi.

MOUNTAIN DESIGNS

Map pp228-9   Outdoor Gear
☎ 9267 3822; 499 Kent St; 🕒 9am-6pm Mon-Wed & Fri, 9am-9pm Thu, 9am-5.30pm Sat, 10am-5pm Sun
If you need top-quality outdoor goods this is a fine place to come. Australian- and US-made backpacks, rock-climbing equipment, camping gear, sleeping bags, hiking shoes and travel books are on offer, and the friendly staff can help you with info about excursions or day trips out of Sydney.

MYER

Map pp228-9   Department Store
☎ 9238 9000; 436 George St, City; 🕒 9am-6pm Mon-Wed, Fri & Sat, 9am-9pm Thu, 11am-5pm Sun
At seven storeys, Myer (ex-Grace Bros) is one of Sydney's largest stores and a prime venue for after-Christmas sales. It's not as swanky as David Jones, but you will still be able to findplenty of high-quality goods, along with slick cafés when you tire of lugging those bags. More branches in the suburbs.

OBJECT

Map pp228-9   Designer Art
☎ 9247 7984; 88 George St, The Rocks; 🕒 10am-5.30pm Mon-Fri, 10am-5pm Sat & Sun
Creative designs dominate the theme at this museum-like store, with everyday items converted into gorgeous pieces of art. Things like aluminium pitchers, hand-blown glass vases, knitted scarves, contemporary lighting and funky jewellery will compete for your attention and dollars. Not cheap, but lovely to look at.

OPAL FIELDS

Map pp228-9   Jewellery
☎ 9247 6800; 190 George St, City; 🕒 9am-6pm
Award-winning jewellery designs incorporating Australia's famous stone are on offer at this fine store. Service is friendly and no-pressure; check out the specimen display case also. They have another store on the 2nd level of shop 19, Queen Victoria Building (Map pp228–9).

PADDY PALLIN

Map pp228-9   Outdoor Gear
☎ 9264 2685; 507 Kent St, City; 🕒 9am-5.30pm Mon-Wed, 9am-9pm Thu, 9am-6pm Fri, 9am-5pm Sat, 9am-4pm Sun
This is another good choice for camping and climbing equipment, ski gear, outdoor wear and travel books (including Lonely Planet ones). Knowledgable staff are on hand to help make your outdoor adventure a memorable one.

PASPALEY PEARLS

Map pp228-9   Jewellery
☎ 9232 7633; 142 King St, City; 🕒 10am-5.30pm Mon-Fri, 10.30am-3.30pm Sat
Glorious South Sea pearls that have been harvested off the West Australian coast are the main attraction here, but you'll need a thick wallet as prices can easily get into the thousands. Expect quality that is second to none, along with knowledgable, professional service.

PUPPET SHOP AT THE ROCKS

Map pp228-9   Children's
☎ 9247 9137; 77 George St, The Rocks; 🕒 10am-5pm
From the ceiling of this wonderful underground treasure chest dangles all manner of stringed things and bizarre, jointed toys. Meet Phillipe, the French owner and world traveller, as he shows you his

Burmese and Thai puppets. Almost every-thing you see is for sale.

QUEEN VICTORIA BUILDING

Map pp228-9   Shopping Centre

☎ 9265 6864; 455 George St, City; ⏰ 9am-6pm Mon-Wed, Fri & Sat, 9am-9pm Thu, 11am-5pm Sun
The magnificent QVB takes up a whole block with its late-19th-century Roman-esque grandeur, and boasts nearly 200 shops on five levels. It's the city's most beautiful shopping centre, and you'll find plenty of fashion outlets along with stores selling Australian knick-knacks. The lower level, which connects to Town Hall Station, has food bars, shoe-repair shops, dry-cleaners and newsagents. Tours are avail-able; check with the information booth.

RED EYE RECORDS

Map pp228-9   Music

☎ 9299 4233; 66 King St, City; ⏰ 9am-6pm Mon-Wed & Fri, 9am-9pm Thu, 9am-5pm Sat, 11am-5pm Sun
A great store for music junkies, as the large and unusual stock covers Japanese, Euro-pean and US imports along with Australian artists and plenty of independent releases. A second-hand section upstairs includes col-lectable CDs, DVDs, vinyl, books and posters. Knowledgable staff take custom mail orders for the hard-to-find. Also at 370 Pitt St.

RM WILLIAMS

Map pp228-9   Australiana

☎ 9262 2228; 389 George St, City; ⏰ 9am-6pm Mon-Wed & Fri, 9am-9pm Thu, 9am-5pm Sat, 11am-5pm Sun
This long-established manufacturer and distributor of Aussie outdoor gear, such

as drought-breakers (oilskin riding coats) and moleskin trousers, attracts every urban cowboy and cowgirl within the city limits. One of their best sellers is of course the classic elastic-sided boot, which is nothing less than an Aussie icon.

STRAND ARCADE

Map pp228-9   Shopping Centre

☎ 9232 4199; Pitt St Mall or 412 George St, City; ⏰ 9am-5.30pm Mon-Wed & Fri, 9am-9pm Thu, 9am-4pm Sat, 11am-4pm Sun
With its stained-glass windows, iron-lace-work balconies and three floors of bou-tique shops (think Luxe, Third Millennium, Wayne Cooper etc.) and the odd Austral-ian store (see Strand Hatters, following), this quirky shopping centre makes for a truly atmospheric shopping trip. Stop for a latte, bleach your hair or have your shoes cobbled.

STRAND HATTERS

Map pp228-9   Australiana

☎ 9231 6884; Shop 8, Strand Arcade, Pitt St Mall, City; ⏰ 9am-6pm Mon-Wed & Fri, 9am-8pm Thu, 9.30am-4pm Sat, 11am-4pm Sun
Wearing a hat to protect oneself from the sun is a good idea in this country – wearing an authentic rabbit-felt Akubra from this place will ensure you'll look like you came straight from the outback. Plenty of other high-quality selections are also ready to top your head.

DARLING HARBOUR & CHINATOWN

See the boxed text on p72 for transport op-tions to/from these areas.

AUSTRALIAN GEOGRAPHIC

Map pp228-9   Australiana

☎ 9212 6539; Shop 428, Harbourside, Darling Harbour; ⏰ 9.30am-9pm Sun-Thu, 9.30am-9.30pm Fri & Sat
Named after a national magazine, this store offers semi-ecological purchases like eucalyptus candles, emu oil lotions, gar-dening stuff, save-the-world books, scien-tific items and plenty of kids' toys. Ten per cent of profits goes towards preserving the environment. They have another store at the Centrepoint shopping mall.

Shopping at Paddy's Markets (p159), Haymarket

TOP FIVE LOCAL SPECIALISTS

Australia excels at kitsch souvenirs involving koalas and the Opera House, but you *can* find useful mementos if you try.

- **Aboriginal & Tribal Art Centre** (p159) From boomerangs to bark paintings, plus exhibitions.
- **Australian Wine Centre** (p160) The best in Aussie drops to bring back home.
- **Gowings** (p160) Stereotypical Australian souvenirs, but some hidden jewels too.
- **RM Williams** (opposite) From catwalks to construction sites, the best foot coverings around.
- **Strand Hatters** (opposite) Grab an Akubra and be talking funny in no time.

CYRIL'S DELICATESSEN

Map pp232-3   Food & Drink
☎ 9211 0994; 183 Hay St, Haymarket; ⏲ 6.30am-5.30pm Mon-Fri, 6.30am-1pm Sat
Run by Czech immigrant Cyril Vincent since 1956, this small, old-style delicatessen offers a large selection (over 4000 different product lines) of imported goodies like jams, cheese, crackers, pickled olives and canned peppers. And his loyal customers love him for it.

GAVALA ABORIGINAL ART

Map pp228-9   Indigenous
☎ 9212 7232; ground level, Harbourside, Darling Harbour; ⏲ 10am-9pm Mon-Sun
Proudly proclaiming itself as Sydney's only Aboriginal-owned retail centre and gallery, this is a great place to source everything from a T-shirt to a bark painting, a boomerang or an Aboriginal flag. Located in Darling Harbour's large Harbourside shopping centre.

MARKET CITY

Map pp228-9   Shopping Centre
☎ 9212 1388; 9-13 Hay St, Haymarket; ⏲ stores 10am-7pm Fri-Wed, 10am-8pm Thu, centre 10am-late
This mammoth shopping centre houses Paddy's Markets, a slew of restaurants, heaps of retail fashion outlets (mostly the end-of-season variety), cinemas and video game parlours. There's something for everyone and multiple floors, so don't get lost!

DARLINGHURST TO POTTS POINT

See the boxed text on p75 for transport options to/from these areas.

BLUE SPINACH Map p235 Clothing & Accessories

☎ 9331 3904; 348 Liverpool St, Darlinghurst; ⏲ 10am-7pm Mon-Sat
Consignment clothing at its most high-end, with penny-pinching label-lovers – both men and women – flocking in droves to this shocking-blue corner shop. They're here to source second-hand designer duds (think YSL, Gucci and Collette Dinnigan) at (relatively) bargain prices. Accessories to complete your 'rich' look include shoes, sunglasses and bags.

THE BOOKSHOP DARLINGHURST

Map pp232-3   Books
☎ 9331 1103; 207 Oxford St, Darlinghurst; ⏲ 10am-10pm Mon-Wed, 10am-11pm Thu, 10am-midnight Fri & Sat, 11am-11pm Sun
This small bookshop specialises in gay and lesbian literature, with everything from queer crime to lesbian fiction to gay life stories to gay glossy coffee-table books to XXX magazines and calendars. A fun browse, to say the least.

KOOKABURRA KIOSK

Map p235   Clothing & Accessories
☎ 9380 5509; 112A Burton St, Darlinghurst; ⏲ 11am-6pm Tue-Wed & Fri & Sat, 11am-8pm Thu
This small, long-running second-hand clothing store has some fab finds from the fashion archives. It concentrates on unique vintage pieces and manages to avoid that fabric-explosion atmosphere that plagues so many of these vintage shops. Sort through the sale racks out the front for bargains.

THE TOOL SHED Map pp228-9 Sex & Fetish

☎ 9332 2792; www.toolshed.com.au; 81 Oxford St, Darlinghurst; ⏲ 10am-1am Mon-Thu & Sun, 10am-3am Fri & Sat
Two-foot dildos, life-size dolls, raunchy codpieces, leather whips and bondage gear and tons of fantasy videos – all respectably displayed. They've got another store nearby at 191 Oxford St if you can't get enough. Shop online if you're shy.

Shopping

DARLINGHURST TO POTTS POINT

SURRY HILLS & EAST SYDNEY

See boxed text p77 for transport options to/from these areas.

REEFER RECORDS Map pp232-3   Music

☎ 9358 6100; 326 Crown St, Surry Hills; ⏰ 11am-7pm Mon-Wed & Fri, 11am-9pm Thu, 11am-6pm Sat, noon-6pm Sun

Turntable enthusiasts will love this small place, which offers wall-to-wall rare and hard-to-find vinyl albums and CDs. Promos, collectables and second-hand DJ specials are on offer, with knowledgable staff there to help you sort through the classic material.

WHEELS & DOLL BABY

Map pp232-3   Clothing & Accessories

☎ 9361 3286; 259 Crown St, Surry Hills; ⏰ 10am-6pm Tue-Sat, noon-5pm Sun

There's nothing like this boutique – it's rock-chick, posh punk or Parisian scruff (your choice), and a great place to snag a costume to prove you're an upmarket girly-girl. Join Pamela Anderson and own a piece of this action, whether it be a polka-dot skirt, floral spaghetti-strap dress, Victorian corset or baby-doll T-shirt. It speaks of pure celebrity-dom, starting with the lovely service.

PADDINGTON & WOOLLAHRA

See the boxed text on p78 for transport options to/from these areas.

AKIRA ISOGAWA

Map pp232-3   Clothing & Accessories

☎ 9361 5221; www.akira.com.au; 12A Queen St, Woollahra; ⏰ 10.30am-6pm Mon-Wed & Fri, 10.30am-7pm Thu, 10am-6pm Sat

One of Sydney's most famous designers, Akira Isogawa creates fastidiously crafted dresses (some utilising his own dyeing techniques) which are true masterpieces

---

TOP FIVE CHILDREN'S SHOPS

- Fragile (opposite)
- Kidstuff (opposite)
- Kite Power (p167)
- Lesley McKay's Bookshop (p166)
- Puppet Shop at The Rocks (p161)

---

of feminine geometry and even worthy of a modern art collection. If you can afford his pieces, you'll be sure to attract some exclusive attention. Check for his clothes at David Jones also.

ANDREW MCDONALD

Map pp232-3   Clothing & Accessories

☎ 9358 6793; www.andrewmcdonald.com.au; 58 William St, Paddington; ⏰ 10am-6pm Tue-Fri, 10am-6pm Sat

Sydney's best in custom footwear for men and women can be had at this small Paddington workshop. Choose your materials, colours and even styles (or they can replicate a desired design) and expect exquisite, long-wearing and perfectly-fitted shoes. Great for those with 'difficult' feet, or just anyone who wants something unique. Prices range from $600 to $1200.

BELINDA Map pp232-3   Clothing & Accessories

☎ 9380 8728; 39 William St, Paddington; ⏰ 10am-6pm Mon-Sat, noon-5pm Sun

Super-stylish überboutiquist Belinda Seper's namesake store offers a small but excellent selection of just-so bags and shoes, along with a few fashions to add to the fun. Men, check out the affiliated menswear shop just a few doors down at number 29.

CALIBRE

Map pp232-3   Clothing & Accessories

☎ 9380 5993; 416 Oxford St, Paddington; ⏰ 9.30am-6pm Mon-Wed & Fri, 9.30am-8pm Thu, 10am-6pm Sat, 11.30am-5.30pm Sun

Smart suits and hip weekend wardrobe supplies for men are the speciality here. Even if you're a complete fashion misfit, the staff – who come complete with slicked-back hair – and full-length mirrors will make you look good enough to walk down Oxford St with confidence.

COLLETTE DINNIGAN

Map pp232-3   Clothing & Accessories

☎ 9360 6691; www.collettedinnigan.com; 33 William St, Paddington; ⏰ 10am-6pm Mon-Wed & Sat, 10am-7pm Thu, noon-4pm Sun

Dinnigan is one of Australia's most successful international designers, and this sugar-coated boudoir of a shop shows why. Her wonderfully slinky designs include beautiful, intricately hand-beaded dresses, all made in Sydney. And it's not just made for size-8-wearing models, either – 'real' women can enjoy her creations as well.

COPELAND & DE SOOS

Map pp232-3 · Antiques

☎ 9363 5288; 64 Queen St, Woollahra; ☉ 11am-6pm Mon-Fri, 11am-4pm Sat

Specialising in late 19th- and 20th-century decorative art and design (think Art Nouveau and Art Deco furniture), this charming store also does a nice line in 20th-century jewellery like big resin bangles and Scandinavian silver. Service is friendly and the staff is knowledgable.

CORNER SHOP

Map pp232-3 · Clothing & Accessories

☎ 9380 9828; 43 William St, Paddington; ☉ 10am-6pm Mon-Sat, noon-5pm Sun

This treasure-trove of a boutique is stocked with unique and original foreign goodies like stylishly torn jeans, cosy turtlenecks and wispy things that go 'slink' in the night. It's a good mix of casual and high end (including some excellent second-hand clothes), with some jewellery for good measure.

DINOSAUR DESIGNS

Map pp232-3 · Jewellery & Homewares

☎ 9361 3776; 339 Oxford St, Paddington; ☉ 10am-6pm Mon-Sat, noon-5pm Sun

If the Flintstones opened a store, this is what it would look like. Oversized, colourful and chunky resin jewellery competes with must-have, vibrantly coloured home accessories (such as salad bowls and vases) that prove your urban coolness. Too bad it's all behind glass, 'cause you'll really want to do some fondling here. Also at the Strand Arcade.

EVA BREUER ART DEALER

Map pp232-3 · Art

☎ 9362 0297; www.evabreuerartdealer.com.au; 83 Moncur St, Woollahra; ☉ 10am-6pm Tue-Fri, 10am-5pm Sat, 1-5pm Sun

This is a well-regarded, friendly gallery stocking a bright selection of modern Australian art. Look for museum-quality works by Grace Cossington Smith, Sidney Nolan, James Coburn, Arthur Boyd and every other big name in the genre. There are works on canvas and paper, plus a selection of artworks for under $5000.

FRAGILE Map pp232-3 · Children's

☎ 9362 0085; cnr Elizabeth & Paddington Sts, Paddington; ☉ 10am-5.30pm Mon-Wed & Fri & Sat, 10am-7pm Thu, 11am-5pm Sun

The cutest in pampering kidswear can be found at this darling shop, which stocks a brilliant array of designer duds like Oilily and Petit Bateau. For mums, there's a good selection of Paul Smith and Diesel maternitywear, along with some spiffy papooses. Find it by the parked prams and coddled babies out the front.

HOGARTH GALLERIES ABORIGINAL ART CENTRE Map pp232-3 · Indigenous

☎ 9360 6839; www.aboriginalartcentres.com.au; 7 Walker Lane, Paddington; ☉ 10am-5pm Tue-Sat

This highly respected gallery has been exhibiting Aboriginal creations from all over Australia since 1973. A wide range of art (bark paintings, weavings, carvings) is on display, including works by young artists Rosella Namok and Fiona Omeenyo; the emphasis is on highlighting top-notch artists and their communities. New exhibits are shown monthly, and lectures can be arranged. To get here from Oxford St turn north onto Shadforth and right onto Walker Lane.

HÖGLUND Map pp232-3 · Art Glass

☎ 9326 1556; www.sydney.hoglund.com.au; 92 Queen St, Woollahra; ☉ 10am-6pm Mon-Sat

Those seeking gorgeous hand-blown glass vases, bowls and glasses should visit this gallery, which showcases Ola Höglund and Marie Simberg-Höglund's high-quality creations. Bright colours and Matisse-like painted designs make for fun, functional and award-winning pieces. Call for a visit outside opening hours.

KIDSTUFF Map pp232-3 · Children's

☎ 9363 2838; 126A Queen St, Woollahra; ☉ 9.30am-5.30pm Mon-Sat, 9am-5pm Sun

A menagerie of toys and books, along with a proliferation of rabbit-related toys at Easter time, ensure that keen young minds will find plenty of fluffy stimulation at this long-serving children's shop. Peek at the very back for sweet little princess and cowboy costumes, or find that perfect doll house for Barbie. Even parents will have fun here.

LESLEY MCKAY'S BOOKSHOP

Map pp232-3   Books

☎ 9328 2733; 118 Queen St, Woollahra; ☼ 9am-6pm Mon-Sat, 9.30am-4pm Sun

It's located a bit out outside the city centre, but if you make it here you'll find an excellent range of fiction, nonfiction, biography and history. There's an especially good selection of children's books, too, and knowledgable staff won't let you down. There's a smaller branch at 14 Macleay St, Potts Point.

MAMBO Map pp232-3   Surf/SkateWear

☎ 9331 8034; 17 Oxford St, Paddington; ☼ 10am-6pm Mon-Wed & Fri & Sat, 10am-8pm Thu, 12-6pm Sun

Bold comic-book graphics from a variety of hip artists adorn street-, skate- and surfwear T-shirts and jeans. They're very popular garments for their original, off-the-wall designs, and Mambo artist Reg Mombasa even designed the casual shirts for the Australian Olympic team in 2000. Expect a wide range of goodies (including watches, backpacks and coffee table books). Also at 80 Campbell Pde, Bondi (Map p238) and at 105 George St, The Rocks (Map pp228–9).

MECCA COSMETICA

Map pp232-3   Perfume & Cosmetics

☎ 9361 4488; 126 Oxford St, Paddington; ☼ 10am-6pm Mon-Wed & Fri & Sat, 10am-8pm Thu, 11am-5pm Sun

The best make-up mecca for beauty junkies that we have ever found. Organic and cult cosmetics along the lines of REN, Prescriptives, Stephane Marais and Serge Lutens, as well as cool scents like Fracas and other hard-to-finds. Test the divine blood-orange lotion ($45) and get a quick make-over if it's not too busy.

NICOLA FINETTI

Map pp232-3   Clothing & Accessories

☎ 9362 1685; 92 Queen St, Woollahra; ☼ 10am-6pm Mon-Wed & Fri & Sat, 10am-7pm Thu, 11am-5pm Sun

Italian-born Nicola Finetti has been creating beautiful women's clothes in Sydney for around 20 years now, offering elegant and feminine designs with a fashionable edge that never wander into the outlandish. Embroidered details, luxe fabrics and smart

cutting all come together beautifully in the casual-to-eveningwear collection.

ORSON & BLAKE

Map pp232-3   Homewares

☎ 9326 1155; 85 Queen St, Woollahra; ☼ 9.30am-5.30pm Mon-Wed & Fri & Sat, 9.30am-6pm Thu, noon-5pm Sun

Sydney's most stylish spot to source homewares, with something for the bath (glorious lotions, soaps, towels), bedroom (sheets, robes, pillows) and garden (statues, urns, pots). Also: stuffed bunnies, scented candles and exotic furniture are definitely present, along with a whole women's fashion collection upstairs. Also at 483 Riley St, Surry Hills; that branch offers more furniture.

QUICK BROWN FOX

Map pp232-3   Clothing & Accessories

☎ 9331 3211; 100 Oxford St, Paddington; ☼ 10am-6pm Mon-Wed & Fri & Sat, 10am-8pm Thu, noon-5pm Sun

No lazy dogs here, that's for sure, but plenty of fast-looking, tanned vixens snapping up a range of funky vintage fashions that veer between Hello Kitty cuteness and indecent exposure sexiness. Catchy patterns and fabrics and very hip boots and bags; they also have a branch at 312 Kings St, Newtown.

SCANLAN & THEODORE

Map pp232-3   Clothing & Accessories

☎ 9361 6722; 443 Oxford St, Paddington; ☼ 10am-6pm Mon-Wed & Fri, 10am-8pm Thu, 10am-6pm Sat, 11.30am-5.30pm Sun

Regularly topping the lists of favourite designers, Scanlan & Theodore excel at beautifully made and finely silhouetted pieces for the evening or for the office. Plenty of sophisticated, feminine patterns and colours (like pinks and reds) complement fabrics you just can't help but fondle.

SIMON JOHNSON

Map pp232-3   Food & Drink

☎ 9328 6888; 55 Queen St, Woollahra; ☼ 10.30am-7pm Mon-Fri, 9am-5pm Sat, 10am-4pm Sun

Stock up your high-class picnic hamper at this gourmet wonderland. You'll find the tastiest Italian olives, creamiest Belgian chocolates and crispiest English biscuits, along with a great selection of imported olive oil and vinegar. The refrigerated case holds prosciutto and salami, along with French cheeses (there's a fromagerie on the premises, and you'll smell it).

TIM OLSEN GALLERY

Map pp232-3   Art
☎ 9360 9854; www.timolsengallery.com; 76 Paddington St, Paddington; ⏰ 11am-6pm Tue-Fri, 11am-5pm Sat

Tim Olsen runs one of Sydney's most important galleries. The airy space holds works by Tim's father, John Olsen (winner of the 2005 Archibald prize), and some dazzlingly beautiful landscapes by Ian Grant and Philip Hunter; also present are abstract paintings by Melinda Harper and Matthew Johnson. Tim's sister owns Dinosaur Designs.

EASTERN SUBURBS

See the boxed text on p80 for transport options to/from this area.

CHRISTENSEN COPENHAGEN

Map pp228-9   Clothing & Accessories
☎ 9328 9755; 2 Guilfoyle Ave, Double Bay; ⏰ 10am-6pm Mon-Wed & Fri & Sat, 10am-7pm Thu, noon-5pm Sun

Owner Marianne Christensen buys up smart and fun imports with UK, Italian and French labels (as well as jewellery from Copenhagen) though Collette Dinnigan frocks can sometimes be seen here too. Expect fun and feminine party dresses and a staff happy to advise with the utmost tact.

EVELYN MILES

Map pp228-9   Clothing & Accessories
☎ 9327 5732; Stamford Plaza, Double Bay, 33 Cross St, Double Bay; ⏰ 10am-6pm Mon-Fri, 10am-5pm Sat

Ensconced in the ground floor of the luxurious Stamford Plaza Hotel is this high-end retailer of footwear for women. It's here that credit cards and chiropodists' nightmares merge into one stiletto-heeled fantasy. Join Naomi Watts and Sarah Murdoch as owners of these stylish, colourful and attention-getting shoes, and be ready to shell out from 500 to 1200 bucks for the pleasure.

MONDO

Map pp228-9   Homewares
☎ 9362 4964; 27 Bay St, Double Bay; ⏰ 10am-5.30pm Mon-Sat

Creative additions to your contemporary lifestyle are found at this cosy boutique, with everything from office accessories to fancy imported perfumes to clothing fashions to small housewares. Owner Ilana Katz makes sure her offerings are affordable and well-designed, and you'll appreciate her efforts.

ZOMP

Map pp228-9   Clothing & Accessories
☎ 9362 3422; 30 Bay St, Double Bay; ⏰ 9.30am-6pm Mon-Wed & Fri, 9.30am-7pm Thu, 9am-5.30pm Sat, noon-5pm Sun

This branch shoe shop is a temptation, with chic imports (Costume National and Pura López) and the less-pricey, just-as-wearable house label, Topouzina. Prices run the gamut from $60 to $900, with the mostly imported fancy labels like Italian Enrico Antinori at the top of the bill. Check out the zebra high heels, spiky boots and spunky handbags. Also at 255 Oxford St in Paddington.

EASTERN BEACHES

See the boxed text on p82 for transport options to/from these areas.

GERTRUDE & ALICE

Map p238   Books
☎ 9130 5155; 40 Hall St, Bondi; ⏰ 9.30am-10pm

A must for beach-reading material, this second-hand bookstore offers good-quality tomes and a wonderfully casual atmosphere. The café (grab a streetside table) makes hanging out easy, and you can sell your book collection here as well. Their shop in Paddington may be open by the time you read this.

KITE POWER

Map p238   Children's
☎ 9315 7894; 126 Beach St, Coogee; ⏰ 9.30am-5.30pm

Whether you're a kid or just a kid at heart, if you're looking for beach entertainment this is the place to come. This small shop is chock-full of beach balls, frisbees, boomerangs, smashball racquets, hula hoops, juggling paraphernalia, games and, of course, lots of kites. Test your purchases in the nearby grassy reserve or at Coogee Beach.

TUCHUZY Map p238   Clothing & Accessories
☎ 9365 5371; 90 Gould St, Bondi; ⏱ 9am-6pm Mon-Sat, 10am-6pm Sun
The place for pricey imported labels: American jeans, embroidered Vietnamese cargos, Italian-designed shirts or Indian textile skirts. Plenty of flashy belts, shoes, bags and lingerie will help accessorise your life, and there are some contemporary vintage selections as well. Next door is Tuchuzy for men.

INNER WEST
See the boxed text on p83 for transport options to/from these areas.

BERKELOUW BOOKS Map pp236-7   Books
☎ 9560 3200; 70 Norton St, Leichhardt; ⏱ 10am-11pm Sun-Thu, 10am-midnight Fri & Sat
Berkelouw and Sons has specialised in second-hand books and printed rarities since 1821, but their modern stores are better for finding new releases and sipping coffee. Another branch in Paddington.

BROADWAY SHOPPING CENTRE
Map pp236-7   Shopping Centre
☎ 9213 3333; cnr Parramatta Rd & Bay St, Glebe; 10am-7pm Mon-Wed & Fri, 10am-9pm Thu, 9am-6pm Sat, 10am-6pm Sun
Located in the grand old Grace Bros building, this large and modern shopping centre offers dozens of shops, a food court, a Hoyts cinema complex and two late-night supermarkets. Medical services are also available, so you can get a massage and dental cleaning with your haircut. Popular with students, as the University of Sydney is nearby.

GLEEBOOKS Map pp236-7   Books
☎ 9660 2333; 49 Glebe Point Rd, Glebe; ⏱ 9am-9pm Mon-Sun
One of Sydney's best, and frequent winner of 'bookshop of the year' awards. Great fiction and academic tomes. Children's books and used books at 191 Glebe Point Rd.

GOULD'S BOOK ARCADE
Map pp236-7   Books
☎ 9519 8947; 32 King St, Newtown; ⏱ 8am-midnight
Jam-packed with musty old out-of-print books, this is easily Newtown's largest bookstore. Sort through the stacks and piles and say hello to Bob, a living legend if ever there was one. It's also worth popping in to see the Diego Rivera–inspired mural.

SCRAGGS HOUSE OF FASHION
Map pp236-7   Clothing & Accessories
☎ 9550 4654; 551E King St, Newtown; ⏱ noon-5pm Mon-Wed & Sun, 11am-6pm Thu-Sat
Excellent 1970s and 1980s fashions for men and women, including jeans, shoes, frilly dresses, fake-fur jackets and new clothes made of vintage fabrics. Cheery service and an authentically second-hand smell make this is a fun place to dawdle.

WALKABOUT GALLERY
Map pp236-7   Indigenous
☎ 9550 9964; 70 Norton St, Leichhardt; ⏱ 10am-6pm Mon-Thu, 10am-9pm Fri & Sat, noon-6pm Sun
This friendly gallery is part of the World Vision Indigenous Programs, which means the Aboriginal artists are getting properly paid. They offer mostly wall art, along with some jewellery, ceramics and small wood statues.

CLOTHING SIZES
Measurements approximate only, try before you buy

Women's Clothing

Aus/UK	8	10	12	14	16	18
Europe	36	38	40	42	44	46
Japan	5	7	9	11	13	15
USA	6	8	10	12	14	16

Women's Shoes

Aus/USA	5	6	7	8	9	10
Europe	35	36	37	38	39	40
France only	35	36	38	39	40	42
Japan	22	23	24	25	26	27
UK	3½	4½	5½	6½	7½	8½

Men's Clothing

Aus	92	96	100	104	108	112
Europe	46	48	50	52	54	56
Japan	S		M	M		L
UK/USA	35	36	37	38	39	40

Men's Shirts (Collar Sizes)

Aus/Japan	38	39	40	41	42	43
Europe	38	39	40	41	42	43
UK/USA	15	15½	16	16½	17	17½

Men's Shoes

Aus/UK	7	8	9	10	11	12
Europe	41	42	43	44½	46	47
Japan	26	27	27½	28	29	30
USA	7½	8½	9½	10½	11½	12½

Sleeping ∎

Sleeping

Sydney has a huge variety of accommodation: you can grab some shuteye at a cheap hostel, cosy B&B, seedy motel, authentic Aussie pub or five-star luxury behemoth with breathtaking harbour views.

Exactly where you stay in Sydney will depend on your budget and holiday needs. For example, those travellers seeking hostels and party atmosphere should think about heading to Kings Cross or the beach destinations of Bondi or Manly, while those willing to spend more and wanting to be closer to tourist sights might wish to stay in The Rocks or the city centre. Areas like Chinatown and Surry Hills are still close to the centre while offering distinctive atmosphere and more culinary and transport options. So, decide what you want and read up a little on Sydney's many neighbourhoods before deciding where to settle in.

Prices are highest during the summer (December and January), and often drop for the slow winter months (June and July). Prices in this chapter reflect mostly high-season – but not peak-season (say, Christmas) – tariffs. Some hotels have many rates that vary during the year and even change with demand, so it's a good idea to call ahead and get a quote – and a reservation. After all, Sydney is a top tourist destination and you'll do well to book. This is especially crucial during Christmas and New Year.

For long-stay accommodation, peruse the 'flats to let' and 'share accommodation' ads in the **Sydney Morning Herald** (www.smh.com.au) on Wednesday and Saturday. Hostel notice boards are also good sources of information, or try these websites: www.gumtree.com.au, www.domain.com.au, www.sleepingwiththeenemy.com or www.flatmates.com.au. Keep in mind that some long-term lodgings require deposits (or bonds) and don't come furnished.

Sydney will present a parking challenge. Many hotels offer a place for your car, but some charge dearly ($15–20 per day) for it. When you make your hotel reservation ask if they offer parking, how much it costs and if you need to reserve a spot.

CITY CENTRE, THE ROCKS & CIRCULAR QUAY

If you've got the bucks and want to be right atop of the action, you'll probably choose to stay either in the historic Rocks, the thriving Central Business District (CBD) or the spectacular Circular Quay area. Many hotels here are part of international chains, such as Park Hyatt, Four Seasons and InterContinental, but there are also some charming little pubs with cosy rooms. And while really cheap accommodation isn't to be found here, there are some very worthy hostels within a stone's throw of Central Station, at the south end of the CBD.

See the boxed text, p59, for transport options to/from these areas.

AUSTRALIAN HOTEL Map pp228-9   Pub
☎ 9247 2229; www.australianheritagehotel.com; 100 Cumberland St, The Rocks; d $125
Ten sweet rooms are on offer here, some with shared bathrooms. There's a rooftop terrace (great views) and cosy communal lounge with tea- and coffee-making facilities, and breakfast is included. The highlight might just be the cool pub downstairs, however (p121).

B&B SYDNEY HARBOUR
Map pp228-9   B&B
☎ 9247 1130; www.bedandbreakfastsydney.com; 142 Cumberland St, The Rocks; s $140-220, d $155-250
Each of the nine rooms in these old, twin heritage buildings is charmingly unique, and all come with soft sheets, a full hot breakfast and relaxing moments in the leafy courtyard. The Rocks location is great,

---

TOP FIVE SLEEPS

- Best Boutique Hotel The Chelsea (p175)
- Best Penny-Pincher Big Hostel (p173)
- Best Pool Observatory Hotel (p172)
- Best Sexy Getaway Medusa (p176)
- Best Views Four Seasons (opposite)

and there's a pleasant kitchen. A couple of rooms share bathrooms.

BLACKET Map pp228-9 — Hotel
☎ 9279 3030; www.theblacket.com; 70 King St, City; d $180-305; ℗
With its sleek split-level suites, the heritage-listed Blacket is dressed to impress. The 42 spacious rooms (some with loft) come with grey and white overtones, and most sport terraces and kitchenettes. Double-bedroom apartments (sleeping four) are available, and the central location is icing on the cake.

CENTRAL PARK HOTEL
Map pp228-9 — Boutique Hotel
☎ 9283 5000; www.centralpark.com.au; 185 Castlereagh St, City; d $135-195
A jewel of a deal in the centre, with gorgeous contemporary rooms sporting dark carpeting, simple lines and great lighting. The airy lofts are even nicer, with full-wall windows, kitchenettes and slick baths. Despite the location it's fairly quiet inside. Rates can be lower during slow times (though rates rise on Saturday nights), so ask.

ESTABLISHMENT HOTEL
Map pp228-9 — Hotel
☎ 9240 3100; www.establishmenthotel.com; 5 Bridge Lane, City; d from $340
You'd never imagine these ultra-slick digs would be hidden behind an inconspicuous entrance off a dark, unwelcoming alley. You could imagine, however, secretive stars and low-key moguls slinking within the 33 silky rooms tricked out in simple modern lines

Four Seasons (right) in The Rocks

and two-colour design schemes. Beds are lined with fine cotton linen, baths are encircled in marble or limestone and two equally extravagant bars right on the premises provide a place to perch and quench your stylish thirst. If you're a celebrity go for the deluxe, split-level penthouse ($1100).

FOUR SEASONS Map pp228-9 — Hotel
☎ 9238 0000; www.fourseasons.com; 199 George St, The Rocks; d from $440; ℗
When money's no object, you stay at the Four Seasons – after all, it's considered by many to be the best hotel in Sydney. The location, next to Circular Quay and The Rocks, can't be beat, and everything you expect from a five-star hotel is at your fingertips. Views from most of its rooms are earth-shattering (city, Opera House, or harbour – take your pick), and after your luxurious spa treatments and massage you'll really be able to appreciate them.

GEORGE STREET PRIVATE HOTEL
Map pp228-9 — Hotel
☎ 9211 1800; www.thegeorge.com.au; 700A George St, City; dm $22-28, d $60-69, ste $80-90
A decent inner-city budget choice is this maze-like, no-frills place with clean dorms (no lockers) and OK doubles – all rooms share bathrooms. There's a cosy kitchen and dining area, and the place is popular with young travellers.

GRACE HOTEL Map pp228-9 — Hotel
☎ 9272 6888; www.gracehotel.com.au; 77 York St, City; d from $320; ℗
This old favourite comes with stunning Art Deco exterior and comfortable, good-sized rooms with muted earth tones and heavenly beds. Business travellers will appreciate the conference rooms and business centre, while tourists can frolic in the pool or work out in the gym. Two bars and a café help everyone mingle. Package deals and rooms with wheelchair access are available.

GRAND HOTEL Map pp228-9 — Pub
☎ 9232 3755; 30 Hunter St, Circular Quay; s/d $77-88
This well-located, heritage-listed hotel offers 19 cosy, flowery rooms above its decent pub. Each is simple but comfortable and comes with its own sink, fridge, tea- and

coffee-making facilities and TV; some have a balcony. All share bathrooms, so you'll be intimate with your fellow travellers. One family room is available for $120.

HOTEL CORONATION

Map pp228-9   Pub

☎ 9267 8362; 5 Park St, City; www.hotelcoronation.com.au; d from $109

Stocked with just 21 small, neat rooms is this well-located hotel. The street out the front is busy, but noise levels aren't bad inside and you can always get a room at the back. A few amenities like fridge, downstairs bar and nearby parking come with the deal, and for this price you couldn't ask for much more.

HYDE PARK INN

Map pp228-9   Serviced Apartments

☎ 9264 6001; www.hydeparkinn.com.au; 271 Elizabeth St, City; s/d from $155/170; P

Nicely located across from Hyde park – the higher of the floors have awesome leafy views – this pleasant hotel offers good spacious rooms with kitchenettes. Deluxe rooms come with balcony and offer the best views (and cost more). Two-bedroom apartments are available.

LORD NELSON BREWERY HOTEL

Map pp228-9   Pub

☎ 9251 4044; www.lordnelson.com.au; 19 Kent St, The Rocks; d $180

This popular swanky pub (see p121) has its own brewery and is in a historic sandstone building in a less-touristy part of The Rocks; there's also a lively restaurant on the first floor. The nine rooms are beautiful, and the one small single with shared bathroom goes for $120. Breakfast is included.

MERCANTILE HOTEL

Map pp228-9   Pub

☎ 9247 3570; www.mercantilehotel.com; 25 George St, The Rocks; s $80-110, d $110-140

This green-tiled hotel is a restored pub with a strong Irish connection. It's well located right near the Harbour Bridge and offers 15 comfortable rooms with shared bathroom; some have fridge and, for the adventurous, jets in the tub. There's also a sunny terrace, and breakfast is included.

METRO HOTEL

Map pp228-9   Hotel

☎ 9283 8088; www.metrohospitalitygroup.com; 300 Pitt St, City; d from $150; P

The location near Central Station and Chinatown is spot-on, and rooms are nice, small, well lit and neatly decorated. There's a restaurant on the premises, but nearby parking costs an extra $21 per 24 hours. Check their website for specials.

OBSERVATORY HOTEL

Map pp228-9   Boutique Hotel

☎ 9256 2226; www.observatoryhotel.com.au; 89-113 Kent St, The Rocks; d from $385; P

Gorgeous five-star rooms, some with balcony, greet you at the lovely 96-room Observatory Hotel. The wonderful indoor pool (complete with starry ceiling constellation), luxury gym and famous day spa will pamper you, and they even have real goldfish to borrow in case you get lonely. Check their website for special packages.

PALISADE HOTEL

Map pp228-9   Pub

☎ 9247 2272; www.palisadehotel.com; 35 Bettington St, The Rocks; d/tw $118/128

Standing sentinel-like at Millers Point, the Palisade Hotel has nine solidly furnished rooms, some with balcony and breathtaking views of the Harbour Bridge and all with shared bathrooms. It's a lovely old heritage building (although the carpet shows its age) in a more isolated part of the Rocks. A decent pub resides downstairs.

PARK HYATT Map pp228-9   Hotel

☎ 9241 1234; www.sydney.park.hyatt.com; 7 Hickson Rd, The Rocks; d from $585; P

Contemporary designs. Futuristic leather furniture. Flat-screen TVs. Absolutely decadent views of the harbour. Around-the-clock butler service. Superluxurious. What more is there to say?

RUSSELL Map pp228-9   Boutique Hotel

☎ 9241 3543; www.therussell.com.au; 143A George St, The Rocks; d $140-280

Located in The Rocks' main tourist drag, this charming 29-room hotel offers creaky floors, modest flowery rooms, pleasant lounge areas and a sunny roof garden. There's an intimate feel and narrow staircase (no elevator), with the cheapest rooms sharing bathrooms. Those who can't climb stairs would not be comfortable here.

SAVILLE 2 BOND ST

Map pp228-9   Serviced Apartments

☎ 1800 222 226; 2 Bond St, City; www.saville suites.com; apts from $220; **P**

Corporate clients and travelling families will appreciate the comfortable studios and one- or two-bedroom apartments on hand here. Baby-sitting is available and all the amenities, including kitchenettes and washer/dryers, are at your disposal, as are the gym, rooftop pool and lobby bar. There's even an executive women's floor, and the location is super. Call ahead for package deals.

SHANGRI-LA HOTEL

Map pp228-9   Hotel

☎ 9250 6000; www.shangri-la.com; 176 Cumberland St, The Rocks; d from $440; **P**

For those seeking unbeatable views at any cost, there's the Shangri-La. Plush rooms offer all the five-star amenities you could hope for, but it's what's out your window that really counts. Choose from city, Darling Harbour, Opera House or Grand Harbour panoramas. For more seduction, head down to the full spa for a relaxing massage, or up to level 36 to the bar and restaurant, where more luxuries and gorgeous views await. Ring them up for special deals.

STELLAR SUITES

Map pp228-9   Boutique Hotel

☎ 9264 9754; www.stellarsuites.com.au; 4 Wentworth Ave, City; d $135-360; **P**

Gorgeous, luxurious rooms in dark rich colours at this hip boutique hotel, located right near Hyde Park. All 38 modern rooms have kitchenette, telephone, safe, Internet connection and access to free movies. A three-bedroom apartment is available.

VIBE HOTEL Map pp228-9   Hotel

☎ 9282 0987; www.vibehotels.com.au; 111 Goulburn St, City; d from $185; **P**

At research time, rooms here were being remodelled in hip designs with three-colour schemes, good use of mirrors and striped quilts; hopefully the dust will have settled by the time you arrive. Important: be sure to investigate the 'vibe-out room' and nifty rooftop pool, and send us your report.

Y ON THE PARK

Map pp228-9   Hotel/Hostel

☎ 9264 2451; www.ywcansw.com.au; 5-11 Wentworth Ave, City; dm $33, s $74-118, d & tw $88-130; **P**

This secure and family-friendly YWCA hotel (men welcome) is ideally located right near Hyde Park and not too far from lively Oxford St. Rooms are clean and modern, with deluxe versions sporting safes. Four-bed dorms (no bunks!) go for $33 per person. Breakfast included; reserve ahead for parking.

Cheap Sleeps
BIG HOSTEL

Map pp232-3   Boutique Hostel/Hotel

☎ 9281 6030; www.bighostel.com; 212 Elizabeth St, City; dm $25-34, d $90

A new concept in accommodation is this 'boutique' hostel. It works, though, so expect good dorms with lockers, a hip TV lounge/kitchen area, great rooftop patio and light breakfast included. Most doubles come with private bathroom, and all rooms have TV and air-con. It's *not* a party hostel.

RAILWAY SQUARE YHA

Map pp232-3   Hostel

☎ 9281-9666; www.yha.com.au; 8-10 Lee St, City; dm $27-33, d $78-88

Housed in a former parcels shed is this tastefully renovated, railroad-themed hostel. Original cargo doors, exposed ceilings and dorms in reproduction train cars add flavour, while the spa, bathroom-floor-warmers, comfortable rooms and trendy common areas make your budget stay

The Russell (opposite)

almost luxurious. It's right next to Central Station (look for it behind the Medina building) and much more intimate than its sister YHA just down the street.

SYDNEY CENTRAL YHA

Map pp232-3   Hostel

☎ 9219 9111; www.yha.com.au; 11 Rawson Pl, City; dm $28-33, d $82-94; Ⓟ
The Cadillac of Sydney hostels, this huge heritage-listed building offers 500-plus beds, swank artsy spaces, a games room, nightly movies, all the services you'd expect (including a full-on travel agency) and even an ATM in the lobby. And don't forget the rooftop swimming pool! It's within spitting distance of Central Station and very popular so be sure to book (especially for private rooms). Wheelchair accessible.

WAKE UP!

Map pp232-3   Hostel

☎ 9288 7888; www.wakeup.com.au; 509 Pitt St, City; dm $24-33, d $88-98
Trendy backpackers flock to this large, modern and artsy hostel right near Central Station. Spiffy spaces await them (the seven floors each have a theme and colour), as do all the services they could ask for. There's a sunny café on the main floor and gloomy restaurant/bar downstairs; access to a small kitchen is also included in the price.

DARLING HARBOUR & CHINATOWN

This central and lively area is home to dozens of well-appointed hotels and serviced apartments that cater to every sort of traveller – from out-of-towners on theatre packages to working holidaymakers to upmarket business travellers. With so much competition there are often good deals available for the asking, so ask!

AARON'S HOTEL Map pp232-3   Hotel

☎ 9281 5555; www.aaronshotel.com.au; 37 Ultimo Rd, Haymarket; d from $100
In the heart of Chinatown and thus close to a plethora of good cheap food is this 94-room heritage-building hotel. Plain rooms all vary in size, but are clean and roomy; some have courtyard views. It's popular with group bookings and rates go up $10

on Friday and Saturday nights. Two rooms with wheelchair access are available.

CAPITOL SQUARE HOTEL

Map pp228-9   Hotel

☎ 9211 8633; www.rydges.com/capitolsquare; cnr George & Campbell Sts, Chinatown; d from $105
Capitol Square is a very convenient place to stay near Chinatown and Darling Harbour, especially given the good deals sometimes available. Small rooms are average and hardly plush, but some do come with balcony. Rates go up on weekends ($150) and tend to change with demand, so call ahead.

FOUR POINTS SHERATON

Map pp228-9   Hotel

☎ 9290 4000; www.fourpoints.com/sydney; 161 Sussex St, Darling Harbour; d from $380; Ⓟ
You'll know the drill as soon as you walk into the Four Points Sheraton – with a lobby as big as this, it's obviously high-class all the way. Expect typical five-star luxury, with over 600 deluxe rooms and all the amenities you can think of. Check for specials and packages as there are bound to be some. Harbour views mean skyrocketing rates, however.

GLASGOW ARMS HOTEL

Map pp228-9   Hotel

☎ 9211 2354; admin@glasgowarmshotel.com.au; 527 Harris St, Ultimo; s/d $120/135
Located just across the road from the excellent Powerhouse Museum, this pub hotel offers 10 comfortable, good-sized and flowery rooms, some with small balcony and one with kitchenette. Tea and coffee are served all day, breakfast is included and there's a great atmospheric pub downstairs.

PACIFIC INTERNATIONAL INN

Map pp232-3   Hotel

☎ 9289 4400; www.pacificinthotels.com.au; 717 George St, City; d $140-225
The 163 small, cosy rooms are comfortable but nothing special at this George St hotel; however, if you want to be close to Chinatown and Central Station the location can't be beat. Get ready to navigate the maze-like halls; a gym and business centre come included.

PENSIONE HOTEL

Map pp228-9   Boutique Hotel

☎ 9265 8888; www.pensione.com.au; 631 George St, City; d $125

A great choice in Chinatown is this hip new boutique hotel, offering stylish and tasteful rooms with minimalist décor and basic services like fridge and cable TV. Friday and Saturday nights see rates go up to $140.

VULCAN HOTEL Map pp232-3   Pub

☎ 9211 3283; www.vulcanhotel.com.au; 500 Wattle St, Ultimo; d $99-150

The location of this budget boutique hotel is a bit off-centre, but the rooms are stunning in their simple design and décor. There's charm in this heritage-listed building, and a pleasant courtyard garden might be finished by the time you read this. This place is great value – you're close enough to the city centre but without the fumes.

WYNYARD HOTEL Map pp228-9   Pub

☎ 9299 1330; www.wynyardhotel.com.au; 107 Clarence St, City; s/d $77/88

Here's a well-located pub offering twelve decent, no-frills rooms with TV, fridge, tea- and coffee-making facilities and shared bathrooms. There's kitchen access and a basic roof terrace, and family rooms are available for $120. A light breakfast is included, and laundry is free; this place is a great deal.

DARLINGHURST TO POTTS POINT

Hipster central, this is the area to hang around if you're hankering for the boutique hotel experience; as a plus, there are plenty of slick modern eateries that won't cramp your style. For a cheap and grungy room you'd head straight to Kings Cross, where dozens of basic hostels cater to what must be central Sydney's biggest backpacker population. Stick to Potts Point and Darlinghurst if you want things a touch quieter.

See the boxed text, p75, for transport options to/from these areas.

THE CHELSEA Map p235   Boutique Hotel

☎ 9380 5994; www.chelsea.citysearch.com.au; 49 Womerah Ave, Darlinghurst; s $94, d $125-195

If you're looking for a special stay, this cosy and intimate boutique hotel won't disappoint. The 13 unique, gorgeous rooms come clean and modern (four share two bathrooms), and some are graced with a balcony. Lovely patios and a residential neighbourhood offer peace, and there's a kitchen available for guest use. German spoken; breakfast included.

CREST HOTEL Map p235   Hotel

☎ 9358 2755; www.cresthotel.com.au; 111 Darlinghurst Rd, Darlinghurst; d from $130; Ⓟ

These sleeps are smack-bang in the middle of Kings Cross, so a comfy bed is just a short stagger away from the area's famous nightlife. Plenty of amenities keep corporate travellers and tourists happy, and there's the wonderful Ginseng Bathhouse (p156) on the premises. Rooms are unspectacular unless you have a harbour view.

HOTEL 59 Map p235   Hotel

☎ 9360 5900; www.hotel59.com.au; 59 Bayswater Rd, Darlinghurst; d $88-165

This small, friendly hotel in the quiet stretch of Bayswater Rd has just nine pleasant rooms, all of which vary in size. The café downstairs whips up great cooked breakfasts (included). Family rooms – some with kitchenette – are available, but call ahead.

HOTEL ALTAMONT Map p235   Hotel

☎ 9360 6000; www.altamont.com.au; 207 Darlinghurst Rd, Darlinghurst; dm $20, d $89-130

Flashy in that rustic sort of way, this modern boutique hotel offers its guests lovely rooms – some with patio – and a smart, intimate lobby strewn with leather chairs. There's a great terrace, and even cheap dorm rooms are available. Continental breakfast is included (dorm residents pay $2). A great deal, considering the surroundings, services and location. Reception open 8am to 8pm.

KIRKETON Map p235   Boutique Hotel

☎ 9332 2011; www.kirketon.com.au; 229 Darlinghurst Rd, Darlinghurst; d $140-190; Ⓟ

Yet another boutique offering in Darlinghurst, this one with equally contemporary designs, fluffy pillows, elegant muted colour scheme and mirrored hallways. Renowned restaurant Salt is next door, and there are two bars on the premises.

Sleeping   DARLINGHURST TO POTTS POINT

MAISONETTE HOTEL

Map pp228-9   Boutique Hotel

☎ 9357 3878; maisonettehotel@bigpond.com; 31 Challis Ave, Potts Point; s/d $60/95

Not a bad deal for this clean, friendly hotel, and the price gets better if you stay longer than one night. The small, bright doubles come with bathrooms, kitchenette and TV, but singles share bathrooms.

MANOR HOUSE Map pp232-3   Boutique Hotel

☎ 9380 6633; www.manorhouse.com.au; 86 Flinders St, Darlinghurst; d $160-320; Ⓟ

The location isn't ideal – right on Darlinghurst's busy Flinders Street – but once you're inside this grand 1850s Victorian mansion it won't matter. Nineteen plush and romantic rooms, including some spacious suites, are downright welcoming. There's a small indoor pool, atrium dining area, and even a conference room. Good service abounds, and breakfast is included.

MEDUSA Map p235   Boutique Hotel

☎ 9331 1000; www.medusa.com.au; 267 Darlinghurst Rd, Darlinghurst; d $270-385

This sultry 18-room boutique hotel is pure Sydney – glamorous, flashy, sexy, decadent and gay-friendly. Lose yourself in the curvaceous furniture, and enjoy the chocolates on your pillow, soft linens on your bed and Aveda toiletries in your bathroom. Design buffs will be in heaven. A lovely, sunny, fountain courtyard offers dreamy lounging.

MORGANS OF SYDNEY

Map p235   Serviced Apartments

☎ 9360 7955; www.morganshotel.com.au; 304 Victoria St, Darlinghurst; studios from $160, 1-bedroom apt from $180

Smartly located in Sydney's coffee belt are these pleasant, large, hotel-like studios and apartments, most with kitchenette. Good security, a rooftop terrace and restaurant are perks, but this place won't rock your world.

REGENTS COURT Map p235   Boutique Hotel

☎ 9358 1533; www.regentscourt.com.au; 18 Springfield Ave, Kings Cross; d $190-255; Ⓟ

A following comes back to the spacious, luxurious rooms at this family-owned place. All are bright and boast fully stocked kitchens and pleasant dining

areas. The highlight, however, is the lush and lovely rooftop garden – it's a relaxing spot in Kings Cross.

SIMPSONS OF POTTS POINT

Map pp228-9   B&B

☎ 9356 2199; www.simpsonshotel.com.au; 8 Challis Ave, Potts Point; d $215-255, ste $355; Ⓟ

Charming B&B it is, and despite the sniffy management, the plush communal areas and luxurious rooms comfort those wishing to be spoiled. Some balconies; the breakfast room is glass-topped.

VICTORIA COURT HOTEL

Map p235   Boutique Hotel

☎ 9357 3200; www.victoriacourt.com.au; 122 Victoria St, Darlinghurst; d $135-165; Ⓟ

Looking for a quiet, comfortable room with a lovely Victorian air? Try this quaint boutique hotel, where at night plush flowery-decorated beds comfort you while in the morning a breakfast buffet is served in the indoor glass-covered patio. Budgeteers should ask for the one room with unattached but private bathroom ($85).

W HOTEL SYDNEY

Map pp228-9   Hotel

☎ 9331 9000; www.whotels.com; 6 Cowper Wharf Rd, Woolloomooloo; d from $335; Ⓟ

Featuring what must be the most impressive lobby in Sydney, this lavish boutique hotel – in an old wool-processing warehouse – offers ultra-chic loft suites with stunning water views. Even standard rooms sport slick minimalist design, and surround an open central space fitted with airy bar and café. The elegant underground pool is a plus.

Cheap Sleeps
HIGHFIELD PRIVATE HOTEL

Map p235   Budget Hotel

☎ 9326 9539; www.highfieldhotel.com; 166 Victoria St, Kings Cross; s $50-65, d $65-80

A clean and welcoming hotel, owned by a Swedish family (it's a magnet to Swedes). This well-run place offers good security, simple bright rooms (shared bathrooms), 24-hour access and a spot-on location. A common lounge offers fridge and microwave.

O'MALLEY'S HOTEL Map p235   Pub

☎ 9357 2211; www.omalleyshotel.com.au; 228
William St, Darlinghurst; s/d $66/99
This friendly Irish pub comes attached to
15 traditionally decorated, well-furnished
rooms with fridge and TV; two have good
harbour views. It's a great deal (breakfast
is included) and surprisingly quiet given
its location. One room with kitchenette is
available.

ORIGINAL BACKPACKERS

Map p235   Hostel
☎ 9356 3232; www.originalbackpackers.com.au;
160-162 Victoria St, Darlinghurst; dm $25-28, d $70
Right in the centre of Kings Cross and set
in a wonderful historic mansion, this long-
running hostel offers 176 beds, friendly
staff, two small kitchens and great outdoor
spaces. It's a mazelike place where rooms
have high ceilings and fridges and all (including the doubles) share bathrooms. Free
pickup from the airport.

ROYAL SOVEREIGN HOTEL

Map p235   Pub
☎ 9331 3672; www.darlobar.com.au; cnr Liverpool
St & Darlinghurst Rd, Darlinghurst; d $77-88
Perched above one of Sydney's favourite
drinking dens, these 19 small but sharply
decorated rooms all come with TV and clean
shared bathrooms. Upper rooms are quieter
but more expensive, and come with fridge
and coffeepot. Even the hallways are nice.

SYDNEY STAR ACCOMMODATION

Map p235   Hostel
☎ 1800 134 455; stay@sydneystar.com.au; 275
Darlinghurst Rd, Darlinghurst; dm $20, s $60-85,
d $80-100
This well-located budget place is especially
great for long-term guests seeking good-
value, personable rooms with TV, fridge
and microwave (some have sinks). There's a
small kitchen and courtyard for socialising.

SURRY HILLS & EAST SYDNEY

If you're looking for the great nightlife that
Oxford St provides – as well as a greater
variety of restaurants than you can toss
your whiskey at – think about staying in
this area. You'll still be relatively close to the
centre, and the eastern beaches are just a
skip away. However, come during Sydney's
internationally famous Mardi Gras (late February to early March), and you'll need to
keep a straight face as you see prices double
(and remember to get reservations way in
advance!).

See the boxed text, p77, for transport options to/from these areas.

CITY CROWN MOTEL

Map pp232-3   Hotel
☎ 9331 2433; www.citycrownmotel.com.au; 289
Crown St, Surry Hills; d $95-115
This basic motel offers clean, simple rooms,
some with balcony or patio, that are ac-
ceptable enough, though unmemorable.
Still, you're a stone's throw from groovy
Oxford St and the city. Reserve well ahead
during Mardi Gras, when prices skyrocket.

COMFORT INN CAMBRIDGE

Map pp232-3   Hotel
☎ 9212 1111; www.cambridgeinn.com.au; 212
Riley St, Surry Hills; d $125-157
Frankly it's not a great deal, with 170 average rooms (though some do have good
views) and boring common areas. However,
it is located close to some of Surry Hills' best
eating options, and comes with amenities
like heated indoor pool, spa, sauna and gym.
Ask for a balcony – it doesn't cost more.

MEDINA ON CROWN

Map pp232-3   Hotel Apartments
☎ 9360 6666; www.medinaapartments.com.au; 359
Crown St, Surry Hills; apartments from $218; P
The comfortable one- and two-bedroom
apartments on offer here are all spacious
and come with well-stocked kitchens, so
they're great for families. Plenty of services
and a peaceful courtyard pool area might
turn Crown St into a holiday spot for you,
especially if you consider the rooftop grass
tennis court.

Cheap Sleeps

GRACELANDS Map pp232-3   Hostel

☎ 9699 1399; 461 Cleveland St, Surry Hills; dm
$22-24, d/tw $60
This intimate hostel is at the edge of Surry
Hills, but close to some of Sydney's best
(and cheapest) Indian and Lebanese cuisine. There are just 10 shared-bath rooms

available, some with balcony, and a pleasant lounge, small kitchen and outside patio provide social atmosphere. Winter rates are about 10% to 20% less, and there's a weekly discount. Internet access available.

PADDINGTON & WOOLLAHRA

Sydney's charming suburbs Paddington and Woollahra have some equally charming small hotels in tastefully renovated and maintained surrounds. Cheap options are like hen's teeth, though.

See the boxed text, p78, for transport options to/from these areas.

HUGHENDEN Map pp232-3   Boutique Hotel

☎ 9363 4863; www.hughendenhotel.com.au; 14 Queen St, Woollahra; s from $128, d from $148; P

For a change of pace stay at this old, 36-room Victorian-era house. All rooms come with en suite and TV, though the smallest rooms are a bit too tight for our taste. Go for a larger suite, preferably with balcony, and cherish your stay. It's not ultraluxurious, but pleasant enough, especially with the included hot English breakfast.

SULLIVANS HOTEL

Map pp232-3   Hotel

☎ 9361 0211; www.sullivans.com.au; 21 Oxford St, Paddington; s/d $135-150; P

Situated in an area often referred to as 'Paddinghurst', this well-managed 64-room motel has simple good rooms and a charming pool courtyard. The pricier rooms face inside, and those in front come with balcony. Wheelchair accessible; bookings essential during Mardi Gras, when gay travellers swamp the area.

HART'S HOMESTAY Map pp232-3   B&B

☎ 9380 5516; www.atn.com.au/harts; 91 Stewart St, Paddington; s $70-110, d $110-150

A great choice for those looking for something a bit more personal is this intimate B&B close to Oxford Street. Only three rooms are available, all differently sized and two sharing a bathroom. It's rather homely, with a hodge-podge of casual yet exotic decoration and a small garden patio out the back. Wonderful fruity breakfasts are included, and it's right near the Paddington markets.

EASTERN SUBURBS

Hotels of high standards are sprinkled liberally throughout the eastern suburbs, and the best can offer stunning harbour vistas. There aren't too many budget choices here.

See the boxed text, p80, for transport options to/from these areas.

DOYLES PALACE HOTEL

Map pp226-7   Pub

☎ 9337 5444; www.doyles.com.au; 1 Military Rd, Watsons Bay; d $145-420; P

Located on some of Sydney's best real estate, this renovated, top-drawer hotel offers either park or water views – guess which costs more? The best thing about this place has to be the drinking and dining empire below, which attracts hordes of both tourists and locals – especially on sunny weekends. Breakfast is included; reserve ahead.

METRO INN Map pp228-9   Hotel

☎ 9328 7977; www.metrohospitalitygroup.com; 230 New South Head Rd, Edgecliff; d $180; bus 324-327; P

Like many creatures of a certain age in this neighbourhood, the three-star Metro Inn has been getting some work done over the years. Some rooms (all neat and tidy and close to Edgecliff train station) have great views of the harbour. Prices are variable during the year so check their website.

SAVOY HOTEL Map pp226-7   Hotel

☎ 9326 1411; www.savoyhotel.com.au; 41 Knox St, Double Bay; d $190-260; P

This three-star hotel lies smack bang in Double Bay's coffee-lounge belt, which is just off busy New South Head Rd, and consequently within spitting distance of many trendy shops and services. Rooms and suites are nicely decorated and some come with balconies. There's a lovely atrium in the common lounge, which gives the whole place a friendly and relaxed feel.

EASTERN BEACHES

Sydney's eastern beaches are an irresistible attraction for many sand-, sun- and surf-seeking travellers, and they can be quickly reached via good transport from the centre. Most accommodation may seem to target rowdy backpackers, but there are plenty of midrange choices for those who want a more subdued vantage point for their ocean view. Be aware that summer is peak season, and rooms can be difficult to find.

See the boxed text, p82, for transport options to/from these areas.

BONDI BEACH B&B Map p238   B&B

☎ 9365 6522; www.bondibeach-bnb.com.au; 110 Roscoe St, Bondi; s from $100, d from $129; P
Just five immaculate (and nonsmoking) rooms, all with TV, fridge, toaster and coffeemaker, are offered by your in-house hosts and owners Nadia and Michael. Two rooms share baths, and one comes with balcony. Plus, all the good stuff in Bondi is only a few minutes' walk away. Light breakfast included; make reservations (and ask about discounts in low season).

BONDI BEACH HOMESTAY Map p238   B&B

☎ 9300 0800; www.bondibeachhomestay.com.au; 10 Forest Knoll Ave, Bondi; s $80, d $125-135; P
Those seeking a charmingly decorated home with friendly owners will find this B&B, located on a quiet residential street, one of Bondi's hidden gems. Immaculate bathrooms are shared among the four homely rooms, and comfortable common areas include a cosy living room and sunny deck. Breakfast is included, and there's a kitchen available for when you want to whip up a special meal.

COOGEE BAY BOUTIQUE HOTEL

Map p238   Pub/Hotel
☎ 9665 0000; www.coogeebayhotel.com.au; 9 Vicar St, Coogee; heritage d from $130, d from $220; P
Those seeking swank on the beach need look no further than these trendy and contemporary digs. Most rooms come with balcony, while some sport jets in the tub – and the extra $10 for an ocean view is definitely worth it. In case the price is too high, call for specials, or check out their more down-to-earth (and noisier) wing at the Coogee Bay Hotel (rooms from $130).

DIVE HOTEL Map p238   Boutique Hotel

☎ 9665 5538; www.divehotel.com.au; 234 Arden St, Coogee; d from $150; P
The 14 modern rooms at this delightful boutique hotel are wonderfully luxurious and come with kitchenette, small groovy bathroom and breakfast; those in front boast ocean views. Some of the original tile work has been preserved, and there's an elegant kitchen along with relaxing, Asian-flavoured back patio that might transport you to a tropical paradise.

HOTEL BONDI Map p238   Hotel

☎ 9130 3271; www.hotelbondi.com.au; 178 Campbell Pde, Bondi; s $75, d $110-120, ste $160-220
The beach-front, peach-coloured Hotel Bondi resembles a tasty layered cake and offers small, tidy rooms a cut above the usual pub standard. Choice front rooms have views, but note that the hotel is also home to three bars and a nightclub – if you want to avoid the action, ask for a quieter room or stay elsewhere. Prices drop from April to September.

RAVESI'S Map p238   Hotel

☎ 9365 4422; www.ravesis.com.au; cnr Campbell Pde & Hall St, Bondi; d $125-275, ste $275-450
Gorgeous and sleek easily describes the 16 contemporary rooms and two-level suites at this posh place. Large and luxurious balconies offer five-star peeps at the ocean, and the modern baths are spotless. It would be a fabulous stay for you and a romantic friend, and with the trendy bar downstairs attracting beautiful crowds you'd be stylin' with the best.

Cheap Sleeps

BONDI BEACHOUSE

Map p238   Hostel
☎ 9365 2088; www.yha.com.au; 63 Fletcher St, Bondi/Tamarama; dm $27, s/d from $60/70
Bondi's best hostel, offering clean rooms (some boasting water views), two TV lounges and an unsurpassable rooftop terrace with spa. Cheap meals, free sports equipment rentals and nightly activities also on tap. Catch bus 380 from the city or Bondi Junction and alight at the Fletcher St stop.

COOGEE BEACHSIDE

ACCOMMODATION Map p238   Budget Hotel

☎ 9315 8511; www.sydneybeachside.com.au; 178 Coogee Bay Rd, Coogee; d from $75
Here's a good option for those seeking clean and simple rooms with fridge, TV and shared bathrooms. There's a small kitchen

with counter seating, and a garden patio below. Family rooms are available ($95). Reception is open between about 8am and noon and 5pm to 8pm.

GRAND PACIFIC PRIVATE HOTEL

Map p238   Hotel

☎ 9665 6301; cnr Beach & Carr Sts, Coogee; s/d $35/45

Curt management rules at this very *un*-grand, gritty and down-and-out smelly joint. Yet that scruffy charm and those dirt-cheap prices keep the hordes coming, so reserve ahead and try to get a balcony (usually snagged up by the regulars). All rooms share bathrooms and come with TV and fridge; kitchen available.

INNER WEST

Close to the city centre, but more laid-back than the inner east, this is a great area to seek out charming B&Bs or intimate guest-houses with an emphasis on personal service. There's less noise, traffic and general bustle, along with a less touristy 'feel' – you can sit back, relax and enjoy the suburban vibe along with the locals.

See the boxed text, p83, for transport options to/from these areas.

ALISHAN INTERNATIONAL GUEST HOUSE Map pp236-7   Guesthouse

☎ 9566 4048; www.alishan.com.au; 100 Glebe Point Rd, Glebe; dm $22-33, s $88-99, d $99-115

This well-run gem is housed in an old building, offering clean rooms with character and a communal kitchen. There's also a beautiful airy balcony and nice garden in which to hang out, along with a bright dining area.

HOTEL UNILODGE Map pp236-7   Hotel

☎ 9338 5000, 1800 500 658; www.unilodge.com.au; cnr Broadway & Bay St, Glebe; s/d $130/190; P

Once you work your way through the maze-like halls, you'll find clean but unmemorable rooms with kitchenettes here. Amenities include a business centre and indoor lap pool, and nearby are plenty of cafés and the Broadway shopping centre. Future renovations might upgrade the place a notch or two, so call in case prices have changed (and ask for discounts). A separate wing houses University of Sydney students.

TRICKETTS B&B Map pp236-7   B&B

☎ 9552 1141; www.tricketts.com.au; 270 Glebe Point Rd, Glebe; s $176-190, d $198-220; P

Seven lovely rooms (each with its private bathroom) and the spacious, antique-filled common areas will make you feel right at home – if your home is a gorgeous 19th-century restored mansion. There's a great deck out the back, plenty of reading materials and your gracious host, Liz Trickett. Breakfast is included; be sure to book.

Cheap Sleeps

BALMAIN LODGE Map pp226-7   Budget Hotel

☎ 9810 3700; www.balmainlodge.com.au; 415 Darling St, Balmain; s/d $65/80; P

Located on Balmain's backbone, Darling St, this place offers capable management and clean, no-frills rooms with kitchenettes and patios. Each two rooms share a bathroom. It's popular with long-term tenants, so call ahead (reception supposedly open Monday to Friday 8am to 6pm, but good luck getting a response). Wheelchair access available.

BILLABONG GARDENS Map pp236-7   Hostel

☎ 9550 3236; www.billabonggardens.com. au; 5-11 Egan St, Newtown; dm $23-25, s $49, d $66-85; P

This brick-and-tile motel/hostel in Newtown has some pleasant common spaces along with a kitchen, cosy TV room and tiny murky pool. Most importantly, though, it's located close to hoppin' King St. This place is popular with backpackers and a good place to socialise.

GLEBE POINT YHA Map pp236-7   Hostel

☎ 9692 8418; www.yha.com.au; 262-264 Glebe Point Rd, Glebe; dm $24-28, d $68

Well run and pleasant, this large, friendly hostel offers good facilities, lots of activities and simple but clean rooms with sinks. There's a covered rooftop area with picnic tables and BBQ, which feel airier than the basement common rooms.

WATTLE HOUSE Map pp236-7   Boutique Hostel

☎ 9552 4997; www.wattlehouse.com.au; 44 Hereford St, Glebe; dm $27, d $85

Here's the homiest, most intimate hostel you could hope for – all wrapped up in a lovely Victorian house accommodating just 26 people. It's also tidy, friendly, efficient and comes with kitchen and sweet little garden. Not your party place, so expect some quiet – and be sure to call ahead (couples: reserve room 4).

NORTH SHORE

Despite the position on the 'other side' of the harbour, staying on the North Shore can often mean a quicker commute into town than one from the inner west or inner east. And the views can be ridiculously sublime.

See the boxed text, p85, for transport options to/from this area.

VIBE HOTEL Map p239   Hotel
☎ 9955 1111; www.vibehotels.com.au; 88 Alfred St S, Milsons Point; d $209-320 Mon-Thu, $140-240 Fri-Sun; P

So cool they've put out their own CD ($21.95), this slick new hotel sports 165 very stylish, contemporary rooms graced with plenty of full-length mirrors. Due to its location it's very business-oriented and offers four conference halls, a ballroom for large events and a 24-hour business centre. A pool with views is a plus.

Cheap Sleeps

GLENFERRIE LODGE Map p239   Hotel
☎ 9955 1685; www.glenferrielodge.com.au; 12A Carabella St, Kirribilli; dm $35, s from $60, d from $105

This large, beautiful old house lies on a quiet residential street and has a wonderfully grassy back garden. Basic rooms come with fridge and shared bathrooms are clean. Breakfast is included and cheap dinners are available, but there's no kitchen access. If you're staying for an extended period, ask for their discount rates. Arrive here via the Milsons Point train station or by ferry from Kirribilli wharf, and look for the white hunter statue out the front.

MANLY

Manly is a relaxing half-hour ferry ride away from the city centre, and thus a great choice if you'd rather make the beach scene than visit every museum in sight. A large share of Sydney's travellers end up here,

along with party drinkers, surfer dudes and a heap of families (especially in summer). Book ahead if you can.

See the boxed text, p88, for transport options to/from this area.

101 ADDISON ROAD Map p240   B&B
☎ 9977 6216; www.bb-manly.com; 101 Addison Rd, Manly; s/d $110/150

Only two lovely rooms are available at this sweet little B&B, and it's intimate, because both share the same bathroom. If you manage to snag a room, though, it'll be a peaceful and cosy stay. There's a large living area with piano, and your host Jill knows the area inside and out. Breakfast is included, and tea/coffee are served all day.

MANLY LODGE Map p240   Hotel
☎ 9977 8655; www.manlylodge.com.au; 22 Victoria Pde, Manly; d $135-200

Vaguely Spanish in appearance, Manly Lodge is a labyrinthine guesthouse with 28 rooms and suites, all with kitchenette and some offering private patio. It's a comfortable though not luxurious set-up and sports a spa, sauna and small, leafy patio. Family rooms are available, starting from $150.

MANLY PACIFIC SYDNEY Map p240   Hotel
☎ 9977 7666; www.accorhotels.com.au; 55 North Steyne, Manly; d from $250; P

This big hotel is across from the beach and holds claim to Manly's fanciest digs. There's a gym, business centre, spa, sauna and a real sense of seaside swank. The most expensive rooms come with balcony and ocean views; check the website for specials.

MANLY PARADISE MOTEL
Map p240   Hotel
☎ 9977 5799; www.manlyparadise.com.au; 54 North Steyne, Manly; d from $110; P

Just looking for a comfortable, bouncy bed right across from the beach? This might be the place for you, especially if you've got kids in tow (children's cots provided and the rooftop pool is a plus). Rooms come with wicker furniture and are narrow but spacious; bathrooms are downright tiny. Some rooms have partial sea views.

PERIWINKLE GUEST HOUSE

Map p240   B&B

☎ 9977 4668; www.periwinkle.citysearch.com.au;
18-19 East Esp, Manly; s from $110, d from $135; ℗
This beautifully restored Victorian house
offers eighteen pleasant, well-appointed
rooms, all with fridge and TV (and some
with stunning water views). There's a family atmosphere and shady courtyard. Cook
in the nifty kitchen, but a light breakfast is
on the house. Reserve ahead, especially on
weekends and holidays.

Cheap Sleeps
MANLY BEACH HOUSE

Map p240   Guesthouse

☎ 9977 7050; www.manlybeachhouse.com.au;
179 Pittwater Rd, Manly; s/d/t $50/70/80; ℗
Nine private rooms (that share bathrooms)
welcome couples and families looking for
an intimate and quiet Manly stay. There's
a homely front living room, small kitchen
and sunny patio. Rooms are basic but
good sized.

THE BUNKHOUSE Map p240   Hostel

☎ 9976 0472; www.bunkhouse.com.au; 35 Pine St,
Manly; dm $25, d $65
Each dorm room comes with TV, kitchenette
and bathroom, making this hostel instantly
unique. There's also a common kitchen, dining area and TV lounge, but you'll have to
walk about 300m to the beach.

GREATER SYDNEY

If staying in the heart of Sydney's overcrowded city and inner suburbs fails to ex-
cite you, there are some great options on
the city's outskirts – some with heavenly
views and bushland surrounds.

BEACHHAVEN B&B   B&B

☎ 9544 1333; www.beachhavenbnb.com.au; 13
Bundeena Dr, Bundeena; d $200; ℗
Just two lavish suites with Jacuzzi tub and
kitchenette are available at this intimate B&B
within Royal National Park. See the boxed
text, p91, for transport options. Lush tropical
grounds include plenty of patios in which
to sit back and relax. Hosts Hans and Maureen Keller live on the premises and attend
to your every need. No smoking. Kids not
catered for. Breakfast is included.

AIRPORT ACCOMMODATION
STAMFORD PLAZA SYDNEY
AIRPORT Map pp226-7   Hotel

☎ 9317 2200; www.stamford.com.au; cnr
O'Riordan & Robey Streets, Mascot; d from
$145; ℗
This comfortable and modern high-
rise hotel is a 10-minute walk from the
airport's domestic terminals or a quick
free shuttle ride from all the terminals.
Service is excellent and there's broad-
band access in many rooms. Check the
website for specials.

OLD RECTORY

Map pp226-7   Guesthouse

☎ 9559 7841; http://oldrectory.idx.com.au;
2 Samuel St, Tempe; s $50-70, d $70-80
A helpful couple manages nine basic,
comfortable rooms (most with shared
bathrooms) in this historic Tempe
house. There's a communal kitchen and
grassy lawn. Traffic (ground vehicles
and aeroplanes) is noisy at times. Free
breakfast but airport pickup is $10.

Cheap Sleeps
CRONULLA BEACHOUSE YHA   Hostel

☎ 9527 7772; www.cronullabeachyha.com; Level
1, 40 Kingsway, Cronulla; dm $25, d/tw $70; ℗
This friendly and intimate hostel offers 48
beds. Facilities are comfy and well maintained, with a cheery vibe. It's a great place
to join others doing the 26km coastal walk
or get your surfing skills up. Catch the train
to Cronulla Station, and walk left until you
reach Kingsway. Wheelchair accessible.

PITTWATER YHA   Hostel

☎ 9999 5748; www.yha.com.au; Ku-ring-gai
National Park via Church Point; dm $23, d/tw $60
This idyllic, beautifully situated hostel,
south of the Basin, is noted for its friendly
wildlife and considerate management.
Book ahead and bring food; reception's
open from 8am to 11am and from 5pm to
8pm. To get here, take bus 156 from Manly
Wharf to Church Point, then the ferry from
Church Point to Halls Wharf – then it's a 10-
minute uphill walk but it's definitely worth
the effort.

Excursions

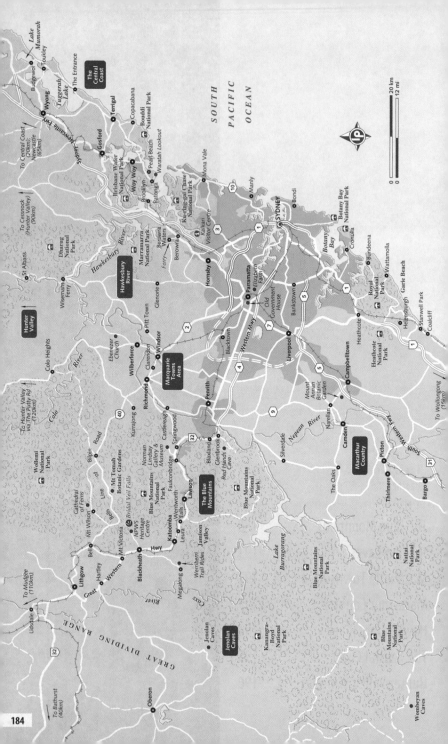

Excursions

If you can manage to tear yourself away from beautiful Sydney, you'll find a treasure trove of day trips just outside the city's outskirts.

Sydney sprawls over a coastal plain, hemmed in by rugged country on three sides and by the Tasman Sea on the fourth. Nearly 25% of Australia's population lives within 150km of Sydney, but despite the sprawl there are still many historic small towns, stunning waterways, uncrowded beaches, superb national parks and vast tracts of forest that haven't become overrun with people. These destinations' proximity to Sydney also means that public transport is pretty good, so day trips are feasible even without a car.

Whether you're hankering for a wine-coloured getaway, a solid dose of sunny surf beaches, a crawl though a limestone cave, a wilderness walkabout or some beautiful colonial architecture, Sydney's day trips offer plenty of rewarding sights, sounds and smells.

NATURE
There are various great options for those needing a nature experience. If time and transport options are tight, the perennial favourite for Sydneysiders and visitors alike is the **Blue Mountains** (p186), with good transport connections, a wealth of tour options and some of the most magnificent scenery in Australia. There are also plenty of accommodation and dining options for any budget. A popular side-trip is a visit to the awe-inspiring grottoes of **Jenolan Caves** (p191). If you prefer serene waterways, then Sydney's stunning **Hawkesbury River** (p194) offers small townships with local charm, along with the chance to sleep on a houseboat.

DRIVING
Bells Line of Rd (p190) is one of the most delightful drives in New South Wales (NSW). It winds its way up through the charming historic township of Richmond, passing through the delightfully enchanting hamlets of Kurrajong Heights and Bilpin. The route is particularly appealing at sunrise and sunset in autumn, and the boxes of orchard-fresh fruit are not to be missed.

Vineyard in the Hunter Valley (p196)

TOWNS

Quaint colonial towns such as **Richmond** (p192) and **Windsor** (p192) can be enjoyed at the western reaches of the Hawkesbury River in the Macquarie towns area. Make every effort to see the **Rouse Hill Estate** (p192) if you fancy soaking up some fascinating local history. The historic site of **Hartley** (p189) has all the right ingredients for a ghost town, but no ghost – as far as we can tell. The towns of the Blue Mountains, past Leura, also offer some pleasant architectural and atmospheric diversions, especially **Katoomba** (p189) and **Mt Victoria** (p189).

BEACHES

The **Central Coast** (p195) is sun, sand, surf and services in one glorious coastal swathe. You can reach most destinations in a day, with good train links between Sydney and Gosford, but an overnight or weekend trip will let you squeeze the most out of the sunshine and surf.

WINE

Hunter Valley reds are famous, and justifiably so. We've included the **Hunter Valley Wineries** (p196) here as a day trip, although the region is a 2½-hour drive from Sydney so overnight stays make more sense – this way, you can really take advantage of the cellar-door tastings and charming scenery. And while there's not a winery option in **Macarthur Country** (p193), you'd be mad not to sample a bottle of beer from the wonderful **George IV Inn** (p193) at Picton.

THE BLUE MOUNTAINS

The Blue Mountains, part of the Great Dividing Range, offer some truly fantastic scenery, excellent bushwalks and gorges, gumtrees and breathtaking cliffs. The foothills begin 65km inland from Sydney and rise up to 1100m, but the mountains are really a sandstone plateau riddled with spectacular gullies that have been formed by erosion over millennia. The blue haze, which gave the mountains their name, is actually a fine mist of evaporated eucalyptus oil from the gumtrees.

For more than a century the area has been a popular getaway for Sydneysiders seeking to escape the summer heat, experience a bit of a winter wonderland, or simply retreat to a bedroom with gorgeous views of the surrounding national parks. Despite intensive tourist development, much of the area is so precipitous that it's still open only to bushwalkers.

Be prepared for the climatic difference between the Blue Mountains and the coast: you can swelter in Sydney but shiver in Katoomba. Autumn's mists and drizzle can make bushwalking a less attractive option. In winter the days are often clear, and in the valleys it can be almost warm. There is usually some snowfall between June and August, and the region has a Yulefest in July, when many restaurants and guesthouses offer 'Christmas' dinners.

The first Europeans to explore found evidence of extensive Aboriginal occupation, but few Aborigines. Probably, catastrophic European-introduced diseases had spread from Sydney to this region long before.

The first white crossing of the mountains was made in 1813 by Gregory Blaxland,

TRAVEL TIP

Sit on the left-hand side of the train going from Sydney to the Blue Mountains, as the views are better than on the right-hand side.

TRANSPORT

Distance from Sydney to Katoomba 109km

Direction West

Travel time 2hrs

Car Take Parramatta Rd and detour onto the Western Motorway tollway (M4; $2.30) at Strathfield. West of Penrith, the motorway becomes the Great Western Hwy, and continues to Lithgow.

Train These run approximately hourly from Central Station. The trip takes two hours ($11.40) to Katoomba, and there are stops at plenty of Blue Mountains townships on the way. Services run roughly hourly between stations east of Katoomba and roughly two-hourly between stations to the west.

Excursions

THE BLUE MOUNTAINS

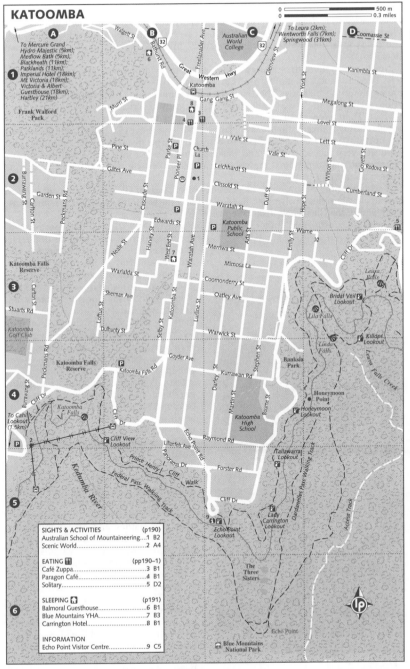

KATOOMBA

0 _____ 500 m
0 _____ 0.3 miles

SIGHTS & ACTIVITIES (p190)
Australian School of Mountaineering...1 B2
Scenic World.................................2 A4

EATING (pp190–1)
Café Zuppa.....................................3 B1
Paragon Café..................................4 B1
Solitary..5 D2

SLEEPING (p191)
Balmoral Guesthouse.......................6 B1
Blue Mountains YHA........................7 B3
Carrington Hotel.............................8 B1

INFORMATION
Echo Point Visitor Centre.................9 C5

William C Wentworth and William Lawson. They followed the mountain ridges and their route was pretty much the same as today's Great Western Hwy.

The Blue Mountains National Park protects large areas to the north and south of the Great Western Hwy. It's the most popular and accessible of the national parks in the area, and offers great bushwalking, scenic lookouts, breathtaking waterfalls and Aboriginal stencils.

North and south of the highway's ridge, the country drops away into precipitous valleys. There is a succession of turn-offs to waterfalls, lookout points and scenic alternative routes along the highway. The roads across the mountains offer tantalising glimpses of the majesty of the area, but the only way to really experience the Blue Mountains is on foot. There are walks lasting from a few minutes to several days, and the two most popular bushwalking destinations are Jamison Valley, south of Katoomba, and Grose Valley, northeast of Katoomba and east of Blackheath. The area south of Glenbrook is also good. It's very rugged country and walkers sometimes get lost, so it's highly advisable to get reliable information at the visitor centres, not to walk alone, and to tell someone where you're going.

A section of the Blue Mountains National Park, south of Glenbrook, contains **Red Hand Cave,** an old Aboriginal shelter with hand stencils on the walls. It's an easy 7km return walk, southwest of the Glenbrook Visitor Centre.

The famous artist and author Norman Lindsay (1879-1969) lived 6km northeast of

Springwood from 1912 until his death. His home is now the **Norman Lindsay Gallery & Museum** and houses many of his risqué paintings, cartoons, illustrations and sculptures. The grounds are well worth a wander.

Just south of the town of **Wentworth Falls,** heading west along the Great Western Hwy, there are great views of the Jamison Valley. You can see the spectacular 300m-high Wentworth Falls from Falls Reserve, which is also the starting point for a network of walking tracks.

Leura, 3km east of Katoomba, is a quaint tree-lined town full of country stores and cafés and home to some of Australia's most beautiful gardens. The **Leuralla Gardens Toy and Railway Museum** is an Art Deco mansion, housing a fine collection of 19th-century Australian art, as well as a toy and model-railway museum. The historic house, set in five hectares of lovely gardens, is a memorial to HV 'Doc' Evatt, a former Labor Party leader and first president of the UN. There's also a nice lookout across the road, with two statues and an amphitheatre. Nearby is the **Everglades Garden,** a magnificent 1930s garden created by Danish 'Master Gardener' Paul Sorenson, with terraces, stone walls, gnarled banksias, waterfalls, grottoes and dramatic views over Jamison Valley. This is a gardener's dream.

Sublime Point, south of Leura, is a great clifftop lookout. Nearby, **Gordon Falls Reserve** is a popular picnic spot, and from here you can take the clifftop path or Cliff Dr 4km west past Leura Cascades to Katoomba's Echo Point, where there is a visitors centre and

The Three Sisters (opposite)

HARTLEY HISTORIC SITE

About 11km west of Mt Victoria, on the western slopes of the Great Dividing Range, is the tiny, sandstone 'ghost' town of **Hartley**, which flourished from the 1830s but declined when it was bypassed by the railway in 1887. There are several buildings of historic interest, including the 1837 Greek Revival **courthouse** (adult $4.40; tours at 10am, 11am, noon, 2pm, 3pm).

There is a **National Parks & Wildlife Service (NPWS) Information Centre** (☎ 6355 2117; 10am-1pm & 2-4.20pm) in the Farmer's Inn (1845). You can wander around the village for free, but to enter the courthouse you must book a tour (minimum four people); call the visitors centre for information. CountryLink buses meet trains at Mt Victoria station on Tuesday and Friday (both at 10.45am) and Sunday (4.25pm) for the run to Hartley – your own transport is a far better option.

Collits' Inn (☎ 6355 2072; www.collitsinn.com.au; Hartley Vale Rd, Hartley Vale; doubles from $160) is a beautifully renovated 1823 inn, where you'll find elegant rooms and cottages, along with excellent French-influenced food. Dinner is the only meal served; reservations are essential. Follow the signs off the Great Western Hwy, along a rough unpaved road (you'll need a vehicle with decent suspension).

the Blue Mountains' most popular sight: the **Three Sisters,** a trio of rocky pinnacles that draw gasps and launch a thousand photographs. They look particularly attractive when floodlit at night.

Katoomba and the adjacent centres of Wentworth Falls and Leura form the tourist centre of the Blue Mountains. Despite the number of visitors and its proximity to Sydney, **Katoomba** retains an otherworldly ambience, an atmosphere accentuated by its Art Deco guesthouses and cafés, its thick mists and occasional snowfalls. A New Age scene has also developed, mixing peaceably with a strong born-again-Christian scene. Steep Katoomba St is the main drag and there are several companies in town, such as the **Australian School of Mountaineering,** that offer rock climbing, abseiling, canyoning and caving adventure activities.

To the west of Echo Point Lookout, at the junction of Cliff Dr and Violet St, is **Scenic World,** which includes a railway, skyway and flyway (both cable cars). All offer breathtaking views from breathtaking heights; nearby eateries offer excellent views. The railway runs to the bottom of the Jamison Valley, where the popular six-hour walk to the **Ruined Castle** rock formation begins. The railway was built in the 1880s to transport coal miners and its 45-degree incline is one of the steepest in the world. The skyway is a cable car that traverses Katoomba Falls gorge 200m above the valley floor. There's also the flyway, an enclosed wheelchair-accessible cable car.

Past Katoomba lies the little town of Blackheath, a good base for visiting the Grose and Megalong valleys. Superb lookouts east of town include **Govetts Leap** (named after a 'daring bushranger'), the adjacent **Bridal Veil Falls** (the highest in the Blue Mountains) and **Evans Lookout** (turn off the highway just south of Blackheath). Northeast of the town, via Hat Hill Rd, are **Pulpit Rock, Perrys Lookdown** and **Anvil Rock**. A long cliff-edge track leads from Govetts Leap to Pulpit Rock and there are walks down into the Grose Valley itself. Perrys Lookdown is at the beginning of the shortest route to the beautiful **Blue Gum Forest** in the bottom of the valley – about four hours return, but you'll want to linger longer.

Details of walks are available from the **Blue Mountains Heritage Centre,** located on Govetts Leap Rd about 3km off the Great Western Hwy. The centre also has an interesting interpretative display on the natural environment and cultural heritage of the Blue Mountains.

Megalong Valley, south of Blackheath, is largely cleared farmland but it's still a beautiful place, with awesome sandstone escarpments. The road down from Blackheath passes through pockets of rainforest and you can walk the beautiful 600m **Coachwood Glen Nature Trail.** A couple of kilometres further on is the small valley settlement of Werriberri, where there are several horse-riding outfits. **Werriberri Trail Rides** can show you the area on a guided horseback ride and, best of all, the horses are well looked after. From Blackheath, it's a 15-minute winding drive into the Megalong Valley via Shipley and Megalong Rds.

Mt Victoria, the highest point in the mountains, is a small, sweet village with a semi-rural atmosphere 16km northwest of Katoomba on the Great Western Hwy.

Excursions

THE BLUE MOUNTAINS

The charming **Mt Vic Flicks** is a cinema of the old school, with a small candy bar, real cups of tea and the occasional piano player.

Sights & Information

Australian School of Mountaineering (ASM; Map p187; ☎ 4782 2014; www.asmguides.com; 166 Katoomba St, Katoomba)

Blue Mountains Heritage Centre (☎ 4787 8877; www.bluemountainstourism.org.au; Govetts Leap Rd, Blackheath; ☻ 9am-4.30pm)

Echo Point Visitor Centre (Map p187; ☎ 1300 653 408; www.bluemountainstourism.org.au; Katoomba; ☻ 9am-5pm; wheelchair access)

Everglades Garden (☎ 4784 1938; 37 Everglades Ave, Leura; adult/child $6/2; ☻ 10am-5pm spring/summer, 10pm-4pm autumn/winter)

Glenbrook Visitor Centre (☎ 1300 653 408; www.bluemountainstourism.org.au; Great Western Hwy; ☻ 9am-5pm Mon-Fri, 8.30am-4.30pm Sat & Sun)

Leuralla Gardens Toy and Railway Museum (☎ 4784 1169; 36 Olympian Pde, Leura; museum & garden adult/child $10/5, garden only $6/3; ☻ 10am-5pm)

Mt Vic Flicks (☎ 4787 1577; Harley Ave; admission $10)

Norman Lindsay Gallery & Museum (☎ 4751 1067; www.hermes.net.au/nlg; 14 Norman Lindsay Crescent, Faulconbridge; adult/child $9/4; ☻ 10am-4pm)

NPWS Centre (☎ 4787 8877; www.nationalparks.nsw.gov.au; Govetts Leap Rd, Blackheath; ☻ 9am-4.30pm)

Scenic World (Map p187; ☎ 4782 2699; www.scenicworld.com.au; each of the three rides roundtrip adult/child/family $14/7/35; ☻ 9am-5pm)

Werriberri Trail Rides (☎ 4787 9171; horse@lisp.com.au; Megalong Rd; rides per hour/day from $40/180)

Eating

Stock Market Café (☎ 4784 3121; 179 The Mall, Leura; ☻ 8am-4.30pm Mon-Fri, 8am-4pm Sat & Sun) A tiny eatery with the best coffee in town and a great range of tasty, affordable snacks, salads, sandwiches and gourmet pies.

Café Zuppa (Map p187; ☎ 4782 9247; 36 Katoomba St, Katoomba; mains $12-20; ☻ breakfast, lunch & dinner) Chalkboard specials proclaim house specialities: burgers, pizza, pasta and sandwiches. Casual, quirky and boasting creaky wood floors, bustling service and good food (breakfasts are delicious).

Leura Gourmet (☎ 4784 1438; 159 The Mall, Leura; mains $3.50-15.50; ☻ 8am-5pm) A great deli/café in which to unwind while you ogle a selection of foodstuffs for an upmarket picnic lunch. Fabulous breakfasts, and lovely views out the back.

Paragon Café (Map p187; ☎ 4782 2928; 65 Katoomba St, Katoomba; mains $15-22; ☻ breakfast, lunch & dinner) Katoomba's undisputed Art Deco masterpiece. Settle in at a dark wood booth and order a sandwich, *frittata*, salad or meat pie – or just pop in for coffee and dessert. Check out the cocktail bar out the back.

DETOUR: THE BELLS LINE OF ROAD

Quieter and much more scenic (and less congested) than the Great Western Hwy, this is a more northerly route between Sydney and the Blue Mountains. The road, constructed in 1841, runs from near Richmond across the mountains to Lithgow. It's recommended if you have your own transport; you can cut across to join the Great Western Hwy near Mt Victoria. There are fine views towards the coast from Kurrajong Heights on the eastern slopes of the range, orchards around Bilpin, and sandstone cliff and bush scenery all the way to Lithgow. The Bells Line of Rd is flanked by bush, small farms and apple orchards, with abundant, affordable fruit stalls.

Midway between Bilpin and Bell, the delightful **Mt Tomah Botanic Gardens** (☎ 4567 2154; www.rbgsyd.nsw.gov.au; adult/child & concession/family $4.40/2.20/8.80; ☻ 10am-4pm Mar-Sep, 10am-5pm Oct-Feb) is a cool-climate annexe of Sydney's Royal Botanic Gardens. As well as native plants there are displays of exotic species, including some magnificent rhododendrons. The views from the deck of the visitors centre are fabulous; it's a great place to sip an espresso from the café. Parts of the gardens are wheelchair accessible.

North of Bells Line of Rd, near the gorgeous little town of **Mt Wilson**, is a remnant of rainforest known as the **Cathedral of Ferns**. Settled by people with a penchant for recreating England, the town itself is a tiny, beautiful village of hedgerows, large gardens and rows of European trees, and is particularly lovely in autumn. Near the Post House there's an information board with details of public gardens and some short walks in the area. The township is 8km north of the Bells Line of Rd; the turn-off is 7km east of Bell.

Wollemi National Park, north of Bells Line of Rd, is the state's largest forested wilderness area (nearly 500,000 hectares). It stretches as far as Denman in the Hunter Valley, and has good rugged bushwalking and lots of wildlife. Access is limited and the park's centre is so isolated that a new species of tree, named the Wollemi pine, was discovered only in 1994. A more recent and equally thrilling discovery was the July 2003 find of a veritable gallery of Aboriginal rock art, dating back 4000 years.

Solitary (Map p187; ☎ 4782 1164; 90 Cliff Dr, Leura Falls; mains $26-32; ☺ breakfast & lunch Mon-Sun, dinner Wed-Sun) Awesomely located, this elegant restaurant offers goats' cheese and herb salad or linguine with roasted tomatoes for lunch, while dinner means quail with pancetta, lamb with sweet potato or asparagus ravioli. Breakfast available; make a reservation for dinner.

Sleeping

Balmoral Guesthouse (Map p187; ☎ 4782 2264; www .balmoralhouse.com.au; 196 Bathurst Rd, Katoomba; d from $110 Sun-Thu, from $125 Fri, Sat, & Sun where Mon is a public holiday) This historic guesthouse has attractive period details, charming rooms (some with wraparound veranda) and lushly overgrown gardens. In winter it's kept cosy with a log fire, and you'll find an electric blanket in your bed.

Blue Mountains YHA (Map p187; ☎ 4782 1416; www .yha.com.au; 207 Katoomba St, Katoomba; dm $26-32, d/ tw $72-80; ℗) An excellent hostel in a heritage-listed building, complete with hip lounge areas in an old dance hall. The sunny terrace with fountain is a major plus. Plenty of services including area tours and activities.

Carrington Hotel (Map p187; ☎ 4782 1111; www.the carrington.com.au; 15-47 Katoomba St, Katoomba; d from $170 Sun-Thu, from $190 Fri & Sat; ℗) This gorgeous heritage-listed hotel has maintained its lavish old style, yet luxurious spa services are also available. Budget rooms with shared bath cost $119-139.

Imperial Hotel (☎ 4787 1878; www.bluemts.com. au/hotelimperial; 1 Station St, Mt Victoria; dm $89, d $125-259) This fine old hotel faces the highway and quiet Station St, and the public bar is pretty good for a

TRANSPORT

Distance from Sydney to Jenolan Caves 190km

Direction West

Travel Time 45min by car from Hartley

Car Turn off the Great Western Hwy at Hartley – the caves are on Jenolan Caves Rd.

Tours The caves are on plenty of tour itineraries available from Sydney or Katoomba.

Walk The Six Foot Track from Katoomba to Jenolan Caves is a fairly easy three-day walk, but make sure you get information from an NPWS visitors centre.

beer or a feed. Accommodation varies from pub-style dorms to heritage rooms with en suite.

Mercure Grand Hydro Majestic (☎ 4788 1002; www .hydromajestic.com.au; Great Western Hwy, Medlow Bath; d from $155) A massive relic of an earlier era (complete with croquet lawn); the more expensive suites ($830-1030) have incredible valley views.

Parklands (☎ 4787 7771; www.parklands-cgl.com.au; Govetts Leap Rd, Blackheath; s/d from $225) A luxurious estate, set about 1km off the Great Western Hwy in some of the loveliest gardens in the Blue Mountains.

Victoria & Albert Guesthouse (☎ 4787 1241; 19 Station St, Mt Victoria; d $140) This lovely and comfortable guesthouse (1914) comes in the grand old style, with upgrades of pool, sauna and spa. It also has cheaper, non-en suite rooms, and a good restaurant.

JENOLAN CAVES

Southwest of Katoomba on the western fringe of **Kanangra Boyd National Park**, **Jenolan** (jeh-*noh*-lan) has the largest publicly accessible network of caves in the world and is well worth a visit. First called *Binoomea* or 'Dark Places' by the Aborigines, the system was formed more than 400 million years ago. One cave has been open to the public since 1860, and eight more are open today, offering a huge variety of stunningly beautiful limestone formations; cave snobs will not be disappointed. Another 300 or so 'rooms' are not publicly accessible. A variety of top-notch guided tours are available, lasting from two to eight hours and including adventure tours, abseiling and spelunking as well as the more sedate kind. It's advisable to book ahead during holiday periods to get the tour you want.

Sights & Information

Jenolan Caves (☎ 6359 3911; www.jenolancaves.org.au; ☺ tours 9.45am-5pm Mon-Fri, 9.30am-5pm Sat & Sun, ghost tour 8pm Sat; adult/child/family per tour $16/10/39)

Eating & Sleeping

Jenolan Caves Cottages (☎ 6359 3311; www .bluemountainstourism.org.au; cottages per 6-8 people

Mon-Thu $89, Fri-Sun $121) These fully self-contained cottages, set in a 2416-hectare reserve, have beautiful views. The main complex is 8km before the caves, but the 1930s Bellbird Cottage is a short stroll from the caves and a lake. No wheelchair access.

Jenolan Caves Resort (☎ 6359 3322; www.jenolan caves.com; GateHouse $90-120, Mountain Lodge Units $210-480, Caves House $165-490) You can't get closer to the cave entrance than this comfortable choice. Prices can vary widely depending on the dates of your stay, so check the website for details. Dating from 1889, this is an atmospheric place to bed down.

Jenolan Cabins (☎ 6335 6239; www.bluemountain stourism.org.au; 42 Edith Rd, Jenolan Caves; d Fri-Sun $98,

Mon-Thu $105) Five kilometres beyond the caves, these comfortably furnished, fully self-contained cottages have log fires and sweeping views of the surrounding national parks. One has wheelchair access and all are subject to visits from the resident wallaby population.

MACQUARIE TOWNS AREA

Windsor, Richmond, Castlereagh, Wilberforce and Pitt Town are the five 'Macquarie Towns' established by Governor Lachlan Macquarie in 1810 on green, fertile agricultural land along the upper Hawkesbury River.

Windsor has some fine old buildings, notably those around the picturesque Thompson Square on the banks of the Hawkesbury River. The **Hawkesbury Museum & Tourist Centre** is in a building that dates from the 1820s and was used as the Daniel O'Connell Inn during the 1840s. There are a variety of displays in the museum.

The **Macquarie Arms Hotel** (1815) has a nice veranda fronting the square and claims (along with some others) to be the oldest pub in Australia. Windsor's other old buildings include the convict-built **St Matthew's Church** (1820), designed – like the **Old Windsor Courthouse** (1822) – by colonial Sydney's greatest architect, Francis Greenway. On Sundays, check out the **Windsor Mall Craft Markets** for more Australiana than you can stand.

A fascinating site in the area is **Rouse Hill Estate**, 15km southeast of Windsor on Guntawong Rd just off Windsor Rd. The historical land was owned and occupied by the same family for almost 200 years. The estate is a wonderful, unspoiled time capsule, unsullied by mass tourism and well worth a stop. Bookings and guided tours are compulsory.

The next largest of the Macquarie towns is **Richmond**, 6km west of Windsor, at the end of the CityRail line and at the start of the Bells Line of Rd that crosses the Blue Mountains. The township dates from 1811 and has some fine Georgian and Victorian buildings around a pleasant village green–like park. These include the **courthouse** and **police station** on Windsor St, and, around the corner on Market St, **St Andrew's Church** (1845). A number of pioneers are buried in the cemetery at **St Peter's Church** (1841).

The pretty **Ebenezer Church** (1809), 5km north of Wilberforce, is said to be the oldest church in Australia still used as a place of worship.

Sights & Information

Cattai National Park (☎ 4572 3100; Wisemans Ferry Rd, Pitt Town)

Ebenezer Church (☎ 4579 9350; Coromandel Rd, Ebenezer; 10am-3.30pm, service 8am Sun)

Hawkesbury Museum & Tourist Centre (☎ 4577 2310; 7 Thompson Sq, Windsor; adult/child $2.50/0.50; 10am-4pm)

Hawkesbury Visitor Centre (☎ 4588 5895; Bicentennial Park, Ham Common, Windsor Rd, Clarendon; 9am-5pm Mon-Fri, 10am-3pm Sat, 10am-2pm Sun) Across from the Richmond Royal Australian Air Force (RAAF) base, this is the main information centre for the upper Hawkesbury area and is immensely helpful.

NPWS Office (☎ 4588 5247; Bowmans Cottage, 370 George St, Richmond; 9am-12.30pm & 1.30-4pm Mon-Fri) Information about national park facilities in the region.

Old Windsor Courthouse (cnr Pitt & Court Sts, Windsor)

Rouse Hill Estate (☎ 9627 6777; www.hht.net.au; Guntawong Rd, Rouse Hill; adult/concession/family $7/3/17; 10am-2pm Wed, Thu & Sun by guided tour only)

St Matthew's Church (☎ 4577 3193; Moses St, Windsor)

Windsor Mall Craft Markets (☎ 0418 869 685; George St Mall, Windsor; 9am-4pm Sun)

TRANSPORT

Distance from Sydney to Windsor 60km

Direction Northwest

Travel time 1hr 15min

Car Heading to Windsor from Sydney is Windsor Rd (Route 40), the northwestern continuation of Parramatta's Church St. In some parts Route 40 is also called the M2, which starts at Sydney Harbour Bridge and runs through Lane Cove in Sydney's northwestern suburbs all the way to Windsor; it costs $3.80 to use. To go via Penrith, head north on the Northern Rd (also called the M9).

Train CityRail trains run from Sydney to Windsor ($6) and Richmond ($6.60).

Eating & Sleeping

Harvest Restaurant (☎ 4577 4222; 61 Richmond Rd, Windsor; mains $25-30) Fireside dining in the Sebel Resort & Spa, with hearty, yet special, meals and a great wine list.

Macquarie Arms Hotel (☎ 4577 2206; 99 George St, Windsor) Enormous pub meals for protein and carbohydrate lovers.

Sebel Resort & Spa Hawkesbury (☎ 4577 4222; www.mirvachotels.com.au; 61 Richmond Rd, Windsor; d from $180) A lovely escape from the city and even from the area, with all plush mod cons and great service.

Windsor Terrace Motel (☎ 4577 5999; 47 George St, Windsor; d from $89) A handy, well-equipped spot.

MACARTHUR COUNTRY

The Hume Hwy (South Western Fwy) heads southwest from Sydney, flanked by the rugged Blue Mountains National Park to the west and the coastal escarpment to the east. This cleared and rolling sheep country has some of the state's oldest towns, although many have been swallowed by Sydney's ever-expanding suburban sprawl. For a more rural vista than the freeway allows, take the **Northern Rd** between Penrith and Narellan (just to the north of Camden).

Liverpool and, 20km further south, **Campbelltown** are unattractive outer suburbs of Sydney, though both do have some interesting old buildings.

Camden is promoted as the 'birthplace of the nation's wealth' because it was here that John and Elizabeth Macarthur conducted the sheep-breeding experiments that laid the foundation for Australia's wool industry. Their house, the oldest surviving home in the country, is open for tours at **Elizabeth Farm** (p92). Camden is on the urban fringe, 50km southwest of the city centre, off the Hume Hwy. **John Oxley Cottage**, a historic house on the town's northern outskirts, contains the Camden visitor centre, which has information on the area's attractions.

Midway between Camden and Campbelltown, the 400-hectare **Mt Annan Botanic Garden** is the native-plant garden of Sydney's Royal Botanic Gardens. The garden displays over 4000 species set among hills and lakes.

South of Camden is the more rural, pretty **Picton**, an old village that was originally called Stonequarry. The first-rate Wollondilly Visitor Information Centre is located in Picton's old post office, with mountains of brochures in the Macarthur Country area and around NSW.

A number of historic buildings still stand in Picton; among them are the **train station** and the **George IV Inn** (1839). The inn has a great local vibe (refreshingly, there are no pokies), brews its own Bavarian-style beer in plain view and provides modest accommodation. Picton's **Menangle St West** is listed by the National Trust and worth a wander; along this street you'll find the sandstone **St Mark's Church** and the **Pioneer Cemetery** (1850). Take a stroll around the old graves belonging to the town's early settlers.

Sights & Information

John Oxley Cottage (☎ 4658 1370; Camden Valley Way, Elderslie; ☷ 9.30am-4pm)

Mt Annan Botanic Garden (☎ 4648 2477; Mt Annan Dr, Mt Annan; adult/child/family $4.40/2.20/8.80; ☷ 10am-6pm Oct-Mar, 10am-4pm Apr-Sep) Picturesque gardens; wheelchair accessible. Guided-tour bookings essential.

Wollondilly Visitor Information Centre (☎ 4677 3962; cnr Argyle & Menangle Sts, Picton; ☷ 9am-5pm)

Sleeping & Eating

George IV Inn (☎ 4677 1415; 180 Old Hume Hwy/Argyle St, Picton; d/tr/f $50/55/66) Food as well as accommodation.

TRANSPORT

Distance from Sydney to Camden 50km

Direction Southwest

Travel Time 1hr

Car From Sydney take Parramatta Rd and turn south onto the Hume Hwy (called Route 31, the M5 or the South Western Fwy at various stages). The Narellan Rd exit on the Hume Hwy runs west to Camden and east to Campbelltown. Alternatively, take the Camden Valley Way (Route 89) as it forks off the Hume Hwy south of Liverpool. For Mt Annan Botanic Garden, take Narellan Rd (Tourist Drive 18) off the Hume Hwy. To reach Picton, stay on the Hume Hwy past Campbelltown and turn off at the Picton exit. From Camden or Narellan, head south on Remembrance Dve (Tourist Drive 12).

Bus Take the **Busways** (☎ 4655 7501) service 895 or 896 from Campbelltown station to Mt Annan Botanic Garden.

Train CityRail trains stop at Liverpool, Campbelltown and Picton. For Mt Annan Botanic Garden get off at Campbelltown.

HAWKESBURY RIVER

This mighty river enters the sea 30km north of Sydney at Broken Bay, shortly after it passes the town of Brooklyn. The Hawkesbury is dotted with coves, beaches and picnic spots, making it one of Australia's most attractive rivers. Much of its lower reaches is lined with mangrove. Before hitting the ocean, the river expands into bays and inlets such as Berowra Creek, Cowan Creek and Pittwater on the southern side, and Brisbane Water on the northern side. The river flows between a succession of national parks – Marramarra and **Ku-ring-gai Chase** (see p89) to the south; and Dharug, Brisbane Water and Bouddi to the north. The town of Windsor is about 120km upstream.

A great way to get a feel for the river is to catch the **Riverboat Postman**. This mail boat does a 40km round trip on weekdays, running upstream as far as Marlow, near Spencer. There are also coffee cruises and all-day cruises (bookings recommended).

The settlements along the river have their own distinct character. Life in **Brooklyn** revolves totally around boats and the river. The town is on the Sydney-Newcastle railway line, just east of the Pacific Hwy. **Berowra Waters** is a quaint community further upstream, clustered around a free 24-hour winch ferry that crosses Berowra Creek. There are a couple of cafés overlooking the water, and a marina where you can hire an outboard boat for about $65 for a half-day. Berowra Waters is 5km west of the Pacific Hwy; there's a train station at Berowra, but it's a 7km hike down a very narrow road to the ferry.

Wisemans Ferry is a tranquil settlement overlooking the Hawkesbury River roughly halfway between Windsor and the mouth of the river. Free 24-hour winch ferries are the only means of crossing the river here.

Yengo National Park, a rugged sandstone area covering the foothills of the Blue Mountains, stretches from Wisemans Ferry to the Hunter Valley. It's a wilderness area with no facilities and limited road access. North of the river, a scenic road leads east from Wisemans Ferry to the Central Coast, following the river before veering north through bushland and orange groves.

An early convict-built road (mostly unsealed, but in good condition) leads north about 21km from Wisemans Ferry to the tiny, delightful settlement of **St Albans**. It's a pretty drive, with bush on one side, and the flats of Webbs Creek, a tributary of the Hawkesbury, on the other. In town it's worth stopping for a drink or meal at the **Settlers Arms Inn**, a charming inn dating from 1836.

Dharug National Park, also on the north side of the river, is a wilderness noted for its Aboriginal rock carvings, which date back nearly 10,000 years, and for the convict-built Old Great North Rd. There's camping at Mill Creek and Ten Mile Hollow (walk-in track only).

Marramarra National Park, south of the Hawkesbury, has vehicle access from the Old Northern Rd south of Wisemans Ferry. Camping is allowed here.

Sights & Information

Riverboat Postman (☎ 9985 7566; Brooklyn Wharf, Brooklyn; adult/child/family $38/20/85; ☼ departs Brooklyn 9.30am, returns approximately 1.15pm, Mon-Fri).

TRANSPORT

Distance from Sydney to Berowra Waters 40km

Direction North and northwest

Travel Time 1hr

Car To reach Berowra Waters, turn off the Sydney-Newcastle Fwy at Berowra, taking Berowra Waters Rd. To reach Brooklyn, take the Sydney-Newcastle Fwy and follow the signs. A road (signposted) leads to Wisemans Ferry from Pitt Town, near Windsor. You can also get there from Sydney on Old Northern Rd, which branches off Windsor Rd north of Parramatta.

Train There are trains running regularly from Central Station to Brooklyn's Hawkesbury River train station; the 8.16am train from Central Station ($6 one way) gets you to the station in time to meet the morning *Riverboat Postman*.

Ferry Free 24-hour car ferries across the Hawkesbury at Wisemans Ferry put you on the road to St Albans. The **Riverboat Postman** runs a ferry service from Brooklyn to Patonga Beach six times a week (not on Friday) for $20/10 return per adult/child. Bookings are recommended. For the *Riverboat Postman* excursion, see above.

Eating & Sleeping

Ripples (☎ 9985 5555; www.ripples.com.au; 87 Brooklyn Rd, Brooklyn; houseboats per weekend for 2-10 people from $640 in the off-season; cheaper midweek) Houseboats for hire, with good facilities.

Settlers Arms Inn (☎ 4568 2111; www.settlersarms .com.au; 1 Wharf St, St Albans; d from $130 during the week) Good food, a lovely pool and a few pleasant rooms.

Wisemans Ferry Inn (☎ 4566 4301; Old Northern Rd; d/tw $60, f $72) This historic inn has decent (if a little cramped) rooms. There's often a lot going on in the pub, from singers to lingerie waitresses, which sort of sums it up.

THE CENTRAL COAST

The central coast has superb surf beaches, lakes and national parks, but its growth as a commuter corridor has meant continuous development and sprawl. Still, it's immensely popular with Sydneysiders at weekends. Beautiful waterways include **Broken Bay** and **Brisbane Water** in the south and three contiguous lakes in the north – **Tuggerah Lake**, **Lake Budgewoi** near Toukley, and **Lake Munmorah**. A few kilometres north of Lake Munmorah is **Lake Macquarie**, which stretches north to Newcastle.

Gosford, the largest town in the area, is 12km inland on the shores of Brisbane Water. Gosford is a good place to pick up tourist information for the area.

On the northern side of the Hawkesbury River, across from Ku-ring-gai Chase National Park, **Brisbane Water National Park** ($7 per car entry fee) is 9km southwest of Gosford. It extends from the Pacific Hwy in the west to Brisbane Water in the east but, despite its name, this national park has only a short frontage onto this body of water. Come here for the **Aboriginal rock engravings** at Bulgandry. These can be accessed by a 30-minute signposted walk off Woy Woy Rd, just near Kariong.

South of the national park is **Patonga**, a small fishing village on Broken Bay, with camping available. Off the road to Patonga is the worthwhile **Warrah Lookout**.

Upmarket **Terrigal**, on the ocean about 12km east of Gosford, is the centre of the region's café and restaurant culture, and offers top-end lodging as well as a YHA hostel.

North of Terrigal, **Bateau Bay** meets the southern section of the small Wyrrabalong National Park. It's popular for surfing.

The Entrance, on the sea inlet of Tuggerah Lake, 15km north of Terrigal, is a slice of suburban sprawl set beside a beautiful lake and superb surf beach. The daily beach-front pelican-feeding (3.30pm) is certainly a crowd-pleaser. You can reach The Entrance either by driving north from Terrigal or by taking the Tuggerah exit off the Sydney–Newcastle Fwy.

North of this are the towns of **Toukley** and **Budgewoi**, popular bases for boating and fishing.

Sights & Information

Brisbane Water National Park (NPWS office ☎ 4320 4200; Suite 36, 207 Albany St North, Gosford; ☻ 8.30am-4.30pm Mon-Fri)

The Entrance Visitor Centre (☎ 4385 4430; www .visitcentralcoast.com.au; Marine Pde, The Entrance; ☻ 9am-5pm)

Gosford Visitor Centre (☎ 4385 4430; www.visitcen tralcoast.com.au; 200 Mann St, Gosford; ☻ 9am-5pm Mon-Fri, 9am-2pm Sat & Sun)

Terrigal Visitor Centre (☎ 4385 4430; www.visitcentral coast.com.au; Rotary Park, Terrigal Dr, Terrigal; ☻ 9am-5pm Mon-Fri, 9am-2pm Sat & Sun)

Eating & Sleeping

Crowne Plaza Terrigal (☎ 4384 9111; www.terrigal .crowneplaza.com; Pine Tree Lane, Terrigal; d from $250) This big hotel, with three restaurants and a luxurious spa facility, dominates the foreshore, and caters to couples looking for a flashy weekend break. Wheelchair accessible.

Terrigal Beach YHA (☎ 4385 3330; www.yha.com .au; 12 Campbell Crescent, Terrigal; dm $25-30, d $60) Located only 50m from the beach, this hostel is a popular spot with surfers (it offers free use of bodyboards and hires out surfboards) and it is a great deal. Clean rooms, good common areas, and a barbie out the back; what more could you ask for?

TRANSPORT

Distance from Sydney to Gosford 85km

Direction North

Travel Time 1hr 15min

Car The Central Coast is easily accessible from Sydney via the Sydney-Newcastle Fwy.

Train Regular CityRail trains connect Sydney with Gosford ($8) and other central coast towns.

Terrigal (p195), central coast

HUNTER VALLEY WINERIES

The Hunter Valley nestles serenely at the foot of the Brokenback Range, just 2½ hours north of Sydney by car. It's a scenic area holding more than 50 vineyards that run the gamut from small, family operations to megaproducers, and from snooty-serious to silly (think of wines labelled 'Old Fart' and 'Old Tart' and you get the picture). The region's attractive guesthouses, numerous restaurants and countless tasting rooms make it a great place to create your own antipodean version of the movie *Sideways*. Or just to indulge yourself in a midweek getaway (overnights are best, and weekends can get uncomfortably crowded).

The bulk of the wineries are concentrated around the picturesque parish of **Pokolbin**, just northwest of Cessnock. Most encourage visits, with free tastings and cellar-door sales of popular varieties like Chardonnay, Semillon and Shiraz. Many have on-site cafés, restaurants or delicatessens as well.

Several wineries also offer tours. They include: **McWilliam's Mt Pleasant Estate, Drayton's Family Wines, McGuigan Cellars** and **Tyrrell's Vineyard**.

The **Hunter Vintage Festival**, held from January to March in the Hunter Valley, attracts hordes of wine enthusiasts for tastings, grape-picking and grape-treading contests.

If you're driving back to Sydney, it's worth taking the scenic route along the old convict-built road that passes through Wollombi, a charming old town in its own right.

Sights & Information

Balloon Aloft (Map p197; ☎ 4938 1955; www.balloon aloft.com; 1443 Wine Country Dr, North Rothbury; balloon flights over the valley per adult/child $280/170)

Drayton's Family Wines (Map p197; ☎ 4998 7513; www.draytonswines.com.au; Oakey Creek Rd, Pokolbin; tours 11am Mon-Fri)

Grapemobile (Map p197; ☎ 0500 804 039; www.grape mobile.com.au; bike hire per half/full day from $22/30)

TRANSPORT

Distance from Sydney to Cessnock 180km

Direction Northwest

Travel Time 2½hrs

Car Take the Sydney-Newcastle Fwy, which starts in Wahroonga on the North Shore, then take Route 82 to Cessnock.

Bus The company **Rover Coaches** (☎ 1800 801 012; www.rovercoaches.com.au) has Xpress buses from Sydney ($25-40).

Train CityRail to Newcastle ($17), then Rover Coaches bus service 160 to Cessnock.

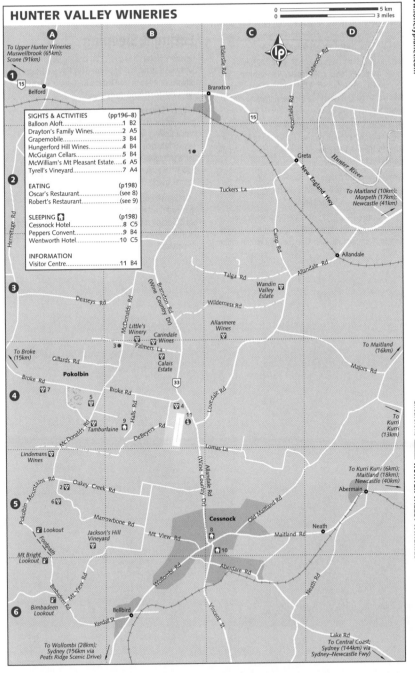

HUNTER VALLEY WINERIES

0 | 5 km
0 | 3 miles

SIGHTS & ACTIVITIES (pp196–8)
Balloon Aloft.........................1 B2
Drayton's Family Wines..............2 A5
Grapemobile...........................3 B4
Hungerford Hill Wines...............4 B4
McGuigan Cellars.....................5 B4
McWilliam's Mt Pleasant Estate...6 A5
Tyrell's Vineyard......................7 A4

EATING (p198)
Oscar's Restaurant...................(see 8)
Robert's Restaurant..................(see 9)

SLEEPING (p198)
Cessnock Hotel........................8 C5
Peppers Convent......................9 B4
Wentworth Hotel....................10 C5

INFORMATION
Visitor Centre........................11 B4

To Upper Hunter Wineries
Muswellbrook (65km);
Scone (91km)

Belford

Branxton

Elderslie Rd

Leconfield Rd

Dalwood Rd

Greta

Hunter River

New England Hwy

To Maitland (10km);
Morpeth (17km);
Newcastle (41km)

Allandale

Tuckers La

Camp Rd

Allandale Rd

Talga Rd

Wandin
Valley
Estate

Hermitage Rd

Branxton Rd
(Wine Country Dr)

McDonalds Rd

Deaseys Rd

Wilderness Rd

Allanmere
Wines

Little's
Winery

Carindale
Wines

Palmers La

To Broke
(15km)

Gillards Rd

Pokolbin

Broke Rd

Calais
Estate

To Maitland
(16km)

Majors Rd

Broke Rd

Halls Rd

Lovedale Rd

To
Kurri
Kurri
(13km)

McDonalds Rd

Tamburlaine

DeBeyers Rd

Lomas La

Lindemans
Wines

Pokolbin Mountains Rd

Oakey Creek Rd

Allandale Rd
(Wine Country Dr)

To Kurri Kurri (6km);
Maitland (18km);
Newcastle (40km)

Abermain

Marrowbone Rd

Cessnock

Neath

Lookout

Jackson's Hill
Vineyard

Mt View Rd

Maitland Rd

Mt Bright
Lookout

Footpath

Mt View Rd

Old Maitland Rd

Aberdare Rd

Neath Rd

Bimbadeen Rd

Bimbadeen
Lookout

Bellbird

Kendall St

Wollombi Rd

Vincent St

To Wollombi (28km);
Sydney (156km via
Peats Ridge Scenic Drive)

Lake Rd
To Central Coast;
Sydney (144km via
Sydney–Newcastle Fwy)

Excursions

HUNTER VALLEY WINERIES

197

Offers advice on pedalling routes through the vines, as well as guided tours.

Hungerford Hill Wines (Map p197; ☎ 4998 7666; www .hungerfordhill.com.au; 1 Broke Rd, Pokolbin; ✆ 9am-5pm Mon-Fri, 10am-5pm Sat & Sun)

McGuigan Cellars (Map p197; ☎ 4998 7402; www .mcguiganwines.com.au; McDonalds Rd, Pokolbin; ✆ tours at noon Mon-Fri, 11am and noon Sat & Sun) Also has an on-site cheese factory serving antipasto platters.

McWilliam's Mt Pleasant Estate (Map p197; ☎ 4998 7505; www.mcwilliams.com.au; Marrowbone Rd, Pokolbin; ✆ 10am-4.30pm, tours 11am; per person $3) A café rounds out the agreeable atmosphere here.

Tyrrell's Vineyard (Map p197; ☎ 4993 7000; www .tyrrells.com.au; 1838 Broke Rd, Pokolbin; ✆ 8.30am-5pm Mon-Sat, tours 1.30pm Mon-Sat)

Visitor Centre (Map p197; ☎ 4990 0900; www.wine country.com.au; 455 Main Rd, Pokolbin; ✆ 9am-5.30pm Mon-Fri, 9am-5pm Sat, 9am-4pm Sun) This visitors centre

has good information on accommodation, attractions and dining in the Hunter Valley region.

Eating & Sleeping

Cessnock Hotel (Map p197; ☎ 4990 1002; 234 Wollombi Rd, Cessnock; r per person $35) This good-value pub offers decent rooms, and **Oscar's Restaurant** (Map p197; ☎ 4991 4414) is right next door.

Peppers Convent (Map p197; ☎ 4998 7764; www.pep pers.com.au; Halls Rd, Pokolbin; d from $372) The romantic Peppers is a lovingly restored period piece: a former Brigidine convent. Very inviting, especially after some strenuous wine tasting and a delicious meal at Robert's Restaurant (Map p197), part of the adjoining Pepper Tree Winery.

Wentworth Hotel (Map p197; ☎ 4990 1364; www .wentworthhotelcessnock.com.au; 36 Vincent St, Cessnock; s/d $75/95) A friendly hotel with refurbished rooms and an Irish-themed bar and restaurant (with good pub grub) downstairs.

Directory

Directory

TRANSPORT

AIR

Sydney's Kingsford Smith Airport is Australia's busiest, taking in flights from all over country and the world. Virgin (☎ 13 67 89; www.virginblue.com.au), Qantas (☎ 13 13 13; www.qantas.com.au) and Qantas' budget alternative, Jetstar (☎ 131 528; www.jetstar.com.au), have frequent flights from other capital cities.

Airlines

Air New Zealand (Map pp228–9; ☎ 13 24 76; 11th fl, 151 Clarence St, City)

Alitalia (Map pp228–9; ☎ 9244 2400; 64 York St, City)

British Airways (Map pp228–9; ☎ 1300 767 177; 19th fl, 259 George St, City)

Japan Airlines (Map pp228–9; ☎ 9272 1111; 14th fl, 201 Sussex St, City)

Jetstar (☎ 131 528; www.jetstar.com.au)

Qantas (Map pp228–9; ☎ 13 13 13; 10 Bridge St, City)

Singapore Airlines (Map pp228–9; ☎ 9350 0100; 17 Bridge St, City)

United Airlines (Map pp228–9; ☎ 9292 4111)

Virgin (☎ 13 67 89)

For other airlines, check under Airlines & Airline Agents in the *Yellow Pages*.

Airport

Sydney airport (☎ 9667 9111; www.sydney airport.com.au) is 10km south of the city centre. The international and domestic terminals are a 4km bus trip apart on either side of the runway. Flights cease between 11pm and 5am due to noise restrictions.

Left-luggage lockers are available in the domestic and international arrivals halls, but oversize items can be stored only in the international lockers. There are many bureaux de change in both the domestic and international terminals of the airport, open from 5.15am to 10.30pm daily.

One of the easiest ways to get from the airport into the city centre is with a shuttle company. These take you straight to your hotel or hostel and cost from $9 to $12. All go into the city centre; some reach surrounding suburbs and beach destinations. Companies include Kingsford Smith Transport (KST; ☎ 9666 9988; www.kst.com .au), Super Shuttle (☎ 0500 513 789, 9311 3789; www.supershuttle.com.au) and Shuttle Bus Services (SBS; ☎ 0500 503 220; www .shuttlebusservices.com).

Airport Link (☎ 8337 8417; www.airportlink .com.au) is a train line which runs to and from city train stations and the domestic ($11) and international ($11.80) airport terminals every 10 to 15 minutes. Trains run from approximately 5am to midnight daily. If you buy a TravelPass (see the boxed text, p202) along with a train ticket into town, your train ticket is discounted to $8.80.

If you're going to Bondi via the cheapest route, take bus 400 or 400 express ($4.30) to Bondi Junction, then the L82, 380, 381 or 382 to Bondi.

Taxi fares from the airport are approximately $25 to Circular Quay, $35 to North Sydney and Bondi, and $50 to Manly. A slew of car-rental booths will greet you after you exit immigration, if you dare to drive.

BICYCLE

Sydney is a big city and thus full of bike-unfriendly traffic; the best spot to get some spoke action is Centennial Park. Many cycle-hire shops require a hefty deposit on a credit card.

Cheeky Monkey (Map pp232–3; ☎ 9212 4460; 456 Pitt St, City; ☻ 8.45am-5.30pm Mon-Fri, 10am-4pm Sat; per day/week from $25/100)

Favourite Cycles (Map p240; ☎ 9977 4590; 22 Darley Rd, Manly; ☻ 9am-6pm Mon-Wed & Fri, 9am-7pm Thu, 9am-5pm Sat, 10am-4pm Sun; per hour/day $9/22)

Inner City Cycles (Map pp236-7; ☎ 9660 6605; 151 Glebe Point Rd, Glebe; ☻ 9.30am-6pm Mon-Wed & Fri, 9.30am-8pm Thu, 9.30am-4pm Sat, 11am-3pm Sun; bus 431, 432, 433, 434) Bicycle hire per day/week $33/90; convenient access to the city and to Central Station.

Wooly's Wheels (Map pp232–3; ☎ 9331 2671; 82 Oxford St, Paddington; ☻ 9am-6pm Mon-Wed & Fri, to 8pm Thu, to 4pm Sat, 11am-4pm Sun; per day/week $39/265) Across from the Victoria Barracks and very handy to Centennial Park.

Bicycles on Public Transport

You can take bicycles free of charge on City-Rail trains, although you will need to purchase a child's ticket for the bike if you are travelling during peak hours (6am to 9am or 3.30pm to 7.30pm Monday to Friday). You can also take your bike on Sydney's ferries, which are equipped with bicycle racks (first come, first served).

BOAT
Ferries

Sydney's **ferries** (☎ 9207 3166; www.syd neyferries.info) provide the most enjoyable way of getting around and have a pretty good reputation as far as reliability, cleanliness and flotation go. Many people use ferries to commute, so there are frequent connecting bus services. Some ferries operate between 6am and midnight, although ferries servicing tourist attractions keep much shorter hours. Popular places accessible by ferry include Darling Harbour, Balmain, Hunters Hill and Parramatta to the west; McMahons Point, Kirribilli, Neutral Bay, Cremorne, Mosman, Taronga Zoo and Manly on the North Shore; and Double Bay, Rose Bay and Watsons Bay in the eastern suburbs.

There are three kinds of ferry: regular STA ferries, fast JetCats that go to Manly ($7.90), and RiverCats, which traverse the Parramatta River to Parramatta ($7.40). All ferries depart from Circular Quay. At Wharf 4 you'll find the **ferry information office** (Map pp228–9; ☎ 9207 3170; 🕑 7am-5.45pm Mon-Sat, 8am-5.45pm Sun), near the ticket booths. The standard single fare for most regular harbour ferries is $4.80, although making the longer trip to Manly costs $6.

ON THE MOVE

The **Transport Infoline** (☎ 13 15 00; www.131500 .com.au) is invaluable when figuring out how to get exactly from here to there on buses, trains and ferries. Call them between 6am and 10pm daily.

If you plan on taking several ferry rides and are keen to save a few bucks, check out the boxed text on p202.

Water Taxis

Water Tours (☎ 9211 7730; www.watertours .com.au) has chartered water taxis from Circular Quay to Watsons Bay for $120 (up to four people, $10 per person after that), or to the islands of Sydney Harbour.

BUS

Sydney's local bus network extends to most suburbs. Fares depend upon the number of 'sections' you pass through; tickets range from $1.60 to $5.70, but most jaunts cost $2.70. Special discount passes (see the boxed text, p202) will save you big bucks. Other than the **Transport Infoline** (☎ 13 15 00; www.131500.com.au), you can call ☎ 9244 1991 or check www.sydneybuses.info for more information.

Regular buses run between 5am and midnight, when Nightrider buses take over. During peak hour, buses get hideously crowded and often fail to pick up passengers at major stops because they can't take any more punters. Try getting on bus 380 on a sunny weekend day (going to or coming from Bondi) and see how close you can get to someone without getting pregnant.

The major starting points for bus routes are Circular Quay, Argyle St in Millers Point, Wynyard Park, the Queen Victoria Building and Railway Square (near Central Station). Most buses head out of the city on George or Castlereagh Sts, and take George or Elizabeth Sts coming in. Pay the driver as you enter, or dunk your prepaid ticket in the green ticket machines by the door.

At Circular Quay there's a **Transit Shop** (Map pp228–9; cnr Alfred & Loftus Sts; 🕑 7am-7pm Mon-Fri, 8.30am-5pm Sat & Sun) which sells passes, along with offering bus information. There are other Transit Shops at Wynyard Park (on Carrington St) and at the Queen Victoria Building.

All long-distance bus services operate from the **Sydney Coach Terminal** (☎ 9281 9366; 🕑 6am-10pm), which is located underneath Central Station. Major bus operators include **Greyhound** (☎ 13 20 30; www. greyhound.com.au), **Premier** (☎ 13 34 10; www.premierms.com.au) and **Murrays** (☎ 13 22 51; www.murrays.com.au).

Directory

TRANSPORT

TRANSPORT DEALS

There's a confusing number of transport deal passes to be had in Sydney. If you decide on your preferences and do some research, you could save big.

The SydneyPass is tourist-oriented and offers three, five or seven days' unlimited travel over a seven-day period on all buses, trains (within the city centre and surrounding suburbs) and ferries as well as Airport Link, the Explorer hop on/off buses, the JetCats, RiverCats and three STA-operated harbour cruises. for an adult/child/family they cost $100/50/250 (three days), $130/65/325 (five days) and $150/75/375 (seven days). These are for people who want to do it all, both on regular and fancy transport.

TravelPasses are more commuter-oriented (but great for tourists who don't need frills) and offer cheaper weekly travel on the regular buses, trains and ferries. There are several colour-coded grades; the **Red TravelPass** ($32) gets to most tourist destinations; the Green TravelPass (which includes the Manly ferry) is $40.

The **Daytripper** (adult/child $15/7.50) is good for one day only, and covers all buses, ferries and trains you're likely to need for sightseeing in central Sydney. It also offers discounts to some popular tourist destinations, like the zoo and aquarium.

If you're just catching occasional buses get a TravelTen ticket, which gives a big discount on 10 bus trips. There are various colour codes for distances so ask which is the most appropriate for you. A brown TravelTen costs $19.70 and covers 5 sections, which should get you to most tourist destinations, but ask at a Transit Shop to make sure.

All the passes above are sold at train stations, Transit Shops and major newsagents.

Ferry Ten tickets are similar and cost $30.30 for 10 inner-harbour (ie short) ferry trips, or $45.10 including the Manly ferry. They can be purchased at Circular Quay.

Several transport-plus-entry tickets are available, which work out cheaper than catching a ferry and paying entry separately. They include the **ZooPass** (adult/child $33.50/16.50) and the **AquariumPass** (adult/child $29.10/14.50). Buy them at Circular Quay.

CAR

Automobile Associations

The **National Roads & Motorists Association** (NRMA; Map pp228–9; ☎ 13 21 32; www.nrma .com.au; 74 King St, City; ☺ 9am-5pm Mon-Fri; train Martin Place or Town Hall) provides 24-hour emergency roadside assistance, road maps, travel advice and insurance, and discounted accommodation. It has reciprocal arrangements with the other state associations and similar organisations overseas – bring proof of membership with you.

Driving & Parking

It's best to avoid driving in central Sydney if you possibly can. The city has an extensive, confusing one-way street system, parking sucks (even at hotels!), parking inspectors are everywhere and tow-away zones are common and have proved to be good revenue-raisers. Having a car in Sydney can be like having an expensive anchor around your neck.

On the other hand, a car is a great way to get to the far reaches of the city and for day trips. For further details on great day trips from Sydney, see p185.

Australians drive on the left-hand side of the road and the minimum driving age (unassisted) is 18 years of age. Overseas visitors are permitted to drive in Australia with their domestic driving licences, but must take a driving test to obtain a New South Wales (NSW) driving licence if they take up temporary or permanent residency. Speed limits in Sydney are generally 60km/h (50km/h in some built-up areas), rising to 100km/h or 110km/h on freeways. It is the law that seat belts must be worn.

The blood-alcohol limit of 0.05% is enforced with random breath-checks and severe punishments. If you're in an accident (even if you didn't cause it) and you're over the alcohol limit, your insurance will be invalidated.

Private car parks are expensive, costing on average around $15 per hour, and even street parking can eat up your coins, at a rate of about $2.20 to $4.40 per hour. Public car parks are signed: look for the large white 'P' on a blue background that lets you know where they are. Many maps indicate with a 'P' where you can park your car. See also the *Yellow Pages* under Parking Stations.

Directory

TRANSPORT

Hire

Car rentals are affordable and relatively consistent with US and European rates. Prices can vary widely depending on time of year and demand, but booking online can sometimes provide savings (as can renting for a longer period). Check the small print on your rental agreement to see exactly where you can take the car (some firms don't allow driving on dirt roads) and what your insurance covers. Also check on any age restrictions.

Avis (☎ 13 63 33; www.avis.com.au), **Budget** (☎ 13 27 27; www.budget.com.au), **Europcar** (☎ 1300 131 390; www.europcar.com.au), **Hertz** (☎ 13 30 90; www.hertz.com.au) and **Thrifty** (☎ 1300 367 227; www.thrifty.com.au) all have desks at the airport, and some have offices in the city centre (mostly on William St). Avis and Hertz also provide hand-controlled cars for disabled travellers. The *Yellow Pages* lists many other car-hire companies, some that specialise in renting near-wrecks at rock-bottom prices – always read the fine print on your rental agreement carefully if you decide on this option.

Toll Roads

The Harbour Tunnel and Harbour Bridge both impose a southbound toll of $3; if you're heading from the North Shore to the eastern suburbs, it's much easier to use the tunnel. The Eastern Distributor imposes a northbound toll of $4.

The new Cross City tunnel connects Darling Harbour to Rushcutters Bay. It's a fully electronic toll road, which means you need a registered vehicle to cross or own a pass (or contact them within 24 hours of crossing to arrange payment). Tariffs to cross vary widely depending on distance travelled and which system of payment you opt for, and may increase quarterly. See www.crosscity.com.au or call ☎ 9033 3999 for more information.

E-Way tags (electronic payment devices that attach to your windscreen) work on the M5, Harbour Bridge and Tunnel, and the Eastern Distributor. To obtain a tag (useful only for longer stays), call ☎ 1300 555 833 or see www.easterndistributor.com.

METRO LIGHT RAIL/ MONORAIL

The **Monorail** (☎ 9285 5600; www.metromonorail.com.au) and **Metro Light Rail** (MLR; ☎ 9285 5600, www.metrolightrail.com.au) are other good means of transport within the city centre.

The Monorail circles Darling Harbour and links it to the Central Business District (CBD). There's a monorail every three to five minutes, and the full loop takes about 14 minutes. A single trip costs $4.20, but for $8 you can have unlimited rides for the day. The monorail operates from 7am to 10pm Monday to Thursday, to midnight

---

BUYING OR SELLING A CAR

Sydney is the capital of car sales for most travellers. **Kings Cross Car Market** (Map p235; ☎ 1800 808 188, 9358-5000; www.carmarket.com.au; cnr Ward Ave & Elizabeth Bay Rd, Kings Cross; 🕑 9am-5pm daily) gets mixed reports, but it seems popular with travellers. Always read the fine print on anything you sign with regards to buying or selling a car. Several dealers will sell you a car with an undertaking to buy it back at an agreed price; do not accept any verbal guarantees – get it in writing.

The *Trading Post*, a weekly rag available from all newsagents, is also a good place to look for second-hand vehicles. You can also check the **Sydney Morning Herald's classified section** (www.smh.com.au). Car prices will probably be a bit cheaper if you buy from a private party.

Yet another option is going to a car auction. One place is **Auto Auctions** (☎ 9724 9111; www.auto-auctions.com.au; 682 Woodville Rd, Guildford).

Before you buy any vehicle, regardless of the seller, we strongly recommend that you have it thoroughly checked by a competent mechanic. The **NRMA** (Map pp228–9; ☎ 13 21 32; www.nrma.com.au; 74 King St, City; 🕑 9am-5pm Mon-Fri) charges $240 for nonmembers ($200 for members). We've heard some real horror stories from readers who've failed to get their vehicles checked.

The **Register of Encumbered Vehicles** (REVS; ☎ 9633 6333; www.revs.nsw.gov.au) is a government organisation that checks whether the car you're buying is fully paid-up and owned by the seller. Other helpful websites, especially if you have problems with your vehicle, are www.fairtrading.nsw.gov.au and www.accc.gov.au.

on Friday and Saturday and from 8am to 10pm Sunday.

The MLR operates 24 hours a day between Central Station and Pyrmont via Darling Harbour and Chinatown. The service runs to Lilyfield via the Fish Market, Wentworth Park, Glebe, Jubilee Park and Rozelle Bay from 6am to 11pm Sunday to Thursday (to midnight Friday and Saturday). Tickets cost from $2.80 to $5.20, but for $8.40 you can have unlimited rides for the day.

TAXI

Taxis are easily flagged down in the city centre and the inner suburbs, except at the boozy hour of 3am, when it's 'changeover time' and you could find yourself standing on the street for what seems like hours. You'll find taxi ranks at Central, Wynyard and Circular Quay train stations, and at other city locations. Flag fall is $2.75, and the metered fare is $1.56 per kilometre. There's a 20% surcharge between 10pm and 6am, for heavy luggage, Harbour Bridge and Tunnel tolls, and a radio booking fee ($1.15). For more on the taxi system in Sydney check out www.nswtaxi.org.au.

The four big taxi companies offer a reliable service:

Legion ☎ 13 14 51
Premier Cabs ☎ 13 10 17
RSL Cabs ☎ 13 22 11
Taxis Combined ☎ 8332 8888

TRAIN

Sydney has a vast suburban rail network and frequent services, making trains much quicker than buses. You can reach practically anywhere within the CBD by train, but lines do not extend to the northern and southern beaches, Balmain or Glebe. Trains run from around 5am to midnight. As a rough guide, a short trip on a CityRail train will cost you $2.20. After 9am Monday to Friday and any time on Saturday and Sunday, you can buy an off-peak return ticket for not much more than a standard one-way fare. For more information check www.cityrail.info.

Central Station has an **information kiosk** (☯ 6am-10pm) near platforms four and five, and there's a **Travellers Aid Society** (☎ 9211 2469; ☎ 8am-2.30pm Mon-Sat) near platform one that provides travel information,

assistance and hot showers. There are **luggage lockers** (☎ 9379 4876; $4-8 per bag; ☯ 5.30am-8.30pm) available near here too.

All long-distance train services arrive and depart from Central Station. Book tickets through **Countrylink Travel Centre** (☎ 9379 9606, after hours 13 22 32; www.countrylink.info; ☯ 6.15am-8.45pm) near platform one. You can get discounts of up to 50% with two weeks' notice. Countrylink has another office at **Circular Quay** (☎ 9224 3400; ☯ 9.45am-5.30pm Mon-Fri), and you can also book online.

PRACTICALITIES
ACCOMMODATION

Accommodation listings in the Sleeping chapter (p170) are ordered by neighbourhood, then in alphabetical order. Midrange and top end places are listed first, while 'cheap sleeps' are last. The average double room with bathroom costs about $150, with seasonal variations (lowest in winter, highest in summer and around Christmas, New Year's Eve, Mardi Gras and Easter). Rooms are also more expensive from Monday to Friday, when business travel is at its peak (outside Sydney, though, weekend rates are often higher because Sydneysiders flee their homes for quick vacations). Generally, we've quoted rack rates for hotels, which tend to be higher than the specials and discounted packages that are often on offer from Sydney's hotels. Always ask a hotel for its 'best rate'. If you're looking for last-minute discounts at higher-end hotels, try www.lastminute.com.au.

BUSINESS HOURS

Most offices and businesses are open weekdays from 9am to 5.30pm. Banking hours are from 9.30am to 4pm Monday to Thursday and until 5pm Friday. Some larger city branches are open from 8am to 6pm weekdays.

Most shops are open from 8.30am or 9am to 5pm or 5.30pm weekdays, with hours extended to 8pm or 9pm Thursday. Many shops open all day Saturday. On Sunday, many shops close, but on Oxford St and in the city you'll find stores open from about 11am to 5pm.

Restaurants generally open from noon to 3pm and then 6pm to 10pm or 11pm from Monday to Saturday. Cafés are often open for day-long breakfasts. See the Eating chapter (p102) for more details.

CHILDREN

With so many natural attractions, Sydney is a good place for kids on vacation, and during school holidays many places put on extra activities for children: the Opera House has an interesting range of entertainment tailored to juniors, and there are some great arty activities for the little ones at the Art Gallery of NSW (p60).

Look for copies of *Sydney's Child,* a free monthly magazine listing activities and businesses catering for ankle biters, in newsagents and other businesses associated with children. For more general information snag a copy of Lonely Planet's *Travel with Children* by Cathy Lanigan.

See the boxed text 'Sydney for Children' (p47) and 'Top Five Children's Shops' (p164) for more details on sights and activities for children.

Baby-sitting

Nannies & Helpers (Map pp232–3; ☎ 9363 4221; www.nanniesandhelpers.com.au; Hughenden Hotel, 14 Queen St, Woollahra; booking fee $20-33, baby-sitting per hr $15-20, 4hr minimum) will send a baby-sitter to your home or hotel, and also helps with domestic duties and parties. They have another base in the northern beaches at 13/20 Bungan St, Mona Vale.

CLIMATE

Sydney is comfortable to visit at any time of year, but unless you enjoy balmy humidity, broken by the odd torrential downpour, keep away in summer. Autumn is delightful, especially around March and April, with clear, warm days and mild nights. In spring (September to November) there's more chance of rain, but it usually clears quickly. Average summer temperatures are around 25°C (77°F), though it can get to over 40°C (104°F) in summer (see the climate chart, p205). Sydneysiders enjoy more than 300 sunny days a year. To help you decide when to visit, also see the City Calendar (p9).

CUSTOMS

When entering Australia you can bring many articles in free of duty, provided that customs is satisfied they're for personal use and that you'll be taking them with you when you leave. There's a duty-free quota per person of 2.25L of alcohol (if you're over 18), 250 cigarettes (ditto) and dutiable goods up to the value of $900 ($450 if you're under 18). Amounts of more than A$10,000 cash must be declared. As these values will change from time to time, it's wise to check current regulations by contacting the Australian Customs Service (☎ 6275 6666; www.customs.gov.au).

Two issues need particular attention: one is illegal drugs – don't bring any in with you; two is animal and plant quarantine – declare all goods of animal or vegetable origin and show them to an official. Authorities are keen to prevent weeds, pests and diseases getting into the country. Fresh food and flowers are also unpopular, and if you've recently visited farmland or rural areas, it might pay to scrub your shoes before you get to the airport.

Weapons and firearms are either prohibited or require a permit and safety testing. Other restricted goods include products made from protected wildlife species, non-approved telecommunications devices and live animals.

When you leave, don't take any protected flora or fauna with you. Customs comes down hard on smugglers.

DISABLED TRAVELLERS

Compared to many other major cities, Sydney has great disabled access for its citizens and visitors. Most of Sydney's main attractions are accessible by wheelchair, and all new or renovated buildings must, by law, include wheelchair access. Older buildings can pose some problems however, and some restaurants and entertainment venues

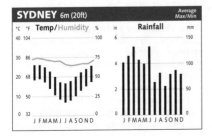

SYDNEY 6m (20ft)   Average Max/Min

°C °F Temp/Humidity %   in   Rainfall   mm

aren't quite up to scratch. A number of taxis accommodate wheelchairs – advise the operator when making a telephone booking.

Most of Sydney's major attractions offer hearing loops and sign language interpreters for hearing-impaired travellers. It's best to make contact with the venues in advance, though.

Many new buildings incorporate architectural features that are helpful to the vision impaired, such as textured floor details at the top and bottom of stairs. Sydney's pedestrian crossings feature sound cues.

Sydney also has lots of parking spaces reserved for disabled drivers.

Organisations

Access Foundation (☎ 9310 5732; www.accessibility .com.au; Suite 33, 61 Marlborough St, Surry Hills)

City of Sydney (www.cityofsydney.nsw.gov.au/cs _disabled_services.asp) Website lists venues with good wheelchair access.

Deaf Society of NSW (☎ 9893 8555; www.deaf societynsw.org.au; 4th fl, 169 Macquarie St, Parramatta)

Royal Blind Society of NSW (☎ 9334 3333; www.rbs .org.au; 4 Mitchell St, Enfield)

Roads and Transport Authority (RTA; ☎ 13 22 13; www.rta.nsw.gov.au) Supplies temporary parking permits for disabled international drivers.

Spinal Cord Injuries Australia (www.spinalcordinjuries .com.au) Publishes the handy **Access Sydney** ($24.95)

ELECTRICITY

Standard voltage throughout Australia is 220 to 240 volts AC (50Hz). Plugs are flat three-pin types. Bring converters for US flat two-pin plugs or European round two-pin plugs, as they can be difficult to find outside airports, outdoors stores, hardware stores and luggage shops.

EMBASSIES

Most foreign embassies are based in Canberra, but many countries also maintain a consulate in Sydney.

American Consulate (Map pp228–9; ☎ 9373 9200; 59th fl, 19-29 Martin Pl, City)

British Consulate (Map pp228–9; ☎ 8247 2238; 16th fl, Gateway Bldg, 1 Macquarie Pl, City)

Canadian High Commission (Map pp228–9; ☎ 9364 3000; 5th fl, Quay West, 111 Harrington St, City)

French Consulate (Map pp228–9; ☎ 9261 5779; 26th fl, St Martins Tower, 31 Market St, City)

German Consulate (Map pp232–3; ☎ 9328 7733; 13 Trelawney St, Woollahra)

Japanese Consulate (Map pp228–9; ☎ 9231 3455; 34th fl, 52 Martin Pl, City)

New Zealand High Commission (Map pp228–9; ☎ 8256 2000; 10th fl, 55 Hunter St, City)

For others see Consulates & Legations in the *Yellow Pages*.

EMERGENCY

In the event of an emergency, call ☎ 000 to contact the police, ambulance and fire authorities. Other useful phone numbers and addresses include the following:

Lifeline (☎ 13 11 14) 24-hour phone counselling services, including suicide prevention.

NRMA (Map pp228–9; ☎ 13 21 32; www.nrma.com.au; 388 George St, City) For auto insurance and roadside service.

Police Stations (Map pp228–9; ☎ 000; 132 George St, The Rocks; 570 George St, City)

Rape Crisis Centre (☎ 1800 424 017, 9819 6565)

Wayside Chapel (Map p235; ☎ 9358 6577; 29 Hughes St, Potts Point; ☺ 7am-10pm) Crisis centre in the heart of Kings Cross.

GAY & LESBIAN TRAVELLERS

Hey, in Sydney, gay is the new straight. Gay and lesbian culture forms a vocal, vital, well-organised and colourful part of Sydney's social fabric. In 2002, Sydney played host to the best-dressed Olympics ever – the Gay Games.

The colourful Gay & Lesbian Mardi Gras is Australia's biggest annual tourist event, and the joyful hedonism-meets-political-protest Oxford St parade is attended by over half a million people. The Sleaze Ball (a Mardi Gras fundraiser) takes place in October, with leather over Lycra. The parties for both events are held in Moore Park. Tickets are restricted to Mardi Gras members. Gay and lesbian international visitors wishing to attend the parties should contact **Mardi Gras Travel** (☎ 9568 8600; www.mardigras.org.au) well in advance – tickets sell fast.

The Taylor Sq region of Oxford St is the hub of gay life in Sydney, although there are 'pockets' in suburbs such as Paddington,

Newtown, Alexandria and Leichhardt. Gay beach life is focused on Lady Bay (nude) and Tamarama (not nude; also known as Glamarama). You may also want to check out Redleaf Pool on New South Head Rd, just past Double Bay, or **Andrew 'Boy' Charlton pool** (p154).

For men, tans and heavy pecs are a 'classic' look. The scene for women is a bit more inclusive. Despite all this, there's still a homophobic side to some 'true blue' Aussies, and violence against homosexuals isn't unheard-of, particularly during holidays.

For the record, in NSW the age of consent for homosexual sex is 16 for both men and women.

The free gay press includes the *Sydney Star Observer* and **Lesbians on the Loose** (www.lotl.com). These can be found in shops and cafés in the inner east and west. Both publications have excellent listings of gay and lesbian organisations, services and events. **Gay & Lesbian Tourism Australia** (GALTA; www.galta.com.au) can provide a wealth of information about gay and lesbian travel in Oz.

Also see the boxed text 'Out & About in Gay & Lesbian Sydney', p135.

HOLIDAYS

On public holidays, government departments, banks, offices, large stores and post offices are closed. On Good Friday and Christmas Day, there is limited newspaper circulation and about the only stores you'll find open are convenience stores. Public holidays include the following:

New Year's Day 1 January

Australia Day 26 January

Easter (Good Friday–Easter Monday) March/April

Anzac Day 25 April

Queen's Birthday 2nd Monday in June

Bank Holiday 1st Monday in August

Labour Day 1st Monday in October

Christmas Day 25 December

Boxing Day 26 December

Most public holidays become long weekends (three days), so if a holiday like New Year's Day falls on a weekend, the following Monday is usually a holiday.

Something else to consider when planning a trip to Sydney is school and public holidays, when everything gets decidedly more crowded and accommodation rates soar. Sydney students have a long summer break that includes Christmas and usually most of January. Other school holidays fall around March to April (Easter), late June to mid-July, and late September to early October. See the City Calendar (p9) for more details.

INTERNET ACCESS

Many hostels and midrange hotels have Internet access for their guests, and practically all top-end hotels will have Internet plugs in rooms. Download the details of your ISP's access numbers before you leave home.

Internet cafés have mushroomed all over Sydney, which means competitive prices for the traveller. Kings Cross has the highest concentration of Internet cafés, but Chinatown and Bondi aren't far behind. Besides allowing you to access the Web, many offer word-processing, fax, scanning and printing services too. Expect to pay around $3 per hour, although night rates are cheaper.

A couple of reliable Internet cafés include the following: **Global Gossip** (Map p235; ☎ 9326 9777; 61 Darlinghurst Rd, Kings Cross; ☺ 9am-1am), with outlets in the city, near Central Station and in Bondi; and **Travellers Contact Point** (Map pp228–9; ☎ 9221 8744; www.travellers.com.au; 7th fl, Dymocks Bldg, 428 George St, City; ☺ 9am-6pm Mon-Fri, 10am-4pm Sat), which has free email (only) access for the first 30 minutes.

Most libraries offer free Internet access, but you need to book ahead.

The local access number for Compuserve is ☎ 9899 1488 or ☎ 8248 5100. For AOL call ☎ 9696 1490. **Telstra Big Pond** (☎ 1800 804 282; www.bigpond.com.au) is a local provider; the access number is given here.

INTERNET RESOURCES

For more information on Sydney, check out these websites:

www.cityofsydney.nsw.gov.au City news and politics.

www.visitnsw.com.au Info on Sydney and NSW, including events.

www.viewsydney.com.au Has live images from around the city.

www.whitepages.com.au Find a business or service anywhere in Australia.

www.sydney.citysearch.com.au What's happening in Sydney.

MAPS

Just about every brochure you pick up includes a map of the city centre, but Lonely Planet's *Sydney City Map* is an exceptional choice. The *Sydney* UBD street directory ($40) is invaluable for drivers.

For a great selection of travel maps (and Lonely Planet guidebooks) check out **Map World** (Map pp228–9; ☎ 9261 3601; www .mapworld.net.au; 280 Pitt St; ⏰ 8.30am-5.30pm Mon-Wed & Fri, 8.30am-6.30pm Thu, 10am-4.30pm Sat, 10am-3pm Sun). For aerial, topographic and many other maps, visit the **Department of Land and Water Conservation** (DLWC; Map pp228–9; ☎ 9228 6360; 23-33 Bridge St, City; ⏰ 8.30am-5pm Mon-Fri). For maps of country areas, see the **NRMA** (p202).

MEDICAL SERVICES

Visitors from Finland, Ireland, Italy, Malta, the Netherlands, New Zealand, Norway, Sweden and the UK have reciprocal health rights and can register at any **Medicare office** (☎ 13 20 11; www.hic .gov.au). Travel insurance is advisable to cover other expenses (such as ambulance and repatriation).

Clinics

If you need to find a dentist in a hurry, call ☎ 9369 7050 (24 hours).

Kings Cross Travellers Clinic (Map p235; ☎ 9358 3066; 13 Springfield Ave, Kings Cross; ⏰ 9am-1pm & 2-6pm Mon-Fri, 10am-noon Sat; train Kings Cross) Bookings advised for morning-after pill scripts and dive medicals.

Travellers Medical & Vaccination Centre (Map pp228-9; ☎ 9221 7133; www.traveldoctor.com.au; 7th fl, 428 George St, City; ⏰ 9am-5.30pm Mon, Wed & Fri, 8am-5.30pm Tue, 9am-7.30pm Thu, 9am-1pm Sat; train Town Hall) Best place to get any travel-related shots and medical advice.

Emergency Rooms

Hospitals with 24-hour accident and emergency departments (generally known as 'casualty wards' in Australia) include:

Royal North Shore Hospital (Map pp226–7; ☎ 9926 7111; Pacific Hwy, St Leonards)

Royal Prince Alfred Hospital (Map pp236–7; ☎ 9515 6111; Missenden Rd, Camperdown)

St Vincent's Public Hospital (Map pp228–9; ☎ 8382 1111; Victoria St, Darlinghurst)

Sydney Children's Hospital (Map pp226–7; ☎ 9382 1111; High St, Randwick)

Sydney Hospital & Sydney Eye Hospital (Map pp228–9; ☎ 9382 7009; 8 Macquarie St, City)

MONEY

The unit of currency is the Australian dollar, which is divided into 100 cents. There are $100, $50, $20, $10 and $5 notes and $2, $1, 50c, 20c, 10c and 5c coins. The 2c and 1c coins have been taken out of circulation, so shops will round prices up (or down) to the nearest 5c on your total bill. Australia's currency is one of the most hi tech in the world. Notes are plastic (which means they don't disintegrate in the washing machine) and every denomination note is a different colour and size. You might hear of the orange-hued $20 note being referred to as a 'lobster' or the yellow $50 as a 'pineapple'.

Travellers cheques have become something of a dinosaur these days, and they won't be accepted everywhere, so don't feel they're crucial to your travels.

ATMs

Central Sydney is chock-full of banks with 24-hour ATMs that will accept all debit cards linked to international network systems, such as Cirrus, Maestro, Barclays Connect and Solo. Most banks place a $1000 limit on the amount you can withdraw daily. You'll also find ATMs in pubs and clubs. Shops and retail outlets will have EFTPOS facilities, which allow you to pay for purchases with your debit card *in situ*.

Changing Money

Both **American Express** (Map pp228–9; ☎ 1300 139 060; 105 Pitt St, City; ⏰ 8.30am-5pm Mon-Fri; train Wynyard) and **Travelex/Thomas Cook** (Map pp228–9; ☎ 9231 2523; 175 Pitt St; ⏰ 9am-5pm Mon-Fri, 10am-2pm Sat; train Martin Place or Town Hall) have branches throughout Sydney.

Exchange bureaus are common in the city centre, but shop around as rates can vary and most charge some sort of commission. Bureaus include the two at **Central Station** (☿ 8am-5pm Mon-Fri, 9am-6pm Sat & Sun) and one opposite Wharf 6 at **Circular Quay** (☿ 8am-8.30pm). There are several in touristy spots like Kings Cross and Bondi, as well as the airport (where they're open until the last flight comes in; rates here aren't quite as good as in the city centre, however).

Credit Cards

Visa, MasterCard, Diners Club and American Express are widely accepted. For lost cards, contact the organisation:

American Express ☎ 1300 132 639

Diners Club ☎ 1300 360 060

MasterCard ☎ 1800 120 113

Visa ☎ 1800 450 346

NEWSPAPERS & MAGAZINES

The *Sydney Morning Herald* is one of the best newspapers in Australia. It's a serious daily, but also captures some of Sydney's larrikinism. The other big Sydney paper is the Murdoch tabloid, the *Daily Telegraph*, which tends to concentrate on the lowest-common-denominator issues, such as kicking refugees when they're down, 'dole bludger' exposés and Nicole Kidman sightings (an obsession with all papers, actually).

Two national newspapers are available in Sydney: *The Australian*, a relatively conservative daily that has an interesting weekend edition; and the business-oriented *Australian Financial Review*. There are also a healthy number of weekly newspapers for Australia's ethnic communities, some published in English; these can be found in most newsagents and in many corner shops and milk bars.

Magazines worth looking out for include *HQ*, a *Vanity Fair*–style number, and *Australian Style*, a fashion- and design-based publication. If it happens to be home-grown Australian political satire you're after, try the Sydney-based newspaper *The Chaser*. Caustically funny some weeks, a sad rip-off of the *Onion* on others, it's definitely going to get you up to speed on local politics faster than the broadsheets will. You can purchase a copy of it at most newsagents.

PHARMACIES

Blake's Pharmacy (Map p235; ☎ 9358 6712; 28 Darlinghurst Rd, Kings Cross; ☿ 9am-midnight)

Darlinghurst Prescription Pharmacy (☎ 9361 5882; 261 Oxford St, Darlinghurst; ☿ 8am-10pm Mon-Sat, 11am-6pm Sun)

Park Pharmacy (Map pp236–7; ☎ 9552 3372; 321 Glebe Point Rd, Glebe; ☿ 8am-8pm)

Wu's Pharmacy (Map pp228–9; ☎ 9211 1805; 629 George St, City; ☿ 9am-9pm Mon-Sat, 9am-7pm Sun)

POST

There are post office branches everywhere throughout the city centre.

Australia Post (www.auspost.com.au)

General post office (GPO; Map pp228–9; 1 Martin Pl, City; ☿ 8.15am-5.30pm Mon-Fri, 10am-2pm Sat) Original central post office.

Poste Restante service (Map pp228–9; 310 George St, City; ☿ 8.15am-5.30pm Mon-Fri) In the Hunter Connection building, level 2A. You'll need identification.

It costs 50c to send a postcard or standard letter within Australia. Airmail letters (weighing up to 50g) cost $1.20 to the Asia/Pacific region and $1.80 to the rest of the world. Mailing postcards anywhere outside Australia costs a flat $1.10.

RADIO

Sydney is not short of radio stations. The Australian Broadcasting Commission (ABC) has the intelligent talk stations Radio National (576AM) and 702 ABC Sydney (702AM), along with the wonderful ABC Classic FM (92.9 FM). Triple J FM (105.7) is the ABC's popular alternative rock station. There are also the SBS multilingual stations (1107AM and 97.7 FM), the multicultural 2000 FM (98.5 FM) and the fabulous subscriber-based 2MBS (102.5 FM). The unique Koori Radio broadcasts on 88.9 FM.

TAX & REFUNDS

There is a 10% goods and services tax (GST) automatically added to almost anything you purchase. If you purchase goods with a total minimum value of $300 from any one store within 30 days of departure from Australia, you are entitled to a refund of any GST paid. Keep your receipts and carry the

Directory

PRACTICALITIES

items on board your flight; you can get a cheque refund at the designated booth located past customs at Sydney airport. Contact the **Australian Taxation Office** (ATO; ☎ 13 63 20) for details.

TELEPHONE

Public telephones, which can be found all over the city, take coins or phonecards and sometimes credit cards. Local calls cost 40c.

Australia's country code is ☎ 61 and Sydney's area code is ☎ 02. Toll-free numbers start with the prefix ☎ 1800, while numbers that start with ☎ 1300 charge only the cost of a local call. Australia's international access code is 0011 (used when dialling other countries from Australia). Drop the zero from the area code when dialling into Australia.

Most hotels will have services that allow you to send or receive faxes. **Global Gossip** (Map p235; ☎ 9326 9777; 61 Darlinghurst Rd, Kings Cross; ☺ 9am-1am) has fax machines too.

Mobile Phones

Phone numbers with four-digit prefixes beginning with 04 are mobiles. Australia's digital network is compatible with GSM 900 and 1800 handsets (used in Europe). Quad-band US phones will work, but to avoid global-roaming charges, you need an unlocked handset that takes prepaid SIM cards from Australian providers such as Telstra, Optus, Virgin or Vodafone.

Most mobiles brought from other states of Australia can be used in the Sydney area, but check roaming charges with your carrier. Sydneysiders will seem glued to their mobiles at all times of the day and night. Despite a reasonable grasp of phone etiquette – not in cinemas, not at the opera, not at funerals – many Sydneysiders will abandon any sign of good manners in mid-conversation should their phone ring.

Phonecards

Local and international phonecards range in value from $5 to $50 – look for the phonecard logo at retail outlets, such as newsagents. There is a bewildering variety of cards available, with all sorts of deals aimed at visitors wanting to get in touch

with loved ones in the UK, Asia and North America. Shop around.

TELEVISION

Sydney has five free-to-air TV channels. ABC (channel 2) is government-funded and relies heavily on BBC material, also offering good local news and current affairs programs, with the occasional documentary, drama or comedy thrown in. Seven and Nine get the biggest ratings, showing a steady run of popular American shows, shock-and-horror news and endless sports like cricket and footy. Ten is similar but targeted to the youth market with profitable reality shows, wacky sit-coms and American reruns. SBS invariably has the most intelligent programming, screening plenty of foreign films, multicultural programs, artistic documentaries, occasional soccer finals and the best news around.

TIME

Sydney is on Eastern Standard Time (EST), which is 10 hours ahead of GMT/UTC. Daylight savings time is one hour ahead of standard time from late October to March. That means when it's noon in Sydney it's 9pm the day before in New York, 6pm the day before in Los Angeles, 2am in London, 4am in Johannesburg, 11am in Tokyo and 2pm in Auckland.

TIPPING

Most services don't expect a tip and you shouldn't be pressured into giving one, even at fancy restaurants. If you want to be remembered, however, you can tip porters ($2 per bag), waiters and waitresses (10%) and taxis (10% or round up to the nearest dollar). If you get your hair cut, it's a nice gesture to give $5 to the underpaid apprentice who washed it. This also goes for those in the beauty therapy trade, who rarely see much of the money they bring into their places of work.

TOURIST INFORMATION

All hours below vary with the seasons; summer hours tend to be longer.

City Host Information Kiosks (Map pp228–9; Circular Quay, Town Hall & Martin Place; ☺ 9am-5pm winter,

10am-6pm summer) Circular Quay's office opens daily, but the others may have more sporadic opening hours/days.

Darling Harbour Visitors Centre (Map pp228-9; ☎ 9281 8788; Darling Harbour; ⏱ 10am-6pm) Behind the IMAX Theatre; specialising in info about NSW, with lots of pamphlets on tours, hotels and entertainment options.

Manly Visitors Information (Map p240; ☎ 9977 1088; Manly Wharf; ⏱ 9am-5pm Mon-Fri, 10am-4pm Sat & Sun; ferry Manly) This helpful visitors centre, just outside the ferry wharf and alongside the bus interchange, has free pamphlets on the 10km **Manly Scenic Walkway** (p96) and other Manly attractions, plus loads of local bus information.

Parramatta Visitors Centre (☎ 9630 3703; 346 Church St, Parramatta; ⏱ 9am-5pm) Incredibly knowledgable, with loads of brochures and leaflets, and plenty of info on access for visitors with impaired mobility and for those with an interest in Aboriginal sites.

Sydney Coach Terminal (Map pp232-3; ☎ 9281 9366; Eddy Ave, Central Station; ⏱ 6am-10pm) Bus and hotel bookings, plus luggage storage. Not radically helpful, but then again, it could just be the location, which has more bad feng shui than one could poke a stick at.

Sydney Harbour National Parks Information Centre (Map pp228–9; ☎ 9247 5033; Cadmans Cottage, 110 George St, The Rocks; ⏱ 9.30am-4.30pm Mon-Fri, 10am-4.30pm Sat & Sun) Organises tours of the harbour islands. See p70.

Sydney Visitor Centre (☎ 9667 6053; Sydney airport; ⏱ 6am-11pm) The first info port of call for many travellers just flying into Sydney. Book discounted hotel rooms, tours, entertainment tickets and even onward travel.

Sydney Visitors Centre (Map pp228-9; ☎ 9240 8788; www.sydneyvisitorscentre.com; 106 George St, The Rocks; ⏱ 9am-6pm) Helpful and knowledgable staff, with tons of brochures and information on aspects of Sydney and NSW. Find a hotel, get the lowdown on restaurants with harbour views, book a tour and arrange transport for day trips out of town. Ask about walking around the neighbourhood.

VISAS

All visitors need a visa. Only New Zealand nationals are exempt, and even they receive a 'special category' visa on arrival. The easiest way to get a visa is online, via the **Electronic Travel Authority** (ETA; www.eta.immi.gov.au). It's quick, costs only $20 and is valid for up to three months (and good for one year).

You must apply for it from outside Australia. Check the website to see if you are eligible.

Regular visa application forms are available from either Australian diplomatic missions overseas or travel agents; you can apply by mail or in person. For further details, call the **Department of Immigration and Multicultural and Indigenous Affairs** (DIMIA; ☎ 9258 4599, 13 18 81; www.immi.gov.au). For the nearest consulate in your country check www.immi.gov.au/contacts/overseas.htm.

WOMEN TRAVELLERS

Sydney is generally safe for women travellers, although you should avoid walking alone late at night. Sexual harassment and discrimination, while uncommon, can occur and shouldn't be tolerated. If you do encounter infantile sexism from drunken louts, the best option is to leave without making any comments. In bars, use good sense and don't accept drinks from people you don't know or leave your drink unattended. Spiking drinks isn't a common practice, but it has occurred in the past.

WORK

Single visitors aged between 18 and 30 from Canada, the UK, the Republic of Ireland, the Netherlands, France, Italy, Germany, Korea, Japan and most Scandinavian countries may be eligible for a Working Holiday Visa. A few other nationalities are also eligible; see www.immi.gov.au for more information.

A Working Holiday Visa allows for a stay of up to 12 months, but the emphasis is on casual, or incidental, employment rather than a full-time job, so working full time for longer than three months with any one employer is not allowed.

There are strict regulations governing overseas visitors working in Australia; see the website above for details. The best place to seek work is in the Saturday Employment section of the *Sydney Morning Herald,* but many hostels will help find you work (though it won't be highly paid). Jobs are also available on www.seek.com.au.

Directory

PRACTICALITIES

Behind the Scenes

THE LONELY PLANET STORY

The story begins with a classic travel adventure: Tony and Maureen Wheeler's 1972 journey across Europe and Asia to Australia. There was no useful information about the overland trail then, so Tony and Maureen published the first Lonely Planet guidebook to meet a growing need.

From a kitchen table, Lonely Planet has grown to become the largest independent travel publisher in the world, with offices in Melbourne (Australia), Oakland (USA) and London (UK). Today Lonely Planet guidebooks cover the globe. There is an ever-growing list of books and information in a variety of media. Some things haven't changed. The main aim is still to make it possible for adventurous travellers to get out there – to explore and better understand the world.

At Lonely Planet we believe travellers can make a positive contribution to the countries they visit – if they respect their host communities and spend their money wisely. Every year 5% of company profit is donated to charities around the world.

THIS BOOK

This 7th edition of the *Sydney* guide was researched and written by Sandra Bao. The 6th and 5th editions were written by Sally O'Brien. Previous editions were written by Meg Mundell, Tom Smallman, Jon Murray and Barbara Whiter. *Sydney* was commissioned from the Lonely Planet's Melbourne office and developed by the following people:

Commissioning Editor Errol Hunt
Coordinating Editor Laura Gibb
Coordinating Cartographer James Ellis
Coordinating Layout Designer Cara Smith
Managing Cartographer Shahara Ahmed
Assisting Editors Sarah Hassall, Emma Gilmour
Assisting Layout Designer Wibowo Rusli
Cover Designer Pepi Bluck
Project Managers Charles Rawlings-Way, Sarah Sloane
Thanks to Susie Ashworth, Glenn Beanland, Rebecca Lalor, Jennifer Mundy-Nordin, Marg Toohey, Lisa Tuckwell, Sally O'Brien, Darren O'Connell, Jane Thompson, Celia Wood, Sally Darmody, Mark Germanchis, Nicholas Stebbing, Mik Ruff

Cover Photographs by Lonely Planet Images: Sydney Opera House detail, Glenn Beanland (top); light showers men in Sydney Gay and Lesbian Mardi Gras, Greg Elms/LPI (bottom). Surf Life Savers Surfboard, Simon Bracken (back).

Internal photographs by Greg Elms/Lonely Planet Images except the following: p2(#1, 3), p16, p31, p36, p51 (#3), p52 (#2, 3),p53 (#4, 5), p55 (#3), p57 (#1), p58 (#1, 3), p71, p94, p116, p139 (#3), p140 (#3), p141 (#1), p142 (#1), p144 (#1, 3), p145 (#1, 3), Glenn Beanland; p54 (#1, 3) Paul Beinssenp; p146 (#2, 3) Chris Bell; p2 (#5), p13, p24, p51 (#2), p52 (#3), p54 (#2), p55 (#2), p58 (#4), p87, p132, p139 (#2), p141 (#2), p144 (#2, 4), p147 Simon Bracken; p196 Manfred Gottschalk; p54 (#4) Dennis Jones; p146 (#4), p185 Oliver Strewe; p55 (#2, 3) Gillianne Tedder; p146 (#1) Hugh Watts, Oliver Strewe.

ACKNOWLEDGMENTS

Many thanks to the following for the use of their content: CityRail's Sydney Suburban Network Map © 2004 RailCorp; Sydney Ferries Corporation Network Map © 2005 Sydney Ferries Corporation.

THANKS
SANDRA BAO

Thanks to Ben Greensfelder, loyal travelling partner, scrupulous editor, grudging tech support and hubbie extraordinaire for over a dozen years - you *know* I couldn't have done it without you, monkey-poo. I very much appreciate Dilip Varma's help, and the companionship of Tricia Wilden, Richie Collins, Juliette Ferrier, and Victoria and Andrew Grimes (and kids). Other helpful folks full of advice and information include Pete Wan, Susan Baker, Sharmila Wood and Eoghan Lewis. A big 'thanks mate' to Andrew Swaffer, who trusted me with his nifty digs. More graces to Vivek Wagle, my real reason for being down under so many damn times. Sally O'Brien's superclean text made this LP job a cruiser. Errol Hunt, you're a super CE and fun to work with, and it was icing to finally meet you at the mother ship.

OUR READERS

Many thanks to the travellers who used the last edition and wrote to us with helpful hints, useful advice and interesting anecdotes:

Kim Ahrend, Alison Anderson, Julia Anten, Helene Apper, Heini Baumgartner, Bob & Jessica Berryman, Michael Bonnet, G Bowyer-Sidwell, Carolyn Brown, Vicky Burling, Andrew Caballero-Reynolds, Dave Cartwright, Joe Cassels, Natasha Cosby, Lynne Coupethwaite, Fe Denton, Heribert Dieter, Joanna Fellows, Tal & Hadas Fuhrer, Emilie Gaboriaud,

Anne Glazier, Michelle Godwin, Dorte Gollek, Helen Gordon, Marie-Adele Nagako Guicharnaud, Liz Hallett, Jim Hamilton, Siobhan Hanbury-Aggs, Jamey Heit, Josh Heuchan, Ieuan Hopper, Nessa Horewitch, Judith Houlihan, PS Johnson, Hilde Keunen, Jan Lane, Gizella Lantai, Simon Lavender, Martin Lerner, Eoghan Lewis, Lorna Macgougan, Mark Martelletti, Trevor Mazzucchelli, Maureen McCarthy, Yasantha Monerawela, TW Mortyn, Maarten Munnik, Phil & Rhonda Murray, Kelly Noyce, S Pathirana, David Patterson, Vikki Peat, Roberta Petri, Kevin Philipson, Scott Phillips, Evan Player, Katie Powell, Suzanne Prymek, Dirk Pueschel, Jean Relph, Jim Revell, Nathan Reynolds, Julie Richards-Fox, Sue Ring, Pierre Sagrafena, Darren Salter, Kathrin Seyer, Stephanie Stevens, Amanda Stillings, Neil Stopforth, George Tam, Jamie Textor, Erik Tjernström, Amanda Townsend, Susan Trenholm, Nick Whyles, Katherine Wilson, Michael Wohl, Kin Yip, Andrew Young, Yvonne Zuidam

SEND US YOUR FEEDBACK

We love to hear from travellers — your comments keep us on our toes and help make our books better. Our well-travelled team reads every word on what you loved or loathed about this book. Although we cannot reply individually to postal submissions, we always guarantee that your feedback goes straight to the appropriate authors, in time for the next edition. Each person who sends us information is thanked in the next edition — and the most useful submissions are rewarded with a free book.

To send us your updates — and find out about Lonely Planet events, newsletters and travel news — visit our award-winning website: www.lonelyplanet.com /feedback

Note: We may edit, reproduce and incorporate your comments in Lonely Planet products such as guidebooks, websites and digital products, so let us know if you don't want your comments reproduced or your name acknowledged. For a copy of our privacy policy visit www.lonelyplanet.com/privacy.

Notes

Notes

Index

See also separate indexes for Eating (p221), Drinking (p221), Shopping (p221) and Sleeping (p222).

Index

Index

000 map pages
000 photographs

MAP LEGEND

ROUTES

Tollway	One-Way Street
Freeway	Mall/Steps
Primary Road	Tunnel
Secondary Road	Walking Tour
Tertiary Road	Walking Tour Detour
Lane	Walking Trail
Under Construction	Walking Path
Track	Pedestrian Overpass
Unsealed Road	

TRANSPORT

Cable Car, Funicular	Rail
Ferry	Rail (Underground)
Monorail	Tram

HYDROGRAPHY

River, Creek	Water

BOUNDARIES

Cliff	Regional, Suburb

AREA FEATURES

Airport	Cemetery, Christian
Area of Interest	Forest
Beach, Desert	Land
Building, Featured	Mall
Building, Information	Park
Building, Other	Sports
Building, Transport	Urban

POPULATION

CAPITAL (NATIONAL)	CAPITAL (STATE)
Large City	Medium City
Small City	Town, Village

SYMBOLS

Sights/Activities
- Beach
- Christian
- Jewish
- Monument
- Museum, Gallery
- Other Site
- Swimming Pool
- Winery, Vineyard
- Zoo, Bird Sanctuary

Eating
- Eating

Drinking
- Drinking
- Café

Entertainment
- Entertainment

Shopping
- Shopping

Sleeping
- Sleeping
- Camping

Transport
- Airport, Airfield
- Bus Station
- Parking Area

Information
- Bank, ATM
- Embassy/Consulate
- Hospital, Medical
- Information
- Internet Facilities
- Police Station
- Post Office, GPO
- Toilets

Geographic
- Lighthouse
- Lookout
- National Park
- Waterfall

Maps

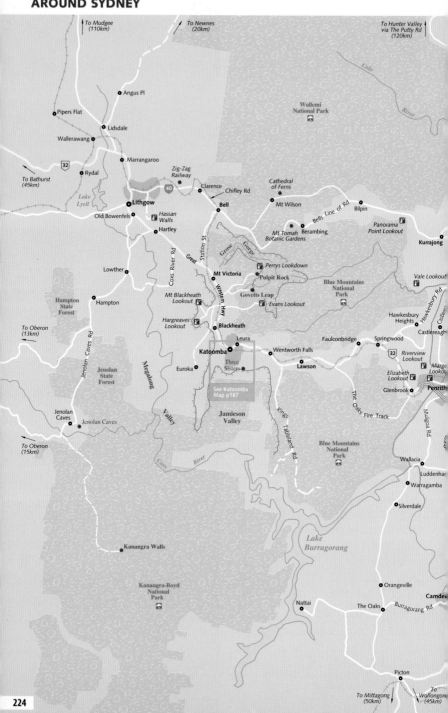

To Cessnock
(Hunter Valley) (90km);
Central Coast (105km)

See Hunter Valley
Wineries Map p197

To Central Coast (20km);
Newcastle (65km)

Yengo
National Park

St Albans

Mangrove
Mountain

Central
Mangrove

Peats
Ridge

Somersby

Wisemans
Ferry

Dharug
National
Park

The Putty Rd

Parr State
Recreation
Area

Colo
Heights

Upper
Colo

Colo

Morans
Rock

Leets
Vale

Maroota
North

Spencer

Calga

Gosford

Sackville
North

Howkesbury

River

Mangrove Creek

Brisbane
Water

Woy Woy

Blaxlands
Ridge

Wilberforce

Marramarra
National
Park

Brisbane
Water
National
Park

Broken Bay

Richmond

Pitt Town

Berowra

West Head

Barrenjoey Lighthouse
Palm Beach
Whale
Beach

The Northern Rd

Windsor

Windsor Rd

Riverstone

Rouse Hill
Estate

Old Northern Rd

Pacific Hwy

Ku-ring-gai Chase
National
Park

Clareville

Avalon
Bilgola
Newport

Richmond Rd

Quakers
Hill

Glenhaven

Hornsby

Rose Seidler
House

Terrey
Hills

Elanora
Heights

Bayview
Rd

Mona Vale

Shanes
Park

Castle
Hill

Normanhurst

Koala Park

Wahroonga

Vale

Belrose

Narrabeen

Dunheved
St Marys

Doonside

Baulkham
Hills

Beecroft

St Ives

Killara

Frenchs
Forest

Cromer

Collaroy

Dee Why

Blacktown

Epping

Lane
Cove
National
Park

Castle
Cove

Curl
Curl

Freshwater Beach

Colyton

Seven
Hills

Girraween

Northmead

West
Ryde

North
Ryde

Chatswood

Manly
Vale

Manly

Erskine
Park

Walgrove Rd

Westlink

Prospect
Reservoir

Dundas

Parramatta

Rosehill Gardens

Ryde

East
Ryde

Parramatta River

Great Western Hwy

Greystanes

Sydney
Olympic
Park

Port Jackson

Elizabeth Dr

Edensor
Park

Smithfield

Cabramatta

Auburn

Berala

Strathfield

SYDNEY

Bondi

Green
Valley

Yagoona

Hume Hwy

Belmore

Bankstown

Enfield
Petersham

See Greater Sydney Map pp226-7

Prestons

Liverpool

Moorebank

Hurstville

Sydney
Airport

Botany

Maroubra

Casula

South Western Mwy

Revesby

Beverly
Hills

Lugarno

Botany
Bay

La Perouse
Cape Banks

Glenfield

Ingleburn

Heathcote Rd

Illawong

Georges

River

Oyster
Bay

Sutherland

Princes Hwy

Kurnell

Botany Bay
National
Park

TASMAN

SEA

Eagle
Vale

Hume Hwy (South-Western Fwy)

Minto

Loftus

Engadine

Caringbah

Narellan

Camden Valley Way

Minto Heights

Lumeah

Campbelltown

Cronulla

Port Hacking
Point

Bundeena

Rosemeadow

Appin Rd

Heathcote
National
Park

Royal
National
Park

Port Hacking

To Melbourne
(830km)

To Southern
Highlands
(45km)

To Wollongong
(40km);
Melbourne via
coast (1100km)

Waterfall

Wattamolla

GREATER SYDNEY

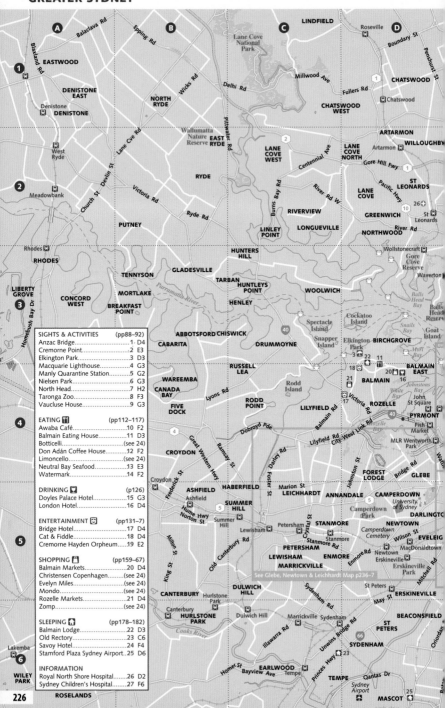

SIGHTS & ACTIVITIES (pp88–92)
Anzac Bridge.................................1 D4
Cremorne Point...........................2 E3
Elkington Park.............................3 D3
Macquarie Lighthouse..................4 G3
Manly Quarantine Station............5 G2
Nielsen Park.................................6 G3
North Head..................................7 H2
Taronga Zoo................................8 F3
Vaucluse House............................9 G3

EATING 🍴 (pp112–117)
Awaba Café................................10 F2
Balmain Eating House.................11 D3
Botticelli...................................(see 24)
Don Adán Coffee House.............12 F2
Limoncello................................(see 24)
Neutral Bay Seafood..................13 E3
Watermark.................................14 F2

DRINKING 🍷 (p126)
Doyles Palace Hotel....................15 G3
London Hotel..............................16 D4

ENTERTAINMENT 🎭 (pp131–7)
Bridge Hotel...............................17 D4
Cat & Fiddle...............................18 D4
Cremorne Hayden Orpheum......19 E2

SHOPPING 🛍 (pp159–67)
Balmain Markets........................20 D4
Christensen Copenhagen.........(see 24)
Evelyn Miles..............................(see 24)
Mondo.....................................(see 24)
Rozelle Markets..........................21 D4
Zomp.......................................(see 24)

SLEEPING 🛏 (pp178–182)
Balmain Lodge...........................22 D3
Old Rectory...............................23 C6
Savoy Hotel...............................24 F4
Stamford Plaza Sydney Airport...25 D6

INFORMATION
Royal North Shore Hospital.......26 D2
Sydney Children's Hospital........27 F6

See Glebe, Newtown & Leichhardt Map p236–7

0 ──────── 2 km
0 ──────── 1.0 miles

E ROSEVILLE CHASE

F

MANLY VALE

G Lagoon Park

Manly Golf Club

H

CASTLE COVE

NORTH BALGOWLAH

NORTH WILLOUGHBY

MIDDLE COVE

BALGOWLAH

FAIRLIGHT

North Steyne Beach

See Manly Map p240

WILLOUGHBY EAST

Crag Cove

SEAFORTH

Sydney Rd

Ivanhoe Park

Manly Beach

Cabbage Tree Bay

CASTLECRAG

Manly Rd

Shelly Beach

1

Alpha Rd

NORTHBRIDGE

Long Bay

Clontarf Beach

CLONTARF

BALGOWLAH HEIGHTS

Smedleys Point

North Harbour

Manly Point

Manly Cove

Little Manly Point

MANLY

Blue Fish Point

AREMBURN

CAMMERAY

CREMORNE

THE SPIT

Middle Harbour

Dobroyd Head

Cannae Point

5

Sydney Harbour National Park

Cammeray Golf Club

Ourimbah Rd

10

BALMORAL

Grotto Point

7

North Head

See North Sydney Map p239

19

12

10

Hunters Bay

Middle Head

Port Jackson (Sydney Harbour)

2

alcon St St

Military Rd

14

Balmoral Beach

ORTH YDNEY

Warringah Fwy

Leonards Park

13

Forsyth Park

MOSMAN

South Head

Hornby Island

SOUTH PACIFIC OCEAN

NEUTRAL BAY

Miller St

Kurraba Rd

Bradleys Head Rd

Georges Head

Lady Bay Beach

North Sydney

Milsons Point

2

CREMORNE POINT

8

Chowder Bay

Camp Cove

Laings Point

WATSONS BAY

Gap Bluff

15

The Gap

3

KIRRIBILLI

Kirribilli Point

2

Sydney Harbour National Park

Chowder Head

Taylors Bay

Vaucluse Point

Parsley Bay

Parsley Bay Beach

Dunbar Head

DAWES POINT

LLERS OINT

Bennelong Point

See Central Sydney Map pp228–31

Bradleys Head

Steel Point

Shark Bay

Shark Bay Beach

6

Old South Head Rd

4

THE ROCKS

Circular Quay

Farm Cove

Clarke Island

Shark Island

Nielsen Park

9

Hermit Point

Wynyard

Royal Botanic Gardens

Point Piper

Felix Bay

Woollahra Point

VAUCLUSE

Diamond Bay

Martin Place

The Domain

POTTS POINT

Clarke Island

4

St James

Hyde Park

KINGS CROSS

Kings Cross

RUSHCUTTERS BAY

William St

POINT PIPER

ROSE BAY

DOVER HEIGHTS

arden aza

Museum

World Square

DARLINGHURST

DARLING POINT

24

Sydney Royal Golf Course

HINATOWN

Crown St

Green Park

EDGECLIFF

Edgecliff

DOUBLE BAY

BELLEVUE HILL

NORTH BONDI

Williams Park

Central Station

PADDINGTON

Walter Reid Gardens

William St

AYMARKET

HIPPENDALE

Oxford St

WOOLLAHRA

BONDI BEACH

Bondi Cliff Park

5

leveland St

SURRY HILLS

Fox Studios

Centennial Park

Bondi Junction

BONDI JUNCTION

BONDI

Bondi Beach

REDFERN

Elizabeth St

South Dowling St

Bondi Rd

Ben Buckler

Moore Park Golf Club

Waverley Park

Bondi Park

WATERLOO

MOORE PARK

TAMARAMA

Mackenzies Point

LEXANDRIA

QUEENS PARK

Cardigan Rd

Tamarama Bay

ZETLAND

Willis Playground

See Surry Hills, Paddington & Woollahra Map pp232–4

BRONTE

Bronte Rd

Bronte Beach

Calga Reserve

Randwick Racecourse

WAVERLEY

Varna Park

Waverley Cemetery

70

Alison Rd

CLOVELLY

KENSINGTON

RANDWICK

Wittle Park

COOGEE

Bundock Park

Shark Point

Australian Golf Club

University of NSW

27

Alby Smith Memorial Reserve

Dunningham Reserve

Coogee Oval

Gordons Bay

Anzac Pde

Coogee Bay Rd

Coogee Beach

6

Gardeners Rd

Kensington Park

1

Coogee Bay

Wedding Cake Island

OSEBERY

DACEYVILLE

Bumerong Rd

Avoca St

KINGSFORD

SOUTH COOGEE

Trenerry Res

See Eastern Beaches Map p238

Southern Cross Dr

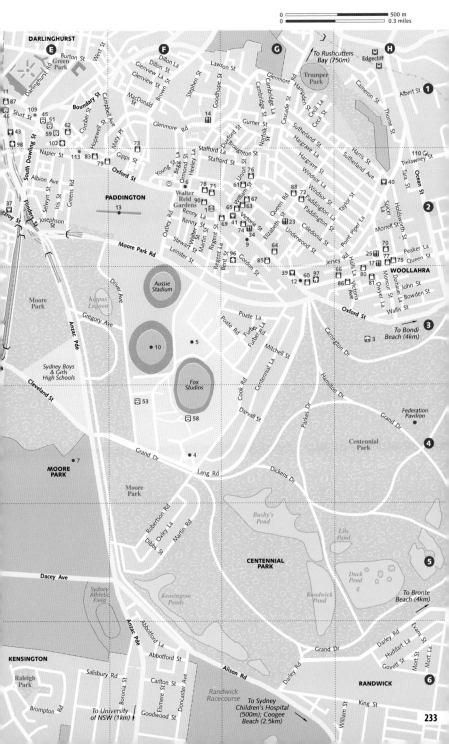

0   500 m
0   0.3 miles

DARLINGHURST

E Burton St
Darlinghurst Rd Green Park

West St

F Dillon La
Dillon St
Glenview La
Glenview St

Lawson St

G Glenmore
Cambridge La
Cambridge St
Cascade St
Hampden St
Cecil La
Cecil

To Rushcutters
Bay (750m)

Trumper
Park

H Edgecliff

Cameron St
Thorne St

Albert St **1**

11
87
Sturt St
46
43
98

109
45
51
62
59
102

Boundary St
Comber St
Campbell Ave
Hopewell St
Mary Pl

MacDonald St
Brown

Stephen St

Goodhope St

Gurner St

Glenmore Rd

14

Sutherland St
Hargrave La
Hargrave St
Windsor St

Norfolk St

Harris St

Sutherland Ave

110
Trelawney St

40

Ocean St **H**

South Dowling St

113 83

73

Gipps St

79

Oxford St

PADDINGTON

Young La
Begg La
Ormond St
Heeley La
Stafford La
Stafford St

Broughton St
Oxford St
Union St

76

Hargrave La
Windsor St

Spicer St
Holdsworth St
Tara St

70

Morrell St

25
17
77
80
75

Queen St

WOOLLAHRA

37
Flinders St
Josephson St

Albion Ave
Selwyn St
Iris St
Greens Rd

78 71
Walter
Reid
Gardens
1
61
65
41
69
74
9
Renny La
Renny
Walter St
Stewart St
Martin St
Regent St
Regent La
Bent St
Gordon St

William St
67
63
Victoria St
34

88
72
Queen Rd
Caledonia St
Paddington St
Taylor St

23

Elizabeth St
Underwood St

64

85

Point Piper La

Peaker La

81

Dwyer St
Moncur St
John St
Bowden St

13

Moore Park Rd

Leinster St

39
12
60 97
86

Jersey Rd
Halls La
Victoria Rd

66

Oxford St

Fitzroy St

Moore
Park

Kippax
Lagoon

Driver Ave
Gregory Ave

Anzac Pde

Aussie
Stadium

10

5

Poate La
Poate Rd
Furber Rd
Furber Rd

Mitchell St

Centennial La

Carrington Dr

3

To Bondi
Beach (4km) **3**

Sydney Boys
& Girls
High Schools

Cleveland St

Fox
Studios

53

58

Cook Rd

Darvall St

Hamilton Dr

Federation
Pavilion

Grand Dr

Centennial
Park **4**

**MOORE
PARK**

7

Grand Dr

4

Lang Rd

Dickens Dr

Parkes Dr

Moore
Park

Robertson Rd
Oxley La
Martin Rd
Dibbs St

Busby's
Pond

Lily
Pond

**CENTENNIAL
PARK**

Duck
Pond **5**

Dacey Ave

Sydney
Athletic
Field

Abbottford La

Abbotford St

Kensington
Ponds

Randwick
Pond

To Bronte
Beach (4km)

Anzac Pde

Alison Rd

Grand Dr

Darley Rd
Huddart La
Govett St

Evans St
Mort St
Mort St **6**

KENSINGTON

Raleigh
Park

Brompton Rd

Salisbury Rd

Carlton St
Boronia St
Elsmere St
Goodwood St
Doncaster Ave

To University
of NSW (1km)

Randwick
Racecourse

To Sydney
Children's Hospital
(500m); Coogee
Beach (2.5km)

Darley Rd

RANDWICK

King St

William St

KINGS CROSS & DARLINGHURST

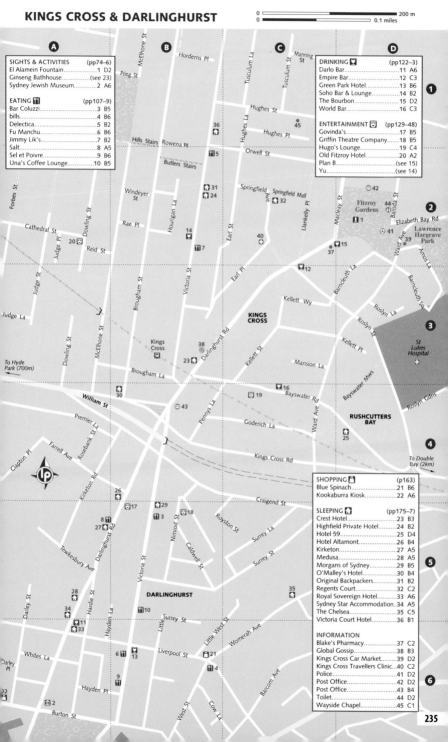

SIGHTS & ACTIVITIES	(pp74–6)	
El Alamein Fountain	1	D2
Ginseng Bathhouse	(see 23)	
Sydney Jewish Museum	2	A6

EATING	(pp107–9)	
Bar Coluzzi	3	B5
bills	4	B6
Delectica	5	B2
Fu Manchu	6	B6
Jimmy Lik's	7	B2
Salt	8	A5
Sel et Poivre	9	B6
Una's Coffee Lounge	10	B5

DRINKING	(pp122–3)	
Darlo Bar	11	A6
Empire Bar	12	C3
Green Park Hotel	13	B6
Soho Bar & Lounge	14	B2
The Bourbon	15	D2
World Bar	16	C3

ENTERTAINMENT	(pp129–48)	
Govinda's	17	B5
Griffin Theatre Company	18	B5
Hugo's Lounge	19	C4
Old Fitzroy Hotel	20	A2
Plan B	(see 15)	
Yu	(see 14)	

SHOPPING	(p163)	
Blue Spinach	21	B6
Kookaburra Kiosk	22	A6

SLEEPING	(pp175–7)	
Crest Hotel	23	B3
Highfield Private Hotel	24	B2
Hotel 59	25	D4
Hotel Altamont	26	B4
Kirketon	27	A5
Medusa	28	A5
Morgans of Sydney	29	B5
O'Malley's Hotel	30	B4
Original Backpackers	31	B2
Regents Court	32	C2
Royal Sovereign Hotel	33	A6
Sydney Star Accommodation	34	A5
The Chelsea	35	C5
Victoria Court Hotel	36	B1

INFORMATION		
Blake's Pharmacy	37	C2
Global Gossip	38	B3
Kings Cross Car Market	39	D2
Kings Cross Travellers Clinic	40	C2
Police	41	D2
Post Office	42	D2
Post Office	43	B4
Toilet	44	D2
Wayside Chapel	45	C1

GLEBE, NEWTOWN & LEICHHARDT

0 ____ 1 km
0 ____ 0.6 miles

SIGHTS & ACTIVITIES   (pp81–2)
Aboriginal Rock Engravings.........1 D1
Bondi Beach................................2 C1
Bondi Golf Club...........................3 D1
Bondi Icebergs Swimming Club....4 C2
Bondi Pavilion.............................5 C1
Bondi Surf Company.....................6 C2
Bronte Beach...............................7 B3
Clovelly Beach.............................8 B5
Clovelly Bowling Club...................9 C4
Coogee Beach............................10 A5
Dunningham Park.......................11 A5
Giles Baths................................12 B5
Let's Go Surfing.........................13 D1
Lookout....................................14 D2
McIver's Baths...........................15 A6
Tamarama Beach........................16 C3
Wylie's Baths.............................17 A6

EATING   (pp113–14)
A Fish Called Coogee..................18 A6
Barzura....................................19 A6
Brown Sugar.............................20 D1
Erciyes 2...................................21 A5
Fishface....................................22 B3
Gelbison...................................23 C2
Hugo's......................................24 C2
Icebergs....................................25 C2
Jack & Jill's Fish Café.................26 A5
La Plage....................................27 B3
Rice.....................................(see 26)
Sean's Panorama.......................28 D1
Swell..29 B3

DRINKING   (p125)
Beach Road Hotel......................30 C1
Bondi Icebergs Club.............(see 25)
Coogee Bay Hotel......................31 A6
Icebergs Bar........................(see 25)

ENTERTAINMENT   (pp135–48)
Hibiscus Lounge...................(see 31)
North Bondi RSL Club................32 D1

SHOPPING   (pp167–8)
Bondi Markets...........................33 C1
Gertrude & Alice........................34 C1
Kite Power.................................35 A5
Mambo......................................36 C2
Tuchuzy.....................................37 C1

SLEEPING   (pp179–80)
Bondi Beach B&B.......................38 C1
Bondi Beach Homestay...............39 B1
Bondi Beachouse.......................40 C2
Coogee Bay Boutique Hotel.......41 A6
Coogee Beachside
   Accommodation....................42 A5
Dive Hotel................................43 A6
Grand Pacific Private Hotel........44 A6
Hotel Bondi..............................45 C1
Ravesi's.....................................46 C1

TRANSPORT   (pp200–4)
Bus Station...............................47 D1

238

NORTH SYDNEY

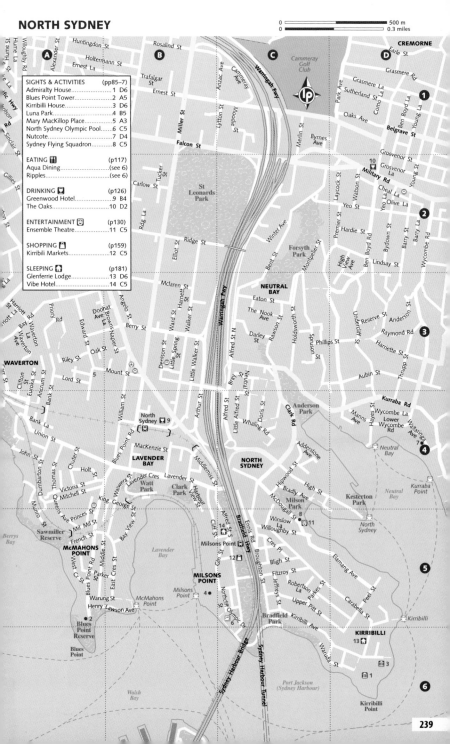

0 _____ 500 m
0 _____ 0.3 miles

SIGHTS & ACTIVITIES	(pp87–8)
Aloha Surf	1 B2
Dive Centre Manly	2 B2
Manly Art Gallery & Museum	3 A2
Manly Blades	4 B2
Manly Surf Life Saving Club	5 B3
Netted Swimming Area	6 A2
Oceanworld	7 A2
Rock Pool	8 C3
St Patrick's College	9 C3

EATING	(pp117–18)
Alhambra	10 A
BarKing Frog	11 B
Beanrush	12 B
Blue Water Café	13 B
Manly Fish Market	14 B

DRINKING	(p126
Ceruti's	15 B
New Brighton Hotel	16 B
Steyne Hotel	17 B

SLEEPING	(pp181–2
101 Addison Road	18 B
Manly Beach House	19 B
Manly Lodge	20 B
Manly Pacific Sydney	21 B
Manly Paradise Motel	22 B
Periwinkle Guest House	23 B
The Bunkhouse	24 A

TRANSPORT	(pp200–4
Bus Interchange	25 B
Favourite Cycles	26 B

INFORMATION	
Manly Visitors Information	27 B

FAIRLIGHT

Kenneth Rd
Rolfe St
Alexander St
Collingwood St
Malvern Ave
Pine La
Balgowlah Rd
Pacific Pde
Smith St
Herbert St
Kangaroo St
Pine St
North Steyne
Francis St
Arthur St
Bundoon
Quinton St
Quinton La
Augusta Rd
Carlton St
North Steyne Beach
Crescent St
Parkview Rd
Birkley La
Birkley Rd
Ocean La
Ocean Rd
Lawson Pl
Raglan St
Augusta La
Denison St
Pittwater Rd
Whistler St
Francis St
Ivanhoe Park
Sydney Rd
Griffin St
George St
James St
Gilbert St
Tower St
Central Ave
Henrietta La
Belgrave St
Market Pl
The Corso
Fairlight St
West Esp
Commonwealth Pde
Manly Cove

Cabbage Tree Bay

Manly Beach
South Steyne

Fairy Bower Beach
Victoria Pde
East Esp
Ashburner St
Cliff St
Bower St
Reddall St
College St
Addison Rd
Darley Rd
Fairbower Rd
High St
Osborne Rd
Woods St
Stuart St

Shelly Beach
Shelly Beach Park

MANLY

Sydney Harbour National Park

SYDNEY TRANSPORT MAP

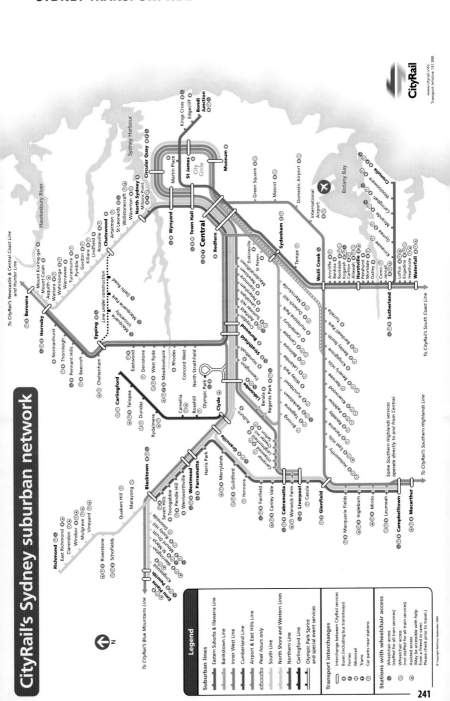

CityRail's Sydney suburban network

CityRail
www.cityrail.info
Transport Infoline 131 500

Legend

Suburban lines
- Eastern Suburbs & Illawarra Line
- Bankstown Line
- Inner West Line
- Cumberland Line
- Airport & East Hills Line
- Peak hours only
- South Line
- North Shore and Western Lines
- Northern Line
- Carlingford Line
- Olympic Park Sprint and special event services

Transport interchanges
- Interchange between CityRail services
- Buses (including bus transitways)
- Ferries
- Monorail
- Trams
- Car parks near stations

Stations with wheelchair access
- Wheelchair access (staffed for all train services)
- Wheelchair access (not staffed for all train services)
- Assisted access (May be accessible with help from a friend or carer. Please check prior to travel.)

© Copyright RailCorp September 2004

SYDNEY FERRIES MAP

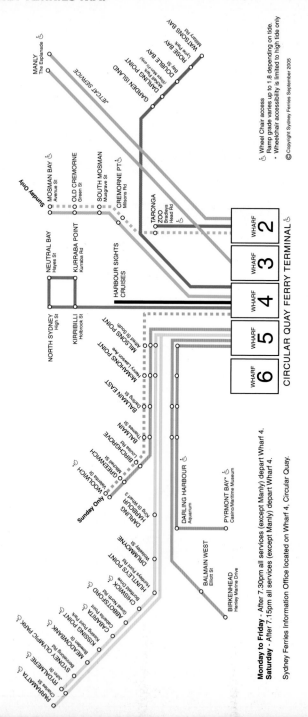

Monday to Friday - After 7.30pm all services (except Manly) depart Wharf 4.
Saturday - After 7.15pm all services (except Manly) depart Wharf 4.

Sydney Ferries Information Office located on Wharf 4, Circular Quay.

- Wheel Chair access
- Ramp grade varies up to 1.8 depending on tide.
- Wheelchair accessibility is limited to high tide only

© Copyright Sydney Ferries September 2005

MANLY
The Esplanade

JETCAT SERVICE

DARLING POINT
GARDEN ISLAND
(Ticket office only)

DOUBLE BAY
Bay St

ROSE BAY
Lyne Park

WATSONS BAY
Military Rd

MOSMAN BAY
Avenue St
OLD CREMORNE
Green St
SOUTH MOSMAN
Musgrave St
CREMORNE PT
Milsons Rd

Sunday Only

TARONGA ZOO
Bradleys Head Rd

NEUTRAL BAY
Hayes St
KURRABA POINT
Kurraba Rd

HARBOUR SIGHTS CRUISES

NORTH SYDNEY
KIRRIBILLI
Holbrook Ave

MILSONS POINT
Alfred St South

McMAHONS POINT
Henry Lawson Ave

BALMAIN EAST
Darling St

BALMAIN
Thames St

BIRCHGROVE
Louisa Rd

GREENWICH
Mitchell St

WOOLWICH
Gale St

DARLING HARBOUR
King St Wharf 3

Sunday Only

DARLING HARBOUR
Aquarium

PYRMONT BAY
Casino/Maritime Museum

DRUMMOYNE
Wolseley St

HUNTLEY'S POINT
Huntleys Point Rd

CHISWICK
Bortfield Drive

ABBOTSFORD
Great North Rd

CABARITA
Cabarita Point

KISSING POINT
Kissing Point Park

MEADOWBANK
Bowden St

BALMAIN WEST
Elliott St

BIRKENHEAD
Henley Marine Drive

SYDNEY OLYMPIC PARK

RYDALMERE
John St

PARRAMATTA
Charles St

WHARF 2
WHARF 3
WHARF 4
WHARF 5
WHARF 6

CIRCULAR QUAY FERRY TERMINAL

242